THE COMPANION GUIDE TO

THE GREEK
ISLANDS

THE COMPANION GUIDES

GENERAL EDITOR: VINCENT CRONIN

*It is the aim of these guides to provide a Companion
in the person of the author, who knows intimately
the places and people of whom he writes, and is able to
communicate this knowledge and affection to his readers.
It is hoped that the text and pictures will aid them
in their preparations and in their travels, and will
help them remember on their return.*

LONDON · EAST ANGLIA · NORTHUMBRIA
THE WEST HIGHLANDS OF SCOTLAND · THE SOUTH OF FRANCE
THE COUNTRY ROUND PARIS · NORMANDY · THE LOIRE
FLORENCE · VENICE · ROME
MAINLAND GREECE · THE GREEK ISLANDS
YUGOSLAVIA · TURKEY · MADRID AND CENTRAL SPAIN
NEW YORK

In Preparation
DEVON · CORNWALL · THE WELSH BORDERS · KENT AND SUSSEX
RUSSIA · THE LAKE DISTRICT
UMBRIA · GASCONY AND THE DORDOGNE

THE COMPANION GUIDE TO

The Greek Islands

ERNLE BRADFORD

Revised and enlarged by
FRANCIS PAGAN

COLLINS
8 Grafton Street, London W1

William Collins Sons and Co. Ltd
London · Glasgow · Sydney · Auckland
Toronto · Johannesburg

BRITISH LIBRARY CATALOGUING IN PUBLICATION DATA
Bradford, Ernle
The companion guide to the Greek Islands.
—4th ed.
1. Aegean Islands (Greece and Turkey)—
Description and travel—Guide-books
2. Ionian Islands (Greece)—Description
and travel—Guide-books
I. Title   II. Pagan, Francis
914.95′0476   DF895

ISBN 0–00–217862–1

First edition 1963
Reprinted 1964
Second edition 1970
Third edition 1975
Fourth edition 1980
Reprinted 1981 and 1985
Fifth edition 1988

Maps by Leslie Robinson
Photoset in Linotron Times by
Ace Filmsetting Ltd, Frome, Somerset
Made and printed in Great Britain
Robert Hartnoll (1985) Ltd, Bodmin

For Marie Blanche

and now for
'Kyria Avdrea'

Acknowledgments

I am in debt to many people for their help, advice and encouragement in the revision of this book. In naming only a few I must include Mr P. Analytis, for many years London head of the National Tourist Organization of Greece, Mr K. Solounas, President of the Dodecanese Hoteliers Association, Mr I. Malliarakis of the Hotel Castello, Athens, Mme Margarita Manolas of the Hermes Hotel, Naxos, and Mr N. Korres and his family, of the Xenia Hotel, Argostoli, Kephalonia.

I am very grateful to Dr Hector Catling, Director of the British School in Athens, for his valuable advice, and to his staff for guidance in the Library there.

Above all I would pay tribute to the people of the islands for their warm-hearted friendship which for more than ten years has made travelling and staying among them such a pleasure. Invidious though it is, I single out with affection Ioannis and Voula Pantazides of Ios, Lambros and Anna Dendrinos of Amorgos, and Ilias and Aneta Perantinos of Paros.

F.P.

Contents

Illustrations

A Note on the Revised Edition

Readers of Ernle Bradford's many books on Mediterranean lore and history will be saddened that he did not live to see the only major revision of his Companion Guide since it was first published a quarter of a century ago. In his note on the third edition of 1975 he called attention to the great changes that have come about in the Greek islands since he travelled in his small yacht between their often primitive harbours in the 1950s and early 1960s. Even greater changes have arrived since then, and whatever may be thought of their effect on the way of life in many of the islands the improvement in communications has made it possible for the traveller to see far more of the interior of these fascinating places than Ernle Bradford was able to encompass in those early days. It is this aspect of the book which the present author has been at pains to develop, while he has also been fortunate in finding his way to a number of less well known and more out-of-the-way islands which did not figure in earlier editions.

At the same time, as Ernle Bradford wrote in 1974, the basic nature of the islands and of island life has not changed: 'The fisherman, squatting on the ruins of a mediaeval quay with a transistor radio for company, still mends his nets and makes his delicate cane fishtraps in the same way as did his remote ancestors who watched the triremes of Athens pass on their way to sacred Delos.' This continuity was what the original book celebrated, and this is what any revision must take account of, together with a clearer idea of what is to be found in likely and unlikely places by the enquiring visitor today.

LONDON 1988   F.P.

The Spelling of Place Names

One problem facing all who write about Greece in English is how to present its place names. We have to cope not only with the different appearance of letters in Greek and English, but with two alphabets which differ even in the number and value of their letters. Some kind of logic must be attempted, even if total consistency is a will-of-the-wisp. Though there are still a few entrenched Anglicisms such as Corfu, Crete and Rhodes (after all, we have not yet learnt to dispense with Vienna and The Hague) the principle here adopted is to keep reasonably close to modern Greek orthography and to stick to those letters which actually appear in the Greek alphabet.

Thus 'f' and the hard 'c', although they have begun to appear on transliterated road signs and maps, do not exist in Greek, while their equivalents *ph* and *k* occur naturally in both alphabets. 'Ch' (sounded as in 'loch') does exist in the form of the Greek letter *chi*, so there seems no need to substitute 'kh' or the simple aspirate 'h' (which modern Greek does not recognize) in a common Greek word like Chora, the island of Chios or the Cretan town Chania. Things are more difficult when we come to Greek vowels and diphthongs. Many are rendered in speech by the single sound 'ee', but it seems unsatisfactory to reproduce all these by a simple 'i', which can conceal the underlying grammar of the word. 'Y' is the capital form of the Greek *upsilon*, and it has been used for centuries in names such as Kerkyra, Kythnos and Zakynthos. This seems a more proper use for 'y' than as a consonant substituting for the silent *gamma* in familiar words like *Agios* and *Agia*. The sounds may be the same, but the visual impact of '*Ayios*' is wrong. One compromise: following most authorities we have used the English letter 'v' to represent the modern sound of the Greek *beta* and of *upsilon* when it occurs in the diphthongs 'au' and 'eu'.

Absolute consistency there can never be, and familiar classical names will be found spelt just as they always have been in English, with some latitude between -us and -os endings. But where sensible we retain the modern Greek forms, and it is hoped that some consistency on these lines will make it easier to consult the index.

Caliban: Be not afeard: the isle is full of noises,
            Sounds and sweet airs, that give delight, and hurt
            not.
            Sometimes a thousand twangling instruments
            Will hum about mine ears; and sometimes voices,
            That, if I then had wak'd after long sleep,
            Will make me sleep again: and then in dreaming,
            The clouds methought would open and show riches
            Ready to drop upon me; that, when I wak'd
            I cried to dream again.
Stephano: This will prove a brave kingdom to me . . .

THE TEMPEST

The Sea
and the Islands

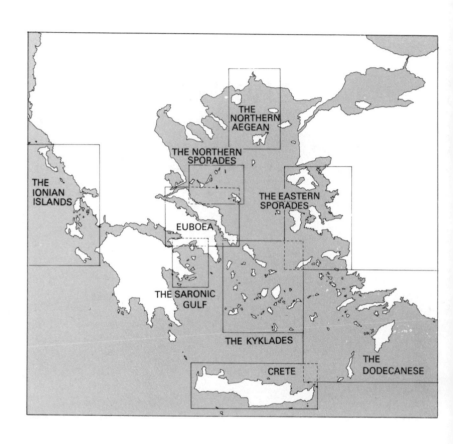

THE
NORTHERN
AEGEAN

THE NORTHERN
SPORADES

THE
IONIAN
ISLANDS

THE EASTERN
SPORADES

EUBOEA

THE SARONIC
GULF

THE KYKLADES

THE
DODECANESE

CRETE

ONE

The Sea and the Islands

It is the sea which determines the islands, and the thing which distinguishes one island or group of islands from another is the quality of the sea. Scientists may find it difficult, if not impossible, to distinguish between one stretch of salt water and another. The traveller knows better, and so does the sailor. The North Sea has an entirely different character from the Caribbean. The Mediterranean, in temperament at any rate, is only a distant relation of the Red Sea or the English Channel.

Even scientifically the Mediterranean has points of difference from the others, for it loses by evaporation two-thirds more than it receives from the rivers which drain into it. This loss is replaced by a steady inflow of water from the Atlantic through the Straits of Gibraltar. The effect of steady evaporation on this almost land-locked sea is that the Mediterranean has a higher salt content than most other seas in the world. The swimmer in the waters round the Greek islands soon appreciates this. The sea is buoyant. It lifts him up as confidently as did the dolphin which carried Arion on its back in safety to Taenarus – or as some say to the island of Lesbos.

The Ionian and the Aegean are very different seas. If the Ionian is female, the Aegean is male. One is soft, enveloped often with that gauze-like haze which hangs so frequently over the Italian landscape. The other is clear and precise. The Aegean engenders an air in which sentimentality and woolly thinking are impossible. The Greeks, with that curious accuracy of theirs which seems to have been as much the result of intuition as of deliberate thought, 'sexed' these two seas by calling one of them after the priestess Io and the other after King Aegeus of Athens. The names have stayed unchanged over the centuries, and so have their separate qualities.

17

Io was a priestess of Hera, the consort of Zeus. It was not surprising, then, that Hera was incensed when she found that Zeus had been deceiving her with one of her own servants. Zeus, to protect his mistress from Hera's anger, changed her into a snow-white heifer. His queen was not deceived and sent a gadfly which chased the unfortunate Io all round the world. Io, after leaving her place of hiding at Dodona, made first – still pursued by the gadfly – for the sea which bears her name.

The Ionian is the central basin of the Mediterranean, and is bounded on the west by Sicily and the toe of Italy, on the east by Greece. In a few places it is as deep as two thousand fathoms. In classical times its importance lay in the fact that the trade routes between the mainland and the new colonies in Sicily and southern Italy ran across it. The seamanship which the early Greek mariners had first learnt by 'island-hopping' in the Aegean was now applied to a larger and more open stretch of water. Even so, in the manner of classical navigation, most of the trade routes followed the coast as far as possible. From Corfu vessels had an open sea crossing of little more than sixty miles to the heel of Italy. Following the coastline of the Gulf of Taranto they came to the rich colonies of Sybaris and Croton, and then to the straits of Messina. Syracuse lay only a little southward down the coast of Sicily.

The character of a sea is determined by its winds and weather, just as these again determine the character of its islands and islanders. In the Ionian two winds predominate, the Sirocco and the Gregale, or the Bora as it is known in Corfu. The Sirocco which blows from the south is a warm, even a hot, wind which originates in north Africa. By the time it reaches the islands it has often picked up a high humidity which restrains physical activity, deadens thought and exacerbates the nerves. Fortunately it is not as virulent on this western coast of Greece as in Malta or Sicily. In Sicily indeed it is said that at one time, if the Sirocco had blown for over ten days, all charges of inexplicable violence and passion were dismissed. Such crimes were considered not to lie within the doer's rational cognizance but to owe their origin solely to the south wind.

The Sirocco blows mostly in spring and autumn, but its counterpart the Gregale is a winter wind. Springing off the mainland mountains, the cold air rushes down to take the place of the warmer air rising off the Ionian. The Gregale is the most dangerous wind in this part of the Mediterranean, though its full effects are fortunately not felt in the Greek islands. It is on the far side of the sea, on the eastern coasts of Sicily, Malta and Gozo, that the full fetch and thunder of these winter gales is felt. This was St Paul's tempestuous wind called Euroclydon, which drove his ship helplessly across from Crete to ground in the Maltese bay that bears his name.

In winter the small-boat sailors and fishermen of the Ionian do not venture far, for apart from the principal winds heavy squalls often descend off their mountainous islands. But in spring and summer the sea round this western coast of Greece is often calm and practically windless for days on end. It is now that the offshore fishermen bring in the excellent fish which make eating a pleasure in these islands. Apart from the magnificent lobsters of Corfu, usually the clawless Mediterranean variety (*astakos* in Greek), the Ionian is rich in mullet, tunny, ray, swordfish, octopus and squid, as well as many others whose names only the locals know.

The Aegean, the island-studded sea of the Greek archipelago, is entered either round Cape Matapan, the ancient Taenarus which contained the entrance to the Underworld, or more often nowadays through the rocky slit of the Corinth canal. Since most cruise ships come first to Athens through the canal, giving travellers their first introduction to the Aegean world, a few words about it will not be out of place.

The emperor Nero, when he visited Greece in AD 66, saw what an advantage to commerce a canal would be, and ordered work to begin on one. His death two years later, as well as the technical difficulties encountered, prevented any further attempts to unite the Aegean with the Ionian by way of the Gulf of Corinth. In classical times ships wishing to cross the isthmus of Corinth, avoiding the long and stormy route round Cape Matapan, could be hauled over the narrow neck of land on rollers. Traces of the tracks used for this purpose have been found, and the position of Corinth astride the isthmus gave it a maritime importance and ultimately a prosperity to rival that of Athens.

It was not until nearly two thousand years after Nero's death that the Corinth canal was opened in 1893. It is a little over three miles long and sixty-nine feet wide at the base, affording passage for ships of up to twenty-two feet in draught. It took twelve years to complete, and by the time it was opened it was not deep enough for the greatly increased tonnage of the merchant ships then being built. Nevertheless for the yachtsmen bound from one coast of Greece to the other the Corinth canal serves a very useful purpose, and the saving in distance is considerable for vessels bound from western Greece for ports in the Aegean and the Black Sea. From Sicily, western Italy and the south of France it is of little use.

At the far end one emerges into the Aegean. The tragic death of Aegeus, father of Theseus, is permanently recorded by the name of the sea. Theseus, triumphant after his conquest of the Minotaur, had left Ariadne behind him on Naxos and was hastening for the shores of Attica and his father's kingdom of Athens. Unfortunately he forgot his promise to hoist the white sail which should have announced his safe return, leaving instead the dark sail which told that the king's son had perished in the Labyrinth of Knossos. Seeing a dark-tanned sail (such as Greek fishing boats still carry) on his son's ship, Aegeus was overwhelmed by grief; he threw himself into the sea from a high rock and was drowned.

The sea to which he gave his name is an arm of the Mediterranean thrust between Asia Minor and Greece – the sea which cradled western civilization and the arts of navigation. It must never be forgotten that the Aegean was the birthplace of Greek seamanship, and hence, directly or indirectly, of almost all western maritime enterprise during the past two thousand years. Out of the Aegean has also come a word that is now part of the English language, 'archipelago'. This has come to mean any large group of islands, but originally it meant the sea which contained the Aegean islands. The word itself is found nowhere in ancient or mediaeval Greek. *Pelagos* is the poetic Greek word for sea, but whether the prefix *archi-* means 'chief' or 'main', or is a corruption of *Aegei*, has not been finally resolved.

The character of this sea is formed principally by two factors: its geographic position and its climate. Geographically it is the sea which divides Europe from Asia, and yet at the same time – because the islands lie like stepping-stones across it – it is not so much a moat between one world and another as a bridge. The closeness of island to island meant that in the infancy of ship-building and navigation man was able, during the clement seasons of the year, to maintain communications across a watery world. Scudding between the rocky islands, traders were able to exchange the goods of one civilization for those of another. Because a ship is hardly ever out of sight of land for more than a few hours, it was possible for these early navigators to bring their cargoes safe to port without compass, chart or sextant.

The climate has played an equally important part in the development of Aegean civilization. Apart from the proximity of island to island, the weather conditions were favourable for primitive navigation. The Etesian winds, as the *Admiralty Pilot* calls them, blow from a northerly direction over this sea for most of the summer months. Without these prevailing winds it is hardly an exaggeration to say that Greek culture would never have spread so widely as to embrace not only the whole mainland but also the coast of Asia Minor. The name derives from the Greek *etos*, meaning 'year', because they can be relied on to blow regularly every year.

Flowing down from Bulgaria, Turkey, and beyond them from Russia, prompted by the hot air rising over the Mediterranean, they carry on southwards all the way to Egypt. It was upon these regular seasonal winds that the Greeks of antiquity based their sailing practices and their navigation. Their ships were hauled ashore in the autumn and were not launched again until the start of the 'prodroms' (or 'forerunners') – the variable winds of spring which herald the return of the Etesians. It was with the Etesians astern that Mycenaean merchants could sail from Argos or other ports in the northern Aegean down to Crete, while from Crete the sailors whose trading had enriched Knossos and Phaistos could run down to Egypt and the Nile delta. Usually a cargo would be taken down during the height of the summer season, and another brought back during the following spring before the Etesians had set in.

However one travels through the Aegean it is impossible to ignore this summer wind. Even the most unobservant landsman cannot help remarking on the extraordinary clarity of the sky, which is unlike any other sky in the world. It is here that one sees at once the difference between the Ionian and the Aegean seas – a difference which is reflected in their respective islands. Even in midsummer there is a briskness in the Aegean air. The blue of the sky is sharp, and broomed by the wind. The softness, the hint of trailing mist over the sea or in the upper reaches of the sky, which is to be found in the Ionian, is absent from the Aegean.

In particular, during July and August the winds which the modern Greeks call *meltemi* begin to blow every day at dawn, reach their maximum about noon, usually dropping off at sunset. The word may derive from the Venetian *bel tempo*, and it is their cool invigorating rush which dissipates the bugbear of so many Mediterranean lands – the noonday lassitude and the high humidity which curb thought and action alike. At midday in an Aegean island one can stand on a rocky peak or sit in a quayside taverna and feel, in a shade-heat of ninety degrees, the stimulating wind which brings freshness to sultry places.

Equally, the *meltemi* can be a source of frustration and even of danger for the unwary. When they are at their noonday height, movement on foot can be difficult and it is as well to look for sheltered places to walk or sit. When at anchor in a north-facing bay it is wise to get under way early in the morning, or to make sure you have enough cable out to stop you dragging in the coming blasts.

Unlike the Ionian, the Aegean is not generally speaking a deep sea. Only in a few places, notably just north of Crete, does it attain to a depth of more than a thousand fathoms. The islands which raise their craggy shoulders out of the sea are remnants of a land mass connecting Europe with Asia Minor. They are peaks of old hills, or the summits of mountain ranges long submerged, and a glance at a map shows how they splay out from Greece or Turkey to follow the lines of the main ranges on either side of the dividing sea. Because it is predominantly shallow, the Aegean can be a very treacherous area, and a dangerous breaking sea can quickly be kicked up on the rocks and shallows round the islands. It is not difficult to understand why the ancient Greeks called a halt to maritime activity during the winter months.

Of the many creatures which share these seas with man, the porpoise or dolphin is the most engaging, playing constantly around the bow waves of ships. They rise close alongside to breathe – that half snorting sigh – and then dive and tumble in the disturbed water. Squeezed along by the water pressure in front of the bows, they will stay there effortlessly just as long as it suits them. Then with a quick flurry they will all be gone. In calm spring weather one of the loveliest sights in the Aegean is the wheeling, planing and banking of a pair of shearwaters, the sharp tips of their wings almost touching the water as they turn and dip. Above all, the Aegean is a clean sea – except where conglomerations of mankind pollute it – and the fathoms-deep sea-bed can be as clear as if seen through glass.

The sea is Greece. Where the first images of other European countries that come to mind may be rural or urban – the Loire or the Champs Elysées, the Lake District or Hyde Park Corner, the image of Greece is the sea. Even the inland shepherd knows it is there, and never far out of sight. From mountain or moorland he can see the shining inlets where the sea marches into the land, or look across a deep blue strait to his nearest island neighbours. Yet Greece is not a romantic land such as the poetry of Keats may suggest. It is a harsher, stronger and more brilliant world, especially in the islands, where the atmosphere – even in Corfu or Rhodes – is never sugared but always astringent.

The Ionian Islands

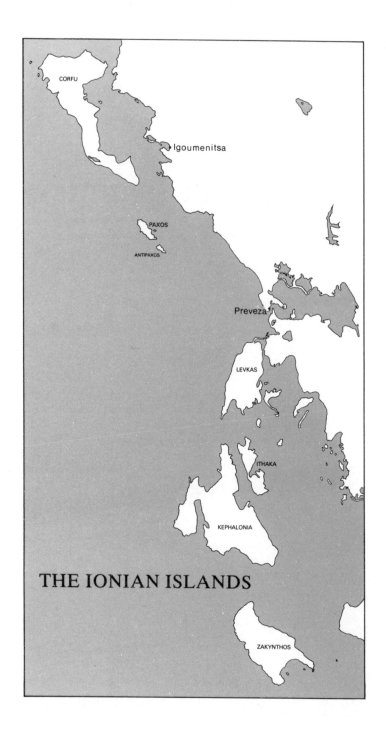

CORFU

Igoumenitsa

PAXOS

ANTIPAXOS

Preveza

LEVKAS

ITHAKA

KEPHALONIA

THE IONIAN ISLANDS

ZAKYNTHOS

THE IONIAN ISLANDS

Seven principal islands form this group; hence their Greek name, *Eptanisi*. The most important are **Corfu**, **Paxos**, **Levkas**, **Kephalonia**, **Ithaka** and **Zakynthos** (or Zante, for those who still prefer the Italian form). Apart from these there are numerous islets, some attractive and fertile like Antipaxos, others no more than sea-washed rocks. The seventh island is Kythera (the Italian Cerigo) but this is a political rather than a geographical connection, as it lies far away off the most easterly peninsula of the Peloponnese.

As we shall see in the subsequent chapters, the main islands all figured in the history of the ancient world from the Bronze Age to the Roman era. Thereafter until the end of the twelfth century the Ionian islands nominally formed part of the eastern empire of Byzantium, but even before the capital fell to the Frankish forces of the Fourth Crusade – diverted to this end by Enrico Dandolo, Doge of Venice – Corfu, Kephalonia, Ithaka and Zante had been captured by Normans from Sicily.

With the proclamation of the Fourth Crusade in 1202 it was natural for its leaders to apply to Venice, the principal maritime power, to furnish their transport. The crusaders' army numbered 9000 knights, 20,000 foot-soldiers and 4500 horsemen. The Doge agreed to provide the warships and the merchantmen for the crusade, in return for the sum of 85,000 silver marks and half of all the conquests. When the money failed to arrive on time, the Doge saw an opportunity to benefit the Republic. The maritime states of Zara and Dalmatia had revolted from Venice in 1166, and Dandolo agreed to postpone the payment on condition that the crusaders should reduce these dissident subjects before proceeding to the Holy Land.

While the crusaders were preparing to attack Dalmatia an even more ambitious scheme was proposed by the Doge. It was decided to attack Byzantium itself. This assault on the eastern bastion of

Christendom, by an army of Christian knights supposedly on their way to rescue the Holy Land from the infidel, has made the Fourth Crusade deservedly infamous, as well as affecting profoundly the course of events in the islands of the Aegean and Ionian seas. In the treaty of partition after the fall of the Empire all the Ionian islands were awarded to Venice, but she was unable or unwilling to establish a lasting authority there.

In the confused century of dynastic rivalry which followed, Corfu became the property of the Greek-born Despots of Epirus, while Kephalonia, Levkas, Ithaka and Zante fell to the Italian Orsini family, who styled themselves Palatine Counts of Kephalonia – all ultimately vassals of the Angevin Kings of Sicily and Naples. Not until 1386 did Venice rouse herself to occupy Corfu by force – a move welcomed by the inhabitants because it gave them better protection against the pirates and corsairs of the Levant – and subsequently the remainder of the group. From then until the end of the eighteenth century the islands were ruled by Venice to their mutual benefit.

With her help, particularly in the form of some magnificent fortifications, Corfu resisted Turkish sieges in 1537, 1570 and 1716, while the other islands suffered no more than occasional harassment by the Turks. It was this Venetian influence which lasted for more than three hundred years that has welded them into a distinct group, and given them an Italian quality which sets them apart from the islands of the Aegean. Venetian architecture, Venetian names and even an aristocracy dating back to the Republic are the legacy of those three centuries.

When Venice fell to Napoleon in 1797 there was a brief French occupation, but a combined operation by Turkey and Russia drove out the French, and in 1800 a treaty between the Tsar and the Sultan created the formidable-sounding 'Septinsular Republic'. Briefly restored to France by the Treaty of Tilsit in 1807, the Ionian islands were captured one by one by the British, and in 1815 they became an independent state under British protection. The first Lord High Commissioner was Sir Thomas Maitland, an efficient if dictatorial character known locally as 'King Tom'. Although this was a period of solid commercial and social progress, Greek national pride made the islanders restive, and by the Treaty of

London in 1864 Britain gave up all her rights and the *Eptanisi* were formally united with Greece.

Their position off the western coast of the Greek mainland, protected from the drying blasts of the north-easterly winds which sweep down through the Aegean, and open to the milder westerlies which cross the Ionian sea from Calabria and Sicily, means that these are green islands, well watered and tree-clad to a degree not found in the exposed waters of the Aegean. Thick pine woods are found in northern Euboea, in Thasos and the northern Sporades, but nowhere else in the Greek world does one find such a constant supply of water to irrigate fruit and vegetables, or such a variety of evergreen and deciduous trees. Some will find the physical atmosphere enervating after the keener edge to life in the Aegean, but there is no denying the beauty of the varied Ionian landscape. Varied it is, and the visitor will be intrigued as much by the physical differences between the islands as by their cultural similarities.

TWO

Corfu, Paxos and Antipaxos

As the first charter plane of the day touches down at **Corfu** airport, there may not be many passengers who will think of comparing their smooth arrival, met by a tourist hotel's special bus, with a morning some three thousand years before when shipwrecked Odysseus woke naked on the shore after ten years of wandering among the islands of the Mediterranean. It is worth a thought, for whatever doubts may hang over Homer's account of those wanderings, there is a consensus to identify Corfu with the island he calls Scheria, the green and prosperous land of the Phaeacians ruled over by King Alcinous.

Scheria was only one of several names borne by this island in its chronicled history. Another early Greek name was Drepanon, 'the sickle', which not inaptly describes its lean and tapering shape. In the classical age its name was Kerkyra, and Greek national feeling has encouraged a return to this use, though only the principal town is generally so called today. Perhaps international airlines find the name Corfu easier to handle. This too was a descriptive word, an Italian corruption of the Byzantine Korypho, from the Greek word *koruphai* meaning 'peaks'. It referred to the two distinctive hill-tops of the headland where the *Palaio Phrourio*, the **Old Fortress**, stands to command the sea approaches to the capital.

This formidable place, joined to the city only by a bridge over a narrow moat, survived all enemy onslaughts but partly succumbed to a controlled explosion by engineers during the British protectorate. Today periodic attempts to restore its rather grim barracks have petered out, and it features mainly as a popular evening excursion from the great **Esplanade**, or *Spianada*, which stretches for nearly half a mile between the fortress and the town. This is

30

where all the approaches to Kerkyra converge, and for most visitors it will provide the first and most lasting impression they have of Corfu. The *Spianada* (the Italian form is still used) is the centre of Kerkyra's social life, and it illustrates the Greek talent for making good use of open spaces. At the northern end is the famous cricket ground, legacy of the British era, now a lush carpet of green turf surrounding a business-like matting pitch, where some excellent and now orthodox matches are played in the summer, and where enthusiastic free-for-all practice goes on every evening. The other much quoted British legacy, *tsintsin bira* (or ginger beer) is no longer in much demand at the café tables which line the western boundary.

In contrast to this wide green space, the southern section is broken up by bright flower beds and flowering trees – in spring the purple clusters of the Judas trees stand out. More architectural features are a splendid bandstand and an Ionic peristyle rotunda which commemorates the first British High Commissioner, Sir Thomas Maitland. From any point along the *Spianada* you can stand back to admire the terrace buildings which overlook it and stamp a distinctive character on Kerkyra town. Eighteenth-century Venetian and French styles blend with English Regency in an elegant vista of tall, iron-balconied, grey-shuttered houses; in particular the arcaded block which fronts the cricket ground, known as the **Liston**, has an almost Parisian sophistication – it was indeed built during the brief French occupation in imitation, it is said, of the Rue de Rivoli.

In strong contrast to this classic elegance is the **Old Town**, an intriguing muddle of narrow streets and alleys (known as *kantounia*) which occupies the rising ground enclosed by the northern walls of the city, which directly overlook the sea. For Kerkyra is still a walled city, and you can trace its fortifications in broken stretches all round its original perimeter. The northern section is the most formidable, if only because it incorporates the scientifically engineered *Neo Phrourio*, or **New Fortress**. In fact both this and the Old Fortress date from the sixteenth century, but here the outlines are sharper and clearer, and the grim grey walls still conceal a military presence.

This may be the earliest view the visitor has of Corfu if he arrives

31

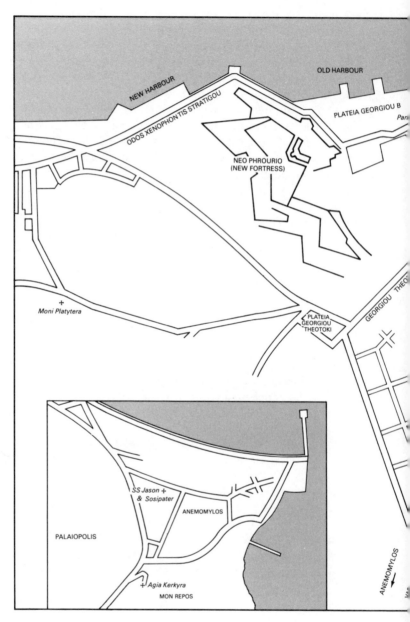

NEW HARBOUR

OLD HARBOUR

ODOS XENOPHONTIS STRATIGOU

PLATEIA GEORGIOU B

Pari

NEO PHROURIO
(NEW FORTRESS)

GEORGIOU THEO

+
Moni Platytera

PLATEIA
GEORGIOU
THEOTOKI

PALAIOPOLIS

SS Jason +
& Sosipater

ANEMOMYLOS

+ Agia Kerkyra
MON REPOS

ANEMOMYLOS

Va

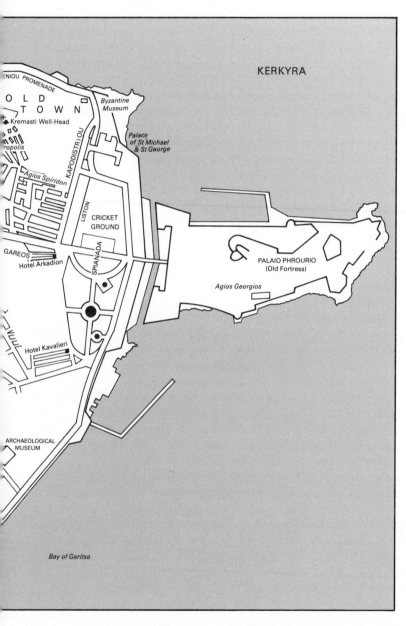

KERKYRA

ENIOU PROMENADE

O L D
  T O W N
Kremasti Well-Head

Byzantine
Museum

ropolis

Palace
of St Michael
& St George

Agios Spiridon

KAPODISTRIOU

LISTON

CRICKET
GROUND

SPIANADA

GAREOS
Hotel Arkadion

PALAIO PHROURIO
(Old Fortress)

Agios Georgios

Hotel Kavalieri

ARCHAEOLOGICAL
MUSEUM

Bay of Garitsa

33

by sea, for the shoreline below has been developed to provide a long line of quays – the western section reserved for international shipping, the smaller eastern end for inter-island ferries. Again good use has been made of open space, the eastern or 'old' harbour being backed by the wide *Plateia Georgiou B* (George II of Greece, that is) and its encroaching cafés. It must be said that much open space in the city was created by a ruthless German bombardment in 1943, when as elsewhere in the Ionian islands they were faced with Italian troops who regarded this as home territory and the Germans as enemy invaders. The Allies then caused further unnecessary destruction from the air. The greatest and irreparable loss was the former university library, a magnificent building containing more than 70,000 volumes.

At the same time Kerkyra lost fourteen of its mediaeval and later churches, which is why not many are left within the walls today. Of those which survive, the one dedicated to Corfu's ubiquitous saint, *Agios Spiridon*, has the most character. Spiridon was Bishop of Cyprus and a member of the Council of Nicaea in AD 325. His embalmed remains were kept in his native island until the Turkish occupation decided the faithful to remove what relics they could to Greece. The mummified body of the saint finally reached safety, they say, strapped to the side of a mule and disguised as a bale of fodder. It was not until Spiridon reached Corfu in 1489 that his career as a miracle-worker seems to have started. The exposure of his relics in a procession through the town saved the island from the plague in 1630. Then in the great siege of 1716 when the city was attacked by the Ottoman fleet he lent his power and strength to the troops fighting under their German commander, Marshal Schulenberg of Saxony, and saved the island from the infidel.

In the now restored church he reposes in an ornate silver sarcophagus, Viennese work of the mid-nineteenth century. Four times a year, on Palm Sunday, Saturday in Holy Week, August 11th and the first Sunday in November, he makes the circuit of his city preceded by the Bishop of Corfu and flanked by priests and acolytes. His church remains an intimate parish church, with a gallery at the west end for an organ and choir to provide music at Sunday masses – an Italianate feature unusual in the Orthodox church.

Deeper into the Old Town, and overlooking the harbour, is the

Mitropolis, the Orthodox Cathedral; this impresses most by its size and the Corinthian grandeur of its portico, and is seen at its best filled with its Sunday congregations. It pays better to explore the recesses of the *kantounia* behind, many of them paved with fine marble slabs; one corner not to miss is the little square containing the Venetian **Kremasti Well-head**, dated 1699. You could easily imagine yourself in a *campiello* in a quiet quarter of Venice, surrounded as it is by high tenement buildings with washing strung out and canaries singing from lofty cages. The well takes its name from the seventeenth-century church beside it of the *Panagia Kremasti*, long ruined but now in process of restoration; the original roof beams survive, and the *templo* has some good early painting.

If you pass along the dull and dusty *Odos Xenophontis Stratigou* past the customs house and the yacht supply station, leaving the Neo Phrourio above you to the left, you reach the suburban village of Mandouki, where there is an excellent seafood restaurant. A turn inland here up the *Odos Napoleontis* will bring you to an oasis in this rather seedy back street area, the **Monastery of Platytera**. An inconspicuous doorway in a high wall (you will see the *campanile* rising behind it) leads into a peaceful courtyard with flowering plants in tubs. The church itself is small and cool, with much dark panelling and stalls with the *misericorde* seats more familiar in the Catholic and Anglican scene; the ceiling is painted in the Venetian manner. Some good seventeenth-century ikons are displayed in the sacristy. You can return to town on foot by way of the big *Plateia Georgiou Theotoki*, though the monastery can easily and cheaply be visited by taxi.

This square is the beginning of the new town centre, laid out conventionally on a grid pattern – a purely commercial quarter except for the leafy green area which accommodates the tennis club. Beyond that again, and close to the long *Vasileos Konstantinou* promenade which skirts the bay of Garitsa, is the **Archaeological Museum**. Before considering what is to be seen there, it may help to give some account of the historical sequence behind the exhibits.

The island's recorded history virtually begins with the foundation of a colony from Corinth in 734 BC. Corinth, strategically spanning the narrow isthmus which divides the Aegean from the Ionian sea, was always particularly interested in the western seaboard of

Greece and the islands which lay in the track of shipping bound for her oldest colony at Syracuse in Sicily. It is ironic that Kerkyra, her most successful colony in these waters, turned into her bitterest enemy. The Greek seafaring tradition was as strong here as anywhere, and as early as 664 BC there took place the first recorded battle of fleets, between Kerkyra and Corinth – and Kerkyra won it. More significant for the future was the naval warfare which broke out again between the two cities in 432 BC and precipitated the Peloponnesian War between their respective allies, Sparta and Athens. Under the Macedonian and Hellenistic monarchies the whole island flourished, and was able to develop its rich natural resources. It was Octavian's base before he defeated Antony at Actium in 31BC, the actual battle being fought in the waters north of Levkas near the modern town of Preveza. This was a disastrous moment for Kerkyra: in order to secure his rear, Octavian (the future emperor Augustus) sent in his chief lieutenant Marcus Agrippa to wipe out its defences. In the process he razed the classical city to the ground.

Almost all the exhibits of importance in the Museum are to be found in the four rooms on the first floor. The central corridor (Room V on the official guide plan) contains a few fragments of Bronze Age pottery from the third millenium, found significantly near the west coast bay of Ermones – significantly because that is where many believe Nausicaa discovered the shipwrecked Odysseus and conducted him to the palace of her father Alcinous.

The centrepiece of this room is a fine stone lion *couchant*, said to have been found on top of the so-called Tomb of Menekrates (a fourth-century BC physician with delusions of grandeur) which is now discreetly housed in the police station south of the city. All that can be said with certainty is that it is a piece of archaic Corinthian sculpture from the end of the seventh century – but he is a pleasantly docile-looking beast. The end room (VI on the plan) is dominated by an extraordinary pediment from a Doric temple of Artemis, dated 580 BC. The central figure is a huge Gorgon, the head so unrestrainedly hideous as to be almost erotically compelling. Her narrow waist is encircled by a pair of intertwined snakes which add to this feeling. By contrast the outer wings of the pediment are occupied by two extremely dignified and amiable panthers, and the

intervening spaces by an assortment of vigorous mythological figures, some of them fragmentary. At the south end of the same room
is a superb collection of silver staters of Kerkyra in fine condition,
minted probably at the end of the sixth century and found in a
deposit dated 480 BC – the year of the battle of Salamis, in which
Kerkyra did not take part.

The North Hall (Room VII) is again dominated by an unusual
pediment from an archaic temple, later in date and a good deal more
naturalistic. Only half of the pediment survives, and shows
Dionysus and a young attendant reclining at a symposium – the
bearded god has a horn of wine, the boy a cup, and underneath their
table crouches a lion. The intriguing thing is that both heads are
turned to look with absorbed expressions at whatever filled the
missing half of the pediment – an insoluble mystery, but a marvellously *vivant* piece of sculpture.

There are of course many cases of pottery from the geometric and
classical periods, which illustrate the sophistication which Kerkyra
shared with Corinth in those days. The ancient city from which most
of the exhibits in the museum were recovered occupied the peninsula which extends south of Garitsa bay, and now has a concentration of holiday hotels centred on the resorts of Analipsis and
Kanoni. It still bears the overall name of **Palaiopolis**, but the ancient
remains are scanty and hard to find, thanks to the destruction
wrought by Agrippa and later by sixth-century Goths. Here stood
the temple of Artemis with its Gorgon pediment, but the main
interest of the site is that one can see – as in so many other parts of
the Mediterranean – how the ancients wherever possible chose a
peninsula for their cities. This one was shut off from the mainland by
a wall; to the north it had the 'harbour of Alcinous' (a doubtful
identity) which has been left dry by the receding sea; to the south a
larger one now cut off from the rest of Lake Chalikiopoulo, a
shallow lagoon across which the airport's only runway has been
rather disconcertingly built.

Just south of the sealed-off mouth of this lagoon is the islet called
Pondikonisi, or Mouse Island. This is the more distant of two islands
which are sometimes confused, as both contain a monastery. The
nearer one, Vlachernes, is connected to the mainland by a causeway, and is used as a staging point for anyone wishing to visit

Pondikonisi by small boat. The latter, with its clump of cypresses half hiding a white-walled monastery, features in countless illustrations of the beauties of Corfu, but few antiquarians today support its claim to be the Phaeacian ship petrified by Poseidon in revenge for its role in returning Odysseus to Ithaka in safety – we have to visit **Palaiokastritsa** on the west coast to judge between this and a rival claimant.

North of what is now known as the Kanoni peninsula (from a platform at the southern end on which a large cannon was once mounted) the attractive modern suburb of **Anemomylos** fills the headland at the foot of the bay of Garitsa. The windmill which gave it its name has disappeared, but in a quiet back street is the best example of a Byzantine church to be found in Corfu. This is the twelfth-century church of the saints *Jason and Sosipater*, disciples of St Paul who first brought Christianity to the island. The exterior is particularly satisfying and well preserved, cruciform in plan with a northern extension and typically Corfiot *campanile*. The stone is warm, picked out with patterns in brick tiling. Inside are two lifesize ikons of local saints, Ioannis Palamas and Ioannis Damaskinos; the cupola is supported by four marble pillars, probably an early eighteenth-century embellishment. Nearby are the grounds of the Government-owned villa of **Mon Repos**, once a summer residence for the Greek royal family, where Prince Philip was born in 1921. There is no admission, but opposite its gates is the interesting ruin of a large early basilica church dedicated to *Agia Kerkyra*, an eponymous saint about whom little is known.

Travellers who come to Greece imbued with some knowledge of her classical history, and eager to see the evidences of it, must never forget Byzantium. The Byzantine traditions and the Orthodox Church mean more to most Greeks than those distant achievements of their classical ancestors. Those have not been forgotten, but rather, under the prompting of foreign visitors since the liberation of Greece in the nineteenth century, re-remembered. Greece has given us so much. First the island culture that culminated in Minoan Crete, then the Ionian culture which produced Periclean Athens; this was followed by Alexandrian or Hellenistic Greece which encompassed most of Asia Minor, the Levant and Egypt. Finally there was the Byzantine Empire with its capital at Constantinople which was the eastern half of the Roman Empire and the first stronghold of Christianity. The Byzantine Greeks defended Europe against her enemies from the east until they were treacherously laid low by the leaders of the Fourth Crusade. Corfu is not, as Crete is, a prime example of this historical sequence, but it can serve as an introduction to a study of it.

Kerkyra has a **Byzantine Museum** housed in the church of the *Panagia Antivouniotissa* at the further end of the Arseniou promenade to the north of the town, set back from the busy road up several flights of steps. There is nothing here from the early Byzantine period, when Kerkyra was part of the eastern Empire, but it has a comprehensive collection of ikons from the thirteenth to the seventeenth century, most of them from churches built or decorated during the Venetian era but continuing the Byzantine traditions of Christian art. The most important group is one of thirteen by the seventeenth-century painter Emanuel Tsanes, who escaped from Crete in 1645 when the Turks first invested Kandia, and spent the next ten years in Corfu. He introduced the Cretan style of church painting to the island. The thirteen were discovered in 1979 in the abandoned church of St George below the Old Fortress – a nineteenth-century neo-classical building which is still only a shell in spite of its dignified exterior. They were cleaned and restored and can be seen now in their splendid original colouring.

The mediaeval history of Corfu begins with its conquest in 1081 by Robert Guiscard, the Norman self-styled 'Duke of Apulia, Calabria and Sicily', as a step in his assault on Dyrrachium to open the Balkan route to Constantinople and the Holy Land. Richard I of England came here in 1193 on his way back from Palestine to Ragusa, and after the fall of Constantinople in 1204 Corfu shared the experiences of the other Ionian islands – except that it was singled out for and successfully resisted the fiercest Turkish attacks in the sixteenth century.

The feeling of the years of British rule is best illustrated by the **Palace of St Michael and St George**, a large and dignified classical building to the north of the cricket ground, with a long Doric portico and two flanking wings which end in archways. The two saints became the patrons of the British Diplomatic Service, and the palace was designed in 1819 to be the treasury of their Order and residence for the Lord High Commissioner. In 1864 it was presented to the Greek king, but during two world wars it became neglected and dilapidated. Great credit is given in Corfu to Sir Charles Peake, British Ambassador to Athens in the 1950s, who had it restored as a memorial to the British connection.

The splendidly ostentatious state rooms are open to visitors, and as an extra bonus one wing houses a remarkable collection of Chinese and Japanese porcelain and bronzes, assembled by Gregorios Manos, Greek Ambassador to France and Austria in the early 1900s. His passion for oriental art led him to buy everything he could find at European auctions, and he offered this unique collection of over 10,000 pieces to the state in 1917. It was ten years before the government agreed to accept and display it suitably, and having spent a fortune on accumulating it Manos died a poor man in 1928. The collection was added to in 1980, when Konstantinos Chiotakis, a Greek merchant from Holland, presented 350 later oriental pieces from the seventeenth, eighteenth and nineteenth centuries. Finally Ambassador Chadzivasilios, who served in India, Japan and Korea between 1954 and 1970, contributed some Indian sculpture and a lovely display of sixteenth-century Japanese screens. The whole scene is an unusual revelation of good taste and generosity in diplomatic circles, Greek and British.

Taste of a different kind is to be found a few miles down the road leading south from Kerkyra town. A turning left just before the village of Kinopiastes, on its way to join the coastal highway, passes the German-inspired extravaganza known as the **Achilleion**. This is a huge neo-classical palace built in 1890–1 by an Italian architect for the Empress Elizabeth of Austria, and subsequently bought by Kaiser William II as a holiday residence. The interior has little interest, and is mainly an adjunct to a casino, but the terraced gardens have more natural charm, in spite of some obtrusively vulgar statuary, and the final 'belvedere' has a marvellous view northwards over Kerkyra.

Before we mount too high a horse over nineteenth-century German taste, we should consider what twentieth-century international tourism has done to parts of this lovely island. Nowhere has more damage occurred than along the eastern coast road between Perama, to the south of the Chalikiopoulo lagoon, and the point

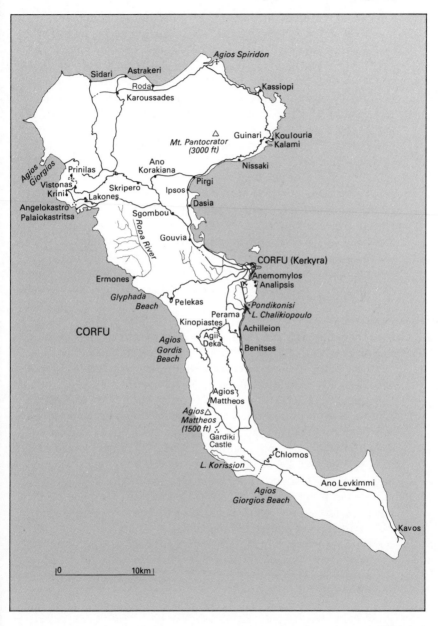

where it turns inland near Messongi. The almost continuous sequence of concrete hotels, bungalows, villas and vulgar restaurants is depressing and not really justified by the narrow, shingly and shallow beaches they command. True, the view across the blue straits to the seemingly uninhabited mountains of Albania is remarkably beautiful – one wonders what an Albanian hill farmer equipped with high-powered binoculars or telescope would make of the reverse view westward. He could only prefer to keep his coastline as it is. Perhaps the biggest loss is the once charming fishing village of **Benitses**, unrecognizable from a visit fifteen years ago, and now on the way to becoming the Benidorm of Corfu.

Happily things improve once the main road leaves the coast and turns inland through Argirades and Levkimmi to reach the southern end of the island at Kavos – not a scenically exciting area, but low-lying, fertile and not over-populated except round Kavos itself. On the way south do not ignore a left-hand turn into the hills at the small hamlet of Linia. This leads to the authentic Greek hill village of **Chlomos**, a marvellous place which Edward Lear visited and painted. With him you can share the view from a balustraded terrace, and even more agreeably over drinks provided by the friendly family who run the village café across the road. Opposite the turning to Chlomos is a track which takes you to the long sand-bar which encloses **Lake Korission**, a shadeless sunbaked spot which belongs to a different world.

If you prefer to give the coast road a miss altogether you can make an attractive tour – and here I emphasize that to make the most of a stay in Corfu you need to hire motor transport – by taking the old road south from Kinopiastes, which follows the central spine of the hills, passing first the nice little village of **Agii Deka**, which inspired an Oscar Wilde poem, and then curves beautifully through olive groves and flowery fields. A return journey can be made by the more westerly route which could take in a visit to a thirteenth-century castle at **Gardiki** and the village of Agios Mattheos under the 1500-foot mountain of the same name. This can also bring you to one of Corfu's genuinely good sandy beaches at **Agios Gordis** on the west coast. Unfortunately it too has suffered badly from overcrowding and development.

A journey like this reveals an unspoilt beauty and richness in the heart of Corfu. The queen of trees here is the olive, many examples having obviously lived for a span of two or three hundred years, born during the Venetian occupation with a subsidy in cash for every new tree put in. The wealth of the country landowner is still measured by the acreage of olives he has inherited or bought. In the south they are saved from monotony by the dark green spears of the cypresses. When the wind passes over the olives, so that their leaves turn in a rustle of silver, the cypresses look like pinnacle rocks rising out of the sea. The oil pressed in Corfu and in nearby Paxos is the best in the Mediterranean, a wonderful green in colour and smooth in texture and taste. The oranges are among the best grown anywhere, and more unusually there are excellent wild strawberries. The local wines are good, but getting hard to find. Roses, clematis, honeysuckle and even wistaria grow in abundance, as well as the full range of Greek wild flowers.

The same prosperous and smiling countryside quickly opens up if you take the western exit from Kerkyra which follows for a time the valley of the river called – surely unnecessarily – Potamos; but then how many rivers in England and Wales are called Avon, which is only the Welsh word for 'river'! There are several branches in the road as it crosses the waist of the island, of which the most southerly leads to Pelekas, a village undistinguished except for its views down to the western coastline. Immediately below is **Glyphada**, still the most glorious of the Corfu beaches, in spite of the huge hotel complex at its southern end. Another branch crosses the green plain of the Ropa, from where its slow-moving river finally tumbles down beside the road into the bay of **Ermones**. This has been a lovely place, and still has charm, but its ancient secrecy has been invaded by tiers of holiday bungalows fixed to the cliff side, with a cable railway saving their occupants the short climb down to and up from the beach. Nevertheless a sufficient aura lingers to encourage those who firmly believe this was where Odysseus was washed ashore and surprised in his nakedness by the princess Nausicaa. Other claims are made, but only here is there the flow of fresh water into the bay which guided Odysseus in his desperate bid to find a safe landing, and in which Nausicaa and her young women came to wash the household linen on that memorable morning.

The northerly branch is a continuation of the most heavily used main road in Corfu, from Kerkyra town diagonally across the island to the triple bay of **Palaiokastritsa**. In essence this is the most beautiful place in Corfu, an entrancing sequence of bays and rocky coves, spread out like some exotic trefoil flower. The beaches are sheltered and sandy at the head of each bay, and the most prominent headland is topped by monastery buildings behind a curtain of trees. Could you one day by magic have it all to yourself, you could dream that close by must have been the palace of Nausicaa's father Alcinous, King of the Phaeacians who dwelt in Scheria, for Homer describes just such an arrangement of bays. True, it is some distance from Ermones, whence Odysseus followed the laundry wagon to the palace, and but for the lack of fresh water one of these bays could equally well have been his landing place. One corroborative detail is the strange low rock which comes into view as you look to seaward – the Phaeacian ship, they say, turned to stone in fury by Poseidon on its return from Ithaka after safely delivering his enemy to his homeland. Its profile is far more convincing than that of flat little Mouse Island, which lies so tamely off the eastern coast.

Sadly, on an ordinary day in summer, you will have to share this still lovely place with more fellow beings than lived in the entire kingdoms of Alcinous or Odysseus – the danger signal is when you find ten coaches parked end to end in the approach lane. Above all try to avoid a visit during the last two weeks of April, a warning which applies to most popular spots in Greece, for then school parties in their thousands are out on educational safari from the mainland.

The best view of Palaiokastritsa – even better than from the well kept and prosperous monastery on the headland – is from the road which climbs northward in steep loops to the village of Lakones. Continuing along a narrow but reasonable road you reach another simple village at **Krini**, from where a track leads downwards to the thirteenth-century castle known today as **Angelokastro**, which the Venetians knew as *Castello Sant'Angelo*, and the Neapolitans in 1272 as the *Castrum Sancti Angeli*. To reach the separate hill on which it stands still needs a short climb, but not such an exhausting one as the old route up from Palaiokastritsa harbour. The view is worth it in any case. Another remote and delightful village up here is **Prinilas**, and the road up from Vistonas is now a good one. A further track will take you down in a mile or two to the sea at **Agios Georgios** bay, which has the best and biggest sandy beach after Glyphada, so far not much visited thanks to its remoteness.

I have left to the last what is perhaps the most interesting and varied expedition you can make in Corfu – and again I stress that without hired transport (on four or two wheels) you will miss the best the island has to offer today. The road running north from Kerkyra at first promises little better than the one which goes south to Benitses. The concentration of hotels at Gouvia, Dasia and Ipsos inevitably obscures and corrupts the coastal views it once enjoyed – though no doubt plenty of fun can be had on their beaches, however crowded.

After Pirgi things improve, when the road begins to skirt the foothills of the mighty **Pantokrator** mountain, 3000 feet of mostly bare rock, which fills up the north-eastern corner of the island. The road winds along as best it can past a minor resort at Nissaki, with the closest views yet of the Albanian coast, less than three miles distant at some points. Do not miss a right hand turn just after Guinari which leads down to a tiny harbour at **Koulouria**, which has a simple taverna, a church and two or three houses in a leafy cove. The same road doubles back to a larger fishing harbour at **Kalami**, where Lawrence Durrell lived in his 'White House' and wrote his diaries for *Prospero's Cell*.

The main road bypasses a rocky headland to reach **Kassiopi**. This was an historic early settlement, with a Venetian castle on its headland, and overlooks a nice beach to the west. It has paid the penalty of fame as a 'picturesque' fishing village by attracting out-of-character and sophisticated attention. A quieter place further on is the landlocked bay below the church of **Agios Spiridon**, only a short detour from the main road. As this turns westward, leaving Pantokrator looming over the driver's left shoulder, the land falls away to a coastal plain with long strips of sand beside a shallow and lifeless sea.

The main resort along here, **Roda**, is busy but not unattractive, and **Astrakeri** has an odd feeling which calls to mind parts of the Norfolk coast. At the time of writing the road from Roda which is signposted to **Sidari** breaks off into chaos just after the village of Karoussades, so that Sidari (another much patronized resort) can be reached only by way of the main road from the south. Instead it is worth taking the minor road southward from Karoussades. From the flat and fertile coastal plain it climbs steadily up wooded valleys to tackle the spiny ridge of mountain which extends westward from Pantokrator. This is glorious country, with views across the eastern straits to Albania, and as you descend gradually past Skripero you can take a left hand turn up to **Ano Korakiana**, a splendid little village straddling the hillside beneath a vast and beetling crag (*korax* is 'crow' or 'raven' in Greek). From there you can return to Kerkyra by way of Sgombou and the main coastal road.

An island as beautiful as this can still withstand the onslaughts of the tourist industry, which must for its own ends keep to its already well publicized areas. Its excesses cannot be blamed on the Greek National Tourist Organization, which does all it can to educate visitors from abroad in the real attractions of the islands. Perhaps the account of Corfu which we give here will help to spread its visitors more widely, without any danger of corrupting the peace of Prospero's island, full of 'sounds and sweet airs that give delight and hurt not'.

From the 'old' harbour of Kerkyra a venerable all-purpose island ferry leaves on most days of the week (every day during the summer season) for **Paxos**, and three hours later ties up conveniently near the main square of **Gaios**, the island's principal town and port. This is not the only link which Paxos has with neighbouring islands, as larger and more modern ferries connect it with Kephalonia, Ithaka and Patras on the mainland of the Peloponnese. These ships come in less conveniently to a new quay nearly half a mile away at the northern entrance to the harbour.

This is an unusual harbour, formed where the island of *Agios Nikolaos* fits neatly into the contours of a wide bay, leaving only a narrow curving channel between it and a long line of quays. Small motor craft, yachts and fishing boats tie up along the quays, which are overlooked by stuccoed, red-roofed houses – a scene at first sight more like Italy than Greece. Over on the island the trees grow thickly, which adds to an already enclosed feeling, and among them you can make out the remains of a fourteenth-century castle partly restored by the French during their brief occupation in the early

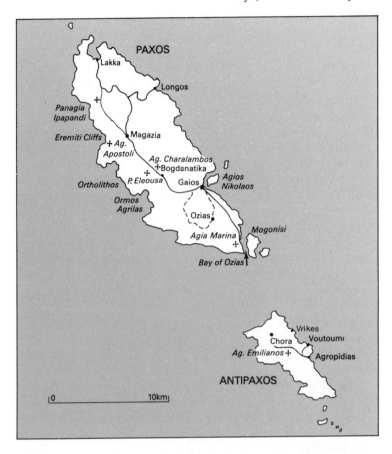

nineteenth century. Beyond again is the smaller island called *Panagia*, with a clean, white-walled convent church which is the starting point of a devout procession – and less devout festivities later in Gaios – to mark the feast of the Assumption on 15 August.

At other times, and especially at weekends and during the long hot afternoons, Gaios is a sleepy place, cut off from enlivening sea breezes by its enclosed position. The only signs of industry are the olive-pressing sheds behind the town, where the fruit of all the millions of trees on Paxos ends up as piles of must, not unlike the rich residue of the French vineyards. Olive must, however, has a life

47

beyond the press, and big lorries take it away for exporting and processing into all sorts of by-products, even ending as solid fuel for stoves.

Paxos is an island given over almost entirely to the cultivation of the olive, and the oil pressed from it has no equal for colour, taste or smoothness. The season lasts from October to April, and well into early spring you can see the black nylon nets spread under practically every tree to catch the fruit as it drops. This ensures a clean crop with little waste, and illustrates how seriously the Paxiots take their great natural asset. As in Corfu, their Venetian rulers in the sixteenth century offered the natives a grant equivalent to five drachmas for every tree planted, and the size and ramifications of some of the specimens you see suggest they are as old as that. Natural generation followed, and a view of Paxos from the air now would show hardly a break in the green cover except on the barer hills of the east coast. This makes it an introspective, even a secretive place, though it can be delightfully shady in the hot summer days, when dappled paths meander through the olive fields past little stone shacks and white-washed cottages.

Some of these qualities may explain why Paxos has become such a favourite with the English, who bought up a great many of its cottages during the 1960s and 1970s, and have formed distinctive communities in the villages. Whether it is cause or effect is hard to tell, but Paxos is still a peaceful uncrowded island, and prices are lower than in its more sophisticated neighbours. Certainly you can eat lobsters here which are as fresh and as cheap as anywhere in the world. Another factor which encourages the island to keep itself to itself is the shortage of water; almost the only source is rainwater collected during the winter. This has so far prevented the building of large hotels – there is one 'bungalow' complex on the cliffs south of Gaios, but it opens only for a limited season and is said to have problems with its water supply.

The wild life too appeals to the country-minded English. Apart from the wild flowers which enjoy both shade and sun, it is quite a draw for ornithologists. Several varieties of hawk, rock doves and skylarks populate the open spaces, and the golden oriole flashes through the grey-green olives. The Skops owl can be heard even in daylight, the two notes of their mating call distinguishing the sexes.

After dark there are glow-worms and some astonishing displays of fireflies.

Under the olive blanket you can make many unexpected discoveries, especially if you are prepared to walk from place to place. One good modern road through the centre of the island connects Gaios with a second and in some ways more attractive harbour at Lakka at its northern tip. There are rewards on the way up in turning aside to look at some isolated churches. They can take a bit of finding, but all of them are worth it. A left hand turn at Bogdanatika winds through the trees to the *Panagia Eleousa*, delightfully placed in total seclusion among olive fields and green flowery paths. A good seventeenth-century bell tower is attached to a typically plain rectangular church.

Instead of the left turn, if you carry on straight on after Bogdanatika, you will see close to the road the tall tower of *Agios Charalambos*. This is a later building (1737) with more classical pretensions, but the body of the church is still a simple rectangle. Charalambos is Paxos's answer to Spiridon of Corfu, and in proportion to their populations just as many boys seem to have been called after him. His usual *persona* depicted on ikons is of a venerable man with an extremely long and narrow white beard, but in Paxos he appears with a witch-like old woman under his feet. This recognizes the part the saint played in ridding Paxos in 1815 from an attack of the plague which has never recurred, for the old woman represents the plague-carrier who went from house to house breathing her poison on the inhabitants. Like all Greeks the Paxiots love myths and symbolism. Their good spirit is the *Liokorni*, or Unicorn, which brings happiness and health wherever it passes. Every other year it visits the olive groves – which explains why the Paxiot trees tend to be biennial croppers.

One of the loveliest walks is through the woodlands west of Bogdanatika, which brings you out in the cliffs overlooking the bay of Agrilas. The headland here is sculptured in natural rock terraces, and you can understand why people who live near come in the evening to sit and watch the sunset. On the way north you come to the bigger village of Magazia, where a road to the left brings you to the west coast again beyond Boikatika. In fact it brings you to a high cliff on the south side of a deep inlet, where in a magnificent

49

situation the tiny church of *Agii Apostoli* looks across at the sheer white **Eremiti Cliffs** beyond the turquoise waters of the inlet. One supposes that somewhere up there lived a hermit with a head for heights. The inside of the church is plain, except for an interesting seventeenth-century *templo* in rough natural stone, painted with figures on a red ochre ground. If you look south from the headland near Boikatika you can see another unusual natural feature, the isolated pillar of rock called **Ortholithos** which sticks up like a finger out of the sea just off the coast.

If you fork left on approaching Lakka you will come to the biggest and oddest of the island churches, the *Panagia Ipapandi*. Odd as the name is (it commemorates a local family and their village rather than an appellation of the Virgin) its architecture is odder. Once the cathedral of the island, a rich foundation of 1602 owning 800 olive trees, it has been given some strange additions over the years. The two cupolas rising from the long rectangular nave have been enclosed in squat drum towers, and the whole fabric washed over in an unattractive brownish-yellow. A very tall and ugly (despite a date given as 1772) bell tower at the end of a cobbled courtyard completes the setting, but if you can find the custodian (a former lighthouse keeper) to open the door it is worth going inside. The chapel to the south of the sanctuary contains an ikon of the Panagia and the Holy Family, covered in silver, which is taken in procession over Easter to various villages, staying for a length of time proportionate to their importance. In the half dome of the apse are remains of an early fresco, a *Christos* with outstretched hands. In the nave is a tall glass case displaying the rich robes of a bishop who found refuge in Paxos from the mainland Turks and died here in 1848. The marble *templo* is in the style of eighteenth-century Venice.

These are only a few of the churches which appear in a series of lists compiled at about fifty-year intervals. The earliest is one of 1686 which contained 39 churches, the latest of 1825 had 61; today the count is 64. The oldest is the seventh-century early Byzantine basilica of *Agia Marina*, whose ruins stand beside the harbour of Ozias at the southern end of Paxos, opposite the large tree-clad island of Mogonisi. This island is the only place where tourism has been overtly encouraged, but outside the holiday season the harbour and its surroundings are delightfully peaceful.

The northern harbour of **Lakka** is a surprise after the shut-in atmosphere at Gaios. It is formed by a deep bay with a narrow entrance, through which the northern breezes find their way in. There is a simple little fishing village at its head, and some inviting-looking houses among the trees which cover the hill behind. An even quieter place is **Longos**, the third harbour of Paxos, which faces north-east a few miles south of Lakka. Like the rest of the island, these little harbours are kept very clean – another factor which must please the English residents. The Paxiots themselves are rightly proud of their island and its history. They share with the Corfiots a distinctive physiognomy, which perhaps suggests an Albanian ancestry. Short of stature and with lightish colouring, they have a broad forehead and a neat nose – not at all like the Aegean Greeks.

The most famous myth connected with Paxos is the one recorded by Plutarch and described by Robert Graves in *The Greek Myths*. The death of Pan is said to have been announced to the Egyptian pilot of a ship passing Paxos on her way to Italy. 'Pan', writes Graves, 'is the only god who has died in our time.' The story is best told in an anonymous comment on Spenser's *Pastoral in May*:

> 'Here, about the time that Our Lord suffered His most bitter Passion, certayne persons sailing from Cypruse to Italie at night heard a voice calling aloud, Thamus, Thamus! Who giving eare to the cry, was bidden (for he was the pilot of the ship) when he came near to Palodas, to tell that the great god Pan was dead; which he doubting to do, yet for that when he came near to Palodas there was such a calme of winde that the ship stood still in the sea unmoored, he was forced to cry out aloud that Pan was dead; wherewithal there was such piteous outcries and dreadful shrieking as hath not been the like. By which Pan of some is understood to have been the great Sathanas, whose kingdom was at that time by Christ conquered, and the gates of hell broken up; for at that time all Oracles surceased, and enchanted spirits that were wont to delude the people henceforth held their peace.'

Plutarch tells us that the scene was the waters off Paxos, while Palodas is identified as a coastal town in Epirus north-east of Corfu. Pausanias, however, describing his visit to Greece a century later, found that the shrines and places sacred to Pan were still active. On this score one can subscribe to the modern theory that what the pilot

51

Thamus heard were the ritual words used in the lament for Tammuz (Adonis): '*Tammuz Pan-Megas tethnike*', which would mean 'The almighty Tammuz is dead' rather than 'Thamus, Great Pan is dead'.

Like Pausanias, we can confirm that Pan today is still alive in the islands. Wherever a fresh stream trickles from the rocks, wherever the best wines are produced, and where the sprightliest goats are to be found, there the wicked little guardian of the flocks sits and plays on his pipes to his devotees and those clever enough to find him. No longer in Paxos, perhaps, but in Kephalonia, in Kea of the western Kyklades, and above all in Thasos and Samothrace away in the north Aegean, he is at home.

He may have found Paxos too uncongenial with the arrival of Venetian busybodies and English reformers. In 1858 Gladstone came to see for himself the state of the Ionian islands. As temporary Lord High Commissioner he was based on the Palace of St Michael and St George in Corfu town, and during a few days on Paxos he puzzled the local dignitaries by his version of religious protocol. The British Residency where he stayed was a small house still to be seen in the main square of Gaios.

A more suitable home for Pan today is the smaller island of **Antipaxos**, a mile or so to the south. There should be no difficulty in getting there from Gaios, for even if the regular inter-island boat is laid up or out of action (as often happens) you can usually find someone to take you with him in his small motor-boat; this is most likely at weekends when he may be going across to look after his family vineyard, or less creditably to take part in the popular 'sport' of shooting at the parties of rock doves which use Antipaxos as a staging point in their migrations. This deplorable practice is now illegal at certain times, but one suspects that the police who should enforce the ban may themselves be culprits when off duty. No retriever dogs are used, so that many birds fall dead or wounded in unreachable places; for whatever reason, the 'bags' are small in proportion to the spent cartridges you see on the ground.

The passage takes about half an hour from Gaios to the little harbour of **Agropidias**, halfway down the east coast, but on the way your boatman may like to show you the spectacular caves under the cliffs at the extreme south of Paxos. He can steer right inside and manoeuvre round a pool of midnight blue sea water and out again into the dazzling sunlight – though naturally it has to be calm weather. On the run down to Agropidias you pass two bays with lovely beaches, **Vrikes** and **Voutoumi**. The latter is an idyllic place – clean sand, cliffs, deep blue water shading to turquoise close in.

It is when you climb the new road up from the harbour to the main inland village – just a few scattered houses and the rustic church of *Agios Emilianos* where the graveyard may be a safe pen for a ewe and her lamb – that you can picture what Paxos must have looked like before the olives grew. The hillsides are scrubby and treeless, but the little homesteads are surrounded by vineyards which produce one of the best wines – a slightly sparkling red – in the Ionian seas. These properties are mostly surrounded by stone walls over six feet high, with grassy lanes between them. To walk through the village, with flowering trees and shrubs peeping or trailing over the walls, is to glimpse a mediaeval paradise untouched by anything except time – one might even accept the mediaeval sanitation which goes with it.

The coastal scenery is glorious, especially on the west side, where high rocky cliffs rise steeply from the sea. There is no access to them, but a second road up from Agropidias leads to the southern end of the island and the lighthouse at its tip. There is nowhere on Antipaxos for the visitor to stay, and one hopes that it will be a long time before familiar notices like 'Rent Rooms' and 'Pizza Bar' are seen in the island.

Access

Most visitors come to CORFU by air, though there are not many scheduled flights direct from London. Ferries from Italy and Yugoslavia dock in the New (international) Harbour; those coming from Igoumenitsa or Patras on the Greek mainland put in at the Old Harbour a little to the east and nearer the town centre. On the way from Patras they call at Kephalonia, Ithaka and Paxos, but this service is only twice weekly. PAXOS is served by a veteran ferry which leaves the Old Harbour in Kerkyra every day during the high season, but less often at other times. You can also get there from Patras, by way of Kephalonia and Ithaka, but only twice a week.

Communications

The road system in CORFU is extensive, though even on the main roads the surface can have alarming pot-holes. Buses and tour coaches cover most of them, and there are plenty of taxis. However, if you can hire a car or a moped you will be able to see more and dodge the crowds.

In PAXOS there is only one modern road, from Gaios in the south to Lakka in the north, with a regular if infrequent bus service. Taxis can be found in either of these two ports; they are helpful and not too expensive, and can usually be raised by telephone.

Accommodation

CORFU   The holiday hotels are too numerous to list. In spite of its size, the GRAND HOTEL GLYPHADA (A, 417 beds) is probably the best. It has every comfort and diversion available, a magnificent beach, and its tariff is reasonable for its class. In Kerkyra town the best hotel is KAVALIERI (A, 91 beds), overlooking the southern esplanade. ARKADION (C) is also well placed and convenient, though not very welcoming. There are rooms of varying quality to let all over the island, and many small houses are let as 'villas' by the agencies.

PAXOS   There is only one hotel, PAXOS BEACH (B) on the cliffs beyond Gaios. This is a summer-only, 'bungalow' hotel, without much character. The most popular accommodation here is in 'villas', of which large numbers are let through international and local travel agents.

Restaurants

CORFU   Again there are too many to list. In Kerkyra, AVEROF near the Cathedral is authentically Greek and deservedly popular. The smartest is the seafood restaurant ARGO, on the northern front beyond the New Harbour, where the food lives up to the elegance. Much simpler but very good value for ordinary Greek food is EUROPE, below the New Fortress and opposite the New Harbour. Plenty of good simple meals can be had in country villages and small harbours round the coast.

PAXOS   There is not much choice, but in Gaios you can be sure of a good meal (if you get there in time) at REX, where the *langoustes* are as fresh and as cheap as you will find anywhere.

Facilities

Banks: Kerkyra has branches of all Greek banks, but there is no other centre big enough to have any. In Gaios, a desk in a shop counts as a 'branch' of the National Bank of Greece, where the cashier is friendly and efficient.

Yachts: Corfu is not a great favourite with the yachtsman. The best harbours are in the bay of Gouvia, north of Kerkyra, and at Kassiopi on the north coast – which can be crowded. In Paxos there are harbours at Gaios, Lakka and Longos where it is a pleasure to lie.

THREE

Levkas, Ithaka and Kephalonia

Levkas, sometimes called Levkada and known to the Venetians as Santa Mavra, lies just, but only just, off the coastline of Acharnania. Homer in the Odyssey refers to it as a promontory of Epirus; at first sight it does appear to be a peninsula leaning out from the mainland, and such it was in early times. Considered as an island it is an oddity. Its backbone is a high mountain ridge, but up in the north the modern capital Levkada is surrounded by low-lying lagoons and marshes where the sea salt whitens in sour-smelling pans. The only approach to it is by way of a causeway across the marshes built by the Turks in the sixteenth century, which goes as far as the mediaeval castle of Santa Mavra – at the time this lent its name to the whole island. Built on a detached spit of land, it still leaves a very narrow channel to cross, which is now done by an electrically operated chain ferry.

The problem with Levkas is how to get there. There are no regular sea communications with Corfu or Paxos, and from Kephalonia there is only a roundabout route which involves an overland bus journey up the mainland coast. Occasionally during the summer a boat-owner in the northern port of Phiskardon on Kephalonia may be persuaded to take a party on a day excursion to Vasiliki in the south-west corner of Levkas. From Athens it would be a daunting 248-mile bus journey by way of Corinth, but there is now an airport at Aktion at the mouth of the Gulf of Arta, with a direct road connection to Levkada by way of the causeway and the chain ferry.

The cord which originally joined Levkas with the mainland was at another very narrow point further south, opposite the site of the ancient capital. The short isthmus there was cut by the Corinthians

55

in the seventh century BC when they founded a colony here – one of several intended to protect their shipping routes along this coastline. The canal they dredged had apparently silted up by 427 BC, thanks to the prevailing north wind, seismic disturbances and the steady drift of mud and sand. It was that year when according to Thucydides the Peloponnesians at war with Kerkyra hauled their ships 'over the Leukadian isthmus'.* Levkas had sent three ships to Salamis in 480 BC, but during the Peloponnesian War the city paid a heavy penalty for siding with Sparta: she was devastated first by Kerkyra in 436 and then by the Athenians ten years later. Life was hard for the smaller city states who had to decide on their alliances almost from year to year, and often decided wrongly. Her final mistake was to back Macedonia against Rome in the second century BC, which finished her as an independent state – though the ever-magnanimous Emperor Hadrian later gave the island back to Athens.

The waterway was opened again by the Romans under Augustus, and from then on Levkas has been, however narrowly, an island. That there is now an airport at Aktion reminds us that from here Antony watched the destruction of his fleet by Octavian's lighter and more easily manoeuvred ships. The rout was completed when the ships of Cleopatra's Egyptian navy fled and were followed by Antony himself. The battle of Actium on 2 September 31 BC made the victor master of the Roman world, and as Augustus Caesar its first Emperor.

Shipping still used the channel in the Middle Ages. Giovanni Orsini added Levkas to his Ionian dominions in the thirteenth century AD, and it was he who built Santa Mavra castle to guard its northern approach, and established the capital on its present site. Being so close to the mainland it had no chance of warding off the Turks, who seized the island in 1479. Not until 1718 was she ceded to Venice, after which she shared the fortunes of the other Ionian islands.

In this century the channel was dredged again to take large coastal steamers and caiques; in 1905 the Levkas Ship Canal was opened. Three miles long, and dredged to a depth of fifteen feet, it

* *Histories* III, 81

follows the ancient route due south from the Ormos Denata to the Ormos Drepanou. Entering it from the north one sees the fort of Santa Mavra dominating the channel on the port side, while the town of Levkada faces it across the mud flats.

Modern **Levkada** (if we may call it that to distinguish it from the island as a whole) is a dull town in a dull position, its character not much enhanced by some restored eighteenth-century churches. To the south is a big expanse of salt-pans, to the north a shallow sea lagoon. There is interest in the rest of the island, though. Beyond the sea lagoon is the fourteenth-century church of *Agios Ioannis* which overlooks a long narrow beach. Here in 1810 the Greek national hero, Theodore Kolokotronis, joined the British in landing to dislodge the French, and was rewarded by our strong support in the Greek War of Independence. The cold springs which empty into the sea make it uncomfortably chilly for bathers, but the local housewives use the fresh water for their laundry.

The road south from the capital is more rewarding. First it passes the site of the ancient city near the village of Kaligoni: the acropolis was built on a flat-topped hill, where you can still see the stonework at the base of its walls, and water cisterns cut out of the rock. The road then follows the coast, skirting a few spurs of the central mountain range to reach the wide valley where two rivers converge on the attractive harbour town of **Nydri**. Nydri offers access by small ferries to an archipelago of lesser islands, the biggest of which is **Meganisi**, an oddly shaped island with a number of deep caves. One of the smaller ones is **Skorpios**, owned by the Onassis family and so not to be visited.

Sea and land seem inextricable in this part of Levkas. Another long inlet, the Ormos Vlychou, is enclosed by the headland of Agia Kyriaki across the water from Nydri. Here is the grave of the nineteenth-century archaeologist Wilhelm Dörpfeld, who endeared himself to the islanders by pursuing one of the longest running Ionian hares – the true location of Homer's Ithaka. He was convinced, in the face of what has always seemed reasonable evidence, that the home and palace of Odysseus was here in Levkas. It was one of those *idées fixes*, passionately believed but based chiefly on his discovery of Mycenaean remains in the Nydri valley. It ignored Odysseus's own description of Ithaka as lying well away to

57

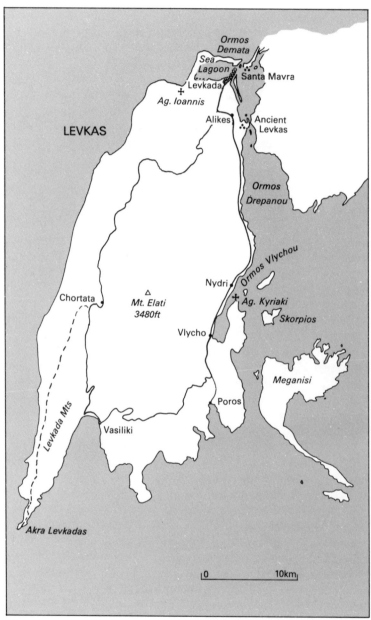

the west, and as 'rugged and unfit for driving horses', while several places named by Homer can be recognized in Ithaka.

Beyond Vlycho the road crosses the wide plains of the south – very suitable, it must be said, for driving horses – to the most attractive place on the island, the harbour, village and beach of **Vasiliki**. The village occupies the higher ground to the south of the point where the considerable river Karouchas enters the bay after its long course down from the towering central mountains.

Across the bay from Vasiliki runs the Levkada ridge which has given its name to the whole island and ends in its most historic spot. Down there at the end of a long tapering finger of land is the white cliff of the Akra Levkadas, the scene of the strange procedure of the *Katapontismos*, or 'Sea Dive'. A temple of Apollo, some remains of which can still be seen, once stood on the headland 230 feet above the sea, and from here the priests of Apollo under some curious compulsion would hurl themselves into space, buoyed up, it is said, by live birds and feathered wings.

There is also a theory that the 'Leukadian Leap' was used as a form of trial by ordeal, or for the disposal of scapegoats. Sappho is reported, on dubious authority, to have thrown herself to her death from here when desperate for unrequited love. There is no record of any priest being harmed in this strange ritual, for boatmen with nets waited below to rescue the divers after what may have been an initiation ceremony. Norman Douglas must have had this spot in mind when he describes in *South Wind* how Mrs Meadows launched the unfaithful father of her daughter into the depths below – there was no waiting boatman then.

The impression remains that Levkas is not a real island, but part of the jumbled coastal scenery of mainland Greece – to which it might still be joined but for historical accident. There is certainly no overall island character, such as we find in all the others of the Ionian group. Its most dramatic impact is when seen from northern Ithaka – the huge bulk of Mt Elati seems to occupy its whole width.

There is no doubt that **Ithaka** is an island, though in the geological past it must have been a part of the much bigger island of Kephalonia, so neatly would its western shoreline fit into the opposite coast. It lies ten miles south of Levkas, small in area but with

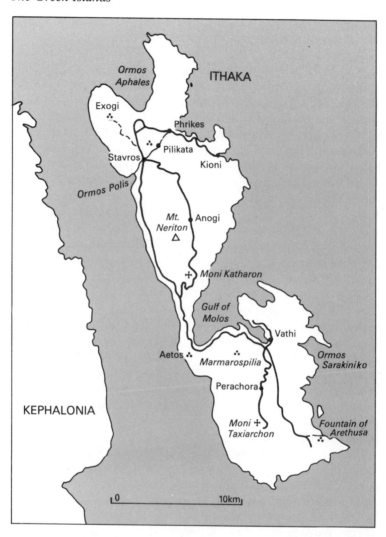

sufficient grandeur to deserve a claim to be the most famous island in the world.

The main harbour and capital is **Vathi**, in a deep narrow inlet off the Gulf of Molos. It was a sixteenth-century foundation, now rebuilt after the disastrous earthquake of 1953 which caused such havoc in Kephalonia and Zakynthos. You can reach it from the mainland at Astakos or from the port of Agia Evphemia on the west coast of Kephalonia. The latter is far the best way to approach Ithaka. As you emerge from the Ithaka channel between the two islands, the dark rounded humps of Odysseus's homeland never fail to excite. Then as you look north up this historic strait, nowadays perhaps dotted with white yacht sails, you may be thinking of Penelope's suitors lying in wait for Telemachus by the islet of **Daskalio**, the most likely candidate for Homer's Asteris. To reach Vathi your little ferry has to round the southern capes of Ithaka, and will pass the sandy bay of Agios Andreas where it seems most likely that the son of Odysseus landed – well out of sight of the waiting suitors, who expected him to make for one of the northern harbours below the palace.

The knowledgeable will be looking up one of the valleys, covered with scrub almost to the water's edge, to see if they can make out where the swineherd Eumaeus had his cottage. Sure enough, just before you round the eastern cape of Agios Ioannis, you can make out a little stone building on one of the upper slopes – nothing unusual in the islands, but somehow reassuring for those who believe that Homer knew Ithaka. Further encouragement comes as you move up the eastern coast: you can see a steep beetling cliff against the skyline, with a green cleft below down which water may be falling – the **Raven's Crag** and the **Fountain of Arethusa**?*

The next sighting on the coast, as we cross the Ormos Sarakiniko (the Bay of the Saracens) jolts us into modern times. A scattering of what look like white plastic beehives dotted among the scrub is a settlement of German nature-lovers, trying to live in Bronze Age conditions – the island authorities refused to let them build new stone cottages. We round the final point for the long run in to Vathi at the head of this very deep bay, and we find a pleasant small town with every modest facility, including a few taxis with informative drivers who are glad to take you up for a look at the northern end of the island.

Ithaka is squeezed into these distinct halves, like an hourglass, and is less than a mile across at its waist. The road from Vathi

* *Odyssey* XIII, 408.

quickly reaches one of the most evocative places, the bay which Homer says was named after Phorkys, the old man of the sea, and which today is called **Dexia** because it lies to the right of a ship entering the Gulf of Molos. It fits the description Homer gives of the bay where the Phaeacian ship was beached to lay the sleeping Odysseus on the shore – a shallow sandy cove guarded by bold headlands on either side. In the hillside above is a roomy cave which could easily have been the Cave of the Nymphs where Athena advised him to hide his treasures. Today it is called **Marmarospilia**, and it faces north to Mt Neriton as Athena implies in her own words to Odysseus.*

Mt Neriton is the long dark backbone of northern Ithaka, so striking when seen from across the strait in early morning light, and the north-bound road is forced close to the western cliff edge to pass it. First, though, it has to cross the narrow isthmus, at whose southern end the separate hilltop of **Aetos** ('eagle' in Greek) suggested to Schliemann and others the site of the Mycenaean palace. Modern opinion tells us to look further north for this, and when we reach the substantial village of **Stavros** we find ourselves on a plateau where a dig by the British School in the 1930s found a good deal of Bronze Age pottery and traces of city walls; recent excavations are still turning up valuable evidence near the village of Pilikata, a mile north-west of Stavros.

In **Pilikata** is a small museum, containing one of those slightly sad little collections of pottery reassembled from the merest fragments with immense care and skill. Amongst it are some charming domestic objects – bowls, cups, beakers, dishes and ladles – of dates ranging from 2000 BC Minoan to 1200 BC Mycenaean, and from 700 BC archaic to fifth-century Corinthian. The devoted custodian is the English-speaking wife of a local schoolmaster, soon to take over after finishing a degree course in Athens. She points bitterly but resignedly to an empty case which until a few years ago contained twelve three-legged bronze cauldrons (*tripoda*). Now Homer says that Odysseus brought thirteen bronze cauldrons with him from Scheria, and one is known to have been stolen after they were found in a cave on the north side of the bay of Polis.

* *Odyssey* XIII, 96–112 and 342–351.

Polis could easily be one of the three harbours which Homer says were used by the rulers of Ithaka and were visible from their palace. It lies south-west of Stavros, facing Kephalonia, and the name shows that here in classical times was a 'city' – and possibly an earlier settlement too. The city was probably an eighth or seventh-century foundation which was wrecked and submerged by an earthquake – the outlines of houses can be seen under the waters of the bay. As for the *tripoda*, they have been dated to about 800 BC, and it seems possible that Homer knew of them or had even seen them in their cavern near the ancient city. Now they have been removed 'for safe keeping' to the big museum in Patras. It was said that the bronze was being eaten away by the salt air of Pilikata – but if so did nobody think of presenting a replica or even a full-scale photograph for display where they were found, and where visitors come from all over the world to look for Odysseus in his homeland?

Due north of the Pilikata site is the bay of **Aphales**; due east is **Phrikes**, now a comfortable little fishing harbour with the towers of windmills on either side of the entrance. All three bays can be seen from the high ground near Pilikata, and would have made convenient beaching harbours in different weather conditions. There is another east-facing harbour at **Kioni** a few miles down the coast – all these are places of individual charm. The southern flanks of the island may be bare and scrubby, but in the northern valleys and round the Gulf of Molos there is much greenery, many fruit trees, vines and flowers. From the higher parts the views are miraculous: eastward the distant mountainous mainland with scattered offshore islands; to the north the spectacular massif of Levkas; to the west the northern peninsula of Kephalonia; to the south Kephalonia's majestic Mt Aenos.

No excuse is offered for presenting Ithaka so far mainly in the context of Homer's *Odyssey*. To see where the climax of this marvellous adventure story happened must be the prime reason for visiting it, though the individual beauty of the island would be almost enough in itself. No apology either for calling the hero of the story by his Greek name – I doubt if one native of Ithaka would know who you meant by Ulysses. At the same time, it is true that no Greek island was untouched by Byzantium. A minor road, rough in places, braves the rocky ridge of Neriton as far as the village of

Anogi, where there is a good *Panagia* church which survived the earthquake of 1953. There are interesting Byzantine frescos in the apse, and an array of later gospel and Old Testament scenes along the walls of the nave which must belong to the seventeenth and eighteenth centuries. In the village you can find some strange semi-cave dwellings, with very low entrances leading into the hillside – mediaeval hide-outs for when pirates were around. From Anogi onwards the road deteriorates, but it passes the *Moni Katharon*, a restored mediaeval monastery which is rarely to be found open. From here there is a superb eagle's eye view across the Gulf of Molos to Vathi – a toy harbour seen from nearly 2000 feet up.

The southern bulge of Ithaka is served now by a reasonable road which forks into two on the outskirts of Vathi. The right hand fork goes by way of Perachori to the *Moni Taxiarchon*, restored after the 1953 earthquake, while the left hand one sticks to the lower foothills on its way to the neighbourhood of the Raven's Crag and the spring of Peripigadi, perhaps the Fountain of Arethusa. The road is still rough in places, following possibly the route which Odysseus took on that first day from the bay of Phorkys to the cottage and piggeries of Eumaeus – the first of the well calculated moves which re-established him as lord of Ithaka, the jewel of the Ionian islands and today a place of heart-warming beauty and friendliness.

If there are those who wonder why a great man like Odysseus should have been content with little Ithaka as his kingdom, a plausible answer is that he may have ruled over a confederacy which included **Kephalonia** and Zakynthos. Homer says that the troops Odysseus led at Troy were 'great-hearted Kephallinians' from Ithaka, Zakynthos and Samos. If so, it seems another proof of the man's ability and reputation that he could control such a confederation from a small base like Ithaka. We must remember that in those days the importance of the city and its ruler counted more than the size of his territory. The name Samos is at first confusing, but when we find there is a modern town and harbour of Sami on the east coast of Kephalonia it falls into place. In classical times this was Same, the chief of the four cities described by Thucydides as a *tetrapolis* – the others being Kranioi, Pale and Pronnoi.

The jetty at Poros

Corfu. Vlachernes I., with *(above left)* Pondikonisi

Sami was the base where Don John of Austria assembled his fleet before the battle of Lepanto in 1571 – the engagement which checked the westward spread of Ottoman power, and did much to keep the Ionian islands out of Turkish hands. Though not the most important town today, it lies conveniently for ferries working between Corfu, Paxos and Patras on the mainland. To land here is not exciting. The town was obliterated by the 1953 earthquake, was rebuilt without much enterprise or taste, and has nowhere to tempt the visitor to stay. The best move after landing is to take a taxi or wait for a bus across to Argostoli on the opposite coast. This journey, which crosses the col of Agropidias, gives you an early idea of what to expect in Kephalonia. The scale has changed dramatically from anything we have seen so far in the Ionian. High rolling hills stretch away on both sides of the road, scrub on the lower slopes and patches of the native Kephalonian pine higher up. When you cross the col the scenery changes to a wide fertile plain, with vineyards, cornfields and olive plantations filling the open spaces as you drop into the Omala valley.

Now you can see clearly the unusual surroundings of **Argostoli**, which is now the capital. The town lies on the farther side of a narrow arm of the sea crossed by a long causeway, really a very low bridge built on the arched foundations laid by British engineers in 1813 during the protectorate. The island profited a good deal at that time from an efficient administration, especially under Sir Charles Napier who was Governor from 1822 to 1830 and concentrated on improving roads and education. They remember him here still, perhaps appreciating the sense of humour which produced his famous despatch after conquering an Indian province: '*Peccavi*, I have Scind!'.

Argostoli was bravely if optimistically laid out afresh after 1953, with spacious squares and avenues lined with palm trees, but the buildings on the whole do no justice to the planners. A wide promenade has been left along the harbour front, with a richly stocked fruit and vegetable market at the southern end, but again the offices, cafés and hotels which overlook it are commonplace. One of the better and more dignified buildings is the **Archaeological Museum**. It has all the virtues of the local Greek museums, though without many notable exhibits. Two of the rooms contain mainly

Mycenaean finds – pottery, jewellery and bronze weapons – from cemetery sites in the south-west. Another room to the right of the entrance has some interesting Roman and Hellenistic exhibits, notably a bronze head of the third century from Sami. In the same room is a collection of silver and gold coins from most of the Greek cities, and two very fine gold pieces from Carthage.

Devotees of Pan will be fascinated to find here a round terracotta plate found at his sanctuary near the east coast. In the centre of the plate is the little horned figure playing on his pipes with a circle of girls dancing round him. In the same case is a larger figure of Silenus, with a wine cup resting on his ample belly and a cornucopia on his left shoulder; he has goat's legs and hooves, but has lost his phallus.

Beyond the short peninsula on which the town stands, a large western extension is almost severed from the body of the island by the deep intrusion of the Gulf of Argostoli. **Kranioi** was the ancient city which controlled the Gulf, and if you walk round the head of the bay south of Argostoli you can reach the site. Just past the small modern waterworks building on the right, a path climbs quite steeply to a ridge where long sections of the old walls stand to a height of several feet; one section survives at road level, where it protected the bottom of the winding approach path. Up there now all is lovely and remote, with bird song and browsing goats – a perfect place for a picnic.

Another of the four cities was close to the sea on the opposite side of the Gulf. **Pale**, two hundred of whose citizens fought the Persians at Plataea, was about a mile north of **Lixourion**, the modern port which faces Argostoli across the water. Unlike Kranioi its site was not defensible, and hardly a trace remains; its stones were plundered to build Lixourion. This is a sad place, low-lying, shadeless and messy, with no building of character to lift its spirits. It seems hardly worth taking the ferry across from Argostoli, though if you go round by the road you will find – not far from where Pale stood – the little church attached to the *Moni Kechrion*. The monastery church is modern, thanks to the earthquake, but the courtyard where it stands is an oasis of peace just off the busy road.

An easy and pleasant walk from Argostoli follows the coastal path to the tip of its peninsula. The cool dark pine woods inland give

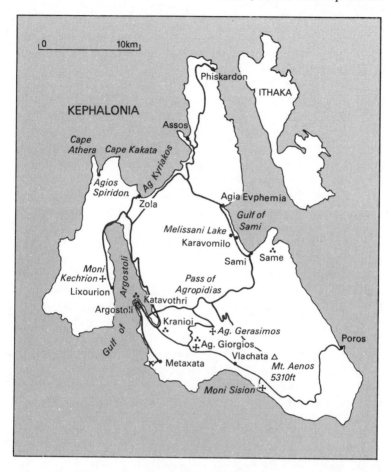

way to flowery slopes between the path and the sea, and before long you come to the most curious feature on this side of the island. A sequence of ditches parallel to the coast receive a constant inflow of sea water which disappears entirely into underground channels which are called *katavothri*. The force of the inrushing sea was enough to drive watermills of the wheel and bucket type, one of which has been reconstructed behind a popular café near the point. The mystery was where the water went to, and the extraordinary solution was only found when a team of Austrian scientists traced it

67

with chemicals to an underground lake on the far eastern side of the island – which it could only reach by doubling back under the intervening arm of the sea and then passing under the highest point of the central mountain range.

The north coast of the Lixourion peninsula is high, bare and rocky, but at two places it gives place to sandy bays. The remote cove of **Agios Spiridon** lies between Capes Athera and Kakata at the end of a long and roughish road. Easier of access is the usually empty expanse of beach at **Agios Kyriakos** below the village of Zola, reached by a short side turning off the main road from Argostoli to the north, soon after the fork for Lixourion.

At that junction the right hand turn is signposted to Phiskardon, and if you take it – by bus or hired transport – you will have the most glorious drive in all the islands. The scale and grandeur of this west coast scenery will not be equalled until you reach Naxos in the Kyklades. The road follows the corniche, with capes and bays unfolding before and behind you, the sea open to the western horizon. Down below, a headland with a double summit comes into sight – almost but not quite an island, for on the narrow connecting neck of land you can see the red roofs of the harbour village of **Assos**.

If you want a change of base from Argostoli, this could hardly be more different or more delightful. The fishing harbour is to the south, it has a sandy bay to the north, and across the double crest of the headland spread the walls of a huge Venetian castle. The village opens out into a wide leafy square, well supplied with cafés and restaurant tables. Crowds come for the day during the summer, but most houses seem to have clean and well equipped rooms to let, which makes it a thoroughly enjoyable place to stay when the crowds have gone.

After Assos the road moves further inland and finally descends in a long right hand curve to the larger harbour of **Phiskardon**. This name has an odd sound in Greek, being derived from the surname of Robert Guiscard, the Norman baron from Sicily who captured Corfu in 1081 and died here four years later. (Almost the same name belongs to a man of our own time, Valéry Giscard d'Estaing.) Phiskardon would be another good place to stay, though its natural charm is beginning to wane just a little as it feels the impact of tourism. There are some beautiful beaches within walking distance, romantic views across to Ithaka, and if you can find a boat to take you there it is only five miles south of Vasiliki and the Leukadian Leap.

There is no choice of roads back south until you reach the turning a few miles beyond Assos, where the left hand road follows a valley across to **Agia Evphemia** in the northern corner of the Gulf of Sami. This is a quiet harbour, without the charm of Assos and Phiskardon, but useful as the ferry terminal between Kephalonia and Ithaka. Committed now to follow the coast down to Sami, you must look for a sign just before the village of Karavomilo directing you to the **Melissani Lake**. This is a fantastic place, an underground sea of deep blue, where it has been proved that the sea water from the Argostoli *katavothri* emerges. A small opening high overhead lets in a little daylight, by which you can see dripping clusters of stalactites, and Charon is at hand to row boatloads of visitors round two underground chambers in a Stygian twilight. The colour underneath the boat is an astonishing aquamarine, and the effect is eerily beautiful. The small entrance fee includes Charon's obol.

Nothing illustrates the scale on which Kephalonia is built better than its central mountains, which reach a climax in Mt Aenos, a dark and threatening mass rising to over 5000 feet at the southern end of the chain. Yet between it and the coastline south of Argostoli is a wide and gentle plain with a network of little roads connecting neat, well cared-for villages. **Metaxata** (not far from the airport) is the best known of them, because Byron lived here in the last year of his life before ending his Greek pilgrimage at Mesolongi in April 1924. It must have been a happy, peaceful time for this naturally restless man. His house vanished in the great earthquake, but you can still see the orchard from which in season he would have enjoyed a choice of oranges, lemons, mulberries, walnuts, figs, almonds and peaches – such are the riches of Kephalonia. He wrote in his journal:

> 'Standing at the window of my apartment in this beautiful village, the calm though cool serenity of a beautiful and transparent Moonlight, showing the Islands, the Mountains, the Sea, with a distant outline of the Morea traced between the double Azure of the waves and skies, has quieted me enough to be able to write.'

On a wall opposite there is a marble plaque which says simply 'Lord Byron's Ivy', and there it is.

The main road to the east runs across the plain from Argostoli before it has to squeeze between Mt Aenos and the sea. As soon as you leave the capital you will see rising from the plain the clear-cut hill of **Agios Georgios**, where in the thirteenth century the Orsini family built a castle – turned later by Venetian experts into one of their finest. At that time it was the centre of the largest mediaeval town in Kephalonia, with a population of 15,000. It was wrecked by an earthquake in 1636, and in 1757 the remaining inhabitants moved down to Argostoli.

A good deal of the castle's impressive system of fortification is intact, the *enceinte* almost complete, with round corner bastions sloping outwards to the base like the curtain walls. The central keep is not much more than a grassy mound, but there is a formidable main gateway at the head of a stone ramp, and on each of the other three sides an underground passage leads to a postern. The chapel walls on the south side of the keep survive almost to their full height. Fortresses can be sour places, but this whole site is sweetened now by wild flowers, waving grasses and pine trees. The views all round are grand, and immediately below the northern ramparts you can see the scattered ruins of all those deserted houses.

On a lower spur of the same hill you will find a baroque Venetian church which has mostly survived the earthquake. The *Evangelistria* is a large rectangular building with a Corinthian pilastered doorway at the west end with a sundial over it and a broken pediment. A separate archway of the same period was all but demolished, and is only kept upright by wooden buttresses. It would be worth restoring, with its semicircular arches, its baroque curlicues and flying angels. Churches in this style are to be found all over Zakynthos, but this is the only one in Kephalonia that has survived.

About two miles after the village of Vlachata (the Greek word *vlachas* means 'stupid', and the Greek sense of humour often shows in their place names) a track leads down to the coast past the monastery of **Sisia**. At first you see only a large, modern, obviously post-earthquake building, but below, concealed by a drop in the road, is the old monastery, ruined beyond repair by earthquakes but with the shell of the church intact except for its roof. The signs are that this was an early Italian foundation, a complete monastic layout with a long refectory, possibly a dorter above, and a courtyard with a well in the centre. Grass and flowers grow among the tumbled blocks of masonry, which must have been in ruins long before 1953 – perhaps as early as 1636 when it still belonged to the Catholic faith. The church was converted to Orthodox use and kept in repair until the last cataclysm – new tiles had been laid on the floor and the roof not long before. There are traces of much earlier Italianate features in the body of the church, and it may not be too fanciful to associate the name Sisia with the Order of St Francis of Assisi.

Rounding the tail end of Mt Aenos the road turns north to reach the coast at **Poros**. The approach is dramatic, the road descending through a narrow gorge between steep cliffs. For a time Poros was used as a ferry harbour connecting Kephalonia with Zakynthos *via* Killini on the mainland, but this service has been transferred to Sami. It remains a clean and sensible place with legitimate claims to be a seaside resort. It was rebuilt after the earthquake with a wide esplanade laid out with creeper-covered canopies and flower beds, overlooking a long beach of sand and shingle.

A monastery which is still very much in business is **Agios Gerasimos**, down in a green offshoot of the Omala valley and easily reached by a turn south off the main Sami–Argostoli road. This is rich farming country, with quietly grazing flocks of sheep, obviously capable of sustaining a rich monastic foundation. Its present wealth has enabled it to build a huge and by no means beautiful church at the end of the valley, but the old monastic enclosures have been converted since the earthquake into a series of spacious gardens through which the nuns (it is properly a convent) flutter in their black habits. The oldest surviving building is a long low church which contains an elaborate silver-covered sarcophagus and an upright 'sentry-box' with an apparently headless mummified body. Both are repositories for the remains of the Ieros Monachos Gerasimos who founded the convent in 1554 and planted three enormous plane trees (at least they are enormous today) – two in the gardens and one in the centre of a ceremonial approach avenue. They should be nearing 450 years old. It is said that his original cell was a space underneath this church, reached by a steep iron ladder from the nave, but he soon established a reputation for miracles and was canonized in 1622.

Besides the road back to Argostoli you may be puzzled to see a

71

row of cavelike openings in the hillside, outlined in white paint, with stone troughs full of flowers set out in front. This was the headquarters of the Italian 'Acqui' division, 9000 Alpine troops who refused to submit to the German command after the Italian government's surrender in 1943. There was a bitter week-long battle, and the 3000 Italians who survived were forced to surrender. During the three following days they were systematically shot in cold blood by the Germans. It is said that thirty-four survived by shamming death and escaped with the help of the Kephalonians, who adopted their former enemies as heroic allies and have kept the memory of this shameful episode alive.

Our final encounter may be with Mt Aenos. This magnificent mountain dominates the south of Kephalonia and the sea for many miles around, but the engineers who have built so many good roads here have contrived a motor route right to the summit at 5310 feet. From the pass of Agropidias it climbs in steep zigzags to run straight along the summit ridge to its peak. If lucky enough to take this road on a clear day you have a view the gods of Olympus might have envied. It confirms that Kephalonia is the grandest of the whole Ionian group, and equalled for individual beauty only by Ithaka.

Access

This is a surprisingly difficult problem, considering the short distance between these islands. LEVKAS has no direct connection with either Ithaka or Kephalonia, but the small daily ferry which connects these two continues to the port of Astakos on the mainland, from where buses run to Vonitsa and across the causeway to Levkada. You can fly from Athens to the airport at Aktio, which has a bus connection with Levkada. ITHAKA is served by the daily ferry from Agia Evphemia in Kephalonia, and also by a larger ship which runs between Patras in the northern Peloponnese and Kerkyra. This sails daily for KEPHALONIA but goes the whole distance and returns from Kerkyra only once a week. Kephalonia can be reached by ferry from Killini on the mainland opposite (which provides a connection with Zakynthos) and by air direct from Athens.

Communications

In LEVKAS there are buses from Levkada to Nydri, Vlycho and Vasiliki. In ITHAKA there are some buses between Vathi and Stavros, but taxis can save a lot of time. To see KEPHALONIA properly it is worth hiring a car in Argostoli, where there is a big choice; the roads cover much of the island and are excellent.

Accommodation

LEVKAS   There are three hotels in Levkada or near it: LEVKAS (B, 186 beds), NIRIKOS (B, 69 beds) and the smaller SANTA MAVRA (C) which has more character. Villas and rooms are let in Nydri and Vasiliki.

ITHAKA   MENTOR (B) at the head of the harbour at Vathi, near the Cathedral, is the pleasantest there. Rooms are readily found in Stavros and in the northern harbours of Phrikes and Kioni.

KEPHALONIA   Of a number of hotels in Argostoli, the family-run XENIA (B) is outstanding for peace and friendliness. KEPHALONIA STAR (C) is modern and well run, but is right on the harbour front. The big tourist hotels are at Lassi and Platys Gialos on the west coast of the Argostoli peninsula, headed by MEDITERRANÉE (A, 430 beds). There are small 'pensions' in Poros and Phiskardon, mostly block-booked, but there and especially in Assos you will find excellent lodging in privately owned guest houses, or simple comfort in rented rooms. In Agia Evphemia there is the convenient PYLAROS (C) and an attractive guest house.

Restaurants

LEVKAS   There are good restaurants both in Levkada and in the east coast villages, which cater for the Greek as well as for the foreign tourist.

ITHAKA   The harbour restaurants in Vathi are much as you will find in holiday places. You will do better in the little northern harbours, and best of all in Stavros next to the big church.

KEPHALONIA   Argostoli comes to life late in the year, with hardly anywhere open till well into May. Later there is a fair choice at different levels around the *Plateia Valianou* – the best is at the south-east corner, and is open most of the year for the inhabitants. You can eat well in Phiskardon and better still in the *plateia* of Assos.

Facilities

Banks: Levkada town has three banks, and so have Vathi in Ithaka and Argostoli in Kephalonia.

Yachts: Levkas has a number of sheltered harbours – at the capital Levkada, at Nydri, Poros and Vasiliki, and at Spartochori on the offshore island of Meganisi. There is a yacht supply station at Levkada and a repair yard at Vlycho.

Vathi harbour in Ithaka is ideal for the yachtsman, though Kioni in the north is quieter and just as good in most weathers.

The extensive Gulf of Argostoli in Kephalonia is safe in all weathers, with shore facilities at Argostoli and Lixourion. The harbours at Sami and Agia Evphemia are more exposed, though the latter is convenient for a short stay. Phiskardon in the north is very popular – crowded but fun.

FOUR

Zakynthos

Levkas to the north, Ithaka and Kephalonia in the middle, to the south **Zakynthos** – this crescent of islands shields the entrance to the Gulf of Patras. The Italian name Zante has almost if not universally given way to the classical Zakynthos, as Homer and Virgil knew it. It is surprising to find that though only eight miles separate their coastlines, and both islands have airfields, there is no direct communication between it and Kephalonia. Instead, a daily ferry chugs across from there to Killini on the mainland and an hour or so later a different ferry completes the journey to the harbour of Zakynthos. An otherwise tiresome wait at Killini is relieved at midday by an excellent restaurant patronized by *routiers*, the drivers of heavy Greek lorries on the way south from Patras.

The town of Zakynthos is in a lovely situation, lying around the gentle curve of the bay, overlooked from the south by Mt Skopos ('the look-out') with the exaggerated pimple on its skyline which gives it its name. Yet more keenly here than in any of the neighbouring islands one is aware of the utter disaster which struck Zakynthos on the night of the 12–13 August 1953. This is in spite of the careful, devoted and skilful restorations carried out since then, which have left us a town still Italianate in character, but with a feeling about it which reflects the best in modern Greek town planning.

To understand the full tragedy of the 1953 earthquake, every visitor should look at – and if possible buy a copy of – the volume which is on display at the Solomos museum in the *Plateia Agiou Markou*. Published in Athens in 1977 it is the work of N. A. Varviani, who has compiled a deeply moving record – complete with unique black and white photographs – of the monuments of Zakynthos before, during and after their destruction by earthquake

75

and fire. The architectural and decorative riches to be found all over the island, mainly of the renaissance and baroque periods, were hardly to be equalled over a comparable area in any European country. Barely a building survived intact, and what could be restored, however lovingly, is only a small fraction of what there was.

It was Venetian architects, complemented by artists who inherited the traditions of Byzantium rather than those of Florence or Siena, who created Zante. The scanty references in Homer and Virgil (which emphasize how thickly wooded it was in ancient times), and in Herodotus and Thucydides, convey nothing of the nature of the island today. Its strategic position, commanding the strait between it and the mainland as well as the waters south of Kephalonia which lead to the Gulf of Corinth, made it important to whatever power wished to control them, so that in turn Athens and Sparta, Macedon and Rome, Vandals, Saracens, Normans and Turks all fought over it – yet today it is of little maritime importance.

The modern era of Zante – that is to say what can still be traced in its monuments – began with the rule of the Orsini family in the thirteenth century, but its flowering waited for the formal takeover by Venice in 1489 and continued until the victory of Napoleon in 1797. Thanks to the faithful restorations carried out after 1953 we can have (at least in the town of Zakynthos) a good idea of what it looked like by the end of the eighteenth century.

The principal feature today is the *Plateia Solomou*, reconstituted with some elegance at the northern end of the harbour. It was first created as a memorial to the poet Dionysios Solomos, who lived from 1798 to 1857. The son of one of the Hellenized Venetian aristocratic families, Solomos went to Italy for his education, returning to Zante when he was twenty. His early poems were written in Italian and showed little sign of his future genius. It was only after his return to Zante that Solomos, at first diffidently and then with growing confidence, began to write in demotic Greek. It was a courageous step to take, for demotic Greek was then considered in the polite circles of Zante rather as English was in the court of our Norman kings. This Greek was the working-class language, and no one had thought before of using it to convey the finer shades of emotion or sentiment. Solomos, like his friends and relations, had been brought up on Italian poetry, and the influence of Dante remained strong with him all his life. A later influence was Byron, to whom Solomos addressed an ode, but it was the legends and the spirit of his native Greece that gave him his real strength. By trial and error he evolved the first great poems in the Greek demotic language – it is said that he found a dialect and left a language. His *Ode to Liberty* was adopted as the national anthem, but his greatest poem was *The Free Besieged*, an incomplete epic dedicated to the defenders of Mesolongi. His statue looks across the bright square open to the sea, where Greek families gather for the *volta* and children ride bicycles like small *valkyries*; he faces his slightly earlier compatriot poet, Ugo Phoskolo (1778–1827).

On two sides of the *Plateia* there are modern replicas of fine arcaded Venetian buildings – that to the north houses the municipal library and other offices, on the west side is the Museum. To seaward of the municipal block, with its busy café tables spilling from the arcades on to the pavement, is the (inevitably restored) sixteenth-century church of *Agios Nikolaos tou Molou*, reminding us that St Nicholas here as always was the saint of harbours and fishermen. Leading away from the sea and past the Museum is the wide and once fashionable boulevard known as the *Plateia Rouga*. Its Venetian elegance has been coarsened somewhat by commercial intrusions, but it leads to the much smaller *Plateia Agiou Markou*, which takes its name from the church of St Mark on the far side – a little eighteenth-century gem (as it was) with two slightly detached towers framing a plain renaissance façade. There is nothing here to recall San Marco of Venice, but this was and still is the Catholic cathedral of Zante, and the little triangular *plateia* has an authentic Zantiot feel about it.

Next to the church is another successful piece of restoration, the neat balconied façade of the **Solomos Museum**. This is both a mausoleum for the poets Solomos and Phoskolo and a home for *memorabilia* concerned with the life and works of island worthies between 1800 and the 1960s. In a vestibule on the first floor is a small room concerned with the life of Dionysios Roma, author, poet and theatrical impresario, a major benefactor and the founder of this museum. He was born in 1906 of an influential Zakynthos family, whose eighteenth-century mansion near the northern sea front was almost the only building in the town to survive the earthquake. There are portraits of Solomos and his family – his brother was a distinguished nineteenth-century diplomat – and a whole room devoted to books from his library and other *personalia*. In a way more interesting is a contemporary portrait of one Dionysios Pelekasis, who is described as '*trophodotis Lordou Bironos*', in other words Lord Byron's steward. This is one more reminder of how much Byron was involved in the Greek independence movement, and we can also see here a dramatic oil painting of Theodore Kolokotronis and his original band of conspirators (known as the *Philikoi*) taking their dedicatory oath at a candle-lit table. Most interesting and most moving of all is the illustrated book called so reticently *Zakynthos Then and Now*.

An alleyway leads off the corner of Agios Markos to the Orthodox Cathedral, the **Mitropolis**, disappointingly restored in the nineteenth-century style associated with the bigger city churches in Greece, and attended by a monstrously forbidding concrete *campanile* – in its justification we guess that its builders were determined it should never fall down again. A visit to the Cathedral is necessary, however, if you want to get inside the most delightful of the smaller churches of Zakynthos. This is the *Panagia ton Angelon* (Our Lady of the Angels) in a side street just below the east end of the Cathedral. It was in fact in the garden of the Roma family mansion, and must have been used as their private chapel. Although the house survived the earthquake, the church was destroyed. It was one of the first reconstructions undertaken and one of the best. Sunk below the level of the modern road, it has a naïvely baroque west doorway, with an outsize pediment featuring the Madonna surrounded by cherubs – hence its name. There is no separate *campanile*, but two bells swing from an iron framework over a smaller door to the left of the main entrance, which has more of this happily vigorous baroque carving above it.

Inside, the gorgeous *templo* was put together again from its surviving pieces, and incorporates some of the finest ikons (miraculously preserved) of this period – in particular the striking crowned head of Christ as 'King of Kings and Great High Priest' which is signed and dated at the back. It was executed in 1691 by Panagiotis Doxara, a notable innovator of the Cretan school of religious painting. The central panel is a Crucifixion, with a Virgin and Child to the left, all flanked by two graceful angels. There is a Cretan flavour in all the painting, and the whole church is in miniature an example of how well Venetian and Spanish baroque combines with the Cretan style of ikonography. Sunday is the best time to see it, and if you ask at the Mitropolis when it opens on Saturday an obliging young acolyte will accompany you next morning and let you in. Incidentally, if you sight a large black Mercedes with a curtained rear window and a registration plate saying just MZ, it belongs to the Metropolitan Archbishop of Zakynthos, and can often be seen standing outside his official residence near the *Plateia Solomou*.

Reconstruction of the long *Lombardou* waterfront has not been so successful architecturally. The quayside itself is accommodating enough for all manner of small craft, but behind it the commercial world of trinket shops and cafés has taken over. A more interesting way to traverse the town is to stick to one of the several shopping streets which run behind and parallel to the harbour. The traffic can be insistently at your heels, but at least these streets have alternate one-way systems, and many of the old arcades have been reconstructed; in the *Odos Philita* the old trades in wood and metal work are still pursued.

The quarter at the far, or southern, end of the harbour contained two of the most important religious buildings in Zakynthos, the churches of *Agios Dionysios* and the *Panagia Phaneromeni.* It will be apparent by now that Dionysios is to Zakynthos what Spiridon is to Corfu and Charalambos to Paxos. The surprise is that in French he becomes St Denis, though there is nothing in common between the twelfth-century romanesque Abbaye Saint-Denis and what we have here. Our Dionysios was a Bishop of Zakynthos belonging to the aristocratic Sigouri family; he was canonized in 1560 and presented by Venice with the *Moni Anaphonitrias*, a delightful rural monastery in the far north of the island. He died in 1622 on one of the Strophades – two small islands thirty miles south of Zakynthos – where his relics were guarded in a Byzantine fortress monastery until 1716, when they were brought here. The great *campanile* (Greek *kodonostasis*) of 1839 which towered over the southern end of the harbour has been faithfully rebuilt, but the big new church is an extreme example of the 'neo-Byzantine' style, from which one would rather avert the eye.

Not so the *Panagia Phaneromeni*, which stands in the corner of a leafy square a little further inland. This is one of the most impressive restorations to be seen anywhere, and the care and money expended on it is the city's tribute to the serene beauty created by its seventeenth-century architect. As you will find in Zakynthiot churches of this period, the long south or north side and its doorway was more richly designed than the west end: here the north side is a harmonious sequence of blind semicircular arches surrounding a noble entrance flanked by restrained Corinthian pilasters, and with a pediment cleverly broken up into three units. Over the doorway is the inscription: '*Anekainisthe 1633*'. What the mediaeval church it replaced looked like, we do not know, but seventeenth-century Italy would find it hard to put up a rival. The whole exterior of the church has been meticulously reproduced in plain biscuit-coloured stone, and work is still going on inside to restore the interior to its exact appearance before the earthquake. The *templo* is practically complete, a unique feat carried out by modern wood-carvers in Athens working from photographs of the original, which can be seen in the narthex of the church. The original *templo* of 1633 was carved by Manios Manganares, a Cretan wood-carver who came as a refugee to Zakynthos.

High above the town is the wooded hillside where the Venetians built their castle. You reach it by a pleasant road which climbs through private properties with olive and citrus orchards. Though not obvious when seen from below, the fortified approach to the **Kastro** and the outer walls have kept their formidable Venetian appearance. A curving ramp leads through three successive gateways, the last displaying a stone plaque with St Mark's lion over the entrance. The walkway round the ramparts is now covered with grass and shaded by pines, while the huge area inside the walls is mostly indistinguishable under a carpet of earth and pine needles. It covers a bigger area than the castle of St George in Kephalonia, which you can see across the strait to the north under the long dark outline of Mt Aenos.

If you look carefully around you can make some historically fascinating finds. On the north side is a grassy area delineated in

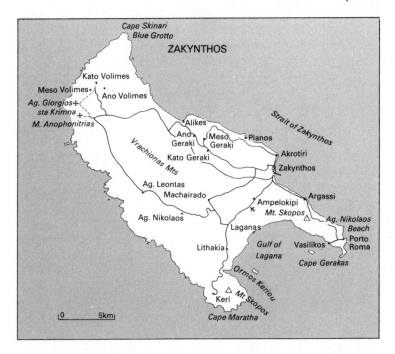

stone, which was set out as a playground for the children of English
service families during the nineteenth-century occupation. Round
to the west are the ruins of the small Byzantine church of San
Salvatore (or *Christos Sotiros* in Greek) which became the Catholic
cathedral for a time. In the central area towards the summit are the
scanty remains of a fourteenth-century Franciscan monastery. The
main keep was on a bluff to the south-west, now a grassy enclosure
with fruit trees, and it has one of the great views of Greece across the
fertile central plain to the Vrachionas mountains, with the sea
closing in from north and south.

Round to the south is an unusual long building with a pitched roof
which proves to be the Venetian munitions store, with alongside it
the foundations of a row of army barracks (which the defenders of
the castle occupied without a break from 1600 to 1900) and of the
main headquarters building. Nearby is the site of the ruined church
of *Agios Ioannis Prodromos* (St John the Baptist), a late basilica

81

built in 1478 just after the fall of Byzantium, but ruined irreparably in 1953. South-east again is the grim stone block which contained the Venetian prisons, with iron barred gates and one high window at the back of each cell. Opposite are arched recesses for the guard-rooms. The corner bastion at this point has a look-out platform, scattered with rusting iron cannons, which affords another great view across the town and harbour to Mt Skopos.

At the head of the approach road to the castle is the rebuilt church of *Agios Georgios ton Philikon* (St George of the Patriots). This is a national monument, because it was here in 1805 that Theodore Kolokotronis administered the oath to his fellow conspirators at the start of the revolution which led to the War of Independence.

The countryside of Zakynthos is benign, though the scenery as a whole is not as beautiful or impressive as it is in Kephalonia. This is partly because the highest point of the Vrachionas ('rocky') mountains is only half as high as the summit of Mt Aenos, and they occupy a smaller area; partly because there is no road to equal in grandeur the east coast route in Kephalonia. The first few miles of road running south-east from the capital follow the coastline, but views to seaward are blotted out by a long and messy line of tourist hotels, bars and discos, culminating in an obtrusive cluster at **Argassi**. The views improve as the road climbs past Mt Skopos into the long south-eastern peninsula.

If you are moved to climb **Mt Skopos**, you will be rewarded by fine views in all directions. The monastery of the *Panagia Skopiotissa* high on its flank was a fifteenth-century foundation, unique in Zakynthos for having a cupola above its cruciform church. The cupola and much of the church fell in 1953, but has been restored. As you climb you are following in the steps of one John Dallam, an English musician who visited Zakynthos in 1599 on his way to deliver as a present from Queen Elizabeth to the Sultan Mehmet III an organ he had built himself. On Easter Sunday that year he left it behind to climb Mt Skopos with two companions. Stories like this (such as the famous despatch in classical Latin from Elizabeth to the Emperor of Ethiopia) confirm the extent of diplomatic relations in the sixteenth century.

Down at the end of the main road, **Porto Roma** is a pleasantly unspoilt fishing harbour with the long beach of Agios Nikolaos to the north. If you cross the tip of the peninsula by way of Vasilikos, a track brings you to the even longer and usually emptier beach enclosed by Cape Gerakas. The surprise here is to find a notice forbidding access to the beach during the hours of darkness, so as to avoid interfering with the breeding practices of the indigenous sea-turtle. These enterprising creatures come ashore at night to deposit their eggs in sand-burrows, from which the infant turtles emerge in due season and scamper down to the sea. All reasonable visitors will surely respect their privacy and obey this explicit notice put up by a scientific research body which is concerned to protect the species against thoughtless or over-inquisitive people. This far end of the peninsula is agreeably cultivated, and a good deal of the land belongs to the Roma family, which explains not only the name of the harbour but possibly also why it has escaped too much development.

The road running south-west from the capital passes the airport and the well-named village of Ampelokipi ('vineyards'), and it is most frequently taken to reach **Laganas**, the most popular beach on the island with a choice of more than twenty hotels nearby. The beach is lovely, but inevitably overcrowded in high summer. The Laganas turning comes early on, leaving the main road to continue past Lithakia and a little holiday settlement at Ormos Keriou, or Keri Bay, to the village of Keri itself. This is a quiet place on the western slopes of the other Mt Skopos which fills the whole end of the south-west peninsula as far as Cape Maratha.

Keri Bay is wide and shallow, backed by water meadows and fed by muddy streams. Boats are still built and mended along its protective spit of land, but there is no call today for the bay's most famous natural product, the pitch once used for caulking seams. This was piped to the base of the mole from 'wells' in the swampy hinterland, but the standpipes have seized up and rusted, and no local resident can be found to indicate the pools where the pitch used to bubble so conveniently to the surface. Described by Herodotus and Pliny, and by every guide book of recent years, they are no longer traceable. Wherever they were, they were nowhere near the village of **Keri**, which is a simple inland community with the fine Venetian renaissance church of the *Koimisis tou Theotokou* (the Assumption of the Virgin Mary) which survived the earthquake. The southern façade

83

is graciously classical, and the tall *campanile* is crowned by a jaunty little spire like a pointed hat.

Zakynthos is not a large island, and with a car at your disposal you can make an interesting round tour by way of the north coast through **Akrotiri** (where Solomos lived in a country villa) which turns inland after the holiday resort at Planos to reach a trio of villages, **Meso, Kato** and **Ano Geraki**. In the angle of the road between the first two is the abandoned church of the *Panagia Evangelistria*, a large and handsome renaissance building with a triple apse and a good south doorway. Continuing north you reach the salt pans and holiday beach at **Alikes**, from where excursions can be made by boat to the **Blue Grotto** just below Cape Skinari, the most northerly point of the island. There are many such seawater caves in the islands, usually as here marked by the intense indigo blue of the water within.

From Alikes onwards the scenery changes to a low rolling countryside, intensively farmed, not unlike parts of Norfolk or Devon. The most interesting bit is the far north-west, centring on another trio of villages, **Ano, Kato** and **Meso Volimes**. Meso Volimes (sometimes just 'Volimes', as it is the most important) is a charming place with pretty cottages and another fine church – this one is *Agia Kiriaki*, in Venetian baroque. Within easy reach are two monasteries of unusual character. A roughish road connects the triangle formed by Meso Volimes and the monasteries of **Agios Georgios** and **Anophonitria**; in fact it is wiser to descend from Volimes to the main road, then turning right for Anophonitria.

The monastery here is a fifteenth-century foundation made famous by Bishop Dionysios Sigouros, who was canonized as Agios Dionysios in 1560. Evidence of his saintliness came when the murderer of his brother arrived at the monastery to confess; Dionysios forgave him and gave him absolution for the crime. The monastery was a gift to Dionysios from Venice, and on his death in 1622 it was transferred to the Abbot Ioannis Moussouran, who paid 150 ducats to supply teachers for the local community. In 1783 it was awarded to a member of the Zantiot aristocracy, Count Stylianas Phlambouriasi – the value of such a property being as much material as spiritual.

The most striking feature of the monastery is the solid, stumpy tower, square in plan and spreading out at the base, which guarded the entrance and provided a refuge from pirate attacks. The church has a majestic *templo* in gilded wood, and some damaged early frescos at the east end. Its most precious content is an ikon of the Panagia found in the wreckage of a ship which had escaped from Byzantium after its final fall to the Turks in 1453. The ikon is taken on a tour of the island to bring an end to periods of severe drought, and must obviously have had some success for the custom to be kept up. The tiny subsidiary church standing close to the west end is also an early foundation, though it was much restored in the 1950s. There was little damage to the monastery in 1953 and it comes as a surprise to be told that the tower stands at its original height. The custodian is usually at hand to show visitors around (she lives conveniently at the nearby café) and she will show you the cell occupied by St Dionysios; it contains his books and a dramatic picture of the scene when he forgave his brother's murderer.

Whether you approach from Meso Volimes (which is difficult) or from Anophonitria, it is worth striking out westward to the other monastery, **Agios Georgios sta Krimna** – to give it its full title, which means 'St George on the Precipice'. The site is no longer precipitous, but it stands comfortably among pine trees on a headland overlooking the sea. Again the most notable feature is a short massive tower, this time a round one. The date of the monastery's foundation is unknown, but it was destroyed by pirates in 1553, which explains why the church is in seventeenth-century Venetian style with an ornamental ceiling and *templo* to match. Otherwise the place is less sophisticated than Anophonitria; there are no resident monks or nuns at either.

From Anophonitria you can return to the capital by a more westerly route, which passes through the villages of Maries, Agios Leontas and Agios Nikolaos. This is the most spectacular drive in Zakynthos, with views to seaward from a considerable height. A warning here about the map most commonly sold here, issued in the usually reliable *Toubis* series, which is far too optimistic about the condition of the roads it marks, invents others which do not exist, and is unreliable about the exact position of important sites. A better buy, if you can find it before going out, is the *Clyde Leisure Map* of Corfu and the Ionian islands.

In particular, there is no road (as yet) connecting Agios Nikolaos with Keri and the southern Skopos peninsula. Instead your main road turns eastward to drop into the great fertile plain sheltered from the winter storms by the Vrachionas mountains. This plain is crossed by a network of minor roads radiating from the capital, and dotted with small villages surrounded by a sea of currant vineyards. But for the extreme lushness of it all, you might imagine yourself in the Medoc, with glimpses of substantial château-like buildings from which this still major island industry is organized. When only in leaf the vines seem much the same as you will find in any wine-producing country, but the grapes are very small and gathered in August early enough to be spread out to dry under the burning summer sun, before the onset of the autumn rains. The presence of so many currant vineyards in Zakynthos and Kephalonia reminds us that the word 'currant' is a corruption of 'Corinth' (in French, *raisins de Corinthe*), the town generally associated with their export. In classical times both islands were closely connected by trade with Corinth, lying as they do right across the mouth of the Gulf.

Among the villages of the plain, **Machairado** stands out as having one of the finest surviving churches. Dedicated to a favourite Ionian saint, *Agia Mavra*, its chief glory is the internal furnishing. The great baroque *templo* soars to the ceiling in elaborate gilded stages: the first storey has a row of projecting balconies with figures of Christ and six saints in cut-out painted wood. The dignified ikon of the principal saint (she is paired here with St Timothy) stands on a separate *ikonostasis* with a richly worked silver surround contributed by Queen Olga of Greece in 1896. The ceiling is painted in the Venetian manner by a nineteenth-century artist who has also contributed a frieze of surprisingly lively and realistic Old Testament scenes, beginning with Adam and Eve in quite explicit poses. Altogether the 1873 restoration of the nave seems for once in keeping with the seventeenth-century *templo* and other fittings, but the plain whitewashed exterior gives no idea of the splendours within. *Agia Mavra* was one of the few churches to survive the earthquake, and so did the huge separate *campanile*. This has a fortress-like base, but its upper works are more decorative than defensive, and it ends like the one at Keri in a pointed top-knot. Its bells are said to have an unusually sweet tone.

Agia Mavra in Machairado, the *Panagia* in Keri, the re-consti-
tuted *Phaneromeni* and *Panagia ton Angelon* in Zakynthos, together with some of the rebuilt exteriors we have noted, may give
the visitor an idea of what was to be seen all over the island before
the tragedy of August 1953. The dominant style was derived from
seventeenth-century Italy, shading from the purer renaissance to
riotous baroque, and with a few exceptions the nineteenth-century
additions seem not as inappropriate as elsewhere. To have a better
idea of what has been lost (though it will still be inadequate) you
must visit the big new **Museum** in Solomos square, one of the most
brilliantly conceived exhibitions in the islands.

No room is found for pottery, marble fragments or other relics of
Zakynthos's somewhat hazy classical past. Here is a unique collection of Byzantine art and church furnishings salvaged from the 1953
debacle. On the ground floor are two complete baroque *templa*, the
finer of the two from *Agios Dimitrios* at Kolla, with original ikons of
1690. On the first floor there is a complete re-assembly of the
interior of *Agios Andreas* at Volimes. The frescos in the half dome
of the apse show the Virgin holding the risen Child in her bosom, the
twelve apostles at the Last Supper, the four evangelists below. Over
the west end is a Second Coming, with appropriate symbolism
including a 'snakes-and-ladders' effect between heaven and hell,
and the sea giving up its dead (a favourite conceit among sea-faring
peoples). In the long gallery overlooking the *plateia* are separate
ikons from various sources, many of them prime examples of their
period. Finest of all is a *Christ pitié*, or *Akra Tapeinosis*, of 1670
from the convent of Agios Georgios – just the head and torso of
Christ seated on the tomb, almost post-Impressionist in its treatment of line and light. There is a dramatic winged St John the
Baptist of the sixteenth century, an unusually large canvas; a
Panagia by Emanuel Tsanes, whose collection of thirteen ikons we
saw in Kerkyra; and a handsome 1670 St George without his horse
but wearing armour made of beaten silver. St George was a favourite subject for ikons, and so was St Demetrios; here you can see how
they are usually distinguished, for Demetrios has to ride a red horse,
George a white one – sometimes with a little Arab 'coffee-boy'
mounted on the crupper behind him.

The oldest and most valuable exhibit was a twelfth-century ikon from the early Byzantine church of *Christos Sotiros* inside the castle precinct, but this is one of several treasures which have been removed to Athens – where they will hardly be noticed. The pleasure of a visit to the Museum is completed by finding some good pieces of eighteenth-century furniture on the ground floor by the entrance, among them a card-table, a sofa-table and a lovely serpentine chest-of-drawers in walnut. This most civilized of Greek islands is still rightly proud of itself, and of the complimentary jingle with which Venice saluted her – '*Zante, fior di Levante*'.

Access

ZAKYNTHOS has an airport, and this is far the easiest approach from Athens. Otherwise there is only a ferry connection with Killini on the mainland, which also provides the only link with Kephalonia.

Communications

The road system is extensive, covering most of the island apart from the Vrachionas range, though the roads in the far north-west are rough. Bus routes radiate from the capital through the villages of the eastern plain; they also serve Vassilikos on the eastern peninsula and Keri to the south. There are plenty of car and moped hire firms in the capital.

Accommodation

The show hotel is the STRADA MARINA (B, 91 beds), well placed on the not too noisy harbour front. The XENIA here (B, 78 beds) is a stark modern building overlooking the sea front north of the harbour. The more discreet PHOENIX (C, 70 beds) is probably the best value for comfort and money, set back on the fringe of the *Plateia Solomou*. One would not like to recommend any of the hotels around Argassi, though they do not lack customers. Those at Laganas, and there are plenty of them, are as a rule better, and they command a beautiful beach. Villas and rooms to let are not so much in evidence as in other islands.

Restaurants

The better restaurants in the capital are in or near the *Plateia Agiou Markou*, though there is not a great choice. A little place worth trying is kept by the brothers STROUZA in the *Odos Desylla* behind the harbour – it has local wine in carafe. Best of all is PANORAMA up on the Kastro hill, where the food, while still Greek, is cooked to French standards.

Facilities

Banks: The principal banks are well represented in Zakynthos town, and the Commercial Bank will cash Eurocheques.

Yachts: There is plenty of room along the quays in Zakynthos harbour. Otherwise there is only Keri Bay, a small fishing harbour where there is not much depth of water, and possibly Porto Roma, though both these are exposed to the east.

The Saronic Gulf

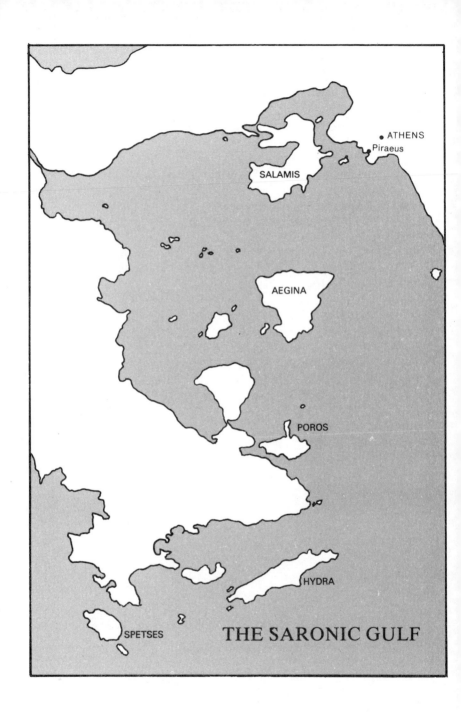

SALAMIS

ATHENS
Piraeus

AEGINA

POROS

HYDRA

SPETSES

THE SARONIC GULF

THE SARONIC GULF

Saron was a legendary king of Troezen, the most important of the early cities on the substantial peninsula which divides the Gulf of Argos from the Saronic Gulf. It seems strange that he should have given his name to the whole Gulf, when the name of Theseus is more vividly connected in legend and literature with both Troezen and Athens. All we know about Saron is that he was so fond of hunting that he chased a stag into this sea and was drowned in it. The adventures of Theseus are too well known to enumerate, but he was brought up in Troezen by his grandfather, and it was there that his son Hippolytus became disastrously entangled with his own step-mother, Phaedra.

The two largest islands in the Gulf, Salamis and Aegina, are closely connected in many ways with Athens, and both figure prominently in classical history; the other three principal members of the group – Poros, Hydra and Spetses – are geographically extensions of the Troezen peninsula and have little independent history. Several lesser islands could strictly be included, but Angistri and Moni are entirely dependent on Aegina, as is Spetsopoula on Spetses, while Dokos off Hydra is all but uninhabited. Methana, the 'all-but-island' of the southern Gulf, only fails to qualify by reason of a very narrow neck of land joining it to the Peloponnese.

The main islands are quickly and easily – some might say too easily – reached from Piraeus, and during the summer they get uncomfortably crowded. That is not to say that away from the harbours there are no places of beauty and interest, and the sheltered waters around them are a profitable fishing ground and a marvellous playground for yachtsmen. Ships of many centuries and many peoples have left their wakes here: Theseus on his way to Crete and back, Agamemnon's fleet bound for Troy, Athenian expeditions against Sparta and Syracuse, invaders from Persia and Rome, traders from Byzantium and Venice, Saracen raiders and

Turkish corsairs, Russian, French, German and British warships. Piraeus has become one of the great commercial harbours of the world, and now the cruise liners of the west queue to enter the Gulf through the Corinth canal on their way to Athens, Delos and the other delights of the Aegean. More than anywhere on the mainland, more than Athens herself, these waters are at the heart of Greece.

FIVE

Salamis and Aegina

In the last week of September 480 BC there occurred one of those momentous battles by which the history of the world is changed. To the men who fought in it, it did seem that their world was at stake, but they could have had no inkling that the result of it would determine the course of European civilization. Salamis, like the destruction of the Spanish Armada or the battle of Trafalgar, was a sea battle which determined for centuries the pattern of life to be lived upon the land.

The island of **Salamis** is easily reached either from Piraeus harbour or from Perama a little further up the coast, after a short bus journey from Athens. In either case you land at the purely functional port of Paloukia, after crossing one of the most historic stretches of water in the world. The Persians, after an indecisive sea engagement off Cape Artemision in Euboea, had occupied Attica; their fleet, now based at Phaleron, was all set to crush the combined forces of Athens and the Peloponnesians which had retreated into the narrow waters between Salamis and the mainland. To show how apparently hopeless was the Greek position, here is Professor H. D. F. Kitto writing in *The Greeks*:

> 'The northern Greeks had all but submitted and were fighting now with Persia; Attica was lost, no one was left but the Peloponnesians, a few islands, and Athens. The Peloponnesian land forces were at the Isthmus, busy fortifying it, and of their sea captains most were in favour of moving the allied fleet back there from Salamis. ... Themistocles saw that the narrow waters inside Salamis would give the Greek fleet a chance of victory, while at the Isthmus they would certainly be defeated – even if the fleet held together which was unlikely.'

King Xerxes had already set up a throne on Mt Aegaleos overlooking the straits, to watch the expected victory of his fleet. At this juncture Themistocles, the master Athenian strategist, devised a plan to prevent the Peloponnesian ships from leaving to defend the Isthmus. He 'leaked' information to the enemy that they were about to do so, whereupon the Persian fleet moved out in force to blockade the channels to west and east of Salamis, at the same time occupying the small island of **Psittaleia** midway between the Kynosura ('Dog's Tail') peninsula and the mainland. This suited Themistocles, as it forced an engagement on his unwilling allies while the enemy fleet was divided, and in waters which favoured the more manoeuvrable Greek triremes – waters which were known to the Greeks as only seamen and fishermen can know a stretch of sea by which they have been born and bred.

The Greek fleet, outnumbered by about two to one, feigned a retreat into the more open waters of the bay of Eleusis, but in fact withdrew only out of sight behind a convenient promontory. As the Persians advanced up the eastern channel, necessarily in close formation, the Greek ships tore into them at full speed, using the long metal rams at their bows to deadly effect. At a critical moment an Athenian force under the exiled Aristides recaptured Psittaleia, and the victory was complete. Only three hundred ships out of a thousand, it has been estimated, managed to reach Phaleron Bay in safety. With the winter coming on, and with the fleet which guarded his supply lines destroyed, there was nothing left for Xerxes but retreat. The fate of the invading army was finally sealed in the following year at the battle of Plataea on the borders of Attica and Boeotia.

The course of the battle can be readily imagined by a visitor today, the only doubt being whether Psittaleia was the island today called Lipsokoutali, or one further north called Agios Georgios. It seems appropriate that a shipyard at Perama has just built and launched a reconstruction of a Greek warship from designs made by scholars. Although the trireme had small square sails for use on passages with a fair wind, in battle they relied entirely on oar power generated by something like two hundred rowers. It has been reckoned that this could produce a speed of eight to ten knots, about the same as a modern racing eight.

Corfu. *Above,* goats coming down to water;
below, Palace of St Michael and St George, Kerkyra

Pothia harbour, Kalymnos

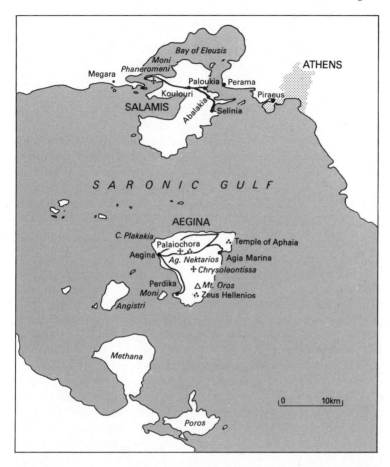

Paloukia, where the little all-purpose ferries land, is of no scenic or other interest, though it is important for the big naval and military base which occupies the whole area to the north of it – the headquarters, in fact, of the modern Greek navy. From Paloukia you can reach by bus or taxi the other centres of this not unattractive island. The least attractive is **Koulouri**, usually shown on the map as Salamina, a big sprawl of concrete houses and characterless bungalows at the head of Salamis Bay, a water which deserves better things, but is chiefly notable for its colonies of Japanese pearl

97

oysters, introduced accidentally in 1959 from far eastern ships laid up here.

Beyond Koulouri the road crosses to the north coast of a finger of land pointing in the direction of the big Isthmus town of Megara – a regular ferry plies between. One vantage point on the Salamis road is the convent of the **Panagia Phaneromeni**. This contains a few surprises, not least on the approach road, which is enlivened on one side by cages for peacocks and other poultry, including sometimes a pair of quails and their family. The farmyard atmosphere is kept up outside the walls to the south, where there are cowsheds and sheep pens.

The main church was originally cruciform with a cupola over a short red-tiled tower, but it was extended westwards later to make a richly decorated basilica with a double row of columns. There is a good deal of wall painting, mostly of the nineteenth century, but the whole of the west end is covered by a fresco of the Second Coming, very faded and blurred, which was the work of Georgios Markos, an artist in the medium who lived in the early eighteenth century. There is a smaller church to the south which contains some authentic early ikons, and heaped in a corner of the grounds is a jumble of marble masonry – columns, capitals and mouldings – which look like the remains of an earlier Christian basilica church. Overall the place is a curious mixture of homeliness and religious opulence.

Looking across from here to the mainland one realizes suddenly that the narrow coastal plain between mountains and sea carried one of the most celebrated highways in history – the only road which joined Athens and the north to Argos and Sparta and the other cities of the Peloponnese. Along it Phidippides must have run on his mission to alert Sparta to the Persian threat in 490 BC; by this way came the Spartan army on its annual foray to devastate Attica during the Peloponnesian War.

There is not much else to see in the island. Abalakia, south of Paloukia, is near the site of classical Salamis; Selinia is a Greek holiday resort, and in the south of the island, reached by road only from Koulouri, there is another monastery, delightfully called *Agios Nikolaos tis Lemonias* ('St Nicholas of the Lemon Tree'), with a basilica church reconstructed from a Byzantine one of the twelfth or thirteenth century. The largest village in the south is

Moulki, whose classical name of Aiantio reminds us that Ajax the son of Telamon was prince of Salamis and took twelve ships with him to the siege of Troy.

Telamon himself was a son of Aeacus, legendary ruler of neighbouring **Aegina**, and was forced into exile in Salamis after his brother Peleus (father of Achilles) had accidentally – or possibly on purpose – killed their half-brother Phocus with a discus. Aegina was the name of one of Zeus's many mistresses, a daughter of the river god Asopus, and Aeacus was their son. It was he who changed the name of the island to honour his mother, for it was previously called Oenopia or Oenona, a word of doubtful origin but probably connected with the nymph Oenone rather than having anything to do with wine. Aeacus acquired a reputation for justice, and first established the dignity of a city state which up to the middle of the fifth century BC rivalled Athens in sea power.

Until the Athenians had secured either the friendship or the destruction of Aegina, they had no security for their own sea routes. The struggle between the two seafaring powers was long and bitter, broken only during the Persian wars when Aegina joined Athens to defeat their common enemy at sea, supplying thirty ships at the battle of Salamis, where they were acknowledged to have fought the best of all the Greeks.

Today the 'flying dolphin' hydrofoils take only forty minutes to reach Aegina from Piraeus, even though they have to round its north-western cape to arrive at the principal harbour on the west coast. As they round Cape Plakakia you see first the headland of **Kolona**, where the sole surviving column of the temple of Apollo stands; then the town itself shows up white against the land, with the blue cupola of St Nicholas church looking like a bubble of the sea that has strayed on to the shore. South and to starboard is the separate island of Angistri, and beyond it the peninsula of Methana, humped against the mainland like a stranded whale. The waters in between are usually alive with yachts and fishing boats.

The small town of Aegina occupies part of the same site as the classical city. The modern harbour was the ancient commercial one, its moles built on a bank of shoal; at the end of the north mole a tiny whitewashed church seems almost to stand in the sea. There is a wide, sweeping front, with some good nineteenth-century houses at the northern end. Along the southern quays local boats tie up, their decks not displaying catches of fish or piles of nets, but heaped with fruit and vegetables for sale like barges on Venetian canals – bright patches of colour under protective canvas awnings.

The old naval harbour was further north, now distinguishable only by its sunken moles – the *kruptos limen* ('hidden harbour') as it is called today. It lies between the commercial harbour and the Kolona headland which sheltered both harbours from northerly winds. This bold natural site, commanding the sea approaches, was fortified in Neolithic times and occupied well into the Christian era, but now it is little more than an extensive muddle of ruins. The single weather-worn tufa column stood in the *opisthodomos* of a big temple to Apollo; the foundations are there, built up to a high level with a walk-way around, but the other buildings are difficult to trace after frequent destruction and reworking in different periods. There is some good walling on the inland side, and one interesting detail stands out – two circular 'eyes' cut on a large stone facing the approach, a psychological addition to the defences.

It may be a surprise to find that the **Archaeological Museum** has been moved to a new site just below the ruins, for the official maps show it in the centre of the town. It contains nothing much of interest – a lot of restored pottery of different periods, and a nice little Sphinx – but is well laid out in rooms built round a courtyard. Another piece of public misinformation is that the curator controls entry to the thirteenth-century **Omorphi Ekklesia**, just outside the town. This is one of the smallest and (on the outside) simplest of island churches, dedicated to the two Saints Theodore and probably built with stones from a classical temple. Its great interest lies inside, with fine frescos of episodes from the life of Christ in the nave, a Crucifixion on the west wall and a Resurrection over the altar. To protect them the church is now kept locked, and it needs a special application to the *demarcheion* to see them – a pity, but Aegina is flooded with tourists in the summer, not all of them reputable or trustworthy.

The destruction of buildings on the headland of Kolona, including the temple of Apollo, was hastened by Ioannis Kapodistrias, the first leader of independent Greece, who in 1826 quarried the site for material to build new quays when Aegina became the seat of a provisional Greek government. Needless to say, it was soon dispossessed by its ancient enemy, Athens, but it was one of the first places over which the Greek national flag was formally hoisted – though its colours were then red and gold, quite different from the blue and white we know today.

Before 1826 – and indeed from the ninth century onwards – the capital of the island was on an acropolis site a few miles inland to the east, now known as **Palaiochora**. The move from the coast was made after frequent Saracen raids, and like the mediaeval capitals of so many Aegean islands it was a witness to the long centuries of piracy and anarchy when to live on or near the sea coast invited disaster. The mediaeval history of Aegina is not greatly different from that of the western Aegean as a whole. In the thirteenth and fourteenth centuries, after the crusaders had split up the Byzantine empire, it was ruled individually by a succession of Venetian and Catalan families. In 1451 Venice herself took over in the hope of stiffening resistance to the conquering Turks, and held it until its formal cession in 1718 by the treaty of Passowitz – though it was captured and devastated in 1537 by Khair-ed-din, the Greek renegade from Lesbos who became a Turkish admiral (generally known as Barbarossa) on his brief but terrible rampage through the Aegean.

The acropolis of Palaiochora is an extraordinary place today. Apart from the ruined castle walls at the top, every vestige of the mediaeval city has disappeared except for some twenty churches scattered on the steep sides of the hill. It seems that empty private houses could be plundered for building material, but not those where God was still present. The result is that you can now examine better than anywhere else the different types of small church architecture, which cover centuries from the thirteenth to the seventeenth, close together and not obscured by other buildings. The most unusual one is *Agios Georgios*, which is rectangular on the north–south axis, but has its apse projecting to the east at the northern end. The most attractive in style and position is the tiny cross-in-square church of *Episkopi*, left like all the others in its original bare stone. In many of them there are frescos, more or less damaged, and it seems a pity that more care is not taken to preserve the whole group as the outstanding mediaeval monument it is.

Apart from their individual interest they illustrate the custom by which different families in the town built and maintained a church at their own expense. Few visitors find their way up here, and the grassy paths between the churches are alive in summer with marbled white butterflies and continental swallowtails.

Palaiochora is just off the main road from Aegina town to **Agia Marina**, the most popular resort in the island. Before you reach the mediaeval acropolis, your eye will be caught by the huge modern church of the monastery of **Agios Nektarios** which spreads across the valley below. He was the Metropolitan bishop of the diocese in the nineteenth century, canonized by the Orthodox church in 1961, so no architectural subtleties can be expected there. The road to Agia Marina gives you a good view of the island's chief product, pistachio nuts. The trees line it on either side, and looking at their copious clusters one wonders who eats them all.

Agia Marina is a lively and colourful place on the east coast opposite the capital, but those interested in the past will want to stop for a look at the Doric **Temple of Aphaia**, which stands on a pine-clad hill above the bay. It is easily the best preserved of classical temples in the islands, and was built about 485 BC on the same site as two earlier ones. A good deal of what we see today depends on the restoration – or rather re-erection – of elements such as columns, triglyphs and metopes, but the clean outlines of soft golden limestone are very satisfying. The pediments at either end of the temple had sculptures depicting two sieges of Troy: the first was mythical, involving Herakles and Telamon against the Trojan king Laomedon; the second was the ten-year siege described by Homer, involving Ajax, the hero of Salamis. The central figure of both pediments was Athena, and this gave rise to the belief that the temple was hers. However in 1901 the German archaeologist Furtwängler discovered an inscription including the name Aphaia, a local variant for the Cretan Britomartis or Dictynna, a nymph in the service of Artemis. The name itself can mean 'dark' or 'invisible', and some have taken it as an appellation of the moon goddess herself in her dark phase.

Greek mythology is a confusing study, especially when it involves gods with legendary and near-historical characters. Wherever such complications lead us, the fate of the sculptures is interesting in view of modern controversy, for they were carried off in 1811 to Zakynthos, which was then under British control, and later bought at auction by Ludwig of Bavaria. He had them restored in Rome and handed them over to the museum of sculpture in Munich, where they are held to this day without to one's knowledge any protest from the Greek Ministry of Culture.

This northern half of the island accounts for most of its population and nearly all its crops, for down in the south a series of mountain summits gradually increase in height to the final cone of **Mt Oros**, one of the classic viewpoints of the Mediterranean. These central mountains contain two important sites, the seventeenth-century convent of **Chrysoleontissa** and considerable remains of a sanctuary of **Zeus Hellenios** which originated in the Mycenaean age – but the whole area is accessible only by rough tracks on foot. Mt Oros is a tautology, as *oros* means mountain in ancient Greek, but its more specific name, Mt Prophitis Ilias, is all too familiar in the Greek islands for an often surly, cloud-capped peak. The sanctuary of Zeus is said to have been established by Aeacus himself when he visited the mountain to pray to his father for rain at a time of desperate drought. He was successful, and local wisdom has it that whenever Ilias (the Jewish Elijah) pulls on his night-cap, rain can be expected in the Gulf and on the southern shores of Attica.

The other two main roads serve chiefly to connect coastal resorts with the capital. The chief centre on the north coast is Souvala, but the road which hugs the western coastline passes holiday centres at Pharos and Moundi Bay, and ends at **Perdika**, perhaps the best spot of all, which looks across at **Moni Island**, home of wild flowers, birds and goats but otherwise hardly inhabited. Boats cross over there from Perdika with parties for swimming, while from Aegina harbour there are excursions to the more distant island of **Angistri**, where there are hotels and more beaches. Aegina has a greater range of attractions and a more interesting history than the more popular islands further down the Saronic Gulf.

The Greek Islands

Access

A number of unscheduled crossings are made to both these islands from Piraeus harbour. The shortest and most frequent service to SALAMIS is by constant car ferry from Perama, north of Piraeus, supported by buses included in the fare from Piraeus – look for the green one. The small boats from Piraeus direct tend to return in the early afternoon.

Hydrofoils ('Flying Dolphins') leave their own quay in Piraeus harbour for AEGINA every hour, beginning at 0700, throughout the week. Return schedules are similar.

Communications

The main roads on SALAMIS are well served by buses, which leave from the harbour at Paloukia. On AEGINA regular buses connect the capital with Agia Marina, and with villages along the north and west coasts. Taxis are available on both islands.

Accommodation

SALAMIS   Hotel accommodation is minimal. There are C class hotels at Aiantio and Selinia, but for the tourist there is not much incentive to stay overnight on the island.

AEGINA   Hotels are all concentrated at Agia Marina on the east coast, where there is a wide choice. Rooms can be found in Aegina town. No camping is allowed.

Restaurants

SALAMIS   ROUMELI, opposite the landing stage at Paloukia, is convenient, good value and well run.

AEGINA   To choose between the many establishments along the harbour front is difficult; go by the usual signs – clean tablecloths and wooden chairs.

Facilities

Banks: There are branches at Salamina in Salamis, and in Aegina harbour.

Yachts: Both islands are well equipped and safe for yachtsmen (from weather, at least).

SIX

Poros, Hydra and Spetses

Though itself only just an island, **Poros** turns out to be two. Unlike the larger Methana peninsula, Poros has allowed a narrow ribbon of sea to divide it from the mainland, and to this (*poros* in Greek means 'strait') it owes its present name. Across a gap of no more than 400 yards the mainland town of Galata presents an almost mirror image of the island's capital. Both have busy waterfronts, and all day long small boats ply between the two. An even narrower channel all but seals off the strait from the north end, so that the waters here are seldom disturbed from their glassy serenity, and they afford one of the safest of all Greek anchorages.

Factors such as these, plus a swift hydrofoil service from Piraeus, have turned both Poros and Galata from quiet fishing harbours into havens for the tourist industry. Galata can claim to be more independent of tourism on account of its profitable citrus orchards – there are around 30,000 lemon trees – which darken and scent a whole hillside nearby. Its waterfront, though, is the more modern and functional; Poros still has the look of an island harbour, with red-roofed houses crowding the narrow space between the quays and the low background ridge – a ridge which culminates to the west in a tall blue-domed *orologio*, or clock tower.

A climb of 150 steps to the base of the tower gives you a fine view of mountains, islands and sea, while down below there is only the clutter and clatter of cafés and their customers. Even by May the scene has become crowded and rather sordid, though it must be said that mechanized traffic has been barred from the quays. Instead, an enterprising firm hires bicycles to all comers, who whizz up and down what is almost a half-mile track from end to end.

105

This is practically all there is of Poros island – at least that part of it which in antiquity was called **Sphaeria**. If you penetrate behind the ridge and the *orologio* you come to a canal between two arms of the sea, which is crossed by a road bridge. This leads to a much larger, virtually separate island known still by its ancient name, **Kalavria**. The western arm of the intruding sea accommodated the naval headquarters of nineteenth-century Greece before they were moved to Salamis in 1877. This fine establishment now incorporates the Naval Training School for Boys – the Greek Dartmouth – whose centrepiece is the famous old cruiser *Averof*, moored in the bay.

While the harbour area has lost most of its natural charm, Kalavria retains an unfading beauty. Its hills are still clothed in rich green pine woods, through which a modern road strikes upwards as far as the monastery of **Zoodochos Pigi** (the 'life-giving spring') where there are peaceful eighteenth-century monastic quarters behind high fortified walls, and a *katholikon* church with a striking seventeenth-century *templo*. There are still monks here – eight of them, of whom seven work in the fields and one (by rota) stays behind to do the household chores. The twentieth century takes advantage of the scenery here as well, for in the valley below there is a big modern hotel which occupies a wide terrace overlooking a small cove – not a bad place for a holiday, if you like plenty of company.

A branch in the road near the hotel carries on upwards through the pines to the **Sanctuary of Poseidon**. Although remains are scanty – the ground plan of the temple and a *stoa* can just be traced – this grassy and flowery plateau is a pleasant place to wander in. You are not seriously hampered by a high perimeter fence which allows only one point of entry – in fact the custodian there can add to your pleasure by his conversation and directions. A surprise bonus may be to put up a cock pheasant in his summer glory, for a few pairs were recently introduced here and given five years immunity from slaughter while they breed. The idea is to exploit them commercially in shoots when there are sufficient numbers to transfer to other suitable sites.

The sanctuary of Kalavria was the meeting place of an early maritime countil, a body formed by Aegina, Athens, Epidaurus,

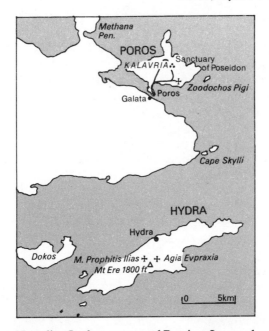

Hermione, Nauplia, Orchomenos and Prasiae. It was also an inviolable sanctuary for refugees and the victims of shipwreck. It was here that Demosthenes, the orator who had vainly urged the Athenians to resist the power of Macedon, took refuge from the soldiers of Alexander's former general, Antipater, when they came to take him from his place of exile in Troezen. They followed him to Kalavria, but trusting that not even Macedonians would dare profane so famous a shrine he refused to be inveigled out of the sanctuary until – as Plutarch tells the story – he had had time to write a letter to his friends: 'He went into the temple, as though he would have despatched some letters, put the end of the quill with which he wrote into his mouth and bit it, as was his habit when he wrote anything. Then he cast his gown over his head and laid him down.'

The soldiers outside taunted him with cowardice, and their leader Archias himself came into the sanctuary and begged him to come out, saying that he would intercede for him with Antipater. While he was speaking Demosthenes felt the poison he had absorbed from the quill beginning to work, and he staggered to his feet saying

'O Poseidon, now I will leave thy temple while I am yet alive and not profane it with my death'. It was not to be. As he stumbled towards the door the poison struck him down and he fell dead at the foot of the altar.

Although the views from the sanctuary are blocked by trees, this is made up for if you follow the loop of the road as it returns to Poros town. At one point especially you are looking out towards Aegina over the long narrow tongue of land which extends to the north. One would like to include Athens and her attendant mountains in the distant view, but the truth is that the sultry miasma which permanently hangs over Athens prevents that. On the other hand, if the light falls right, you can make out Cape Sounion across the open sea to the north-east, where stands another famous temple to Poseidon. Between them they guarded the wide entrance to the whole Saronic Gulf.

From Poros the hydrofoils speed on round Cape Skylli to **Hydra**, a baffling and sometimes infuriating island fashioned from uncompromising grey rock. Though barely five miles wide it is nearly twenty in length, yet few of its throngs of summer visitors penetrate beyond the harbour on the north coast. There are good reasons for this, the chief one being the harbour's overwhelming beauty, partly natural and partly man-made. The rocky amphitheatre which encloses it is perfectly proportioned, the horseshoe inlet is deep and still, and without any conscious planning the houses rise harmoniously like the crowded seats of a Greek theatre. What is more, many of the houses on the lower tiers are buildings of distinction – the *archontika*, nineteenth-century homes of the Greek sea captains, or *kapetanaioi*, who made the island, its sailors and its shipbuilders famous. Some are still lived in by their descendants, while two of the finest are open to visitors. Out of this small island have come some of the greatest sailors the Mediterranean has bred. Admirals, shipbuilders and fighters, their ships drove the Turks out of the Aegean, while they and their statesmen were largely responsible for the ultimate liberation of Greece.

There is no evidence that Venice ever controlled Hydra, though Venetian traders would have used the harbour, which has an Italianate air; there are said to be Venetian names among the

Hydriot families, and Venetian terms are used in shipbuilding and sailing – though that is true of most harbours in the Aegean. An important event, however, was an influx of Albanian refugees during the sixteenth and seventeenth centuries, a stream of vigorous highland blood which may have contributed to the island's later triumphs.

The foundation of Hydra's greatness was laid in the eighteenth century, when the reviving commerce of the Peloponnese, together with the grain trade with southern Russia, provided the islanders with an outlet for their energy and ability. 'From here', as one of them exclaimed, 'we ruled the Aegean. From this harbour our *sakturias* swept between island and island. We carried all the trade that passed between Asia and Europe!' There may be some Greek hyperbole here, but the *sakturia*, a fast and seaworthy sailing ship of about fifteen tons, was the Hydriots' great contribution to maritime progress in these waters. With the expansion of trade they turned to building a larger type of merchant ship, the *latinadika*, a lateen-rigged vessel of about fifty tons. They began to trade as far afield as Constantinople in the north and Alexandria in the south. Venice and Trieste in the Adriatic were ports of call, and soon Marseilles and the southern coast of France came to know the seamen of the Aegean.

Hydra, Spetses and Psara (off the western coast of Chios) became known as the 'Three Naval Islands', and they provided a large part of the Greek navy during the War of Independence. Hydra in particular had grown wealthy during the British blockade of Europe during the Napoleonic wars, when she was able to trade freely with both sides; when Psara was attacked and depopulated by the Turks in 1822 she and Syros inherited much of its trade. Hydra's wealth, which had depended latterly on the grain trade with southern Russia, declined during the nineteenth century, as the Russians took to building their own ships. It declined even further as the ports of Ermoupolis in Syros and then Piraeus gradually monopolized the trade of the Aegean.

Hydra revolted from the Turkish rule in April 1821. Her fleets and admirals immediately flung themselves into the struggle, including the Greek naval Commander-in-Chief, Andreas Miaoulis, whose statue stands in the great Plateia Miaoulis on Syros. It is no exaggeration to say, as a Greek historian has put it, that 'the final deliverance of Greece was mainly due to the fleets of Hydra'. It was the Hydriot fleet which supplied and eventually relieved Mesolongi, where Byron died during its long ordeal under siege. The *archontikon* which today houses the Academy of Fine Arts belonged to Iakovos Tombasis, the admiral who sank the first Turkish battleship. Another belonged to one of the Tsamados brothers who fought in nearly all the sea battles of the war, and is now the Merchant Seamen's Training college. Of the two which are open to the public, one belonged to the wealthy Koundouriotis brothers, also prominent in the war at sea, the other to Demetrios Voulgaris, who was Prime Minister of Greece from 1855 to 1857.

Little of the dignity of those days survives, but one refuge from the crowds who drink and guzzle on the waterfront, or spill out from cruise liners to wander mostly mindlessly along the quays, peering into the depressingly trivial curio shops, is the monastery of the **Koimisis tou Theotokou** (the Assumption of the Virgin Mary), whose entrance from the harbour goes mercifully unnoticed for most of the time. The gateway leads into a peaceful courtyard with an orange tree; the *katholikon* is modern inside but has an impressive *templo* in grey marble with some elaborate carving. The rooms around the upper storey of the courtyard are no longer monks' quarters, but offices of the Mitropolis, for this is an important religious centre where you may see a gathering of venerable priests on special occasions. Then the bells on the *campanile* above the gateway ring out, and if some patriarch of the Church is arriving or departing then the cannon mounted on the platform at the entrance to the harbour will fire a resounding salute.

Another reason why most visitors stay put in the harbour is that there are no motor roads and no motor vehicles apart from a few trucks engaged on essential services. To reach the isolated monasteries high among the inland hills – one is just visible from the harbour – you must walk or hire a donkey. Nearest (about an hour's climb) are those of **Prophitis Ilias** and **Agia Evpraxia**, the latter a convent where the nuns weave and embroider fabrics for sale. Beaches are slightly more accessible – or rather you can swim from rocky stretches of coast to the west of the town, and there is one sandy beach at Mandraki, about a mile to the east.

Mt Ere is the highest peak of Hydra, but Prophitis Ilias is the second highest, and the monastery which takes its name is only just below the summit at 1953 feet. The real reward for the climb is the view, especially in the early light. To the east, Seriphos and Siphnos are just visible, outriders of the circling Kyklades. North lies the headland of Skylli, behind which Poros shelters. To the west the bay of Hydra and the barren island of Dokos are shadowed by the mountains on which you stand. Southwards the sea is empty, all the way to Crete and Africa.

Down below, the glory has not altogether departed, but the days when genuine artists and fashionable folk made their homes or took their pleasure here are gone. The tourists come and go, but the Hydriots are still here and proud to be, drying and mending their fishing nets on the new concrete mole which defines the limits of the modern harbour, watching the cameras click to record the moods of their beautiful town. The tills in their bars and restaurants click too – or now, as everywhere, they 'ping' – so why should they mind? Arriving or departing, the view from seaward of this historic place is the thing you will remember most.

Spetsai or **Spetses**? Both are feminine plural endings, the former classical and official, the latter modern demotic Greek. 'Spetsai' still appears on maps, but 'Spetses' is the local and popular name. Its history has been much bound up with that of Hydra, but physically they are very different islands. Spetses is comparatively low-lying, and it is well wooded. Its classical attribute was *pityoussa*, meaning 'pine-clad', and the Aleppo pine still softens the outlines of its hills. The air itself is resinous and has a tang and an uplift which is such a contrast to the sullen heat of the mainland in midsummer that you can understand why the inhabitants of Navplio and other towns in the Gulf of Argos first built summer houses here. Spetses in truth belongs less to the Saronic than to the Argolic Gulf. An airfield has been built at Porto Heli on the mainland only a few miles away, and frequent 'flying dolphins' bring holidaymakers across to Spetses after a short flight from Athens. This can be a useful link in reverse, as expeditions can be booked from here to Epidavros and Mycenae.

The landing point for the hydrofoils, whether they come from Porto Heli or Piraeus, is the long concrete jetty which forms the tiny harbour of **Dapia**. It is not only small but shallow, and visiting yachts have to anchor in a bay to the east, sheltered by a headland with a lighthouse at its tip. This was the old harbour, or Limani, which is still a centre for shipbuilding.

From the quay the ground rises at once, and you sense a more relaxed atmosphere than prevails on Hydra, with a sequence of café tables ranged along a shaded terrace which overlooks the harbour. Not that they are not desperately crowded at times, when service seems impossible within half an hour of an order, but again in contrast with Hydra the town has space to expand along a lower coastline in either direction. Its streets ramble pleasantly away from the sea, with no motorized traffic to disturb them, but as you move further along the front to the east standards begin to drop: bars and restaurants become cruder, and the town beach of Agios Mamas is as unattractive as most of its usual occupants, if that is possible.

However, if you persist in that direction, you come round a headland to the bay of **Agios Nikolaos**, called after a dignified and peaceful monastery which overlooks it. The *katholikon* is still in use, with an interior in the modern Greek style, but not as grating as some. The distinctive thing here is the black and white pebble decoration which paves the approach road and the large open courtyard at the west end of the church. Its designs of anchors and ships, birds and beasts, are much more lively and imaginative than the formal pebble patterns you see elsewhere – in the forecourts of the Evangelistria on Tinos, for example. There is even a portrait of Bouboulina, the Spetsiot heroine of the War of Independence.

Beyond Agios Nikolaos the road follows the coastline to the head of the bay which formed the ancient harbour of Spetses. Here you can better imagine the days of her commercial and naval importance: ships of all kinds at anchor, smaller boats drawn up on the hard, warehouses along the shore, and above all the skeletons of ships under construction in builders' yards. It was one of these yards which gladly accepted a commission from Tim Severin, that indefatigable retracer of ancient steps, to build a twenty-oar galley such as might have carried the Argonauts to Colchis in search of the Golden Fleece.

The new *Argo* was built here in the yard of Vasilis Delimitros by traditional methods with traditional tools, from technical drawings

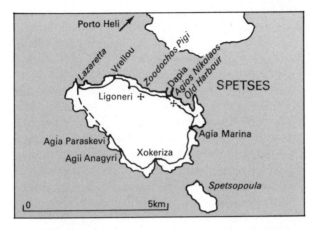

made by scholars in England. You can visualize the scene – two or three men (never more, or they impede each other) at work, shaping the stern and paring them with adzes. Like all the old hand instruments, scythe, plane or axe, the adze evokes from its operator a satisfying and beautiful rhythm. The arms swing, the wrists twist and the body sways deeply. Whether the launching was attended by the equally traditional ceremony of cutting a cockerel's neck and smearing the bows with its blood is not recorded.

On the far side of the headland where the lighthouse stands is the bay of **Agia Marina**, the most popular of the island beach resorts. You reach it by one of the main town thoroughfares which continues to the coast past a line of noisy tavernas. The metalled road ends shortly after, but a fairly good unmetalled road continues all round the island, taking in a few other holiday resorts on the south coast. These places are generally reached by small boats plying for hire in Dapia harbour, for the only wheeled transport in Spetses is the horse-drawn 'garry' which prefers to keep to the metalled surfaces. The general ban on motorized traffic does not include mopeds, an exception which some think suits only those who use them, but which does allow the enterprising to see more of the island.

The horse carriages are just as popular with the Spetsiots as with the tourists, and are not, as in other islands, seedy contraptions only intended to provide expensive local colour. You may be passed

113

anywhere in the neighbourhood of Dapia by a well sprung vehicle rattling along behind a well groomed and high stepping animal. A modern hydrofoil may be met on the jetty by a carriage which embarks a whole family – granny, children, dogs and all – on the way to spend a weekend with relations.

The name Dapia properly belongs to the broad esplanade to the west of the harbour, where the eye is at once caught by a more than lifesize statue of the Spetsiot heroine, Lascarina Bouboulina. Her story is bound up with the outbreak of the War of Independence, when on 3 April 1821 Spetses claims to have been the first of all the islands to join the revolt against Turkey. She took command of her husband's ship after he had been killed in action, using it as a privateer in irregular warfare against the enemy. She is presented here in the baggy-trousered piratical gear of the period, with a pistol and a cutlass stuck in her belt. A pair of flashing eyes commands the scene, the pupils emphasized in black, just as they are in the pebble portrait outside the church of St Nicholas. A casket containing her bones is one of the exhibits in the Museum, which occupies the former residence of a Spetsiot notable called Hadzi-Ioannis Mexis. This is a somewhat gloomy neo-classical building in one of the back streets, which seldom seems to be open.

The other story of the period is of the day when a Turkish fleet appeared off Spetses to the dismay of the islanders, because their own troops were away on another operation. The women responded to the crisis by putting red fezes (worn by Greek as well as by Turkish soldiers) on all the asphodel plants which grew along the shore. The ruse worked, and the Turks sailed away without daring to attack.

The more civilized quarter of the town spreads out past Dapia to the west through the greener suburb of Sourbouti. This is where Greeks have built their holiday homes, where the restaurants are in a higher class, and where several hotels occupy pleasant sites. The metalled road passes below the extensive estate of **Anargyrios College**, half-a-dozen very large residential blocks in neo-classical style set in formal gardens. Until the advent of the Socialist government this was the Greek equivalent of an English 'Public School', and must have been made an enjoyable start to life for those lucky enough to enjoy it. Only the young inmates are missing, for the gardens are well kept up, and the accommodation can be used for residential courses of further education. The boys also enjoyed the use of an athletics stadium and an open-air theatre built after ancient Greek models on the hillside above. The whole institution owes its existence to a Greek adventure-seeker called Anargyros, who left Spetses for America in the 1900s as a penniless boy and returned to his native island a very rich man. It was he who built the enormous 'Edwardian' hotel which overlooks the esplanade and the statue of Bouboulina – a hotel which is still in business and discreetly patronized by those who can afford it.

Beyond the College is the well placed Xenia hotel, and then the road climbs by way of 'Blueberry Hill' (really a beach-cum-chalet development) into the most attractive part of the island. It winds through pine woods several hundred feet above the indented coastline, where only a scramble is needed to reach some lovely coves. A few houses show up among the pines, and the road turns inland by a shady valley to the small church of *Zoodochos Pigi* at **Ligoneri** (both are suitable names, for Ligoneri means 'little water'). This part is well served by streams and springs, and close behind the church is a water-filled cave in the rock face which is said to have been connected by an underground passage with the monastery of Prophitis Ilias (which you will not be surprised to find in the centre of the island) – later blocked by an earthquake.

The road becomes even more beautiful as the asphalt surface ends and you enter an area justifiably called Paradissos. A rough track diverses downwards to the bay of **Vrellou**, with a sandy beach at the foot of a leafy valley. Thereafter the coast road becomes rudimentary, but it does continue to the distant bay of Zogaria and the beautiful inlet of Lazaretta. It cuts across the extreme western headland to complete a circuit along the south coast by way of bays at Agia Paraskevi and Agii Anargyri, and the more sophisticated centre of Xokeriza (next to the island's main football ground).

It would take some time to explore Spetses properly – there is another rough road which climbs from Dapia into the central hills and winds its way down to Vrellou on the north coast – but it would be time more agreeably spent, perhaps, than in the crowded harbour bars and cafés. An ideal island for a holiday, one concludes, if only other people would stay away!

The Greek Islands

Access

All three islands have a fast and frequent service by Flying Dolphin from *Zea Port*, close to Piraeus. SPETSES can also be reached from Porto Heli on the mainland of the Peloponnese, after a short flight from Athens.

Communications

POROS has a limited road system on the south coast; taxis are available, but not as a rule buses. In the other two islands motor traffic is barred, except fore hired mopeds in SPETSES. Bicycles can be hired in HYDRA, while the chief form of local transport in SPETSES is the horse carriage.

Accommodation

POROS   A number of B class hotels cater for package tourists, of which the best is probably SIRENE (228 beds) in a fine position below the monastery of Zoodochos Pigi. Those in the C class would need careful inspection before booking. No camping.

HYDRA   Again the B class hotels are the most satisfactory, though they are all 'pensions' catering for all-in holidays. The best could be MIRAMARE (50 beds) at Mandraki, but this is not a personal recommendation. No camping.

SPETSES   The general picture is the same. An exception is POSIDONION (A, 83 beds), overlooking the Dapia esplanade. Its vast Edwardian exterior contains all modern comforts in a peaceful if rarefied ambience. No camping.

Restaurants

There is too much choice in the most popular places and too little elsewhere for useful guidance.

Facilities

Banks: There are branches in all three main harbours.

Yachts: Poros and Hydra are popular with yachtsmen in all categories. In Spetses, Dapia harbour can only accommodate small craft. Yachts are diverted to the Old Harbour, with a safe anchorage and facilities ashore, including repairs.

The Kyklades

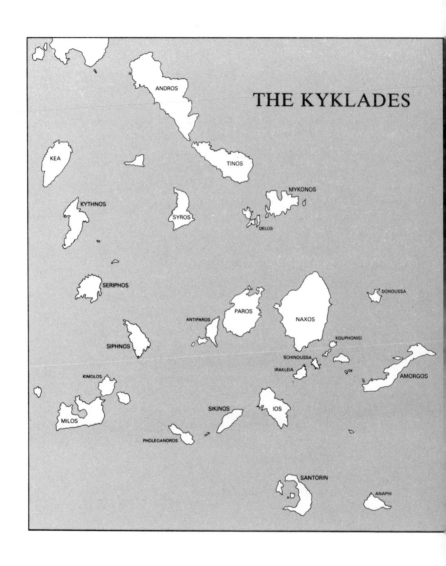

THE KYKLADES

ANDROS

KEA

TINOS

MYKONOS

KYTHNOS

SYROS

DELOS

SERIPHOS

DONOUSSA

ANTIPAROS

PAROS

NAXOS

KOUPHONISI

SIPHNOS

SCHINOUSSA

IRAKLEIA

AMORGOS

KIMOLOS

SIKINOS

IOS

MILOS

PHOLEGANDROS

SANTORIN

ANAPHI

THE KYKLADES

The best impression of the Kyklades as a whole would probably be from an aircraft on its way from Athens to Rhodes, but it is hard to better the view from the top of Mount Kynthos on Delos, ringed as it is by this constellation of inviting yet mysterious grey-brown humps rising out of the blue Aegean. The word Kyklades comes from the Greek *kyklos*, meaning a ring or circle, and in classical times Delos – the birthplace of Apollo – was regarded as the nucleus of the ring. Geographically this is not far out, though if you follow the chain of islands from Andros in the north to Santorin far away to the south it looks more like an oval than a true circle, and Syros (the modern administrative capital) lies closer to its centre line.

Except for Andros, which is more an extension of its northern neighbour Euboea, and Santorin, which is an exotic geological freak, these islands have much in common physically. There are no big pine forests and very few deciduous trees; the land is mostly dry and barren, and they seem bare to the natural elements which surround them – the wind and the sea. These are what have shaped their character and contribute to their charm. The air above is exhilaratingly fresh, the sea around transparently clear.

The history of the Kyklades has had a common pattern. Today there are few remains of centuries under Cretan, Mycenaean, Athenian, Macedonian and Roman supremacy. Nor has the long period of Byzantine rule left many traces except in a few monasteries like the *Panachrantou* on Andros, the *Kechrovouniou* on Tinos, the *Chozoviotissa* on Amorgos and the *Taxiarchon* on Seriphos. These survived barbarian attacks because as a rule they occupied remote or strongly defensive positions.

It was the fateful year 1204, when Venice managed to divert the leaders of the Fourth Crusade to attack and destroy their commercial rival Byzantium, that changed life in the Aegean generally and most particularly in the Kyklades. By the treaty of partition which followed, they were awarded to Venice, but Venice had no wish to subdue and administer these outlandish places herself. Instead she let it be known that adventurous members of Venetian families were welcome to found what amounted to small personal kingdoms, provided they remained friendly to the Republic and gave it trading facilities.

Many of them were already on the scene, having joined the Crusade as younger sons in search of fortune. In particular the Doge Enrico Dandolo had an enterprising nephew, Marco Sanudo, who lost no time in establishing himself as lord of Naxos. Within ten years he was master of all the present Kyklades, plus Astypalaia, and had proclaimed himself Duke of Naxos and the Archipelago.* He was joined by members of other Venetian families, whom he promised to instal in minor fiefdoms within the Duchy. His cousin Marino Dandolo was allowed to capture and rule Andros; the Barozzi took over Santorin; Astypalaia fell to the Quirini family; Tinos, Amorgos, Seriphos and Kea to the powerful Ghisi. Most of the other islands came under the direct control of Marco Sanudo and his descendants, who acknowledged not Venice but the French-born Princes of Achaea (and through them the Angevin Kings of Naples) as their suzerains.

From then on the different islands had different fates, as pirate attacks, inter-family quarrels and intervention by western or eastern powers unseated or restored their rulers and depleted their populations. Nevertheless, thanks to the diplomatic protection of Venice, the Duchy of Naxos survived at least in name for another hundred years after Byzantium and most of the rest of the Aegean fell to the Turks in the fifteenth century. Yet by 1566 the Sultan was master of the whole Aegean, and in 1580 the Kyklades were formally annexed to the Turkish Empire.

This period of Turkish rule, which lasted until the successful War of Independence in the nineteenth century, was on the whole a happier one than the islands had enjoyed under their Italian overlords, who had treated their people like serfs. Safe in their castles

---

* This word has come to mean any large group of islands; its derivation is doubtful, but it may have originally been a corruption of *Aegei Pelagos*, the Sea of Aegeus.

the nobles did nothing to protect their subjects from pirate attacks which laid waste their shores and decimated their populations, whereas the Turkish fleets kept the seas free for their own commerce. The Greek Orthodox church was allowed to re-establish its authority, although a large Catholic community survived in Naxos and Syros.

Two features strike the visitor today as characteristic of the Kyklades – the harbours and the inland capitals, or *Choras*. The natural and often land-locked harbours with their ring of buildings are simple and charming in the smaller islands like Ios, Seriphos and Amorgos, more pretentious and commercial in the larger ones like Syros and Tinos. The *Chora* embodies the Kykladic spirit more than anything – the dazzling white houses and churches crowding and clinging to the nearest convenient hillside, the narrow lanes twisting and climbing by alleys or steps, the paving stones edged with whitewash and spattered with donkey droppings. Sadly the white-sailed windmills have vanished from the ridges above, and only a few of the terraced cornfields are still sown to provide fodder for animals. Flour today comes ready milled from the mainland, though the island bakers do wonders with it.

Life in the Kyklades now is a mixture of mediaeval and modern. Theodore Bent, who travelled here at the end of the nineteenth century, gave a unique account of the still mediaeval conditions a hundred years ago – *The Cyclades* was published in 1884 and remains the best book ever written about these islands. The life he saw has not altogether vanished, nor has the poverty which went with it. Tourism has brought prosperity to the fringes, and some money is beginning to seep through to the inland villages, but the life of the islanders is hard and their ways simple.

THE NORTHERN KYKLADES

SEVEN

Andros

Although **Andros** is second only to Naxos in size and historical importance, it is unlikely to be the first of the Kyklades you visit, if only because there is no direct ferry connection with Piraeus and there is no airport. So much out of the way does Andros seem at first sight that it may be the last of the group to claim attention. Yet it is only a two-hour passage from the modern port of Rafina on the east coast of Attica, and it practically touches the more popular island of Tinos to the south.

In many ways Andros is untypical of the Kyklades, but as the one with the most varied and largely unspoilt attractions it could be a pleasantly convenient introduction to them all. A green and well watered island, it is outstandingly beautiful in spring, mellow and still fresh in autumn. The mountainous interior confines the road system to the west coast and the two deep valleys which cross from west to east, but the roads are excellently engineered and surfaced, which means that buses, taxis and private transport can take you swiftly from one centre to another. The sandy beaches and warm sea-splashed rocks are ideal for swimming, except when (and this is the only warning) the ferocious north winds drive you inland for shelter.

It is the prevalence of these winds – more violent and unpredict-able than the Etesian *meltemi* – which have turned **Gavrion** into the principal harbour, rather than the mediaeval capital of Andros on the exposed north-west coast. The harbour is a deep inlet within the wider *Ormos Gavriou*, itself protected from the south by a fringe of islets, which with their rings of submerged rocks remind one of a coral reef guarding the entrance to the bay. The village behind the harbour is insignificant and unsightly, quite subordinate to the business of loading and unloading vehicles and passengers on the quay.

Now that even the heaviest goods can be packed in lorries and transported in the gigantic holds of the modern ferries, you no longer see the various types of trading ships which used to frequent such a harbour. The old name *vapori* ('steamer') for the commonest form of inter-island transport has given way to the less specific word *karavi*. Happily the traditional design of the island *kaïki* has survived, even though these graceful and practical boats now surge through the seas driven by powerful marine engines. The generic term *varka* (or *varkoula*, according to size) is still used for the fishing boats, and the low flowing lines of their bulwarks, rising gently to stem and stern, are a familiar sight in the harbours of Andros and elsewhere. Despite their modern engines (I have sailed in one powered by a Lister marine engine made in Gloucestershire) the steersman still stands high in the stern, as in the days of sail, working the vertical rudder by a long wooden tiller, often nicely carved to give a good grip. It makes an inspiring silhouette against the morning or evening sunlight.

The fishing industry in the islands is highly organized these days. The larger boats are in radio contact with each other and their base, and companies often operate in groups of one large and two or three smaller boats. The parent boat may anchor offshore for her catch to be packed up in ice and transferred to the smaller ones, who will nip into harbour where lorries are waiting to transport the fish on board ferries bound for the mainland. This explains why the larger fish are hard to find (and very expensive) in island restaurants, which rely on the little open boats you see everywhere round the coast.

Landing inevitably at Gavrion, you are most likely to travel by bus or taxi the five miles down the coast to **Batsi**, which is a very different kind of place. There are few scenes in the islands more suitable for a summer holiday – a bright and cheerful town built round a sand-lined bay and well sheltered from the north. A mainly red-roofed old quarter climbs the hill to the south, and overlooks the small but busy fishing quay. There is a backing of shapely mountains, and a choice of hotels and attractive villas for the tourist. Within easy reach between Batsi and Gavrion are more fine sandy beaches, and with all these advantages it is not surprising that there is a real danger in summer of overdevelopment and overcrowding. However, if beaches get too crowded there are accommodating rocks to lie on out of sight of everyone – the writer doing just this one day had his best view yet of the Aegean kingfisher, a blue flash round the rock into a hole in the cliff behind. The *alkyon*, whose 'halcyon days' of winter are proverbial, is a reality whatever its breeding season.

Another five miles along the coast road to the south from Batsi was the ancient city and one-time capital, **Palaiopolis**, founded in the seventh century BC. It has been much written up in the guidebooks, and in the late nineteenth century Theodore Bent could write:

> 'When the temples and public buildings stood here it must have been one of those ideal places which we see depicted on theatrical drop-scenes. Everything that nature can provide is granted to this spot. Behind it rise the precipitous heights of Mount Petalos. Two clear streams dash down the slopes amidst olives, cypresses and lemons, which grow in profusion here. Below is the sea – and not a breath of that biting north wind which had tormented us so on the heights – everything was genial and pleasant except, perhaps, the interior of the peasant's house where we had to sleep.'

Bent's description reminds us that the Greeks were the most brilliant site-choosers in history. Imagine the good fortune that gave men of good taste and sensibility the chance to build in an almost virgin world – unsullied canvases for their temples, theatres and cities. In the case of Palaiopolis it was also a natural and practical choice, because (as will be seen) its founders came from an arid site not far away on the same coast, while here they had water which still flows without stint or interruption.

The site is indeed magnificent, but of the extensive classical town which crowded its steep slopes there is hardly a trace today. Soil has washed down from the mountain above to cover its remains, and terraced olive patches conceal all but a length of strongly built acropolis wall. To reach this you have to leave the end of the concrete track leading down from the modern village from the main road, and follow a long sequence of overgrown steps and stony paths. Your first sight of antiquity may be a group of three huge

blocks of stone by a water tank – all that survives of one of the gateways to the town below.

The proof that there were once streets, houses and marble-columned temples here lies in the fine new **Archaeological Museum** in the Chora of Andros town, where among many marble fragments you can see a statue of Hermes – a second-century copy of a Praxiteles original – dug out of this hillside by a farmer in 1833. It seems likely that the soil was washed down further to form a narrow alluvial plain which all but obliterated the harbour. Today it is only possible to beach a few small fishing boats on the foreshore.

The coastal road south from Gavrion is one of the loveliest in the Kyklades. It follows the enfolding lines of the hills at a considerable

125

height, with trees and rich vegetation above and below. The coastline here faces mainly south-west, and across a wide blue channel
you can see the clear outlines of other island sisters. Closest is
Giaros, which looks interesting, but being waterless is almost uninhabited. To the left of Giaros is the more familiar outline of Syros,
to the right the long irregular shape of Kea, first in the chain of the
western Kyklades. In between, and shadowy against the midday
sun, you can make out Kythnos, while to the right of Kea begins the
eastern coastline of Attica, from Pentelikon down to Cape Sounion.
The Archipelago is a family concern, like so much of Greek life.

After rounding the 3000-feet massif of Mt Petalon the road
divides at a point known as *Stavropeda* ('crossways'). Most of the
traffic will turn left here for Andros town, or Chora as it is still
generally called. Once over the watershed the road drops down the
wide and fruitful valley of Messaria. On either side of it scattered
villages appear in green settings, while down in the depths a massed
regiment of tall cypresses shields the floor of the valley from the
north winds which bring the waves bristling into the harbour
beyond.

Andros Chora is an unusual town, and one of the best kept in the
islands. The oldest part occupies a rocky tongue of land between
two bays, and it was here that Marino Dandolo, nephew of the Doge
of Venice who engineered the fall of the Byzantine Empire in 1204,
built a strong castle – strong enough for its final tower to have
survived the attacks of wind and waves for nearly eight hundred
years. A jagged foursquare ruin, its base is a rocky islet joined to the
narrow headland by a curious high-arched bridge.

The seventeenth-century English traveller Randolph describes
what he saw here: 'The inhabitants are all Greeks, having a good
large town to the north-east with no other walls but those of their
houses, which join together. At the end of the lanes are Gates,
which every night are shut to keep out the Privateers.' Andros owed
its considerable prosperity in the Middle Ages and later to its
remarkable fertility, and not least to a silk industry based on a
widespread plantation of mulberry trees. According to Randolph,
in some years they made more than 3000 lbs of silk.

The upper Chora is a later foundation, but an attractive and
sensible one. The long sloping main street is closed to traffic and

paved with large smooth slabs, swept clean every day. At the lower end the *Plateia Kaïris*, shaded by wide-branched plane trees, extends at right angles, and a good restaurant overlooks the southern bay and its long sandy beach. From here an arched gateway leads into the old walled town, or *Kato Kastro*, and as this narrows to a point you reach the windswept *Plateia Riva*, where a huge bronze statue of an 'unknown seaman' rocks disconcertingly on his heels when he meets the gale head on.

On the left of the main street, just before the *Plateia Kaïris*, is the **Archaeological Museum**, one of the finest small museums in Greece. Its scope is limited, and the greater part of the exhibition is taken up with finds from the early Geometric site of Zagora, which occupies a headland just south of the Stavropeda crossroads. This was the earliest settlement discovered in Andros, apart from vestiges of a Mycenaean presence in the Bronze Age. Legends of a Cretan occupation are too sketchy to convince, and a Phoenician presence would be limited to traders on their constant errands across the Mediterranean.

When Zagora was excavated by the Athens Archaeological Society and a team from the University of Sydney in the 1960s and 1970s, it proved to be a unique find – a self-contained town established by Ionian colonists about 900 BC which flourished until its evacuation in 700 BC, after which the site was never disturbed. The pottery and small objects displayed in the Museum show the high level of artistic civilization the Ionians brought with them or developed. In our appreciation of the glories of Periclean Athens we tend to overlook the charms and skills of the Geometric and Archaic periods which led the way. As one of the excellent charts in the Museum reminds us, we owe to those times the introduction of the Greek alphabet (which they owed to those Phoenician traders) and the poetry of Homer – as well as the first celebration of the Olympic Games, traditionally put in 776 BC. The whole exhibition is beautifully set out and catalogued. The same is true of the **Museum of Contemporary Art**, a modern building in one of the byways of the Kato Kastro, and the **Maritime Museum** down on the Plateia Riva. The loyalty to Andros of its natives who have prospered abroad has been shown by their support for these and all kinds of undertakings, great and small.

127

The Archaeological Museum was finished in 1981, thanks to the generosity of two of them, Basil and Elise Goulandris, and its opening was marked by the return from Athens of its most famous exhibit, the marble Hermes from Palaiopolis. This is the centrepiece of the ground floor exhibits, which include marble fragments of the Classical and Hellenistic periods also found at Palaiopolis, the site almost certainly occupied by the population of Zagora when – for whatever reason – they abandoned the earlier town.

The site of **Zagora** is fascinating, and not difficult to find, though the defences put up by the excavators when they finished work are as properly discouraging to the intruder as was the massive wall built across the neck of the headland by the original settlers. Five hundred yards beyond Stavropeda in the direction of Korthi, a path to the right between stone walls leads first past a small church and then up and down hill – it takes about forty minutes to walk it – until you emerge on to a curious flattened promontory, sloping gently back to the north. Surrounded on three sides by sheer cliffs descending to the sea, the only other defence it needed was this cleverly built wall with just one narrow and easily covered entrance, while ships could be beached in a deep sandy bay to the north. Sad to say the natural beauty of the site has been spoilt by a brush fire which has turned all the evergreen scrub to a few blackened stalks; even then the ground is covered early in the year with the small blue *iris pumila*, and in autumn by bright yellow patches of the crocus-like *sternbergia colchiflora*, pushing up bravely between the piles of blackened stones.

Three main groups of houses were discovered, of uniform and practical design, and clear reconstructions of them are illustrated in the Museum Guide. The most interesting and best preserved building is the temple, a touchingly small forerunner of the great pillared structures of the sixth and fifth centuries. Only the ground plan survives, the size of a large house, beautifully built of finely cut schist stone and divided simply into a plain *pronaos*, or antechamber, and a *cella* with a rough altar in the centre. The roof, as in all the houses, was flat, supported on wooden columns (the stone bases survive) with a ceiling of natural wood poles carrying heavy schist slabs and sealed by a layer of waterproof clay. This kind of roofing can still be seen in countless houses and small churches in Andros and other islands.

Siphnos. *templo* of the *Panagia Eleoussa*, Kastro

Above, Zakynthos. The Church of the Assumption, Keri;
below, Astypalaia

Why was such a marvellous site abandoned? Enemy attack or earthquake must be ruled out, for the new settlement at Palaiopolis was far less defensible and just as susceptible to earth tremors. Most probably it was the failure of the water supply, which depended on catchment cisterns for rain water, or long journeys to fetch spring water from elsewhere. There are no springs on the headland itself, while at Palaiopolis water gushes liberally from the hillside. Even so the new site was not far away, and Zagora was not entirely abandoned, for the temple and its surrounding sanctuary was maintained and used at least for another two hundred years by the descendants of those who built it. In fact the latest form of the temple as revealed by the excavation is probably a sixth-century building, not unlike a temple of that date found at Emborio in Chios. Both seem to have been dedicated to Athena, the most popular Olympian of the Archaic period in those parts.

With one exception the other places worth visiting in Andros have a mediaeval origin. The exception is an extraordinary circular tower which stands near the head of the valley above Gavrion near the hamlet of **Agios Petros**. Although the natural stone blends with the stony hillside behind, the tower can be clearly seen from the main road below, and is easily reached by way of the road signposted to Vitali at the back of Gavrion. At first sight it seems to be a homogeneous construction, rising to about 65 feet with window spaces representing five distinct storeys, and most authorities classify it either vaguely as 'Hellenic' or mistakenly as 'Hellenistic'.

In fact, if you look closely you will see that the stones forming the lower courses are colossal and roughly put together, whereas the upper part which forms the tower is built of smaller, carefully graded stones tapering towards the top. The entrance on the south side is low, enclosed by two huge stone jambs and a lintel, and it leads directly into a domed chamber rising to about 20 feet in the centre. You look up – and you could imagine yourself inside the 'Tomb of Agamemnon' at Mycenae! True, the entrance is lower, and lacks the triangular weight-bearer above it, but the external and internal stonework is Mycenaean or Pelasgian in scale and style. So what do we have? Why not an original *tholos* or 'beehive' chamber, possibly a royal tomb of that period, on whose massive foundations later builders have added a more useful structure – perhaps a fortified look-out tower to command the approaches to Gavrion? In any case there was no connection between the domed chamber and the upper storeys – you had to climb through a gap made in the roof of the entry passage to reach a series of stone stairways, spiralling round the inside of the tower. This left the lower chamber totally enclosed, and it could have been retained as a refuge for animals. As far as one knows the floor has never been excavated.

The two chief mediaeval monuments of Andros are the monasteries of **Zoodochos Pigi** and **Panachrantou**. The former is not far from the tower of Agios Petros, and can be reached either by a fairly stiff climb from the main road behind Batsi – it lies just over the brow of the hill at the head of a typical walled pathway, or *dromaki* – or more easily (if you can persuade a taxi driver to tackle a roughish road) by way of an unmarked turning halfway between Batsi and Gavrion. Thought to have been originally a Byzantine school, it was converted to a monastery during the fourteenth century. Theodore Bent had a warm welcome from the monks in the 1800s, but it declined after the First World War and in 1928 it became a convent for nuns.

Only six nuns are left of the sixty who were a happy community here twenty years ago, but the Mother Superior is a distinguished figure, well educated and a good linguist. The name Zoodochos Pigi means 'Life-giving Spring', and this often explains the choice of a site for a Christian church. Next to the monastery church is a marble fountain, from which flows the *agiasma*, a miraculous stream of water. Inside the church is a delightful ikon worked in fine petit-point embroidery, embellished with gold and silver thread, of which the subject is a miracle wrought by the holy water. A man lies spreadeagled on his back while the water is poured on his head from a pitcher, and a vigorous little black devil shoots out of his mouth in defeat. The southern range of the mediaeval fortress-like walls survives, with one dramatic ruined tower. The inner precincts have a sad decaying charm.

The Panachrantou monastery is in a wilder and more remote situation, just over the top of the mountain ridge which separates the valleys of Messaria and Korthi. The long trek up from the bottom of the Messaria valley is no longer necessary, for a rough road over the mountain branches off the new highway between Andros Chora and the southern harbour of Korthi, near the village of Exo Vouni. It is a very rough track at present, and horribly steep in places, but a weekly tourist bus which leaves Gavrion in the early morning brings visitors most of the way. Even in summer it is a grim place to come to, but inside it is more cheerful and domestic, and there is a spectacular view down the Messaria valley and out to sea beyond Andros harbour. The senior monk is a genial character and will show you round the complicated interior. Founded possibly as early as the tenth century, it is like a small village, with two principal churches (both later foundations) and narrow lanes connecting the monastic buildings.

You can reach the bay of Korthi either by this way from the Chora or by continuing straight on past the Stavropeda crossroads from Batsi. In the first case the road continues past Exo Vouni and in its descent it passes three sites which must have been important in mediaeval times. First comes a rock-crowned peak above the village of **Kochylou**, where at nearly 2000 feet you can make out the ruined walls and two towers of a considerable fortress – the *Epanokastro* ('upper castle') and the final refuge of the dwellers in the Korthi valley. Further down on the left, below the road, you pass the significantly named **Palaiokastro** ('ancient castle') and soon afterwards the equally significant **Episkopio** ('look-out place') above the road on the right. The three places must have been a chain of defensive positions subordinate to the *Kato Kastro* of the capital.

The two villages are worth exploring if you have the time. In Palaiokastro the most obvious building is the Byzantine church of *Christos*, but behind it are the remains of a largely deserted mediaeval village. Episkopio is more substantial, with the ruins of large mediaeval houses and towers, dwarfing small modern villas surrounded by orchards and well watered vegetable plots. A lane leads through it past a mediaeval arcaded washplace to a leafy ravine where water still flows past a ruined mill – the only watermill I remember seeing in the islands, apart from the 'sea-mills' on Kephalonia.

Down in **Korthi** one is reminded of a fishing village in the west of Scotland. An uncompromising stone-paved street runs parallel to the sea, with glimpses of it through narrow alleyways. It makes a better harbour than Andros town, with two breakwaters to shelter it from the north. There is a plain grey stone hotel, quite a number of rooms to let in summer, and a long sandy beach stretching away to the south.

We have left to the last the modern aspect of the beautiful Messaria valley, and the sequence of lovely villages which line its southern slopes. **Messaria** itself is a busy little place almost joined on to the outskirts of the Chora, with a main street which gets frequently jammed by lorries, but gives a friendly passage to donkeys. The main church of *Agios Nikolaos* has been dully modernized, but a lane opposite leads to the delightful twelfth-century one of the *Taxiarch Michailis*. This has been stripped of its disfiguring whitewash, and you can see both the beauty of its natural stonework and the elegance of its later marble doorway. An inscription in the church records that it was built in 1158, during the reign of the Emperor Manuel Comnenus, and therefore by a strange calculation 6666 years after the creation of the world.

The line of hill villages begins in the north with **Stenies**, overlooking from some height the harbour and sandy bay of the same name. This is a village paradise, with tiers of well built houses rising in stages round the folds of the hillside, sunny and sheltered even in the blustering north winds. Winding lanes connect houses on each level, and flowery gardens alternate with luscious orchards – lemons, oranges, almonds, quinces, figs, walnuts and pomegranates. No traffic is allowed or possible, though buses and cars can reach either end of the village.

Next in line is **Ipsilou**, a poor relation as it were of Stenies. The situation is just as beautiful and even more peaceful, but the houses are poorer and more dilapidated. Water gushes in channels and spouts from top to bottom, wild cyclamen grow in the cracks of the steps, and if you follow one channelled stream downhill you come to another Byzantine church dedicated to the *Taxiarch Michailis*. The Archangel Michael was obviously a special patron of Andros. This church was built in the eleventh century, but has been modernized within. Above Ipsilou is **Apoikia**, better known because of the famous Sariza mineral water it produces. It has two hotels, but except for its position and superb views it is less attractive than its neighbours. Below again is **Lamira**, now a more sophisticated through still attractive village, and from here you regain the main road up the valley.

Almost at once a short side road takes you to **Menites**, a naturally beautiful spring-watered hamlet, deeply shaded and cool in mid-summer. A mile or two further on you see above the road the beautifully proportioned white shape of yet another *Taxiarch Michailis* identified with the nearby village of **Melida**. This forms part of the cemetery of Pitrophoros; beyond the west end there is a delightful domed ossuary to contain the bones of the departed when room can no longer be found for them in the ground. Apart from that it is another good example of eleventh-century Byzantine work, and even the blanketing effect of total whitewash fails to conceal the beauty of its lines.

Although there is a good bus service operating between Chora, Gavrion, Batsi and Korthi, Andros is a big enough island to warrant hiring a car or moped. This enables you to turn aside at will, explore more distant places, and enjoy one of the most welcoming countrysides the islands can present to the traveller. Apart from its trees, its flowers and its springs of fresh water, man has contributed a collection of decorative dovecotes bettered only in Tinos, and a unique system of dry stone walling. This interrupts the line of the wall every three or four feet with a pointed slab set on its broad end, lined with smaller stones to wedge it in, thus preventing any tendency of the wall to collapse laterally. For hundreds of miles this walling, still in good condition, surrounds the fields and lanes and orchards, and marches over the hills in all directions. The labour of building it passes belief, but it is one of the chief features of Andros.

You will notice too that there are as many horses here as donkeys, as well as plenty of cattle in the fertile valleys. When you do see donkeys, as often as not the riders will be seated astride at a purposeful canter instead of being slumped across the saddle drumming with their heels against the animal's flanks. Altogether life seems more open and confident, less of a struggle, perhaps, than elsewhere. The Andriot responds in a detached manner to the visitor, but with a slow-kindling warmth and a gentleness you do not always find in islands where life is harder. They are proud of their island, which preserves its own charm and dignity in all seasons.

The Greek Islands

Access

There is no direct connection with Piraeus, but ferries leave Rafina, the new port on the east coast of Attica, every afternoon for Andros; the passage usually takes under two hours. There is a regular bus connection between Rafina and the centre of Athens. In the other direction, ferries call two or three times a week from Tinos and Syros. There is no airfield.

Communications

Good roads and buses connect the principal centres. Taxis can be found at Andros Chora, Batsi and Gavrion. Cars and mopeds can be hired at Batsi and the Chora, though there is not a lot of choice.

Accommodation

The principal holiday centre is Batsi, where there is a wide choice of hotels, guest houses and villas. The biggest hotel is CHRYSSI AKTI (B, with 118 beds), which is only concerned with the tourist industry; so is the smaller LYKION (B, pension only). SKOUNA (C) is more individual, and more personal still is the recently built KARANASOS (C), obligingly run by a married couple. All these have immediate access to the sandy town beach, which is clean and suitable for children.

Andros town, or Chora, is less well provided. XENIA (B) is quiet and comfortable, if showing signs of wear. It occupies a dramatically sea-swept position almost on the harbour rocks (no beach). EGLI (C) is more old-fashioned, but a cosier place off the main street, and open all year. The owner rents cars.

Restaurants

There is only one good restaurant in the Chora, KAIRIS, in the plateia of the same name, with tables inside and outside. As a change, DIONYSOS in Messaria village is fun and has good food.

In Batsi there are several eating places, but the best restaurant is the STAMATIS taverna, popular with Greek families (tables inside only), and open all year.

In Korthi there is a remarkable café-bar where you can buy litre bottles of local wine, red and white.

Facilities

Banks: There are branches in the principal centres.

Yachts: Andros and Korthi harbours are exposed to the north. There are good berths and anchorages at Batsi and Gavrion, though shore facilities are better at Gavrion.

EIGHT

Tinos and Syros

Tinos, some fifteen miles long by five broad, is separated from Andros only by the narrow Steno Strait. Ferries from Rafina on the east coast of Attica call here after Andros, but most of the big modern ships come straight here from Piraeus and pass on to Mykonos. The capital and port, once the town of St Nicholas, lies on the south-west coast and looks across towards Syros, only ten miles away. The entrance to the harbour is awkward for the bigger ships, and extensive concrete quays have been built further along the shoreline to the north.

What Delos was to the ancient world, Tinos is to modern Greece. This is the centre of Orthodox piety, for the miraculous ikon of Our Lady is contained in the great church of the *Panagia Evangelistria.* On 25 March and 15 August (the feasts of the Annunciation and the Assumption) pilgrims come from all over Greece, for on those two days the ikon is brought out from its shrine to the church, and innumerable are the cures attesting to the healing power of the Panagia – witness the multitude of gold and silver votive offerings suspended within.

You might well think that the history of Tinos began in June 1822, when a sister in the convent of Kechrovounio dreamed one night that she was visited by the Panagia, who told her that an ikon bearing her picture was buried on a farm just outside the town (as it was then). The nuns joined in excavations which uncovered the ruins of a Byzantine church – and there on 30 January 1823 a workman found the ikon. Building of the present church began at once on the site. These events established the character of Tinos town from then on, and the intensity of feeling at the time was increased by the outbreak and progress of the War of Independence – in which the Tiniots played an energetic part.

135

In an early nineteenth-century foundation you might expect something of the qualities you find in nearby Syros, and indeed not so long ago descriptions of the harbour front spoke of the elegance of its buildings, backed by the lacy white elevations of its churches. Sadly it is not so today. Almost all that range of buildings has been demolished to make room for half a dozen large and poorly planned hotels, each with an enormous restaurant area at street level. The churches nearby are deserted or neglected, and in the parallel back streets there are pseudo-tavernas and bars from which hideous 'music' comes at night.

There are still quiet and clearly paved little streets, overlooked by balconies, which lead upwards and away from the harbour, though the narrow market thoroughfare – narrow enough to carry an awning over it in summer – has sacrificed all but a few of its traditional stalls to displays of trinkets, baubles and commemorative crockery. Beside it in a steep gradient rises the ceremonial highway which leads to the cause of it all – Our Lady of the Good Tidings.

What you see in Tinos today is an extreme manifestation of the Greek home tourist industry – designed for and enjoyed by the Greeks themselves, wherever they may live. Huge modern ships bring thousands of good Greek people from Athens and its sultry suburbs for a family weekend which is different, and into which can be woven strands of the strong religious enthusiasm which animates the Orthodox church. Visitors from Germany, England, France, America and Australia, who seem to overrun most of the islands in the summer, are lost among the hordes which disembark in Tinos every weekend, and above all at the two great festivals in March and August.

Those are occasions for more than a weekend jaunt, when the chronically sick and the maimed come hoping for a miraculous cure, but even at other times one may see some poor blighted creature, barefoot and bandaged, falling on hands and knees to crawl the length of the quay and up to the shrine itself.

It is this factor which has saved the whole scene from becoming a mixture of Margate and Disneyland – this and the essential dignity which surrounds the rituals of the Orthodox church. If the harbour area suggests Margate, the approach to the Panagia on a Sunday or feast day is Disneyland. You leave the last of the trinket stalls to cross an area of intricate black and white pebble designs. In front of you rises a white wedding-cake wall, in which a wide rococo arch-way leads directly to a flight of ceremonial steps with a red carpet down the centre. At the foot of the steps stands an attendant selling four or six-foot-high candles at appropriate prices, while pho-tographers offer to take you and your family against the monumen-tal background of the church itself.

The church has arcaded entrances on two levels, the upper one being a balustraded terrace leading to the interior of a typical nineteenth-century Orthodox cathedral, only with every feature twice as rich and grand. The ikon itself, when displayed, is almost indistinguishable under its covering of gold and silver, with a rope of pearls strung across it. On the lower (ground) level is the entrance to the church of the *Evresios*, or 'Discovery'. This is a simpler low-vaulted place; to the right of it there is a chapel in memory of the crew of the Greek cruiser *Helle*, torpedoed by an Italian submarine just before the outbreak of war in 1940; beyond again is a baptistry with a huge copper font. If you are approaching on a Sunday or a festival morning you will have heard from afar the rich baritones of the presiding priests sonorously intoning the liturgy of the day. Overamplified they may be, but they make a reality of what might be an elaborate make-believe.

The upper court, where the throngs gather to enter, is like the *cour d'honneur* of a French château, though softened by shady green corners and flowering bushes. The low building to the right as you face the church houses an exhibition of ikons, mainly of the eighteenth century, but with a few rather battered specimens of the seventeenth.

Perhaps more interesting than any of these is a document dis-played on a table at the far end. This is a facsimile of an unusual despatch dated December 1940 from Sir Michael Palairet at the British Legation in Athens to the then Foreign Secretary, Lord Halifax. It records the incalculable inspiration given by Our Lady of Tinos to the Greek troops resisting the Italian invasion, and how the victories they quickly recorded on successive feast days of the Virgin Mary seemed a clear reply to the outrage she and they suffered when on 15 August that year – two months before war was declared – that Greek cruiser was torpedoed in home waters.

In fact, the circumstances were more remarkable than Sir Michael had room for in his despatch. Mussolini finally declared war on 28 October, and Italian troops invaded Greece through Albania. The Greek army checked the invaders near the town of Konitsa, and on 21 November, which was the feast of the Presentation of the Virgin, they re-entered it and threw the Italians back over the border into Albania. On 6 December the people of Tinos agreed among themselves to hand over five million drachmas worth of offerings from the church – gold, silver and precious stones – to help to finance the war effort. On the same day, which was also the fortieth day of the war, the army captured the port of Santi Quaranta, the 'Forty Saints', on the Albanian coast. Two days later they won another decisive victory at Argyrokastro inside Albania. It is good to record that the Bank of Greece indemnified Tinos for its sacrifice, and her treasures were restored to the Panagia.

The coast road out of town to the north brings you after a mile and a half to **Kionia**, where the largest hotel in the island commands an excellent beach. Just before you reach it there is a rather sad archaeological site enclosed by a wire fence. This is the **Sanctuary of Poseidon and Amphitrite**, suitable patrons of the seaside, first excavated by the Belgians in 1900. Unfortunately since the last visits by the French School in the 1970s it has been totally neglected, and the curator's hut is unmanned. You can trace a few temple foundations, and two *exedrae* show up forlornly amid the long grass and the thistles.

It is a relief to escape into the countryside, which has some of the most beautiful of all Greek island scenery, and almost for the first time you can appreciate that it had a history before 1822. A short tour round the nearer villages will demonstrate both points. The main exit road from the town heads east at first, then turns north up and across some lovely valleys. At the head of one is **Tripotamos**, where 'three rivers' do meet, then comes **Xinara**, home of the Catholic Archbishop of the Kyklades, after which the road circles the distinctive isolated peak of **Xombourgo**. This was the mediaeval acropolis, where after their arrival in 1207 the Ghisi of Venice built the castle which protected the whole island and withstood all assaults for five hundred years. After the fall of Byzantium and most

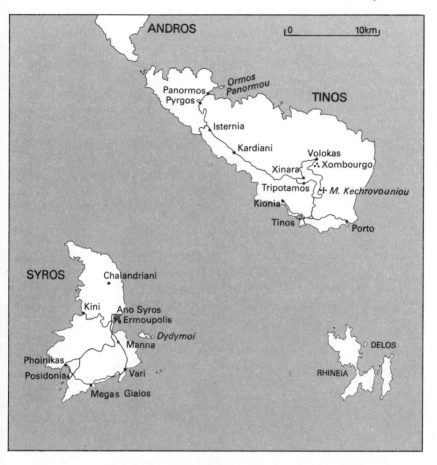

of the Greek mainland to the Turks in the fifteenth century, Tinos (with Mykonos) reverted to the direct rule of Venice. It outlasted all the other Aegean islands in resisting the Turks, and only fell to them in 1715 through the feebleness of the Venetian governor. A substantial town with two churches sheltered under its walls, but castle and town are now only ruins.

Round comes the road through a succession of little hill villages, past scattered white churches, with the typical square Tinos dovecotes rising everywhere on the flowery slopes. These are the most

139

elaborate dovecotes in the Aegean, with machicolated tops and three or four bands of elaborately fretted stonework masking the entry holes. What is more, they all seem to be as fully booked as the hotels in summer, but with far more attractive residents – a cloud of white when they take off against the blue sky.

After the village of Volakas the road winds south through the hills and along the western shoulder of the Kechrovouni range. As you come within sight of the sea again, you can see what looks like another fortress above you on the left. This is the **Kechrovouniou** monastery, the convent where the vision of sister Pelagia made the island's history. Tradition says there was a monastic foundation as early as 842. The convent was founded in the twelfth century and seems always to have enjoyed wealth and fame. Even today there are still a dozen nuns.

Once inside the gate you will see why it looks like a fortress from a distance. It is really a walled village which contains several churches and the living quarters of the nuns – which they keep beautifully, with bright patches of flowers. The main church, or *katholikon*, has an elaborate fifteenth-century *templo* covered in gold leaf and displaying the ancient ikon of the *Panagia tis Kolonas* (Our Lady of the Pillar). Outside is an old walnut tree, and the stalls inside are of the same wood. If this interior is too gaudy for you, there is more feeling in the little underground church next to it. This is the *Zoodochos Pigi*, or 'life-giving spring', probably built round the fountain which was the origin of the whole place, now beautified with modern marble surrounds.

Most interesting of all is the cell where Saint Pelagia (she was beatified in 1971) had her vision. It is reached up a narrow stairway and consists of a tiny bare bedroom with a small but comfortable-looking living room next door, including a washplace and a cooking alcove. Underneath is a chamber with relics illustrating the discovery of the ikon, and next to the cell is the nineteenth-century church, now dedicated to *Agia Pelagia*. The feature of this is the wide gleaming *templo* carved in local marble by local craftsmen – white above, with a green mottled base. The effect is striking, but the carving seems lifeless. These distinctive veins of marble are still quarried in the north of the island, though not to the same extent as on Thasos or Naxos.

A longer and more ambitious bus journey will take you right up to the north of Tinos, ending in the lovely Ormos Panormou below the hill village of Pyrgos, which is also known as Panormos. This is a very enjoyable hour's ride. The road first circles a few inland villages, then follows a corniche route up the west coast through Kardiani to Isternia, and finally crosses the northern watershed to Pyrgos. All these villages are built on narrow shelves below the crest of the hills, bypassed by the modern asphalt road. No journey in Tinos gives such an idea of the beauty and fertility of the landscape. In spring the whole range of Aegean flowers is in bloom, in summer it blazes with golden Spanish broom and bright patches of thyme. Every hillside has been terraced from top to bottom for cultivation, the valleys densely green with olives and splashed with pink oleander.

From Pyrgos the road winds down one of those lovely valleys to end at the little harbour of **Panormos**, a picture-postcard fishing harbour with two good restaurants (the further one is the better) and a large modern jetty for yachts. A walk along the cliffs to the south reveals a number of little rocky coves ideal for swimming, while sandy beaches on the far northern side can be reached by small boat. There are a few simple rooms to be had; a wonderful place for a week's holiday, or worth it for a day's expedition.

A much shorter journey (only a quarter of an hour by bus or taxi) takes you to **Porto**, another attractive bay on the south-east corner of the island. The village straggles round the shore, with a good many new houses offering rooms. It has less character than Panormos, but there are two wide sandy beaches separated by a neck of land, and there is easy access to the sea from rocks to the south. It also has a good, large and shady restaurant.

To return to Tinos town, the developments north of the harbour are more attractive than its immediate background, but nowhere is one tempted to linger. One contented inhabitant is Petros of Tinos, the pelican who mostly sits on a wall in the middle of a small *plateia* within comfortable reach of an outdoor restaurant which specializes in fish. As pelicans fly, it is not very far to Mykonos harbour, where Petros of Mykonos has a bigger public. For my money Petros of Tinos is better looking.

For all ferry passengers sailing south through the eastern Kyklades bound, maybe, for Paros, Ios or Santorin, the first port of call after leaving Piraeus will be **Syros** (the old spelling 'Syra' has been discarded). Unless they are Greeks who live there, not many will disembark. Instead, the stern rails will be crowded with people gazing curiously at what for many of them is their first island harbour. However familiar that first view may become, it is always fascinating.

Away to the left, on the far side of the harbour, are all the appurtenances of a dockyard – machine sheds, cranes, warehouses and rusting ironwork. In contrast there may be a white-hulled cruise liner, Greek or even Russian, being refitted alongside a distant wharf. Closer to the right is the nineteenth-century Customs House; across the road the inviting front of the Hermes hotel, one of the best in the islands; stretching away towards the docks a mostly shabby waterfront. Behind that you glimpse a long neo-classical façade framed by tall houses; behind that again are two conical hills, their sides packed with white and ochre-washed houses, both summits crowned by churches. This is **Ermoupolis**, capital and administrative centre of the Kyklades – its position is no less central to the group than Delos – and most of its remarkable history can be traced in this first view.

Ano Syros, the hill on the left with its clustering houses and the Cathedral of St George which crowns it, is a foundation of the early thirteenth century when Marco Sanudo from Venice established the Duchy of Naxos and the Archipelago, and introduced a junior member of the family to rule in Syros. The Cathedral was built for one of the first four suffragan bishops of the Duchy, but of more significance for the island was a convent and its church built by Capuchin monks in the seventeenth century. The hundred years which followed was a time of widespread piracy in the Aegean, involving mainly Turkish corsairs looking for goods and slaves. The monks appealed for protection to any western power which had influence at the Sublime Porte, and it was Louis XIII who took them under his wing. The French flag was flown from the convent buildings, and the islanders were saved not only from pirates but from any interference by the Turkish masters of the Aegean.

It was thanks to the continued protection by the 'Most Christian' kings of France that the population increased from barely five hundred at the end of the fifteenth century to several thousand by 1700. A high proportion were Catholic descendants of the original Venetian or Genoese settlers, and it was they who built their homes round the mediaeval acropolis of Ano Syros. **Vrontado,** the second hill, was occupied in the same way by the Greek Orthodox community, which is why today St George looks across and slightly down on his Orthodox rival there.

Until the beginning of the nineteenth century these were the only populated areas. Before then there was no proper harbour, only a wide bay sheltered from the east by a long natural breakwater. The beach was empty but for a few shacks, and the low-lying area between it and Ano Syros had only some scattered remains which archaeologists suggest were of a classical city. The modern town and harbour of Ermoupolis was the result of a later historical accident.

When the Greek War of Independence broke out in 1821 the five thousand Greek Catholics were still protected by the successors of Napoleon, so it was understandable that the Syriots, Catholic and Orthodox alike, were not eager to join in the actual hostilities. Andreas Miaoulis, whose statue stands in the *plateia* which takes his name, and who commanded the greater part of the Greek fleet in the war, was a native of Hydra. At the same time the islanders were in a good position to give shelter to fellow Greeks from islands which had suffered for their revolt at the hands of the infuriated Turks.

The first shiploads of refugees began arriving from Chios and its small neighbour Psara, where there had been a savage massacre of the prosperous Christian population. The Chians in particular were great traders and businessmen, and finding the bay and its hinterland almost uninhabited they set about building a new town for themselves there. Soon they were joined by Greeks from Crete and Rhodes, from Smyrna and the Greek mainland, and in no time they had created a fine new city. As the other islands recovered their freedom the later arrivals went home, but the Chians remained – it was ninety years before their homeland was restored to Greece. They called the new town Hermoupolis (the aspirate is ignored in modern Greek), the city of the winged communicator and protector of commerce in the ancient world. The name also happily commemorated the ship *Hermes* which had brought many of them to safety in Syros.

The early nineteenth century was an ideal time for commercial enterprise, with the Industrial Revolution under way, and here was a splendid natural harbour with room around it to build huge warehouses. It became the first free port zone in Greece. Iron foundries, mills and tanneries followed, then banks, insurance offices and printers, with a Chamber of Commerce to control the port's activities. Today the shipping industry is in decline, as it is everywhere, but the population is largely professional – bankers, lawyers and accountants – and almost alone in the islands (Milos is another exception) it has no urgent need of the tourist to stoke the economy.

The modern town spreads all the way round and behind the wide curve of the harbour front, and it is a good mile from the Customs House on the eastern mole, near where the ferries berth, to the end of the sprawling shipyards to the south. The long waterfront is disappointing at close quarters, the buildings almost universally seedy, with few bars or restaurants of a kind to tempt the visitor. Take any street radiating off the front, though, and you are in a world of solid nineteenth-century elegance. The transition is extraordinary. These streets are entirely different from those in any other Kykladic town – with the possible exception of the main street in Andros Chora. They are paved with smooth, square stone slabs, and the tall houses, even those with shops on the ground floor, have balconies and window shutters in the French style. The whole town has a quiet dignity: the traffic is orderly and not too noisy, and even in the busy summer months the foreign tourist is hardly visible.

The focal point to which most of the streets lead is the *Plateia Miaoulis*, a superb open space almost as long as the Piazza San Marco in Venice, beautifully paved and shaded on two sides by rows of palm trees. In the centre at the back is the enormous but well proportioned neo-classical *Nomarcheion* – a County rather than a Town Hall, for here the governing council of the Kyklades meets. There are café tables set out on each side, and in the evenings the Greek families take their *volta* in these dignified surroundings. On the near side of the square is the statue of Admiral Miaoulis; though not a Syriot, he reminds us of the Greek fight for freedom and the time when Ermoupolis was born.

Under the clock tower at the top of a flight of steps to the left of the *Nomarcheion* is a small **Museum** where entry is free. There are exhibits from various Kykladic islands, among them a lively marble relief of a boar hunt from Minoa on Amorgos. The most significant object is a marble slab from Ios, which bears the inscription (transliterated): *Thuseis minos Omirionos.* The translation seems to be 'You will sacrifice in the month Omirion', suggesting a spring festival of unknown origin. This inscription confirmed the Dutch Count Pasch van Krienen in the belief that in 1771 he had found Homer's tomb on Ios, and it is the only discovery he made which has been verified by later archaeologists. It was seen by Ludwig Ross in the nineteenth century, and from it the German scholar Welcker deduced that there was at least a Homeric School on Ios – fanciful as that seems today. The inscription is framed by upright snakes to left and right, and a trefoil flower above.

In a glass case are some little early Kykladic idols of great charm from Chalandriani in north-east Syros. They have a remarkable affinity with primitive African sculpture and even with 'modern' European art. The curious flat dishes displayed here have been variously explained as the backs of mirrors, dishes for religious offerings, and the backs of tambourines tapped with the fingers – the last explanation wins my vote as being the most unexpected.

The part of Ermoupolis which more than any other shows the French influence on its architecture is the quarter known as **Vaporia**, perhaps because former steamer captains built their houses here. French influence began with the arrival of the Capuchins and the foundation of their monastery in 1633, but architecturally speaking it was the nineteenth century which gave Ermoupolis its distinctive appearance.

The centrepiece of the quarter is the dignified and spacious church of *Agios Nikolaos*, reached by quite a steep climb from the northern end of the harbour by way of the quiet tree-lined *Plateia Tsipopina,* The rise in the ground means that the church and the streets beyond it look down on what is virtually a second harbour; flights of steps lead down from a wide terrace to a line of quays where small boats can tie up. The view down the shoreline, right to the end of the main harbour mole, reminds one more of French or Italian seaports, and the substantial mansions on the *Odos Babagiotou* which command it might be found in many French provincial towns – one thinks of Aix-en-Provence. They are beautifully proportioned, solidly built, with elegant iron balconies and tall grey-blue shutters. Most of them are now occupied by offices connected with the *Nomarcheia*, though one of them actually advertises rooms to let.

From up here you have a good view of the two small islands off the eastern approaches to the harbour, which figured in one of the few happenings which made news on Syros in the Middle Ages. These days they are called *Didymoi*, 'the twins', but their earlier name was *Gaidaronisi*, 'the Asses' Islands'. Briefly the story goes that a valuable donkey belonging to the powerful Ghisi family of Mykonos was stolen by pirates and sold to the Sanudi of Syros. They refused to return it, though it was clearly marked with the Ghisi initial, whereupon the troops of the Ghisi landed and besieged the citadel. The siege was raised by an admiral of Charles II of Naples, now the suzerain of the Sanudi, who happened to be in Milos with his fleet. The case was submitted to the judgment of the bailie of Negroponte in Euboea, and the two great families were eventually reconciled, but not before 'more than 30,000 heavy *soldi* had been expended for the sake of the animal, which had probably died in the interval'.* So ended the War of the Ass, as it was called, and the likelihood is that the poor creature was first landed by the pirates according to custom on the Gaidaronisi.

If the lower town is French neo-classical, Ano Syros is mediaeval Greek Kykladic – irregular whitewashed houses and steep narrow streets often blocked by donkeys with paniers of fruit and vegetables for sale. So different are its needs and its problems that it has the status of an independent *deme* which makes its own by-laws and regulates its own water supply. Only in the churches does the Catholic influence show, with open access to the high altar and romantic oil paintings on the walls instead of frescos and ikons. The Cathedral of St George at the very top is a great barn-like basilica in goldenish stone, and the view from there takes in the whole town and harbour area below; across the straits are the mountains of Tinos, with Delos indistinguishable against the bulk of Mykonos.

Naturally the city of Hermes has rapid communications with

* William Miller, *The Latins in the Levant*, p. 581 (John Murray 1908).

Greek ports in all directions, though so far they do not include air travel. This is possibly a mercy, for the busy flights from Athens go whizzing overhead to Mykonos, leaving the traditional sea routes as the only way of getting there. A ship leaves Syros every day for almost any island in the Aegean, or calls on her way back to Piraeus.

Inland communications are well organized too, though as yet there are no feasible roads in the northern half of the island. The motor roads which do exist cross to the western and south-western coast. Almost directly opposite Ermoupolis on the west coast is **Kini**, at the head of the Ormos Kiniou, where a long sheltered beach is being successfully and so far inoffensively developed as a holiday spot. The monastic-looking buildings at the side of the road as it begins to wind down to the bay constitute the convent of *Agia Varvara*, built as late as 1922, which serves today as an orphanage and primary school. The mural decorations in the church are hideous, but all other arrangements for the boarding and education of children and teenagers look sensible, and the atmosphere is a happy one. The harbour below is bright and cheerful, with a small hotel and at least one excellent restaurant.

Another bus route goes south through the village of Manna to **Vari**, on the Ormos Ampela (or 'Vineyard Bay'), which is one of the regions of Syros fertile enough for a number of vineyards. Syriot wine is extremely good when you can find it from the *bareli* – dry but unresinated. Interest at Vari centres on the bay and small harbour. They are not a patch on Kini, and the holiday development is not inspiring, though there are some delightful smaller bays on the indented coast to the south.

The reputation Syros had in the nineteenth and early twentieth century as a bleak and barren island is no longer just. True, the low hillsides are scrubby, dry and treeless, but down in the valleys much has been made of a scanty water supply to keep market gardens going, and there are luscious-looking fig trees everywhere. Vegetation, including trees, has been replanted extensively in the area between **Posidonia** and **Phoinikas** on the south-west coast, where for a long time Greeks have built holiday homes, some on a very ambitious scale. Posidonia is still sometimes called Delagratsia – originally 'Delle Grazie' in more correct Italian – and certainly some of these villas are flamboyantly Italian in style.

147

Today the whole of the bay is fringed with strips of rather muddy sand, from which clouds of wind-surfers take off to decorate the usually calm waters in kaleidoscopic criss-cross patterns. Several hotels are concentrated between Posidonia and the sea, and a line of bars and restaurants is spreading along the coastal road to Phoinikas. This is a more engaging place, with a quay for small yachts and a fishing harbour, and as at Vari there are little sandy coves along the south-facing coastline beyond, The good road which connects Posidonia and Vari passes through **Megas Gialos**, another fishing harbour with sheltered beaches each side of it.

Posidonia and Phoinikas have been identified as the principal cities of the Homeric Age, ruled over by Ctesius the father of Eumaeus, who turns up as the faithful swineherd and first of the household of Odysseus to greet him on his return to Ithaka. Eumaeus himself tells the disguised Odysseus how he was captured as a child by Phoenician traders (who must have been regular visitors to Phoinikas) and sold in slavery to Laertes, king of Ithaka and father of Odysseus. He describes Syros in terms which contradict some later opinions:

> 'Not very thickly peopled is the same,
> but a good land, with oxen and with sheep
> well stocked, with laden vines and cornfields deep.'*

Syros is an island apart from its fellows, though central to them all. It has great character, much interest and much beauty, but you have to make an effort to find the best of it. As for Ermoupolis, it is unique among island capitals.

Access
Ferries from Piraeus call daily at both islands, operated by several different lines. In each case the passage takes about four hours. Neither island has an airfield.

Communications
The road systems are good when the terrain allows, and bus services are regular – though they tend to be on 'winter' schedules in mid-June. There

---

* Homer, *Odyssey XV*, 405–6 (trans. J. W. Mackail).

are plenty of taxis in both capitals, and cars and mopeds for hire. There are frequent day excursions by sea to Delos and Mykonos.

Accommodation

TINOS Hotels in the capital are heavily booked at weekends and throughout the summer season. The big TINOS BEACH (A, 339 beds) is well run and provides transport into the town and for road excursions. Of the smaller and quieter hotels MELTEMI (C) on the way up to the Evangelistria church, and ASTERIA (C) overlooking the sea to the north of the harbour, are both good value.

SYROS There is not much choice in Ermoupolis, but easily the best hotel is HERMES (B), where the quietest rooms overlook a garden at the back. Also quiet is EUROPE (C) beside a main street but built round an internal courtyard. Hotels at Posidonia, Vari, Phoinikas and Galisis are comfortable but lack character. The CYCLADES restaurant at Phoinikas lets rooms which are comfortable and modestly priced.

Restaurants

TINOS The better kind of restaurant which caters for real Greek taste is hard to find in the capital, though you can eat reasonably well in a few places in the narrow streets behind the harbour. Best of these is PERISTE-RION ('Dovecote') where they have Tinos wine in carafe.

SYROS Apart from the rather expensive CAVO D'ORO, which takes in the best fish on the harbour front, there is nowhere inviting in Ermoupolis. For real Greek food there are small tavernas near the upper town of Ano Syros, especially VAPORAKI, where man and wife cook and serve just two or three special dishes every evening (not fish) with local wine in the carafe. Taxi drivers know it, and there is a wonderful view down to the harbour. Kini has a good restaurant at the far end of the harbour, and at Phoinikas the CYCLADES is excellent value.

Facilities

Banks: Branches of all Greek banks in Tinos town and Ermoupolis.

Yachts: Tinos harbour is crowded and noisy, but new quays have been built a little further north. There are anchorages for small yachts in the bays of Agios Nikolaos to the south and Stavros to the north. At Panormos in the far north there are excellent berths alongside, but the anchorage can be exposed in a north-easterly blow.

In Syros, Ermoupolis harbour is dirty as well as noisy. The best berths for small yachts are at Phoinikas, with good shore facilities and a secure anchorage in most weathers. Kini is another attractive harbour, and there is also Megas Gialos, a small fishing port on the sheltered south coast.

149

NINE

Mykonos and Delos

Ask anyone about Greek islands they know or have heard of, and the first likely name to come up is **Mykonos**. If you can shut your eyes to the human element and try to put your visual clock back some years, you can see why. The town rises in a natural amphitheatre around a picturesque harbour, a half-moon city that is in itself one of the most enchanting in the Aegean. Architecturally it presents a pure and dazzling example of the cubist Kykladic style, though to appreciate that you have to penetrate behind the garish line of bars and restaurants which have grown up around the wide quayside. The whitewashed, blue- or red-domed churches are still there, and the little back streets tumble happily into each other in shifting sun and shadow. Even now it has moments of enchantment, and you can see what a discovery it must have been and why so many visitors fell for it at first sight.

The trouble is that Mykonos is now all too accessible – by sea from Athens and from four large and popular neighbour islands, but most of all through its airport. During the summer several flights a day come in from Athens, every cruise liner disgorges passengers by the hundred, and day excursions pour in from any island within two or three hours sailing distance. The hotel and package holiday industry has taken up the challenge, and the town has become a well organized machine for absorbing tourist money. For most of the day it is impossible to cross the promenade without dodging streams of people moving in every direction. Early morning is the best time; by evening the neon lights take over from the sun-lit white walls, and the bars and discos turn up the volume of their cacophony.

Yet behind all this, and to a certain extent because of it, there is a feeling abroad of a vigorous and multifarious life which still retains a good deal of Greek character. Certainly it is possible to eat well if you shun the front and find where Greeks eat in side street or back alley. There is no doubt that you can have a good time here, if that is the kind of time you want, and there are interesting things and places to see away from the crowds.

The convenient figure of 365 for the tally of churches on Mykonos is probably too low. There must be nearer four hundred – both figures include the whole of the island. The first you see is little *Agios Nikolaos*, in the middle of the quay. Once he had an island to himself, reached by a causeway, but now the modern quay has expanded to include him. St Nicholas is the patron saint of sailors, and he can be sure of a good position in any harbour. One of the strangest churches is on the headland beyond the outer mole, called the *Paraportiani*. The word *Paraporti* means a postern or private door, so that is probably how the church was reached from inside the harbour wall. It is an almost pyramidal group of four separate churches, and it would look like a mad confectioner's dream were it not redeemed by the austerity of its steps and vertical lines. How often in the Aegean one finds the marriage of Byzantium and the classical world, and marvels that so different a mingling of dogma and outlook has produced such fine offspring. Often in Mykonos one can find, where plaster and lime have peeled away, fragments or antique blocks of marble built into the houses – probably plundered from the ruined buildings of deserted Delos.

In a similar position on the opposite side of the harbour is the **Archaeological Museum**, an attractive place with an enclosed garden. Most of the finds come from the cemeteries on Rhineia, the island on the far side of Delos where bodies were exported to beat the ban on death in the sacred island, but the proudest place is taken by a seventh-century *pithos* on the neck of which is carved in relief a spirited Trojan horse, with Odysseus and his companions peeping out of square openings in its sides. The horse has a knowing look, with its ears well cocked for trouble.

The most striking view of Mykonos town is not from the main harbour, but just round the point where the Paraportiani stands. Here the old balconied houses line up in a graceful crescent with their feet washed by the sea – those balconies must be damp in a westerly blow. Still further round are the three windmills which feature in almost every illustration; actually there are five, but only three have been kept in good condition as one of the island's chief attractions, and it is a very long time since their sails revolved to grind corn. The *Kato Myli*, as they are called, stand on a ridge between the Catholic cathedral and the church of *Agios Charalambos*. Built into the lintel of the main door of the Catholic cathedral are the arms of the Ghisi family, who held Mykonos since the partition of the Byzantine Empire until their extinction in 1390, when it was bequeathed to the Venetian Republic. Like the other Kyklades it passed to Turkish control in the sixteenth century, though Venice continued to claim it until it was formally ceded in 1718. One of the prettiest yet simplest corners is round the *Tria Pigadia*, the 'three wells', which also figure in many photographs. You come upon them well back in the town, beyond the largest *plateia*.

The tourist attractions of Mykonos include some very popular beaches. There is **Agios Stephanos** on the north side of Tourlos bay, and several on the long south-facing coast. The most accessible by road, and therefore the most crowded, is **Platy Gialos**, about three miles south of the town and served by frequent buses. Others, such as the appallingly named 'Super Paradise', can be reached by morning boat trips from the harbour, but far the best and quietest are at **Kalaphatis**, at the end of a roughish track down from the village of Ano Mera. There are some attractive apartments to let here (at a price) and a not so attractive hotel. They look across at a distinctive headland known officially as Cape Tarsana, but locally as 'the breasts of Aphrodite'. The sandy beaches on either side look ready to welcome the goddess.

Ano Mera, though the largest village in the island, is an undistinguished place. It contains the rather dull convent of *Tourliani* which makes a great display of ecclesiastical vestments, embroidery and woodcarving, but the *Moni Palaiokastrou* just to the north of the village is well worth a visit even if you have to take a taxi there. There is no sign today of ancient fortifications, but once you step inside this little convent (there are just three nuns) you will find it a refuge from all the brashness and noise elsewhere. A shady paved courtyard slopes gently upwards to the church of the *Panagia*, passing the poor but cosy quarters where the sisters sit at their

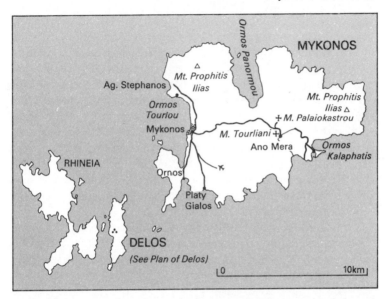

embroidery or sewing. Age creeps on, and at least one of them is wandering in her wits, but there must be peace and comfort for them here.

The Ormos Panormou is a good deep bay which cuts into the northern coast with a not easily reached beach, but the rest of the interior of Mykonos is uninspiring, with sporadic building spreading over the low scrubby hills. Only above Agios Stephanos can you climb over a thousand feet to the top of Mount Prophitis Ilias (there are two of them on this island) and enjoy a panorama of Mykonos and the surrounding islands. Delos and Rhineia lie to the south, and the bulk of Tinos fills the northern horizon. Ships and *kaïkis* trail across the windy sea, and the Mykonos channel is usually scuttering with small white waves as the current pushes down from the north.

Finally, the Mykonos Pelican. It may be the original Petros you see here on the quay, once stolen by the Tiniots and awarded back to Mykonos in a famous lawsuit, but he has a very handsome rival in Tinos today – or is it the same bird commuting between the two islands for a large and fishy fee?

153

From Mykonos it is only five miles by boat to **Delos**, the heart of the Aegean. If one asks why this tiny wisp of ground, with no natural resources, ever became what it did, then the answer can be given by any sailor. Delos is the last and best anchorage between Europe and Asia. To the east it is sheltered by Mykonos, to the north by Tinos and to the west by Rhineia. Looking at the chart you can see how the direct sea route between the Gulf of Nauplia (with Argos at its head) and the principal harbours on the Asiatic coast flows directly along the latitude of 37° 10', with Delos at the halfway mark. At the same time it is just about half way along the north–south trading route between the Dardanelles and Crete. Religious centres may sometimes attract trade, but more often one will find that where the trade is, there also come the temples.

It was the Ionians from the east who colonized the Kyklades in the tenth and ninth centuries BC, and they brought with them to Delos the cult of Leto, one of the many mistresses of Zeus, who gave birth to both Artemis and Apollo. 'Artemis', according to Robert Graves, 'originally an orgiastic goddess, had the lascivious quail as her sacred bird. Flocks of quail will have made Ortygia a resting place on their way north during the spring migration.'* He later identifies Ortygia with Rhineia, the deserted island close to the west coast of Delos, where Artemis was said to have been born before crossing with her mother to Delos to assist at the birth of Apollo. Quail still alight on Rhineia and Delos in spring, which makes the connection plausible.

It was the jealousy of Hera which led to Apollo and Artemis being born here. Pursued throughout the world by the angry goddess, Leto was carried on the wings of the wind until she found herself over Delos, the 'wandering island' as it was called because it had drifted through the Aegean since the dawn of time, waiting for the birth of the divine twins. Poseidon, in one of his rare fits of generosity, struck Delos with his trident and anchored it to the bed of the sea.

Leto gave birth to Apollo on Delos, below the north side of Mount Kynthos in the shade of a date palm – another sacred symbol of Artemis. Immediately the barren island was transformed,

* *The Greek Myths* I, 14, 2 (Penguin 1955).

flowers and fruit burst from the rocks, the Bird of Dawning crowed his delight at the sun, and swans circled the sacred lake. Apollo's worship was established here before the days of Homer, for Odysseus says to Nausicaa that he can only compare her beauty to 'a young palm tree which I saw when I was in Delos, growing close to the altar of Apollo'.*

Coming to historic times, we find that in the seventh century BC Delos was an important Ionian religious centre protected by Naxos. The rising power of Athens was not long in seeing its equal importance as a trading centre. In 543 Pisistratus, dictator of Athens, purified the sanctuary of Apollo by digging up all the tombs in sight and removing the bones to another part of the island. A further and more elaborate purification followed in 426, when the elected Athenian leader Nikias removed all the burials on the island and ordained that it was never to be defiled by human birth or death. Anyone in danger of dying, or a woman nearing childbirth, was ferried across to Rhineia before the worst happened. Four years later all the remaining natives were expelled, presumably to leave Athens with a free hand on the island. The Persians granted them a refuge on the Ionian coast, but after an appeal to the Delphic oracle Athens had to allow them back.

The first period of prosperity for Delos was immediately after the Persian wars, when its position in the centre of the Aegean made it strategically and commercially important. In 478 the Athenians made it the base for their confederacy of Aegean and Ionian states, and a common treasury was established there to receive and bank the agreed contributions from the various cities and islands. It began as an alliance to consolidate their success against the Persians, but during the next twenty years it became more and more openly the base for an Athenian empire, and in 454 the treasury was transferred to Athens itself.

However, the religious festival of the 'Delia', which had been celebrated since earliest times, was revived by Nikias in 426, perhaps in the hope that Apollo would spare Athens another outbreak of the plague which had decimated the city a few years before. In its new form the festival included games in the classical tradition,

* *Odyssey* IV, 165–6.

and even horse-racing was introduced. It took place in the third year of every Olympiad, and began when a convoy of ships set sail for the island, full of priests and sacred choirs, some also carrying oxen for the ritual slaughter. Leading the convoy was the sacred ship *Theoris* with the head of the Athenian delegation on board. Disembarking near the beginning of the Sacred Way, the priests, choirs and other principals went in procession to the Sanctuary of Apollo. Here hymns to Leto and her two children were sung, and after the sacrifices the games and competitions began. The stadium and gymnasium were built well away – about five hundred yards to the north-east – from the religious centre of events. The whole festival was something of a mixture of a pilgrimage to Lourdes, an Eisteddfod and an athletics meeting.

These days the modern cruise liners anchor offshore and send their passengers in by small boat, but the day excursions still come directly into the sacred harbour, a little north of the ancient commercial port. The latter is easy to recognize from the ruins of old warehouses, granaries and quays around its sides. The **Sanctuary of Apollo** lies inland from the modern jetty, a very big area in which the foundations of three temples have been found. The entrance was through a Propylaea, and immediately on the right is the sixth-century **House of the Naxians**, divided into two aisles by a row of marble columns. Outside this is the base of the great statue of Apollo, an offering from Naxos and made of Naxian marble. Two fragments of the torso are preserved on the spot, while a part of the left hand and the toes of the left foot have found their way to the British Museum. The archaic inscription on the base reads 'I am of the same marble, statue and base'.

It needs an effort of the imagination to see the sanctuary as it was, with the giant bronze palm tree set up by Nikias in 417, the colossal figure of the god, and the treasuries of the cities rich in carving and gold. But Delos is one of those places where one feels the past very close.

Leaving the Sanctuary and walking a hundred yards or so to the north, we cross the large **Agora of the Italians**, with a rectangular peristyle of a hundred and twelve Doric columns, to reach the **Sacred Lake**, now dry and dusty under the sun. Against a sky of blinding blue its guardian lions lift their heads and roar. They are

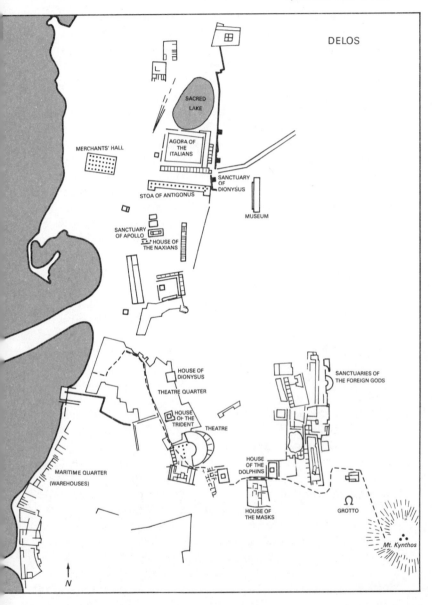

DELOS

SACRED
LAKE

MERCHANTS' HALL

AGORA OF
THE
ITALIANS

SANCTUARY
OF
DIONYSUS

STOA OF ANTIGONUS

MUSEUM

SANCTUARY
OF APOLLO
HOUSE OF
THE NAXIANS

HOUSE OF
DIONYSUS

THEATRE QUARTER

SANCTUARIES OF
THE FOREIGN GODS

HOUSE
OF THE
TRIDENT

THEATRE

HOUSE
OF THE
DOLPHINS

MARITIME QUARTER
(WAREHOUSES)

HOUSE OF
THE MASKS

Ω
GROTTO

Mt. Kynthos

N

157

long-bodied, lean archaic lions, carved from Naxian marble in the seventh century, and they look to have a trace of panther in their ancestry. Only five of what are thought to have been sixteen are left; a sixth was taken away in the seventeenth century to guard the Arsenale in Venice. Mounted on a ridge of flinty tussocks they seem indifferent to the modern intruder.

Birth and death may not have been permitted on this sacred island, but the spring of life, the act of procreation itself, is celebrated. At the north-east corner of the main Sanctuary is the small **Sanctuary of Dionysus**. Here stood a row of choragic monuments crowned by marble phalluses (those surviving have been truncated) rising white and triumphant against the skyline. Around the base of one is carved a light-hearted scene of a bride being carried to her new husband's home. Another has Dionysus himself with a dancing Bacchante in attendance – all joyful celebrations of wine and love-making.

Standing on its own to the east of the Sanctuary and Sacred Lake is the **Delos Museum**. The exhibits are a mixed lot, with the finest sculptures understandably removed to Athens. The oldest substantial object is an archaic marble sphinx from Naxos. Otherwise there is a lot to do with Dionysus – two kneeling satyrs wearing shorts made of ivy leaves, actors dressed as Silenus and a seated statue of the god. But the real wonders of Delos are outside – the broken marbles, the barley grass, the golden thistles, all charged with true Apollonian radiance.

The second great period of prosperity was during the Hellenistic age, from the third to the first century BC. Delos enjoyed virtual independence under Macedonian rule, and had special commercial privileges under the Romans. It was then that the residential quarter grew up around the theatre, with every appearance of wealth among the inhabitants. It is very unlikely that the veto on births held good at this time, though for practical reasons the bodies of the dead would have been carried across the straits to Rhineia.

During the same period the commercial harbour was enlarged and developed as something akin to a free port for trade between east and west. A more notorious function of the port area was as the biggest slave market in Greece. Strabo, the first century historian and geographer, tells us that as many as ten thousand slaves were bought and sold there in a day.

The end came suddenly. In 88 BC Delos was attacked by the forces of Rome's chief Asiatic enemy, King Mithridates of Pontus. They massacred the male population, enslaved the women and children, looted the sanctuary and the warehouses, and destroyed the city. Although Sulla recaptured the island in the following year, it never recovered its wealth or position, and by the second century AD Pausanias found it almost uninhabited.

The **Theatre** was built in the early third century BC for over five thousand spectators, but only the lower tiers of seats survive. The *orchestra* has recently been restored, but to get the feeling of an audience you must climb to where the top seats were – the 'Gods' – and look down over Rhineia to the sea beyond, where the sun sets in evening glory. The **Theatre Quarter** was thickly populated in Hellenistic times, and here some of the finest private houses were built.

In the heart of it is the **House of Dionysus**, with part of a pavement in the courtyard showing the god with wings and riding a (striped) tiger. Above the theatre to the south-east he appears again in the **House of the Masks**, this time more fully preserved and riding a (spotted) panther. Here he has no wings, but he holds a tambourine in his left hand and the *thyrsos* in his right. Another pavement in the same house has designs of comic and satyric masks, and it seems to have been used as a sort of green room club, or a hostel for performers. Beyond that again is the **House of the Dolphins**, where the atrium has a pavement with an exquisite circular design within a square whose corners are filled by pairs of dolphins in harness, ridden by a tiny winged figure – maybe Eros, maybe a mini-Hermes. The craftsmanship is remarkable, considering how intractable the mosaic medium must have been for such a delicately designed subject. The artist signed the work, and it is believed to have come from a studio in Beirut. Another fine set of mosaics is in the **House of the Trident**, back in the centre of the quarter. It has some intricate geometric motifs and yet more dolphins curling themselves round ships' anchors. The trident is a most elegant affair, with a ribbon tied nonchalantly round the shaft.

The visitor today has been well served both by the archaeologist and by the custodians of Delos. The huge complex of buildings, sacred and secular, adding up to no less than a great city, can be surveyed and taken in without too much difficulty with the help of an excellent booklet on sale at the entrance. Restorations are clean and clear, buildings are identified on the site, marble columns and bright mosaic floors gleam in the sunshine. With no mediaeval or modern accretions to distract the eye, you can recapture a great deal of the atmosphere of its heyday – perhaps one of the most gracious periods in the history of the eastern Mediterranean.

The best preserved temples are also of this period, to be found in the area known as the **Sanctuaries of Foreign Gods** on the way up to Mount Kynthos. Many of these deities were Egyptian – Serapis, Isis and their like – though the most impressive building here was devoted to the Syrian goddess Atargates and her consort Hadad (an eastern equivalent of Demeter and Hermes) which included a small theatre with seating for four or five hundred people to watch the ceremonies. The Hellenistic age liked a touch of the exotic and mystical in its observances, and sure enough we find a *Samothrakion* where the Kabeiroi and the Great Gods of Samothrace were given their expected rites.

Through this area ran the stream of Inopus, which fed a number of cisterns, some for secular use, some for purificatory rites and some as a home for sacred fish or reptiles. Today they still hold water, and especially at sunset and in the cool hours which follow you can hear the bull-frogs begin to croak – the classic 'brekekekek-koax-koax' realized by the chorus in *The Frogs* of Aristophanes. Echoing out of the stagnant water, the yellowing weeds and the hollow places where houses and temples stood, their voices survive.

A silent survivor, except for the quick dry rustle as he slips behind a rock, is the Delian lizard. His only equals for size are to be found in Rhodes and Kos, and if any creature is a prehistoric survival this is it. They may belong to the family *varanidae*, or 'monitor lizards', in which case they are likely to have been imported originally from north Africa. They confront you with a cold stare at the windings of the pathways, and not until you are right on top of them do they give a wag of their fat tails and move off into the scrub. The statue of Apollo Sauroktonos (the 'lizard-slayer') by Pheidias has a large lizard climbing the tree on which the god is leaning. Is this the 'old dragon' which Christian saints later confronted? Whatever the message, Delos is an island where the sun and the lizard seem both more potent than anywhere else.

One of the surviving windmills on Mykonos

Delos. *Above,* the Lions of the Sacred Lake;
below, detail of a mosaic floor in the House of the Trident

Whenever you come to Delos, do not for anything miss the **Cave** or **Grotto** on the north side of the mountain just below the peak. From above it is invisible: you reach it by taking a path to the right before you begin to climb the last long flight of steps. A natural fault in the rock has been turned into a holy place by wedging great slabs of stone together to form a crudely arched roof – the architectural fore-runner perhaps of the triangular weight-bearing slabs of Mycenae.

Ignore the large round marble column base by the entrance, and look inside. Right at the back of this cavern stands a lump of rock with a flat upper surface stained a dark reddish brown, and when the sun climbs over the mountain behind you will see that the light strikes it through the gap between the roof and the rear wall. Argue as modern scholars may that this was only a Hellenistic shrine of Herakles, the visitor with imagination is invited to believe that it is an ancient rock temple, older perhaps than anything on Delos. Neither Apollo nor Artemis were strangers to the blood of sacrifice, and maybe here the return of the year was ensured by the blood of a chosen victim – even a human one. In any case you are more likely to find a grotto of Herakles near a place devoted to athletics, as at Archaia Thera on Santorin, than in this place of highly charged mystery.

The Sacred Way reaches the summit of **Mount Kynthos** by long flights of easy steps. A mountain it is, though less than five hundred feet high – who would dare call it a hill? At midday the sun beats down and the lizards reluctantly move aside before the feet of perspiring tourists. If you are ever able to spend a night within range, then sunset or dawn are the times to climb to the top of this bare but intensely numinous height. In the evening you can watch the sun go down behind Syros into the western sea, but if you have once seen the sun come up over the Aegean, and the islands quicken into colour and shape, you have a memory that can be taken anywhere in the world. It is a seascape which one revisits in dreams, and in the midst of great cities. One can be reabsorbed into it, and there is no other region into which one can slip back so happily.

On the peak of Mount Kynthos one understands and feels the whole of the Aegean. The sketchy outlines of temples built up here for the chief Athenian gods, Zeus and Athena, seem irrelevant

161

compared with the view from the final rocky outcrop. Close to the north is Tinos, to the east Mykonos. Westward is Syros, and beyond that you know that only Kea and Kythnos lie between you and Cape Sounion. South, across a fifteen-mile channel, are the two humps of Paros and Naxos. Away to the east, already lit by the rising sun, but invisible behind Mykonos are Ikaria, Patmos and Samos – the end of the long chain of stepping-stones which join Europe to Asia.

Access

It is easy to reach MYKONOS from any direction. Ferries from Piraeus call every day by way of Tinos or Syros, and there are day excursions from a number of nearby islands. DELOS is only reached by excursion boats or by constant sailings of small craft across from Mykonos. There are frequent flights from Athens to Mykonos airport.

Communications

On MYKONOS roads and buses connect the harbour with the main beaches and resorts, and so does a large fleet of taxis – which are much in demand. Small boats ply between Mykonos and DELOS, where there is no road or transport.

Accommodation

MYKONOS   Most accommodation is taken up by travel agencies. There are two hotels in the A category, ANO MERA (124 beds) in the village of the same name, and the smaller LETO (48 beds) in the harbour. It is difficult to make distinctions otherwise, but most houses seem to have rooms to let. There is an attractive set of apartments at Kalaphatis, with good swimming to hand; they are expensive and tend to be booked up a year ahead.

DELOS   There is no overnight accommodation ashore.

Restaurants

MYKONOS   Bars and restaurants round the harbour front are an affront to the ear and the palate, but if you explore the back streets you can still find a good small place with proper Greek food at modest prices.

DELOS   There is a tourist pavilion where you can buy refreshments during the day.

Facilities

Banks: In Mykonos harbour only.

Yachts: Mykonos harbour is crowded and noisy at night. There are anchorages around the coast, the best being at Kalaphatis and Ornos in the south. Ormos Panormou on the north coast is exposed, and without facilities ashore. On Delos, Ormos Phourniou to the south of the ancient harbour provides a sheltered anchorage, but without shore facilities.

THE WESTERN KYKLADES

TEN

Kea and Kythnos

The western group of the Kyklades is quite distinct from its northern and eastern neighbours. The nearest island to Athens is **Kea**, which the inhabitants often still call Zia, the name by which it was known during the centuries when it was ruled by Italian family dynasties. Its classical name was Keos, and it was once the most important of all the Kyklades; only thirteen miles south of Cape Sounion, with a fine natural harbour on the north-west coast, it has always been exceptionally fertile, with a constant natural water supply.

Keos was much more a part of Athenian life than the smaller islands of the Saronic Gulf which are now so quickly reached from Piraeus. Aristotle praised her constitution, and among her sons were Simonides and his nephew Bacchylides, two of the most famous poets of the sixth and fifth centuries. Aristophanes originated a punning proverb which distinguished between the drunken and dishonest Chians and the honest and sober Keans* which no doubt gives satisfaction in Kea today. In more recent times it was the emporium of the Kyklades long before the Chian refugees built Ermoupolis on Syros; they had been refused asylum in Keos, being perhaps still distrusted for the reputation Aristophanes gave them. Keos was the first island to aid Athens in the Persian war of 480 – her ships fought at both Artemision and Salamis – and the first of the Kyklades to join the revolt against Turkey in 1821.

Today it seems improbable that Kea was ever important, though it is still beautiful. The ordinary tourist is discouraged from coming by the shipping companies, who ignore it when scheduling the ferry

* *Frogs*, 970.

164

services down through the western Kyklades. Instead it is served only by a small local ferry based on the distant port of Lavrio at the southern end of the Attic peninsula, grudgingly connected by bus with central Athens. The passage takes two and a half hours, longer than the distance warrants because the ship has to negotiate the northern cape of Makronisi, the strange long barren island (not even goats find sustenance there) off the eastern coast of Attica. Yet once there you will find it a good deal more interesting and attractive than its nearest and more favoured neighbour, Kythnos. Kea is uniformly hilly, with a largely barren ridge running down the eastern coast, but the feature of the western countryside is a chain of deep narrow green valleys between softly rounded hills. There are fruit trees in plenty, much water (with springs actually flowing in summer) and all you need to live on is in good supply.

The harbour of St Nicholas is one of the finest in the Aegean, a sea which has so many fine ones. A fairly narrow entrance widens out into a double-ended bay, with the main harbour of **Korissia** to the south. This is where the ferry lands you, but there is nothing much to catch the eye. The waterfront is pleasant but undistinguished, offering little else but a row of bars, cafés and shops. What life there is comes from the yachts which tie up often double-banked along the quay, while the fishing fleet is confined to a smaller mole nearer the harbour entrance. This tendency to favour the yachtsman is even more obvious at the north end of the bay, where a deeper inlet reaches the once quiet fishing village of **Vourkari**. Here life can be frenetic, with yachts of all sizes squeezed together like sardines, while the bars and cafés do their best to supply the needs of the crews.

It would be a mistake to let this put you off, if it does, for though swimming is officially discouraged because of human pollution, it is a lovely stretch of water, and on a low headland opposite there is a remarkable survival, no less than a substantial Bronze Age settlement incorporating a late Minoan palace and possibly a temple, where Linear A inscriptions were found by excavators from the University of Cincinnati in the 1960s. Work still goes on, and it proves to be one of those delightful sites of the period, close to the sea, sheltered but indefensible. Its inheritor is the little church of **Agia Irene** which crowns a low tree-clad promontory; although you

165

are not allowed into the fenced-off site you can clearly see the big blocks of schist which line a ceremonial way.

After Vourkari the road from Korissa turns inland to reach the northern coast at the bay of **Otzias**. This is not a long walk (though taxis are available) and it gives you a good idea of the gentle countryside in this part of Kea – once you have passed a couple of brash-looking 'discos' on the outskirts of Vourkari. Mostly agricultural, it grows corn, pistachios, apricots, figs and vines, and it supports some healthy-looking cattle. Beside the road you will see a few examples of the island's once famous and prolific product, the oak tree. Theodore Bent, writing in the 1880s, says that there were then some 1,500,000 of them, covering all but the northern slopes. The acorns were huge, 'as big as eggs', but the export trade dealt mainly with the cups, which provided a juice used in the tanning of leather. The acorns themselves sustained the island's gourmet pigs, and of course the timber was of great value in ship-building. There are still plenty of oak trees all over the island, if not in such numbers, and some of them are marvellously ancient specimens. No one knows why they grew almost exclusively in Keos, but one result is that the olive is comparatively rare.

The beach at the head of the Otzias bay is messy, but the few houses of the village nestle among trees on the east side, where families come to swim and splash, and the cliff path beyond looks down over the rock-fringed bay. There is an excellent taverna in the village.

The same road continues past Otzias, though with a rougher surface, as far as Ormos Kastri, a bay which took its name from a mediaeval castle poised on a rocky outcrop. In the eighteenth century this was demolished to build the monastery of the **Panagia Kastriani**. The older of its two churches dates from 1708, and it contains one of those ikons of the Virgin which are miraculously discovered by shepherds at the centre of a mysterious glow – in this case they saw it on top of the headland, so that is where the monastery had to be built. The church which is most used is larger and later, built in 1910, but there is a harmony between all the monastery buildings on this exceptionally beautiful site.

The road across from Otzias has lovely views to seaward, though the hills behind are bare and brown. About a mile inland from the

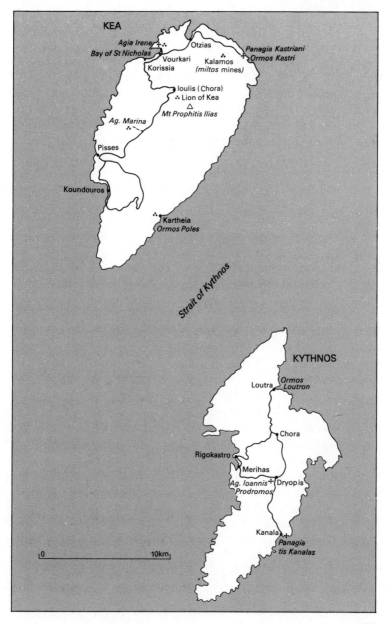

KEA

Agia Irene
Bay of St Nicholas
Otzias
Panagia Kastriani
Ormos Kastri
Vourkari
Kalamos
(*miltos* mines)
Korissia

Ioulis (Chora)
Lion of Kea
△
Mt Prophitis Ilias

Ag. Marina

Pisses

Koundouros

Kartheia
Ormos Poles

Strait of Kythnos

KYTHNOS

Loutra
Ormos
Loutron

Chora

Rigokastro

Merihas
Ag. Ioannis
Prodromos
Dryopis

Kanala
Panagia
tis Kanalas

0   10km

halfway point in the road is the village of **Kalamos**, near which can be seen the 'miltos mines' which produced another of the island's major exports. *Miltos* was a red ochre dye extracted by heat from a reddish-brown ferrous rock, chiselled away from deep cavities in the hillside. Athens imported it as a paint, and it was widely used to decorate the bows of ships. They are called *miltoparioi*, or 'red-cheeked' by Homer, so it must have been a very ancient industry.

Keos, like Kephalonia, was a *tetrapolis*. Its four cities were Korissia, Poiessa, Kartheia and Ioulis. All four can be traced, though there is little to be found at the first two sites. Ancient Korissia was on the ridge to the west of the harbour, and a few sections of wall can be seen from below. Poiessa was at the foot of a long, deep, almost Alpine valley near the west coast, a place now occupied by the village of **Pisses**, which has a holiday beach below it. Further down the coast is the big modern Kea Beach hotel at **Koundouros**. The most important of the four cities was **Kartheia**, in the bay of Poles (probably originally Polis) at the south-eastern end of the island. Ruins of temples, a theatre and the city walls were unearthed by the Danish archaeologist Bronsted in 1811, and it was clearly a major centre of Greek civilization. Unfortunately the old road which connected it with Ioulis (the modern capital and *Chora*) has never been rebuilt for wheeled traffic, and there is no practical access for visitors, who can no longer count on hiring a donkey or mule for cross-country journeys.

Ioulis is a different matter. As you approach the entrance to St Nicholas harbour you will see a patchwork of white-walled, red-roofed houses apparently stuck in tiers to the hillside above and looking as though they might slide downwards at any moment. Here was the ancient city and the mediaeval *kastro*; here is now the Chora, easily reached by a short modern road from the harbour. It is perhaps the finest of the island Choras, light and airy, with an engaging mixture of alleyways and open spaces, and the most magnificent views to the north and west. The *kastro* was built on a separate high point by Domenico Michelli as early as 1210, but it was demolished in 1865, while the earlier temple of Apollo had long ago been plundered for material. Only the gateway and one section of the wall are preserved, and most of the space it occupied is now taken by a hotel. The main *plateia* is next to the *demarcheion*, or town hall; it is adorned by a glorious spreading oleander tree and ministered to by a delightful taverna which serves authentic Kean wine (red and white) from the barrel.

Above the town a footpath leads past a church and cemetery to an amphitheatre facing north, terraced to grow a few olive trees. On the same level as the path you come upon the **Lion of Kea**, a unique sight. He is a charming creature, carved from grey granite, lying on his side in a natural pose with the most amiable expression on his face. This is no maned and lordly African animal, but a smooth-backed Assyrian lion with body and legs carved in lovely flowing lines. His 'happy fellow' expression comes of course from the archaic representation of the mouth which features in human statuary of the period (probably seventh century BC) but the effect is remarkably benign, as though he had just had a good meal of Nereids. The story is that the neighbourhood was so much troubled by these creatures (in Greek mythology Nereids are always malignant influences) that the people imported a lion to drive them out or otherwise get rid of them. This he did, and the carving was made as a perpetual deterrent.

Near a spring higher up there is thought to have been a sanctuary of Pan, one of several in Kea. This ancient cult of the patron of flocks and herds was transferred to the Christian St Anargyris, who has churches near secret grottos in both Kea and Kythnos. Myth also associates Kea with Aristaeus, Virgil's patron of bee-keeping and agriculture* who successfully countered a devastating drought by sacrificing on the top of Mt Ilias to Zeus and Sirius, the Dog Star of *Canis Major* which rules over the hot dry months. The result of his sacrifice was a period of cooling winds which lasted for forty days, just as the *meltemi* do today in the months of July and August.

The main road up from Korissia goes on past Ioulis to Pisses and Koundouros. At about the halfway point a rougher track leads downhill to the right as far as the church (once a convent) of **Agia Marina**. The convent buildings have almost disappeared, and the plain little church is dwarfed by an enormous square tower. Built of huge blocks of schist in the lower courses, their size reduced higher up, it still climbs to a height of more than three storeys. Today it is a

---

* *Georgics* IV, *passim.*

shell, but the dark yellowish stone walls, built without mortar, constitute a unique fortified monument of the early classical period. The original height, estimated at about 300 feet, would have been enough to afford a clear view from the battlements down to the western sea, while the tower itself would have been invisible against its background. The tower had an internal stairway which in 1840 was in good enough condition for King Otto and Queen Olga of the Hellenes to climb it and write their names at the top. Unfortunately the King asked for a piece of carved stone to be removed and given him as a memento, whereupon a good deal more masonry collapsed. It was built not only as a watch tower but as a refuge in times of danger, and seems to have had accommodation on a par with Norman keeps in Britain.

It is to the Chora one feels drawn to return, most of all in the evening, when from the lower *plateia* where wheeled traffic ends you can watch the red sunset path spread across the strait between Kea and the dark outline of Makronisi, with distant Euboea and the historic mountains of Attica filling in beyond. It is said that in the great days of Kean sea trade merchant ships would lie up in the harbour of St Nicholas waiting for a beacon to be lit on Mt Hymettus – a signal that a ship was wanted for loading at Piraeus. As near darkness falls the scene is incomparably beautiful, the sea still gleaming between sculptured slopes which gradually deepen from grey to black.

The whole aspect of any Greek island, especially those most recently opened to tourism, was changed once they were included in a regular ferry service connecting them with Athens; the next stage was when the improved harbour facilities attracted small boat sailors within a weekend's sailing distance. **Kythnos** is a good example of the second stage, where in the past all a yachtsman might do was to anchor briefly in the bay of Loutra, and after a visit on foot to the inland Chora, leave for more immediately attractive or welcoming islands.

Within the past decade a substantial harbour has been built at **Merihas**, half way up the western coast, and this has completely changed the character of Kythnos for the visitor. From seaward neither the western nor the eastern coastline is arresting. The background hills are low, the vegetation you see is scrubby, and nobody seems to live there – not even a whitewashed church breaks the sequence of empty rocky coves. Merihas though is a lovely harbour. The enfolding shores look inviting as you turn in from seaward, and the slopes on the northern side have been pleasantly developed. At the head of the bay a line of tamarisks provides shade for the tables of a very good restaurant, some of them standing almost in the water. It is the town behind the harbour which spoils the effect. It has grown up too quickly in the wake of a summertime rush of not very discriminating tourists and weekend yachtsmen. The houses have been hurriedly built with no style or character, their surroundings are messy, and the big hotel in the far corner is a monstrosity.

Nevertheless the interior of the island is unexpectedly beautiful, and once inland you are happily aware of the sea which closely enwraps it to east and west. The bus service from Merihas, as in many islands, is secretive and unpredictable. If time is short, and you want to go somewhere and return at a reasonable time, it is best to find a taxi. 'Find' is the word, for they are few and elusive, but if you do see one you would be wise to engage the driver well ahead for a fixed time and price.

The most interesting journey is to the village of **Kanala** on the south-east coast. The road crosses the low spine of the island (which rises to only 1000 feet at the highest point), and it runs up to the col through a series of sheltered green valleys, ablaze in the summer with Spanish broom. There are plenty of vines and olives, but most noticeable are the fig trees, some of them enormous.

Across the watershed you see the red-roofed village of **Dryopis** – notice the appealing little isolated church of *Agios Ioannis Prodromos* above the road just before the village. Dryopis has lovely views over the eastern sea below, and the road winds down to a deep inlet – or rather a double inlet with a tongue of land in between – which is occupied by Kanala. This is mostly a modern settlement, but unlike Merihas it is extremely attractive, with well built houses and flowery gardens. The hillside overlooking the harbour is green with pines, and you can take a shady path to the end of the point, which is (or was) occupied by the monastery of the *Panagia tis Kanalas*.

The only part of the monastery still in use is the church, which has been rather too gaudily restored but contains one treasure – a very holy and impressive ikon of St Luke, possibly of the sixteenth century, which is kept for safety in the inner sanctuary. Beyond the church are the now deserted monastery buildings, and beyond again is a rocky headland pointing due north. Across a deceptively short-looking expanse of wind-flecked sea rises the rounded hump of Seriphos, the next in line of the western Kyklades.

The larger bay beneath Kanala has a little fishermen's jetty, and a sandy beach with just a few holiday buildings on it. The smaller bay to the north is called *Kalo Livadi*, or 'Good Harbour', and has a sheltered beach at its head. The road leading north from Merihas follows the western coastline for a time, passing several bays with good swimming beaches, as well as the site of the ancient island capital at **Rigokastro** on the cliff above the bay of Episkopi. There is nothing to see there now, and only in the far north of the island have any substantial remains of earlier ages survived. On the headland which terminates in Cape Kephalos is the mediaeval *kastro*, which was abandoned about 1650. There are said to be ruins of towers, churches and a monastery to be seen there, but it is an hour's walk up the valley from Loutra.

The present-day **Chora** lies some way inland from Rigokastro, and is a pleasant but unremarkable village. It repays a visit because it is typical of so many island villages – ordinary, unspectacular and unwritten-about. It helps one to understand the life that goes on in all those others one will never visit, far away and white in the hills.

From there you continue northward to the great bay of **Loutra**. In the nineteenth century this was a well known centre for thermal baths, with a unique combination of hot and cold springs, one of 75°F and the other of 47°F – you bathe in the hot and drink the cold. The mediaeval name of Kythnos was Thermia, and it was held for many centuries by the Gozzadini dynasty from Bologna, acting as vassals of the Dukes of Naxos. In those days the baths were reckoned by a Venetian visitor to be superior to those at Padua, but they must have been in use as far back as 1142, when the island was already referred to as Thermia. They were popular with the Turks during their occupation, and after the liberation King Otto built a double 'hydro' over the springs. These substantial buildings are still used during the high summer, for the middle-aged city Greek tends to be a compulsive valetudinarian.

In the village street leading up from the harbour, the owner of a small shop introduced himself to the writer in 1984 as the holder of a certificate signed by Field-Marshal Alexander, thanking him for his services in rescuing British servicemen during the last war. One forgets that the islanders of the Aegean were as much involved in the resistance at that time as the people in many parts of France.

Kythnos more than most islands shows the strain of being caught between two worlds – the old island ways and the new commercial life based on tourism. Many people you meet around Merihas seem rough and lazy – not characteristics you expect to find in the Kyklades, but quite possibly there was always a tendency that way in their nature. Yet there is much to enjoy in a short holiday here, and in the evening when outlines are softened, and the Skops owl sets up his persistent one-note cry of '*Gkion, Gkion*', you can be well content at your table by the edge of the quiet harbour.

Access

Although they belong to the same geographical group, these two islands are treated separately by the shipping lines. KEA can only be reached by a daily sailing from the port of Lavrio on the south-east coast of Attica, connected by a bus service with Athens. KYTHNOS is directly connected with Piraeus, and is the usual first call on the run down through the western Kyklades. The two lines involved ensure that ships visit on five days a week, while the smaller ferries from Lavrio continue twice a week from Kea to Kythnos, but no further.

Communications

There are some good roads in KEA where the terrain allows, but no reliable bus service. Taxis are available in Korissia and the Chora, with reliable and helpful drivers. In KYTHNOS there are good roads connecting Merihas, the Chora and Loutra, but bus services are irregular to say the least. Taxis are very hard to find, and the drivers suit themselves.

Accommodation

KEA   As a base for exploring the island there is no better value than KARTHEIA (C) in Korissia. Its rooms are large and comfortable, though the

173

management is elusive and breakfast is not provided. The most attractive position is enjoyed by IOULIS (B, pension) on the site of the *kastro* in the Chora, but no vehicle can reach it with your luggage. Most agency bookings are at the KEA BEACH (B, 150 beds) at Koundouros, or at TZIA MAS (B) at the far end of Korissia bay; the latter calls itself a Motel, and the rooms are very cramped, but the outlook is pleasant and it has a restaurant overlooking its own beach.

KYTHNOS The only places which advertise accommodation are Merihas and Loutra. At Merihas, POSIDONION (C, 158 beds) is large, ugly and uninviting. Smaller and more agreeable is KYTHNOS (C) in a good position above the landing point. Rooms are to be had in the town, but it would be wise to inspect them before booking. At Loutra there is a Xenia and a better choice of rooms.

Restaurants

KEA The DIONYSOS in Korissia suffers from having no competition, though it is large and convenient. Infinitely better is NIKO'S taverna in the Chora, while the OTZIAS taverna is also excellent value. Both these are genuine tavernas which serve local wine from the barrel.

KYTHNOS The outstanding place is GIALOS, at the head of Merihas bay, which has tables both inside, on a terrace, and under the tamarisks at the water's edge. It is much patronized by visiting yachtsmen, but maintains a high professional standard. The same family runs the principal restaurant at Loutra. In the Chora there is one good restaurant which caters chiefly for the villagers.

Facilities

Banks: Kea has one branch in the Chora. In Kythnos you can change money and cheques at the tourist office in Merihas.

Yachts: The two harbours in the bay of St Nicholas in Kea are popular with yachtsmen – particularly Vourkari, while Korissia is a good deal quieter – and they have every facility alongside. Otzias is quieter still, but there is shelter only for small boats. The safest and pleasantest anchorage would be in Poles bay off the site of ancient Kartheia, but there is no civilization ashore there today. In Kythnos, Merihas has well organized berths. There is a good anchorage in the Agia Irene inlet, a sheltered arm of the bay of Loutra, but there are no shore facilities nearer than Loutra itself, which is more exposed to the north-east.

ELEVEN

Seriphos and Siphnos

The first view of **Seriphos**, as you approach the main harbour of **Livadi** at its south-eastern corner, is enchanting. The eye rises from the sheltered blue waters of the bay, alive with the masts of small yachts and fishing boats, to the conical hill beyond, up which climb the white houses of the Chora. At the very top, perched or stranded on the highest pinnacle of rock, is a gleaming white church. In any light – morning, evening or mid-afternoon – it is one of the loveliest sights in the Kyklades and could well represent the ideal Greek island.

At this end of Seriphos there are no traces of the trade in iron ore from which until thirty or forty years ago its people still earned a hard and tenuous living. More wealth comes now from tourism, yet much less than in other islands has this distorted, swamped or spoiled the naturalness of the place and its people.

This is principally because the most frequent visitors are yachtsmen – individual or charter-borne – who sail down from Piraeus through this comparatively little known chain of islands. They can anchor out in the bay or tie up at a convenient and well equipped jetty, backed by a line of good simple shops, cafés and restaurants. The big ferries come in with a great sweep to a long quay only just inside the harbour mole, but this and the yacht basin further in are kept spotless – quite the cleanest landing you will find in all the islands.

If you have landed as a passenger from a ferry without accommodation already booked, it is best to walk down the long quayside till you come to the main group of shops and cafés opposite the yacht berths. There are three hotels around the perimeter of the bay which cater for different kinds of patron, but at any of the cafés they will tell you what rooms there are to let.

175

From the pleasant open space behind the yacht basin a bus leaves at irregular hours for the **Chora** – the only fixed one may be the school bus which leaves at 8 a.m. during term time. Alternatively there is a stirring walk up long flights of ancient steps which cut impatiently across the loops of the modern road; this takes about half an hour and gives you increasingly beautiful views when you stop to look back over the harbour below.

There are two villages up there. The lower, or *Kato Chora*, is distinct from the upper, or *Pano Chora*, which is far more interesting. It proves to occupy a long ridge, rather than a peak, and if from the bus stop you walk along the *Odos Kyklopon* to its western end you come to the ruined walls of the mediaeval *Kastro*, spliced as it were into the solid rock.

Here at different levels are several churches, difficult to enter and interesting mainly for their situation. On the lower level you will see the domed church of *Christos*, with remains of classical pillars outside; this proves to have two dedications inside, one to *Agia Sophia*, the other to *Agia Zaras*. Slightly higher up is *Agia Varvara*, handsome enough, but restored in 1890. The gem of the group is the little one at the very top of the final rocky path, *Agios Ioannis Theologos* (St John the Evangelist, or 'Word of God'), said to be on the site of a classical temple to Athena. It was last restored in 1928, and is well kept but contains nothing of interest.

The charm is in the proportions of the gleaming white building, and the excitement comes when you look around you from this rocky eyrie. Close to the south-east lies Siphnos; to the south you can see Kimolos, Poliegos and Milos; to the east Paros and Antiparos. Only to the north is the view blocked by mountains. Down below you to the south-east you can catch a glimpse of a triangle of sand, part of the lovely beach of *Psili Ammos*.

As you come down from Agios Ioannis you will find another church, disused and converted into a small museum. This is *Agios Konstantinos*, built not on but into the rock, with jagged bits projecting under the ceiling. If you carry on back eastwards from this point you will find yourself in the *Odos Perseos*, which leads to the main *plateia* of the Pano Chora, dominated by two buildings. One is the fine blue-domed principal church of *Agios Athanasios*, the other a grand 'town hall' in the neo-classical style of 1912. Less obtrusive

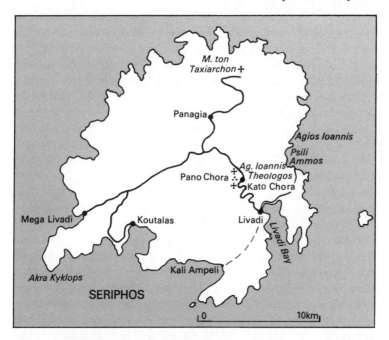

is an important library of manuscripts belonging to the church, and a school of further education which offers classes in Homer and other classical Greek authors.

The *Odos Kyklopon* suggests a variant in the voyages of Odysseus (the south-western point of Seriphos is called *Akra Kyklops*, or Cape Cyclops), but the *Odos Perseos* reminds you that this is the island of Perseus, washed ashore with his mother Danaë after her husband Acrisius had disowned them and cast them adrift in a wooden chest. A street nearby is named after Polydectes the king of Seriphos who at first received them kindly, but later despatched Perseus on the apparently impossible mission to kill Medusa the Gorgon. Perseus enlisted the help of Athena (whose temple, we have seen, crowned the Chora) and of the Graiae, gorgon-like creatures who lived in a cave whose mouth you can see as you sail past the southern coast of the island. With the aid of the mirror-like shield and other devices given by Athena, Perseus killed Medusa and returned with her head to Seriphos. Finding that Polydectes had

177

meanwhile been planning to violate his mother, he used the Gorgon's head to turn him and his associates to stone – which naturally explains the rocky outcrops which mark the surrounding hills.

If you go back from the *plateia* along the Odos Perseos you will find that half way along the ridge it drops down steeply to the right through quiet deserted alleys and flowery flights of steps, eventually turning south to join the old way up from Livadi. On its way it passes between the church of *Agios Elevtherios* and an unusually fine private house with a balustraded terrace giving a wonderful view down over the harbour to the sea beyond. On the wall is a plaque which reads 'Uffizio del R. V. Console Sirpho, 1819' – in other words the Consulate of the Republic of Venice at that date. Now deserted, it is owned by a local family who have so far failed either to spoil or to improve the property.

There are some fine beaches on Seriphos. Most obvious is the wide tree-fringed sweep of sand which runs round the inside of Livadi bay. This is clean and safe, though a more secluded beach can be found across the headland to the south of the harbour entrance. Better than either is **Psili Ammos**, which we have glimpsed from the high rocks of Pano Chora. It can now be reached by a roundabout road leading off the far end of the main beach. Quicker for the walker, and far more pleasant, is to strike off the beach before you come quite to the end, and make your way up beside a partly dried-up watercourse which leads through a lovely flowery valley. The lower part may still have water flowing, but if you negotiate this a sandy path will take you through tufts of cistus, thyme, lavender, purple vetch, scarlet poppies and the low-growing thorny broom – all in full bloom during May. In the swampier parts you may see white egrets, and skylarks will urge you on your way.

After the valley narrows and turns right, cross a low wall on your right and take any of several goat tracks which climb to the saddle between you and the sea. From there you look down on one of the loveliest bays in any island, and at the edge of the soft sand is a tiny bar-restaurant where the fisherman (whose boat is on the beach) or his wife will give you to eat whatever they have. It may not be much, but you can wash it down with a copper canful of true Seriphos wine. You can swim off the beach or off the rocks further on, and in fine calm weather the sea is like champagne. If you swim a little way out you get the reverse view of Pano Chora, topped by the church of Ioannis Theologos, while sometimes a pair of buzzards wheel hundreds of feet overhead. Another ten minutes over the far headland will bring you to the smaller beach of **Agios Ioannis**, lovely and peaceful too, but with nowhere to eat or rest.

There is a pleasant walk in the other direction from Livadi, beyond the southern beach. After the first half mile, which takes you by a metalled road through an outlying part of Livadi, the way follows goat and donkey tracks across a green headland to the few houses which constitute the well named hamlet of **Kali Ampeli**, or the 'Good Vineyard'. There are little beaches below, but no easy way down.

Two more distant places are worth much effort to get to see. The harbour of **Mega Livadi** is the old centre of the vanished mining industry on the south-west coast, and the only place on Seriphos where a hint of sadness remains. A deserted pier and a rusting gantry mark where the ore was shipped, but now it has reverted to a quiet life for fishermen, and for the smallholders who cultivate the fertile little valley which opens out into a delightful sheltered bay. There are many ruined houses, and the grand neo-classical building which housed the mining administration is a picturesque shell, but life is returning. New houses are being built, and there is an increasing number of rooms to let. There is a good little bar-restaurant on the water front.

A drivable road goes all the way to Mega Livadi, and from it you can diverge down to another charming bay and beach at **Koutalas**, but before midsummer it is not easy to find transport to either. The best method is to take the early school bus to the Chora, and near where it stops to look for a covered van which takes local men and their families' bread to Mega Livadi and places on the way. The driver runs the restaurant in the harbour, and will serve you with refreshment before returning at midday. Later in the summer boat trips are advertised from Livadi to both Koutalas and Mega Livadi, with views of the rugged southern coastline.

The monastery known as the **Moni ton Taxiarchon** is easier to get to, and it is an astonishing place. You can catch an early afternoon bus either from Livadi or more reliably from Pano Chora bound for the village of Kalitsos. It will set you down beside the monastery and

179

pick you up some three hours later on the way back. High above the northern coast, looking out towards Kythnos and its sister monastery, the *Panagia tis Kanalas*, it has a plain fortress-like exterior, foursquare with high walls and tiny cell windows. A low doorway leads into a tree-shaded space, with the old monks' cells all round, up and down irregular flights of steps. In the centre is the monastery church; this building is of the seventeenth century, having replaced one contemporary with the sixteenth-century monastery. The dedication is to the archangels Michael and Gabriel, and there is a rich *templo* of seventeenth-century woodwork with a carved Abbot's chair to match.

The surprise in this beautiful place is that it is cared for by one man, an all-purpose monk whose name is Makarios. You may meet him collecting merchandise off the bus, dressed in overalls. To show you the church he will put on a grey cassock, then take you up to the little modern kitchen in his living quarters for a cup of coffee. Later you will see him come out in jacket and breeches with a swill bucket to feed his sleek black and pink pigs. His flock of sheep and goats will be sheltering under a broad ilex, a white horse grazes below with an attendant donkey, and all kinds of poultry strut and cluck around outside the walls. There are vines and figs in abundance. *Makarios* in Greek means 'blessed', and he is a happy man – only in his forties now, he came as a boy of sixteen.

Not long ago Makarios buried the last of his fellow monks in the graveyard of the little church outside the gates. It is not a beautiful church, and neither is the plain building next to it. If the door is open you can see that around the walls are stacked in modern steel racks rows of wooden or tin boxes, each marked by a photograph, a name and a date. If you are curious enough to open one, you may be startled. They are depositories for the bones of departed Seriphiots. A sensible practice, you may agree, to bury and leave your relative in the tiny flowery graveyard for a year or two, then allow the bones to be removed to leave room for others, yet still have them handy to be reconstituted on the Last Day.

Somehow none of this seems gruesome in the context of the place – the sunlit peace of the monastery within, the sweep of fertile fields falling to the strait that runs between Seriphos and Kythnos, the contented family of animals. Here Makarios (and his visitors) can every day consider the greatness of God and the beauty of his works.

On the way back to Livadi look out for the village of **Panagia**, clinging to the hillside below the road. It has a sweet little early Byzantine church, dedicated to the Virgin and built between AD 950 and 1000. This is a Greek cruciform church with a low round central tower, all roofed in red tiles. The very early frescos have now almost disappeared. To see Panagia you may have to find a room for the night – never impossible in the islands. The people of Seriphos are not as immediately friendly and forthcoming as they are, say, in Ios or Amorgos, but the right approach will usually meet a warm response. Certainly there are few more delightful islands.

Siphnos is equidistant from Seriphos and Kimolos, in this western chain of islands. The only modern harbour is at **Kamares**, where a deep inlet cuts into the mountains on the west coast, with only just room for a small village beside it and for the big concrete quay where the ferries berth.

Although there is still a fishing fleet, with all the activity which goes with it, it is no longer mainly a fishing village. Gone is the waterborne *volta*, or evening parade of boats which was seen with surprise and delight on an earlier visit. To balance that loss, the mining village to the left of the harbour has vanished, and only the white gleam of an occasional house or church lights up the brown hillside. Now the not unattractive modern buildings beside the inner quay are for cafés and small restaurants, with guest houses and rooms to let filling in the space behind.

Perhaps fortunately, there is little room for further development, and most visitors will board bus or taxi to take them the few miles up the modern road to the chief centres of Apollonia and Artemona. On the way you will soon see how Siphnos differs from its neighbours. The road climbs by the side of a long steep valley, green and well watered below, with clumps of pink oleander growing high up its sides.

Apollonia and Artemona, on the watershed of the island, straggle into one another in much the same way as the religious territories of Apollo and Artemis once overlapped. You come first to **Apollonia**, a village without much obvious grace, but the most

181

convenient place to stay if you want to get to know Siphnos. It straggles on a north–south axis, and the most attractive part follows the narrow street leading from behind the bus stop towards the southern quarter of Katavati.

Not unlike the quieter streets of Paroikia on Paros, it has no 'tourist-trap' shops – only a few of those marvellously muddled *pantopoleia*, or general stores, where the owner will go immediately to a topheavy pile of assorted goods and pick out exactly what you want, then write out clearly on the back of an envelope the price of every purchase.

At this point you are likely to meet a Pappas with flowing beard and flying soutane, striding down from one of the churches which stand higher up on either side of the street. After two small ones to right and left, the way gets steeper, and steps lead up past the much bigger church of *Agios Spiridon* in a garden of glorious flowers. The best thing in the ornate and conventional interior is a long-case clock with a fine brass pendulum – made in London. The clock face stands (permanently) at five past three. Finally comes the primary school, a fine building in a fine position, and then you come out on to the main road leading south past the half-deserted village of Exembela and the big square monastery of Vrissi.

Exembela is a strange place, well worth a detour to the left of the main road. Once, apparently, it was the artistic and entertainment centre of Siphnos. Poets, musicians and singers congregated in its cafés, and the resulting high spirits led their Turkish masters to call the village *Aksham Bela*, meaning 'Trouble in the Evening'. A story which credits the Turk with unexpected humour, but whether it really explains the name is doubtful.

There is little merriment now. Many of its cottages are ruins, and two big schools in the neo-classical style stand deserted; in the grounds of one a family of goats seem to be the only pupils. Yet one can see life returning. The schools will never reopen, but young couples have come out from Apollonia to newly built houses, and at every corner are gardens old and new. There are banks of white marguerite daisies, beds of Madonna lilies, masses of wistaria – and roses everywhere. With no lack of water Siphnos has a show of garden flowers far more varied than the geraniums and bougainvillea which brighten the dryer islands.

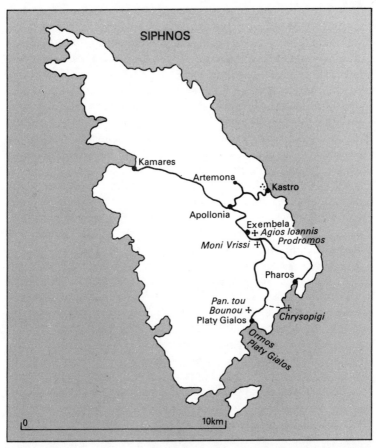

The biggest church in Exembela is *Agios Nikolaos*, high-domed and handsome, but with modern decoration inside. Not far away is the smaller *Agios Ioannis Prodromos*, where the Baptist appears in an ikon, winged and carrying his own head on a charger. The **Vrissi monastery** down the road is conventional in plan: a door in the high wall leads to a courtyard, and the church within has an arcaded porch. Its foundation by a wealthy Siphniot in the seventeenth century has ensured it a good wooden *templo*, but the most interesting thing in the monastery is its museum of religious arts – early gospels, documents, embroidered vestments and decorated vessels.

183

There are only three monks now, and as they spend much of their time in the fields it may be difficult to find one to let you in.

The road you are on leads in about six miles to the long sandy beach of **Platy Gialos** on the south coast. To reach it you need a bus, which leaves the crossroads in Apollonia several times a day – make sure you know when the last one returns. There are rooms to let down there, and two or three friendly restaurants on the edge of the sand. At the far end is a hotel (open only from June to September) and beyond that a cliff path passes above some enticing rocky coves. The neat modern farmhouse at the end of the path has pigeons on the roof, while quantities of chickens, sheep and goats share the shade of the big tree behind. In a shed beyond the house they make goat's cheese on a commercial scale, dripping the congealing milk into low round wicker baskets to set, and putting them to mature on frames hung from the roof. The young wife of the farmer, well dressed and educated, shows you round with pleasure.

If you see piles of dry brushwood stacked behind one of the houses along the sea front, they are there to fire the kiln of an adventurous potter. He is trying to revive an industry for which Siphnos was famous in the first century BC, according to Pliny. It became a thriving export trade during the eighteenth century. During the following century it steadily expanded, and between the two world wars even the potters themselves went abroad to set up ceramic centres on the mainland and on other islands. In Siphnos the industry declined suddenly during and after the last war, and without national help it may never recover. The story of this industry is told in an excellent guide, *Siphnos, the Potter's Island*, by Georgios Moussas, written in English and on sale in Apollonia. It would be a good idea to buy it as soon as you arrive.

You can leave the bus a mile before the road descends to Platy Gialos, and walk down to the monastery church of **Chrysopigi**, beyond which there is another good sandy beach. The monastery is no more, but the church of the *Panagia* is kept up, standing with its feet almost in the water at the end of a rocky promontory. The causeway leading to the church is interrupted by a gap in the rocks, which leaves it confined on a virtual island. There is a good legend about this gap. Three local women, as the custom still is, came down one evening to make the usual preparations before the next day's service, only to find seven pirates asleep on the floor. The pirates woke, the women fled, the pirates pursued hot foot. The women prayed to the Virgin, the Virgin split the rock behind them and let in the sea. Foiled and awestricken, the pirates took to their boat and vanished. Both parties would have had a good story to tell their friends.

The beach beyond the church is inviting, and there is a large bar-café for refreshments before or after swimming. From the promontory you look north into another bay, at the head of which is the pleasant fishing village of **Pharos**. To reach it you must take a different bus down from Apollonia, as the road to it forks left shortly after the Moni Vrissis. There is of course a lighthouse (*pharos*) on the cliff to seaward (though this consists only of a light fixed on a post) and beyond it a path from where you can scramble down for a swim. The village beach is a nice one, small and sheltered, with a farmhouse above it which has a terrace restaurant where the family serves good local produce. On a recent visit a baby pig had just been born, but the poor mite was destined for some unfeeling restaurant in Apollonia or Kamares. Far fewer people come to Pharos than to Platy Gialos or Chrysopigi, and it must be said that the mid-morning and late afternoon buses to and from those popular places can be appallingly crowded.

'Chrysopigi' means 'gold spring', and Siphnos in antiquity was described as 'rich in gold and silver, and adorned with Parian marble'. But the mines were worked out, or submerged by a volcanic change in the seabed, during classical times. Pausanias attributes the destruction of the mines of Siphnos to the anger of Apollo. The people of Siphnos had been accustomed to offer Apollo an annual gift of a gold egg, but on one unfortunate occasion they attempted to deceive the god by presenting him with an imitation gilt one. No doubt there was an efficient assay-master at Delphi, for the ruse was at once discovered. Hence, legend has it, the anger of the god and the destruction of the mines of Siphnos. As for Parian marble, Antiparos is almost as close to the east as Seriphos is to the north, and the Prophet Ilias on Paros glowers at his opposite number on Siphnos across no great stretch of water.

Another less crowded bus journey will take you from the crossroads in Apollonia to **Kastro**, the old capital and one of the most

185

special places in the Aegean. It lies on the eastern side of the island, clinging like all these old townships to its protective hill, and hedged round with a fourteenth-century wall. Unfortunately, as from so many of its date, the glory is departed, the older mediaeval buildings are in ruins, and the streets have an abandoned air. The most distinctive houses are those built into the wall itself, facing across the sea to Paros and Antiparos. Here, unusually in the Kyklades, one finds enclosed wooden balconies (somewhat reminiscent of Malta) built out beyond the walls. One is also reminded of Rhodes, and it is true that the walls were built by a member of the Spanish family of Da Corogna who had served there with the Knights of St John. In 1307 he established a sovereign state on Siphnos, independent of the Duchy of Naxos.

John Da Corogna's castle on Siphnos (or Siphanto as it became known by one of the many corruptions from Greek to Italian at this time) stood intact for three hundred years. In 1465 it passed to the more powerful Bolognese family of the Gozzadini, who managed by diplomacy to keep it out of the hands of the Turks until 1617. The castle and its owners, however, were unable to protect the people of the island from the murderous inroads of Turkish freebooters – and this was true of most of the islands of the central Aegean. We read that during the fifteenth century:

> 'At both Naxos and Siphnos there was such a lack of men that many women were unable to find husbands; in fact the small and wretched population of the latter island, still the absolute property of the Da Corogna, who had a tower there in a lovely garden, was mainly composed of females, who were zealous Catholics, though they did not understand a word of the Latin language in which their services were held.'*

In that tower and garden war and terror must have seemed far away, and today there are few quieter or more peaceful places. Three arched gateways, or *loggias*, pierce the wall on the landward side. The bus stops below the middle one, and you can spend a happy morning wandering through the narrow streets, sometimes passing under small bridges, thrown out by the houses to connect

---

* William Miller, *op. cit.*, pp. 598–9.

them with the higher ground where the next street runs. You can explore the ruins of stately houses at the northern end, where the big window spaces of the upper storeys still illustrate the elegance of their owners' lives. On the highest ground of all, from where you look north along the rocky coast, are the marble foundations of a classical temple, probably of the seventh century BC, which would have been a landmark for sailors approaching from Paros to Seriphos.

In the village below it is easy to get lost, and here Georgios Moussa's guide to Siphnos is invaluable, because it has a detailed map of Kastro on the last page. With its help you should be able to find some of the many fascinating churches which have survived from the sixteenth century, and although not many people are about in the streets you can usually trace the key to a house nearby.

The pick of them is the *Panagia Eleoùssa* (Our Lady of Mercy) in the broader central street leading down from the old quarter. The key is kept in a house beyond and round the corner to the left. The carved lunette over the doorway has on each side the bows of a ship under sail. The date there is 1635, but this only marks the year when it was last restored – a sign of some prosperity under Turkish rule. Indeed one must remember that, though the Turkish conquest was a disaster for the Latin overlords, it brought peace to the islands by eliminating all resistance and silencing the constant feuding between ambitious families. Once in control, the authorities put a stop to most of the piracy and allowed the Greeks to worship as they pleased. How soon they were able to replace Greek for Latin in their services we do not know for certain.

The loveliest thing in the Panagia – and in the whole village – is an ikon of the Virgin. Her face goes right back to Duccio or Giotto, and the eyes look at you sideways with an inner light behind them. The Child is independent, even perky, and holds a scroll in one hand. You should also look for the **Museum**, which after temporary lodging in a disused church has at last found a home of its own. So far not many inhabitants know it is there, but there is a good collection of pieces from all periods, including Greek and Roman items which are not otherwise given much publicity here.

There are just two cafés in Kastro, by no means always open, and you can never count on getting a meal there in the middle of the day.

After 2.30 p.m. you will probably have to walk back to Apollonia if you want to stay longer.

The most distinctive part of modern Siphnos is the district of **Artemona**, a barely separate village on higher ground to the north of Apollonia. Here, as occasionally on Paros, you find substantial neo-classical houses standing in large gardens behind high walls. Some are now put to municipal use; many were built by wealthy citizens at the beginning of the century, or as country houses for Athenian families. Empty for most of the year, if not already deserted, they contrast a little sombrely with the clean and lively intricacies of the more typical Kykladic streets around them.

The island buses all begin and end their journeys at the *plateia* of Pano Artemona, a quiet spot with an authentic *kapheneion* and a good basic Greek restaurant. Much more interesting is to walk up there from the corresponding *plateia* in Apollonia, taking the narrow stepped street which begins between the Hotel Sophia and the café Lakis. This way takes you through the quiet suburb of Ano Petali, across the deep bed of the stream which cuts it off from Artemona, passes the far end of the *plateia* and carries on higher and higher till you come out among farm cottages and open fields. A restored windmill is the only building now between you and the eastern cliffs, and the view back over the white houses and churches of Siphnos is one to remember. Not many people find their way up here, or enter the half dozen very individual churches you pass.

One relishes even their names, though each has something of special interest inside or outside. There is the *Panagia Ouranophotia* (Our Lady of the Heavenly Light), which stands on the site of a seventh-century BC temple to Apollo; the *Panagia ta Gournia* (Our Lady of the Troughs) above the stream where frogs croak in the spring; *Agios Georgios tou Afendi* (the Effendi's St George) away in the eastern quarter called Agios Loukas, on the other side of the main road; the *Panagia tis Ammou* (Our Lady of the Sand); the *Kochi*, another Panagia on the site of a temple to Artemis; and the *Panagia tou Vali*, built by a Greek governor of that name under the Turkish regime in the eighteenth century, and still privately owned by his descendants.

The oddest church name, with an odd story behind it, is the *Panagia tou Barou* (Our Lady of the Baron), said to be a miniature replica of the mediaeval convent *Theologos tou Mongou*, which still stands outside the town to the west. Apocryphally its wealthy founder, scolded for extravagance by his wife, replied '*Je l'ai fait à mon goût*'. The nuns' taste however was for a good life, and according to the great Kykladic traveller, Theodore Bent, the convent became 'the favourite rendezvous of all the gallants of Siphnos'. The further story goes that one of their recruits had been pursued to the convent by a Frankish baron, who built the little church nearby so that he could continue his suit disguised as a monk. As he could make no progress in the convent, despite its reputation, he took to seducing other ladies of Siphnos, until he was reputedly the father of a quarter of the children in Apollonia, who were given the surname *Barades*.

However you take all this, Siphnos must have been a lively place to live during the Turkish occupation. The liveliness is not so obvious now, although its people are warm and friendly. The impression you get is rather of a dignity and independence which comes from a long and often prosperous history – a kind of 'style' which you do not often find in this part of the Aegean.

Access

Both islands are served by the two ferry lines which operate between Piraeus and Milos through the western Kyklades; this means that ships call frequently during the week in either direction. The odd strategy of the shipping companies may result in rival ships calling at different times on the same day, and on some days not at all.

Communications

SIPHNOS is better equipped with roads than Seriphos, and a frequent and regular bus service connects Artemona and Apollonia with Kamares, Kastro, Pharos and Platy Gialos. In SERIPHOS the bus service is very limited. The only buses belong to private owners who decide when and where they run, but in term time one always leaves the harbour for the Chora at 8 a.m. to take children to school, returning in the early afternoon. A new road has been built to connect Livadi with some of the villages and beaches on the east coast. A still rough road goes from the Chora past the Taxiarchon monastery to the village of Kalitsos; an early afternoon bus usually goes this way and returns later. A much rougher road connects the Chora with Koutalas and Mega Livadi on the west coast – taxis are reluctant to take it, but during the summer season you can reach both places by small boat excursions from Livadi. Mopeds can be hired at Apollonia in Siphnos, but nowhere in Seriphos.

Accommodation

SERIPHOS   There are three hotels in Livadi, but none in the Chora. PERSEUS (B, pension only) is small and inconvenient, and is usually fully booked by agencies. SERIPHOS BEACH (C) is bigger but has the same disadvantages, and no outlook to the sea. The best is MAISTRALI (C), overlooking the long sandy beach. It has large airy rooms and balconies back and front, but is open only from June to September. A convenient and well run guest house, ARETE, overlooks the landing quay; breakfast and snacks can be had at the café below. There are rooms to let in Livadi and the Chora, but not a lot of choice.

SIPHNOS   In Artemona, ARTEMON (C) is a modern and comfortable hotel, though only six rooms have private shower and WC. It has a restaurant, with some tables in a nice garden, but the cooking is dull.

In Apollonia the best hotel is SIPHNOS (C), with a friendly and efficient management. APOLLONIA (B, pension only) has the disadvantages of its class, and SOPHIA (C) is rather poky, with uncertain service. At Kamares there is KAMARI (B, pension only), but there are also well equipped apartments and rooms to let. At Platy Gialos, XENIA (B), with restaurant, has a fine position at the end of the long beach; open from June to September only.

Restaurants

SERIPHOS   There is a big choice around the harbour. The quality varies from year to year, as most managers, cooks and staff are seasonal visitors. Easily the most reliable is TELES MATTES with a small sheltered terrace and tables out under the tamarisks beyond the yacht station. In the Chora the best cook is STAVROS – he lives there and has real Seriphos wine. His restaurant is plain and there are no waiters, but it has a wonderful view.

SIPHNOS   In Artemona the little MANGANAS is simple and does genuine Greek food. In Apollonia the best food is found at KREBATINA, where the management is eccentric but pleasantly so.

Facilities

Banks: There are none in either island. Travellers' cheques and currency can be changed at some hotels and at shipping agents; in Seriphos at the

'Seriphos Gift Shop' in Livadi, where the proprietress speaks good English and has better goods for sale than you will usually find at this kind of place.

Yachts: Seriphos has some of the best and cleanest facilities in the islands. The small jetty gets crowded in summer, but there is safe anchorage out in the bay in all weathers. A popular port of call for small yachts and charter cruises. In Siphnos yachts are catered for only in Kamares harbour, where there are good berths and shore facilities.

TWELVE

Milos and Kimolos

At **Milos** you come to the southern end of the western chain of islands which began in Kea. This large and important place has always been prominent in the affairs of the Aegean, and even today it can support its economy without relying at all heavily on tourism. Merchant ships outnumber the car and passenger ships which call here; loading and unloading goes on all day in the busy harbour.

The big ferries are frequent visitors, though, and bring stores and passengers down from Piraeus and the intervening islands, up from Santorin, or across from Ios and the eastern Kyklades. Whether you approach from north, south or east, the last stage of the journey seems interminable. The only entry to the huge landlocked harbour is from the west, so that after calling first at Kimolos off the north-eastern tip of Milos the ships have to plough their way round by the long northern coastline before they can turn into this vast bay, which almost cuts the island in two.

Although volcanic rock occurs here, it is now believed that this basin was formed by the faulting and collapsing of geological plates rather than by the kind of volcanic explosion which blew Santorin apart. Certainly the aspect which meets the traveller here is totally different. The land is on the whole low-lying, except in the unfrequented south-western quarter, where the inevitable mountain of the Prophet Ilias rises to a little over 2000 feet. The landscape, away from the harsher rock formations on the seaward side, is gentle, fertile and flowery in spring.

As you round the rocky north-western cape you will see inland the soaring conical hill which at one time formed the defensive Kastro of a mediaeval town. Then comes the long haul past the sloping, overgrown site of the fifth-century Greek city state, and the

192

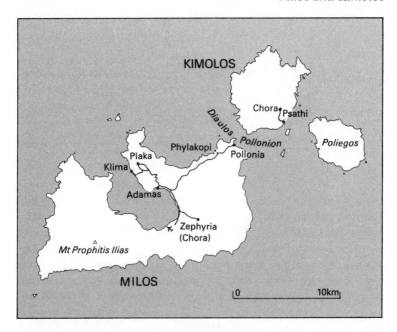

brightly painted houses of the fishing village **Klima**, where the Melians of that period beached their ships, and where a considerable Roman and early Byzantine harbour was built. Finally you turn up past the lighthouse into the modern harbour of **Adamas**, now a town which has usurped the position of principal centre from the older town of Plaka beneath the Kastro. This is because it has become a major industrial port and entrepôt for the south-western Aegean. Few tourists disembark from the ferries here; instead there is a stream of heavy vehicles carrying building materials or other essential supplies.

Mining is still the principal industry of Milos, for it produces not the now unwanted iron ore but metals and chemicals much needed in the modern world. There is salt, sulphur and alum to be won, while more unusual minerals such as bensonite, barium, perlite and the feldspar derivative kaolin are mined in different parts of the island, and exported in quantity. Yet the mining areas are set discreetly away among the rolling hills, or on a distant and little visited coast. You would think at first sight that agriculture and

193

market gardening were the main occupations, so unspoilt is the landscape that meets the eye. Milos has its own life, and the age of the tourist has affected it little.

The fertility of Milos is witnessed to by Theophrastus, who wrote in his work *On Plants*:

> 'There at Milos they reap apparently thirty or forty days after sowing, wherefore is a saying of these islanders that one should go on sowing until one sees the sheaves. ... However it is said that pulses in their country do not grow like this, nor are they abundant. Yet they say that the soil is wonderfully fertile, for it is good for both corn and olives.'

It is the Greek city state of Milos which stands vividly out in the history of the Aegean in the fifth century BC. If you take the bus (which starts and stops round the corner to the east of the harbour) up to the town of **Plaka**, and wander south through its attractive little streets until you are looking right across the entrance to the bay, you will see below you the sloping green fields which cover the ancient city of the Melians. It occupied the saddle between the craggy cliff face of Pyrgaki and the little conical hill to seaward which is now crowned by a church dedicated to – guess whom? – the Prophet Ilias. Apart from the limited security of this mini-acropolis the town was not naturally defensible from the sea. In the Greek manner therefore substantial walls were built to the north and south, running almost down to the sea itself. Some of the impressive masonry of the northern wall can still be seen in places.

It was this city which twice defied the established military powers of the Aegean during the fifth century BC. Milos and the other Kyklades lay in the path of the Persian fleet as it sailed to attack the Greek mainland in 480 BC. The Melians joined the people of Seriphos, Siphnos and Kythnos in refusing to give the symbols of submission to the Persians, and later that year they fought alongside the Athenians at Salamis.

Then they were on the winning side, and incurred no retribution. Fifty years later, having refused to join the Athenian League (centred nominally on Delos) they and nearby Thera stayed neutral at the outbreak of the Peloponnesian War between Athens and Sparta. This was because both islands had ties with the Dorian

peoples of the Peloponnese, and may have been originally colonized from Sparta.

The great harbour had immense strategic importance in a war
fought largely at sea, and Athens could not afford to let her enemies
use it. Repeated attempts to persuade or coerce Milos into joining
the League failed. At last in 416 BC an Athenian delegation was sent
to argue its case before the council and magistrates of Milos. The
ensuing dialogue was recreated (rather than actually recorded) by
Thucydides, and has become a classic example of a clash between
principle and reality.

The Athenians argued simply that might gave them right, and the
Melians were foolish to resist. The Melian case is summed up in
their final reply after hours of deliberation among themselves:

> 'Our decision, Athenians, is just the same as it was at first. We
> are not prepared to give up in a short moment the liberty which
> our city has enjoyed from its foundation for seven hundred
> years. We put our trust in the fortune that the gods will send
> and which has saved us up to now, and in the help of men – that
> is, of the Spartans; and so we shall try to save ourselves. But we
> invite you to allow us to be friends of yours and enemies to
> neither side, to make a treaty which shall be agreeable to both
> you and us, and so to leave our country.'*

The compromise was refused, and the Athenians and their allies
besieged the city. After several months of successful resistance,
during which no help came from Sparta, they were worn down by
lack of food and overrun through treachery. They capitulated un-
conditionally, the men were massacred and the women and children sold into slavery.

We must remember that this bitter war was now in its sixteenth
year, and the high principles set out by Pericles in his funeral oration
at the end of the first year had collapsed in an increasingly cynical
pursuit of power and victory. But twelve years later Athens had lost
the war, the five hundred new Athenian settlers were expelled by
the Spartan Lysander, and a colony of surviving Melians was re-
established under a Spartan constitution.

The next masters of the Aegean were the Hellenistic royal house

---

* Thucydides, *Histories* V, 112 (trans. Rex Warner).

of Macedon, to be routed and evicted in their turn by the Romans in the second century BC. To those periods belong other remains discovered and still to be seen on the site of the old city. Most notable are a massive temple podium littered with the drums of fallen columns, a stadium with a well preserved retaining wall, and the substantial theatre where the famous statue of Venus (the Venus de Milo, now in the Louvre) was discovered in 1820.

The site is a romantic one, both for its tragic history and for its natural beaty. In its heyday it would have looked not unlike the Greek city of Kameiros in Rhodes, though in that gentle place there was no need for fortifications. I shall remember it for the sudden flash of a pair of golden orioles against a leafy background in the evening sunlight. In Plaka itself, which is still the administrative centre, you should be able to see some of the treasures found here and at the Bronze Age site of Phylakopi on the north coast. Unfortunately the Archaeological Museum was at the time of writing in abeyance and out of use while room was being made for a large extension to it.

The other expedition not to miss is to **Phylakopi** (modern Phlakopi). An infrequent bus service runs along a good modern road from Adamas to Pollonia, the fishing village on the north-eastern tip of Milos, just across the narrow strait from Kimolos. The bus will put you down only a few yards from the entrance to the excavations – though you must make it clear that is what you want, and not the village of Phlakopi half a mile before you get there.

An inconspicuous rise in the ground between the road and the sea marks a site which was inhabited from the beginning of the second milennium BC. This phase coincides with the early palace period in Crete, when Milos must have been closely connected with, if not subject to, the kingdom of 'Minos'. The site was first excavated by Duncan Mackenzie, chief lieutenant of Sir Arthur Evans at Knossos, between 1896 and 1899. He distinguished three separate periods of building, ranging from a fairly big unfortified settlement around 2000 BC, followed by a more sophisticated community between 2000 and 1600. After 1600 major fortifications were built, and the discovery of tablet fragments in Linear A script showed there was a written recording system, comparable with that operating in Minoan Crete at the same time.

Later excavations by the British school in 1967–8 clearly distinguished a fourth period, or 'city', after 1400 BC – that is to say after
the second destruction of the Cretan palaces around 1450. The
evidence from this period shows typical Mycenaean rather than
Minoan features, as at Knossos, while unlike Knossos the fourth city
of Phylakopi survived almost into the last milennium and the ensuing 'dark ages'. So in this very small compass you can trace in its
tumbled and jumbled masonry nearly a thousand years of human
occupation.

That the folk of this period shared the taste and artistry of the rest
of the Minoan world, as found in Crete and Thera, can be seen from
some of the objects discovered here. The most delicate date from
about 1500 BC, like the fragments of a fresco of flying fishes, and a
vase painted with the kind of wavy reed decoration you find in the
Thera collection in Athens. A splendid figurine, the 'Lady of
Phylakopi', of about 1350 may have been imported from the mainland. Some of these things should be on show in the reconstituted
Plaka museum, but others have inevitably gone to the National
Museum in Athens.

The excavations are difficult to follow without help or a detailed
ground plan, but it is an evocative place, with the sea now almost
washing into the lower houses, in the shelter of the bold headland of
Kalogeros to the north-east. The hinterland is fertile, with a stream
running through it to the sea, and like the Cretan dwellers in Mallia
and Gournia the people of Phylakopi must have lived for centuries
in undisturbed peace. For building their walls they had hardly to
look beyond the beach, today still littered with huge black and grey
boulders, though some great slabs of volcanic rock must have come
from further away.

If while you are wandering round the site you should pick up an
object which looks like a piece of chipped dark bottle glass washed
up by the sea, look at it more carefully. It is probably a stone age
artefact made from obsidian, perhaps the head of an arrow, the
blade of a knife or axe. The occupation of many places in Milos goes
back far beyond the Bronze Age into Neolithic times. Then Milos
prospered and was famous through its trade in obsidian, a stone
formed by the rapid cooling of molten rock, with a black smooth
surface which can be chipped into sharp sections more easily and

durably than flint. Obsidian implements chipped with the identifiable technique of Milos have been found on the mainland across nearly a hundred miles of open sea.

Another good modern road leads round the eastern shore of the bay to the little airport and the nearby salt works. Just before the airport a left fork takes you to the village of **Zephyria**. This is a place which played a curious and enigmatic part in the history of Milos. When the old city by the harbour entrance was abandoned, some time after the fifth century AD, little is known about the history of the island. It was nominally part of the Byzantine Empire until the fall of Byzantium in 1204, but like most of the lands of the southern Aegean it was open to frequent attacks by the Arabs.

At some time during the Byzantine era a new settlement was formed at Zephyria, set well back from the harbour in low-lying country, with a small but defensible acropolis. During the Middle Ages, under the aegis of the Duchy of Naxos, there is evidence that the Kastro hill above ancient Milos was also occupied and defended, but the overlords of the Crispi family who succeeded to the Duchy in 1383 set up a capital seat at the place they called simply Chora – which is the modern Zephyria.

During the seventeenth and early eighteenth centuries the island economy and population flourished, but towards the end of the eighteenth century a mysterious depression seems to have set in. The population dwindled, and most of the Chora was in ruins. One explanation suggests that the unhealthy marshy site, surrounded by sulphurous rocks, produced a level of atmospheric pollution which led to widespread and epidemic disease. Or it could have been a shift of the population back to the shipping routes entering the harbour.

At all events the site was abandoned, and the remnants of its population migrated back to the old Kastro area, and founded the modern village of Plaka above the ruins of the ancient Greek city. It was a strange turnabout, and one of the oddest sequels is to be found in the church of *Agia Triada* in Adamas town. There at the west end of this splendid three-aisled church hang four heavy battered oak panels, painted with the likenesses of the four evangelists, surrounded by gilded scrolls. These are said to be ikons brought by Cretan refugees escaping from the Turks in the seventeenth century, and they first adorned the principal church in Zephyria. When that was abandoned they found a secure home here at last. The teller of this tale was one of three 'weird sisters' who sit endlessly doing their lace work in a poor little house close to Agia Triada. They have been entrusted with the key of the church, and must be glad to earn a few drachmas by showing it to visitors.

The church itself is a good example of mediaeval building and seventeenth-century decoration. Of the three aisles one is dedicated to the *Trias*, or Holy Trinity, the north aisle to *Agios Nikolaos* and the south to *Agios Athanasios*. There are no frescos, but the wooden *templo* has some lovely painting. There is St Nicholas in the white robe with black crosses which marks the hierarchy of the Orthodox Church, a beautiful Virgin and Child, and on the far right hand panel John the Baptist wearing more clothes and looking better nourished than usual. Other regular features are present – the frieze above the *templo* shows the main scenes in the life of Christ; the two upper panels on the flaps of the sanctuary gate have the Annunciation (archangel to the left, the Virgin to the right) and the two lower ones are portraits of St Peter and St Paul. The setting is handsome too, with a wide courtyard outside the south entrance, a peaceful spot just around the corner from the commercial harbour. This part of Adamas is attractive. It has a tree-lined promenade running along the sea front, an open-air restaurant near at hand and an even better one down at the far end, only the width of the road from the water's edge.

Out there in the bay of Milos was fought the first naval action of the War of Independence, for Milos was one of the first islands to join the Greek revolt from Turkish rule in 1821. It became a major base for British and French naval squadrons and a rendezvous for European and American convoys during the early nineteenth century – when there were plenty of pirates around in those waters. The allies used it during the Crimean War and again in the First World War. The German occupation during the Second World War left trenches and gun emplacements covering the harbour.

We come finally to the fishing village of **Pollonia** – finally because from there you can take passage by small boat to neighbouring Kimolos. The harbour is charming, a sheltered bay fringed with tamarisks; a group of nice-looking modern houses to the north, two or three bar-restaurants lining the curving foreshore to the south, which ends in a jetty for the fishing boats to land their catch.

The best of the restaurants is at the far end, run by a friendly old couple – Granny bakes her own bread and has a wicked gap-toothed grin. You soon come to recognize the simpler and homelier places in the islands by certain signs, one being the type of chairs set out by the tables. If they look as though Van Gogh could have painted them, with wooden backs and rush seats, go in there for good value. If they are in ugly shapes made of brightly coloured or shabby plastic, you may be wise to try elsewhere. At any rate here you can eat fish straight out of the sea at very moderate prices, under the shade of a bamboo awning in the heat of the day.

In summer there are rooms to let behind the harbour front. This can be useful if you plan to take the short cut across to **Kimolos** by way of the *Diaulos Pollonion*, to give the little strait its grand name. You can get to Kimolos by the regular ferry on the run between Milos and Siphnos, but unless you are prepared to stay three or four days you will be stuck there until the next ferry calls. In any case it will be a much longer passage.

You must be ready for an early start. Every weekday morning at 7.30 a fishing boat leaves the jetty at Pollonia with about half a dozen workmen bound for a day's work on Kimolos. Except during holidays they will be joined by the young schoolmistress who has charge of the little school up in Kimolos Chora. There is two-way traffic, and the boat will return about 1 p.m. with more workmen for the afternoon shift at the American-run mineral plant just down the coast. The same process is repeated in the afternoon, though it is as well to make sure that the boat does return to Milos in the evening, as the skipper lives on Kimolos.

Given the early start you can spend four very pleasant hours exploring this attractive small island. The passengers gather about 7.15 in Granny's place for an early coffee, and then you chug across the usually limpid water for no more than half an hour before landing at **Psathi**, where a new concrete quay has now been built for big ships to use, instead of lying off at anchor to be tended by small boats.

There is a little café by the quay, but most people will set out on an easy twenty-minute walk up the road to the **Chora**. The village is quiet, clean and peaceful in the early morning. There are more donkeys than vehicles, very few tourists find their way up there, and the men are mostly at work already in the fields. Women may be hanging out washing from houses with pretty balconies; there are a few shops – one splendid butcher's – and a couple of simple bar-restaurants where you can get breakfast or lunch.

If you walk on through the Chora, you can take a path which leads uphill to a lovely stretch of open fields, full of flowers and butterflies in spring. A pleasant surprise is to find that one of the usual row of dilapidated windmills is in working order, with furled sails waiting for action. The view from the top over Psathi harbour and across the channel to Milos is superb.

We went there first with a mission to seek out a long lost relation for a Greek friend in Ios. This was his half brother, who had been born and brought up with him here in boyhood, but had emigrated and spent most of his working life as a bar-tender in New York state. Now in his fifties, the Greek homing urge had taken over and we found him here in Kimolos Chora, living the simplest of lives in great content.

Without him we might have missed the two most interesting things in Kimolos. First he flushed out Maria, who guards somewhat jealously the key to the church of *Agios Chrysostomos*. This is a fourteenth-century Byzantine church, unusually fine for so small a place. The outside is the real attraction, with excellently preserved stonework and a really beautiful main doorway on the south side. A clue, if you have no guide, is to look or ask for the *Plateia Oikonomou Spiridionos Ramphou* – a sometime mayor who obviously left his mark on Kimolos.

Even more unexpected was to be shown round a deserted mediaeval quarter up behind the main houses of the Chora. It has gates on both sides, set in strongly fortified walls, ruined doorways and windows with a Venetian look. Above one doorway a coat of arms is carved, suggesting some offshoot of the Duchy of Naxos. Our guide said it had been the island's refuge from attacks by pirates, and he deplored the attitude of the Greek Arts ministry which did nothing to preserve the remaining buildings but refused to allow the local people to restore and make use of them.

As we came down, the children spilled happily out of school behind their serious young mistress, singing a song they had just learnt, to play in the courtyard of a different church. So down the gentle slope of the road again to Psathi harbour and across the channel to lunch off Granny's fresh fish and home-baked bread with goat's cheese.

A full account of Kimolos should record that it has a flourishing export business in *choma*, the hard chalky substance which is quarried around the coast, and in that more old-fashioned product, Fuller's earth. There are also radio-active springs to be found at **Prassa**, a short way north of Psathi. If you are tempted, they can be reached by boat most easily in about fifteen minutes. Of outlying islands, one ought to mention **Poliegos**, if only because its almost uninhabited bulk is the first landfall if you are coming from the east. Away to the west of Milos is **Antimilos**, quite uninhabited by man, but a reserve for a rare variety of chamois, or more likely wild goat.

Finally never let anyone tell you, as one well known authority has written, that Milos (or Kimolos) is a dull place. They are islands of quiet beauty and enduring interest.

Access

Both islands are on the north–south ferry route through the western Kyklades, and have frequent visits at all times of year. They can also be reached from Ios by the only line which connects the eastern with the western Kyklades, but this service is only twice a week.

Communications

The roads in MILOS are good and there is a reasonable bus service. Taxis in Adamas are plentiful and not expensive. There is one short metalled road between KIMOLOS Chora and its harbour at Psathi, but few wheeled vehicles. A small fishing boat ferries passengers between Pollonia in Milos and Psathi, but at awkward times for tourists.

Accommodation

MILOS   Three or four hotels face the water to the left of Adamas harbour as you come in, but the quietest and most agreeable is CORALI (C) on higher ground behind the town. The hotel's own minibus meets the ferries. There are rooms to let in Plaka and in Pollonia during the season.

KIMOLOS   You can find rooms to let in the Chora, but they will be very simple.

Restaurants

MILOS   There is little choice in Adamas, and nothing around the harbour. Although there is a popular open-air restaurant just round the corner, easily the best food is at TRAPETSELIS, a few hundred yards along the coast road leading east.

KIMOLOS   Breakfast or a snack can be had in the Chora. In the evening the inhabitants eat at home.

Facilities

Banks: The only exchange facilities are in Adamas, where there are the usual branches. There is nothing in Kimolos.

Yachts: There should be plenty of room to anchor in Milos bay, but its very size means it can be a stormy place to lie. The eastern side of the big quay at Adamas is kept for yachts, where all facilities are at hand. Otherwise Pollonia would be an attractive base, and the same is true of Psathi on Kimolos, though facilities there are minimal and there is nowhere to eat ashore.

THE EASTERN KYKLADES

THIRTEEN

Paros, Antiparos and Naxos

Whether you come upon them from the north, direct from Piraeus, or you approach from the south through the Sikinos–Ios channel, the dark humps of Paros and Naxos are a distinctive sight. Both are dominated by massifs in the south-east, from which the land slopes away evenly to fertile plains. The mountains of Marpissa on Paros and of Zeus (usually 'Zia' or 'Zas' today) on Naxos are 2500 feet and over 3000 feet high respectively, formidable figures watching over the often stormy sea gate between.

Paros like Naxos is on the 'main line' of ferry services between Piraeus and Santorin, and they are both calling points for ships going farther east by way of Amorgos to the Dodecanese. The capital and port of Paros is **Paroikia**, which lies in a deeply indented bay on the north-western coast. Like Mykonos it is a town by the water, clean and sparkling, with the life that always revolves round boats and engines, nets and sails, arrivals and departures. Unlike the towns of Naxos and Syros it stays by the water instead of climbing to a peak above it, and its buildings are gradually extending round the long low coastline to the north.

There is a lightness and freshness about the whole of Paros, so that while there are no obvious beauty spots in the island, and it is only half the size of Naxos, it attracts more visitors. In high summer Paroikia teems with them, and it seems that every year six new hotels are completed and immediately filled by holiday agencies. Yet the council which controls the tourist industry does so with a firm good taste which should be an example to other islands. They have left a wide open space behind the fishing and small boat harbour which allows plenty of room for the long rows of yellow and dark red nets spread out along the edge, as well as for some of the boats to be pulled up on the hard.

Further on into the bay there is a line of feathery tamarisks between the road and a respectable if sometimes crowded beach. This is where most of the newest hotels have been built, and though some look better than others they all enjoy the general freshness of atmosphere. There are no monstrosities and there is space between them. In the evenings and the early mornings you can still hear the soft pad-pad of a donkey going past – as smooth and sure a method of transport as man has devised for himself – or see an old man sitting by an upturned boat with an ever hopeful rod and line. It is strictly forbidden to camp or sleep out on the beach.

Most tourist activity centres on the cafés and bars near the distinctive windmill on the main quayside, or round a *plateia* planted with trees and formal flowerbeds. Leading off this is the inevitable street flanked by tourist trade shops, but if you dive off to right or left from that you will find some pretty and unspoiled corners. To the right the ground rises to accommodate the remains of a thirteenth-century *kastro* – plundered but not ruined. The lower walls are in good condition and incorporate the drums of columns taken from a nearby classical temple of Demeter. They look like giant cotton reels, tucked in as they are between the rectangular blocks of marble. Beyond the *kastro* there are narrow winding alleys which rise gently to what was the highest point of the ancient acropolis, overlooking the sea front. Here there is an intriguing and delightfully arranged double church with a shallow blue dome, dedicated to the royal saints *Agios Konstantinos* and *Agia Eleni*. A short arcade masks the entrance on the south side, and inside there are some fine early ikons.

In the alleyways below there are several other churches of varying interest and confusing identity. It was on a balcony next to one of these that one Sunday I saw a strange sight. A very thin old woman wearing a conical grey woollen cap was standing with a small figure – perhaps a doll – in her hands. Looking fixedly towards a new restaurant on the far side of the square she was swaying from side to side and crooning audibly. Sensing she was being watched she turned on us a disturbingly evil eye. When we asked a resident casually whether there were still any witches (*magisses*) in Paros the reply was evasive – perhaps there were one or two poor crazy old creatures, but harmless.

A more individually interesting street goes off to the left at the beginning of the main thoroughfare. This is the *Odos Lochagou Graveri*, and it passes the church of the *Panagia Septembriani*, dated 1590, with a carved marble doorway. A few yards further on is a decorative marble fountain of 1770, and on the right are some handsome nineteenth-century houses with large gardens. It is good to see that some of the old wooden balconies in the side streets are being rebuilt in wood instead of the usual concrete.

The informed or well guided tourist will most of all want to see the finest, or at least the most famous, church in the Kyklades – outside Tinos that is, where the Panagia Evangelistria is famous for other than architectural reasons. Here we have the cathedral of the *Panagia Ekatontapiliani*, a title which seems to mean 'Our Lady of a Hundred Doors', though it is more likely to be a corruption of *Katapoliani*, meaning simply 'in the town below'. The legend says that while ninety-nine doors have been discovered (but where?) the hundredth will not be found till the Turks return Constantinople to the Christians. Another legend has it that the Empress Helena, widowed mother of Constantine the Great, having taken shelter in Paros from a storm, had a vision of finding the True Cross and vowed to build a great church on this site.

There is some uncertainty about what happened next, and when. Some say that the main church was not built till the reign of Justinian I, by a pupil of the architect of Santa Sophia, an account embellished by a tale of the jealous master quarrelling with his pupil and of them both falling to their death from the roof. This would put the date early in the sixth century, a good two hundred years later than Helena's visit. Whoever built it, it was severely damaged by an earthquake and rebuilt in the tenth century, which makes dating difficult. The same is true of the rather charming baptistry, which has an authentic cruciform basin, and a separate entrance on the south side of the church.

However, built into the north side, beyond the *templo* and apse, is the much earlier basilica church of *Agios Nikolaos*, with a double row of Doric columns and some classical-looking entablature. This may narrow the gap between Constantine and Justinian, but there

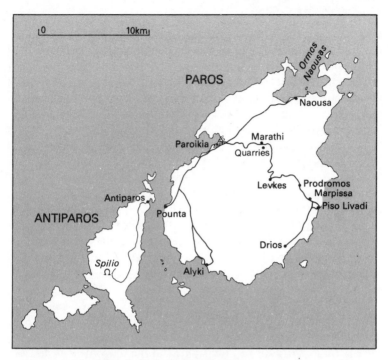

was a very significant find during the most recent restoration – a tesselated pavement of about AD 300. The subject was the labours of Hercules, so it was a reasonable guess that they had found the atrium of a private villa. A nice fancy would be that Helena was entertained here by the owner.

Later history is clearer. Under the Duchy of Naxos the Byzantine church was eventually altered to Venetian baroque, and the marble *templo* was built in 1911. An earthquake in 1773 during the Turkish occupation left it more or less derelict, and when a thorough restoration was undertaken in the 1960s it was very much overdue. The plan was to restore as far as possible the Byzantine character of the church, and although it was carried out a little harshly one feels that a great deal of the early atmosphere has been regained. Simple and dignified, the cool grey stone interior is welcome in the summer heat, and if left undisturbed in the ancient basilica of St Nicholas for half an hour you are enfolded in great peace. It is a place for visions.

207

There is an annual pilgrimage to the cathedral on 15 August, yet despite its greater antiquity, beauty and interest the 'Katapoliani' has nothing like the same appeal in the Orthodox church as the 'Evangelistria' on Tinos.

The courtyard to the west of the church has an upper gallery for the former monastic cells. One of these was converted to a small museum of Byzantine art, but the door seems to be permanently locked. Down below informality reigns: there is a spreading pine tree with a tangle of bell-ropes caught up in its branches, and wayward patches of bright flowers. The real **Archaeological Museum** is not far away, beyond the large High School playing ground. It has an excellent and well displayed collection of sculpture and the notable Roman mosaic of the Labours of Hercules.

The temple of Demeter, from which so much marble was plundered, has been confidently located on the top of the acropolis, where the church of Constantine and Helena now stands. So perhaps it was an earlier sanctuary which figured in a strange episode recorded by Herodotus.* He tells us that Miltiades son of Cimon, one of the heroes of the Athenian victory at Marathon in 490 BC, afterwards organized a punitive expedition against Paros for having contributed a trireme to the Persian fleet. His real motives were perhaps more for personal gain, but the outcome was disastrous.

The Parians played at first for time, and succeeded in strengthening their walls, which enclosed the acropolis and much of the modern town of Paroikia. Miltiades was held at bay for twenty-six days, and then one night he paid a visit to the sanctuary of Demeter which (according to Herodotus) lay outside the walls, having been enticed there by an under-priestess who had promised to show him a way through the defences. A likely story, we may think, but on finding himself inside the sacred precinct where the mysteries were displayed he took fright and managed to break his thigh while escaping over the outer wall. He was carried back ignominiously to his ship and abandoned the siege. The Athenians, who never appreciated failure (especially by members of the arrogant Alcmaeonid family), imprisoned him and imposed a fine of fifty talents for dereliction of

* *Histories* VI, 134–6.

duty, but the leg went gangrenous and Miltiades died before he could pay the fine.

There are two classical sites near the coast just south of Paroikia, an Asklepeion and a temple of Pythian Apollo. Local tradition puts the Miltiades episode near to the former, on a hill now called after St Anne the mother of Mary – is there a connection with Demeter perhaps? In any case there is practically nothing to see at either of these sites.

Inland, while Naxos has a more varied grandeur of mountain scenery, and a romantic beauty in its valleys, Paros is more of a classical unity. Its central mass has a sculptured quality suitable for the island which produced Parian marble – that lovely white grainy translucent stone in which Praxiteles worked, and which was used for tiles to let in light from above to the temples of fifth-century Athens. It would have been used too by the sculptor Skopas, a contemporary of Praxiteles who was born in Paros about 400 BC. He had a wide reputation as both sculptor and architect, and he was employed on the 'Mausoleum' of Halicarnassus (one of the seven wonders of the world) built by the Carian queen Artemisia in memory of her husband Mausolus – hence the use of the word today as a common noun. Another well known artist born in Paros was the satiric poet Archilochus, who later emigrated to Thasos with a party of colonists in the seventh century BC.

The Kyklades, unlike the mainland, were never overrun by northern barbarians during the 'dark ages' of the tenth and ninth centuries. Instead they were able to develop undisturbed the Ionian culture which gave us Homer and later generations of great artists, and Paros had its share. This is illustrated by the 'Parian Chronicle', discovered in the early seventeenth century by the chaplain to the Earl of Arundel. It consists of ninety-three lines cut in a block of Parian marble which give an outline of Greek history from the sixteenth to the third century BC. Whoever was the author, he showed a proper disrespect for the achievements of politicians and soldiers, most of the recorded events being the births and deaths of poets, the dates of festivals and when different kinds of poetry were introduced. 'Important political and military events,' says one commentator rather sadly, 'are often omitted' – a pleasant change from the custom of later chroniclers. A small part of the Chronicle can be seen in the Archaeological Museum here, but the major part is in the Ashmolean Museum in Oxford.

The quarries are easily found today on the slopes of Mount Prophitis Ilias, the northern extension of Mount Marpissa. They lie to the south of the main road from Paroikia to the east coast, only a few hundred yards from the bus stop in the village of **Marathi**. In the nineteenth century quite a settlement grew up on the spot while the French were working the quarries to provide marble for Napoleon's tomb. Their ruined headquarters building has an unusual elegance for the context, but what is surprising is that the quarries – there are three entrances – are totally underground.

The marble was hacked away in the bowels of the mountain and brought to the surface originally by slave labour and primitive tackles. In the nineteenth century they used mechanical winches, and a mule-drawn tramway to take the blocks down to the harbour. So extensive are the workings that they say it takes three hours to reach the farthest point. There is marble around still, but of a lower quality than those precious seams of *lychnites*, as it was called. When Theodore Bent visited the quarries in the 1880s he was told there was still a vein of it extending a hundred and fifty metres into the mountain, but to go on working it must have become un-economic when ordinary marble could be won so much more easily from quarries on Naxos and Thasos.

The road past the quarries continues round the mountain slopes to **Leukes**, a good clean hill village with nice little alleys and flowery gardens. The big church in its present form dates from 1835, but there are some earlier panels on the *templo*, including two views of Adam and Eve – first naked, then sketchily clothed and clearly under notice to quit. A few miles further on is **Prodromos**, a more unusual place. It was originally a walled village which gave protec-tion against the pirates who infested the coast in the seventeenth century, and the only entrance is still through a gateway between the blank walls of two churches. There is an almost mediaeval atmosphere about it, with empty lanes and introspective houses. The church which gives the village its name is *Agios Ioannis Pro-dromos* (St John the Baptist), dated 1690 and typical of the period.

The road bypasses Marpissa, a village of no great interest, and continues to the coast at **Piso Livadi**. This small fishing village has been extended southwards round the fringe of a sandy bay, with a good deal of modern building which includes restaurants and a few hotels – not a bad place for a holiday. Another favourite place is **Naousa**, which is also served by buses from Paroikia. It has the most distinctive of fishing harbours, backed by a very attractive town, and ships passing along the north coast of Paros have a good view of it on the far side of a very extensive bay. The actual harbour is tiny, but somehow the colourful fishing fleet finds room not only for its boats but for the patient unravelling and mending of nets on the quay. There are good beaches in either direction as well as across on the far side of the bay. Naousa harbour is a convenient starting point for day excursions by small boat to Delos and Mykonos, which cuts out the long run up the coast from Paroikia.

All these villages are included in a 'round-the-island' bus tour starting in Paroikia. However it does not at present go farther down the east coast than **Drios**, which is a recently developed seaside village with holiday accommodation. It was off Cape Drio that the Turkish Kapitan Pasha used to anchor to receive the annual tribute of the islands. This was almost the only outside interference with their life during the occupation, though the Russian fleet under Admiral Orloff spent the winter of 1770–71 in Paros. Catherine the Great had taken advantage of her war with Turkey to try to recapture the Aegean for the west, and for five years Orloff's fleet, with the assistance of his squadron commander Antonis Psaros of Mykonos, virtually controlled the Kyklades. The peace concluded in 1775 put an end to the venture.

Drios lies at the foot of a fertile valley, and to reach the sea you walk through green gardens with all kinds of vegetables and flowers. This corner of Paros is good farming land, much of it arable, and when all the roads shown on the map come true there will be a pleasant circuit round through **Alyki**, another new holiday village, and back into Paroikia from the south.

A journey like this, through cornfields, orchards, market gardens and vineyards, explains why the fruit and vegetable stores in the town are so well stocked – hardly anything is imported. Some local wine is produced, but the dark red (*mavro*) which used to be offered by the carafe has disappeared from the restaurants, and even the Paros *retsina* is hard to find. They say the small producers can no longer compete for price with the big imported names in this market, and what they make they drink themselves – lucky people.

Paros is flanked by a sister islet, **Antiparos**, which has a celebrated cave. It has more than that to offer, though, in particular a simple fishing harbour with berths for small yachts, and a sequence of lovely sandy beaches for a mile or more to the south. Behind the beaches are reed beds and swampy pools, not good for campers but thronged with small birds of many species. The harbour is easily reached by taking a bus to **Pounta**, which connects with frequent small boat crossings of the mile-wide strait, and there are excursions direct from Paroikia harbour which include a visit to the cave.

This cave is not a coastal grotto, but goes deep into a rocky hillside about four miles south of Antiparos harbour and a mile in from the coast. The entrance is framed by huge stalactites, dwarfing the little church of *Agios Ioannis Theologos* which stands just inside. Beyond it you descend into a series of connecting caverns decorated by both stalactites and stalagmites. There is a theory that if you insert a goat into one of the many crannies in the caverns it will turn up two hours later at the church of the Taxiarch Michael on the far side of the hill.

Finally you reach an enormous cathedral-like chamber with stalactites hanging like chandeliers from a roof so high as to be almost invisible. There was an extraordinary scene here at Christmas 1673, when an eccentric French nobleman, who was at the time Ambassador to the Sublime Porte, persuaded a congregation of five hundred to attend a midnight mass inside it. This must have been an eerie occasion, even when lit by hundreds of wax torches and oil lamps. Today the natural gloom and mystery has been dissipated by electric light and a prosaic sequence of concrete steps.

Although the opposite coasts of Paros and Naxos are only six miles apart, it always seems a long way by sea from Paroikia to the harbour of **Naxos**. When you get there it is a very different scene. The harbour is as big if not bigger, and the waterfront is wide and deep, but the town is closely concentrated around the steep hill behind it which culminates in a mediaeval castle – the castle which was the headquarters of the central power in the Aegean for over three hundred years, and contained the palace of its rulers. As so much of the islands' history depended on the fact, it is worth reiterating how it came about.

After the fall of Constantinople in 1204 to the armies of the Fourth Crusade, backed by Venice, the Byzantine Empire was divided among its conquerors. Most of the Greek islands, including the Kyklades, were awarded by treaty to Venice. Venice however preferred to leave their occupation to private citizens of the Republic, and the first man to take advantage of this was Marco Sanudo, a nephew of the Venetian Doge Dandolo, who had successfully diverted the crusaders to attack Constantinople. This enterprising character equipped eight galleys at his own expense and set out for the Aegean to annex as many islands as he could. Here is William Miller's account of the establishment of the Duchy of Naxos:

'Seventeen islands speedily submitted, and at one point alone did Sanudo meet with any real resistance. Naxos has always been the pearl of the Aegean: poets placed there the beautiful myth of Ariadne and Dionysus; Herodotus describes it as "excelling the other islands in prosperity"; even today, when so many of the Cyclades are barren rocks, the orange and lemon groves of Naxos entitle it, even more than Zante, to the proud name of "flower of the Levant". This was the island which now opposed the Venetian filibuster, as centuries before it had opposed the Persians. A body of Genoese pirates had occupied the Byzantine castle before Sanudo's arrival, but that shrewd leader, who knew the value of rashness in an emergency, burnt his galleys, and then bade his companions conquer or die. The castle surrendered after a five weeks' siege, so that by 1207 Sanudo and his comrades had conquered a duchy, which lasted between three and four centuries. His duchy included, besides Naxos, where he fixed his capital, the famous marble island of Paros; Antiparos, with its curious grotto; Kimolos, celebrated for its fuller's earth; Melos, whose sad fortunes had furnished Thucydides with one of the most curious passages in his history; Amorgos, the home of Simonides; Ios, or Nio, the supposed tomb of Homer; Kythnos, Sikinos and Siphnos; and Syra, destined at a much later date to be the most important of all the Cyclades.'

* *op. cit.*, pp 43–4.

What a catalogue of islands, with their characters in a nutshell!

The Byzantine castle was at **Apalyri**, in the central and southern part of the island. The town, harbour, castle and even the Catholic cathedral we see as we arrive were all founded by Marco Sanudo I. The Sanudi remained nominal masters of the Archipelago (although other Italian families occupied and built their castles on many different islands) until 1383, when the last and worst of the line was murdered. Francesco Crispo, who had married into the Sanudo family, founded a new dynasty which had a closer association with Venice, and a hundred years later, under constant attack by Turkish corsairs which almost depopulated the islands, the people of Naxos invited Venice to take over the Duchy. In 1500 the senate re-established the descendants of the Crispi for a time, but in 1536 Giovanni IV surrendered Naxos to a Turkish force of overwhelming strength. From then on the Dukes were merely vassals of the Sultan. In 1564 the last of the Crispi was ousted by his own people, who had come to prefer Turkish rule to a dissipated Italian tyrant, and in 1580 the islands were formally annexed to the Ottoman Empire.

In the upper part of the **Chora** of Naxos you can see traces of the Dukes and their noble retainers inside the castle walls – of which only two gateways, a tower and a few short lengths remain. You will come across coats of arms on a few house fronts, a range of buildings which remind you of Venice, and the Catholic cathedral has rows of tombstones with the names and titles of the Italian nobility (and pseudo-nobility) who worshipped there. They include two members of the Barozzi family, principally known as lords of Santorin, and the earliest is dated 1619. Outside, this is a typical neo-Byzantine building, but the inside is simpler and more interesting. The nave and the two side aisles are divided by low, squat pillars, two of them carrying their original capitals. Above the altar is a fifteenth-century ikon of the Madonna, with unusually severe features, but the joy of the place is the seventeenth-century *Notre Dame du Rosaire* in the southern side chapel, a delicate composition which shows the virgin enclosed in the expanded trunk of a rose tree – the lower branches bare and thorny, but springing to life in the upper half in an exquisite design of rose buds and peacock feathers.

The Cathedral is usually locked, but if you ask persistently round

214

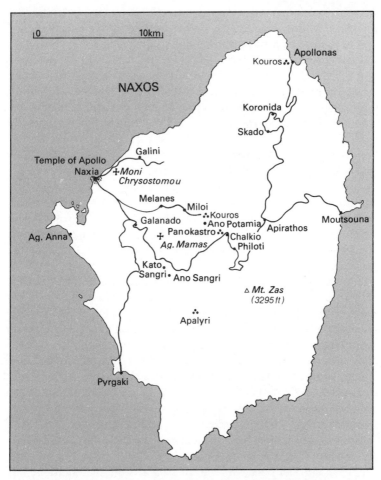

about you should be able to find either the priest in charge or the lady in a nearby street who has a key. The trouble is that the Kastro area is a lifeless place: the Museum is poorly housed and unhelpfully manned (never open on Tuesdays), and the former French Ursuline Convent appears deserted and impenetrable.

The town below is far more lively, and thoroughly Greek in character, with bewildering alleys, sudden corners and baffling culs-de-sac. Even along the harbour front, where it looks as if the

215

foreign tourist has taken over, you will find as many traditional shops as you will supermarkets and trinket stores. You can still see in one corner of a busy restaurant the revolving *kokkoretsi*, spits twined with sheep and goats' guts and stuffed with herb-flavoured pork. In a street behind, next to a depressing modern *pizzeria*, there will be a real Greek butcher's shop with its round wooden block scored with the marks of the cleaver. You can still buy from the general stores or the wine shops the special Naxian liqueur, *kitron*, a miraculous distillation of lemons and sugar.

When evening comes and the sun is setting across the harbour, all traffic is barred and the families of **Naxia** (the traditional name for the capital) begin their slow *volta* along the wide front where an hour before heavy trucks were crashing their way to the commercial quays. Later the restaurant tables along the waterside will fill with as many Greeks as tourists. Naxia harbour can be noisy, dusty and even smelly, but it is real and has not yet surrendered to the barbarians.

One quickly recognizable feature of Naxos is the marble doorway of the **Temple of Apollo**, which stands on the islet of Palatia at the north end of the harbour, framing a blue rectangle of sky between its huge white pillars. Once this was thought to be a temple of Dionysus, connected with the mythical story of Ariadne deserted by Theseus, and the projecting point of the islet is still called Cape Bacchus on the map. In fact this temple was a late fifth-century construction which never got further than the foundations and the doorway we see today. Work stopped when Naxos went to war with Samos and lost – and it was never restarted. The beautiful myth of Dionysus and Ariadne belongs to a more suitable part of the island, a romantic valley far away to the north.

The Kastro of Naxos was a Latin and Catholic creation. The centre of Greek life was the northern quarter known as **Bourgos**, on the far side of Cape Bacchus. Here is the nineteenth-century Metropolitan Cathedral, and the older *Panagia Chrysopolitissa* with an exceptionally long nave. It is a bright and lively, if chronically untidy place. The coastline beyond rises to a series of rocky cliffs with fine views northward to Delos and Mykonos. The name **Grotta** applies not only to traces of Mycenaean buildings found submerged beneath the cliffs, but to a new hotel which enjoys this splendid situation.

If you take the road leading from this quarter towards Galini, soon after leaving the town you will see above you on the right the whitewashed walls of the **Moni Chrysostomou** wedged high up between jagged outcrops of rock. This is an eighteenth-century convent which is not normally open to tourists, but if you can persuade someone of influence in Naxos to write a letter of introduction it is worth climbing the zig-zag track up to it. You will probably be challenged by a loquacious shepherd who acts as scout and guardian, and you may have to wait till the duty nun has finished milking the goats.

The *katholikon* church is dated 1756, with a barrel-vaulted nave – stuccoed, but curiously painted to imitate black marble veined with white. The *templo* in carved wood looks older, probably seventeenth century, with an ikon of Agios Chrysostomos sheathed in silver. It is all very peaceful, with a wonderful view down over Naxia and across to Paros. Into the head come words from that wonderful prayer of St Chrysostom: 'and dost promise that when two or three are gathered together in thy name thou wilt grant their requests'. There are five nuns in residence, and they keep the premises beautifully, bright with flowers and spotless stone paving.

The long western coast of Naxos offers a choice of some enticing sandy beaches, some reached directly by bus, like that at Agia Anna, others like Kastraki after a short walk from the main road, which ends in the south-facing bay of **Pyrgaki**. Right at the end is a big holiday hotel complex, but so wide and long is the seashore that there is room for all. Not only that, you can have a true Greek meal with a carafe or can of Naxos wine at a little family restaurant beside the road a mile before the hotel – they are never short of fish.

The heart of the island is the great mountain of **Zas** (a variant of Zeus) and the glorious valleys which surround it. There is no scenery to equal it in the Aegean north of Crete, and no one can claim to know Naxos without exploring it. Fortunately some of the most splendid prospects and interesting places are accessible from the modern highway, which penetrates high into the central mountains before dropping through a spectacular valley to the northern sea. Cars are easy to hire, but there may be no need for this expense, as during the summer organized coach tours are laid on by one of the travel agencies on the front of the harbour. They follow this route all the way to the seaside village of Apollonas and back.

217

The road we take leaves the coastal road to Pyrgaki just before the village of Galanado, and soon it passes close to a typical example of a Naxian 'Venetian' tower, known as the *Pyrgos Mpelonia*. You will find these foursquare crenellated buildings all over Naxos, and they were nearly all built during the seventeenth century, well after the Turkish conquest. A mile further on, to the left of the road and below it, is the historic church of **Agios Mamas**. No one knows how early it was built, but in the ninth century it was the centre of the Orthodox bishopric. A lovely little building in plain grey stone on the Greek Cross plan, it has the most beautiful situation at the foot of the Potamies valley.

Next on the right come the two villages of Kato and Ano Zangri, the former with another 'Venetian' tower, the latter with the monastery church of *Agios Elevtherias* – and beyond that was found a classical temple to Demeter, said to have been a model for the Parthenon. As the road turns north-east you see the sixteenth-century *Moni Timiou Stavrou* (the convent of the Holy Cross). It looks like just another *pyrgos* from outside, but it has been an active community teaching centre and school – now maintained by only one or two nuns.

After the village of Vourvouria you can see on a peak away to your left the ruined fortress of *Pano Kastro*, a genuine Venetian stronghold built by Marco Sanudo II in the mid-thirteenth century; then you come to the small town of **Chalkio**, or Halki. This contains the very early and very lovely church of the *Panagia Protothrono* (Our Lady of the Highest Majesty). The oldest part is the sixth-century apse, with unusual arched openings into side chapels and concentric steps rising to a *kathedra*. The rest of the church is of the eleventh to thirteenth centuries, originally a Greek Cross but later extended westward with a second cupola above the nave. There are a few early frescos, the most remarkable being an extraordinary scene of the forty martyrs of Albania going to their death by immersion in an ice-cold lake. Their pallid flesh seems actually to be shivering at the prospect. The earliest ikons of Christ and the Panagia – said to have been retrieved from the sea after the ikono-klasts had thrown them out – are covered, all but their faces, in local beaten silver. There is another 'Venetian' *pyrgos* which overlooks the church, and away to the north you can see the white scars made by the marble quarry workings on the slopes of Korakia.

The road now enters a fertile basin, planted with ancient olives and ringed by high mountains, before reaching **Philoti**, a busy small town with a decorative eighteenth-century church. Here begins the most spectacular part of the journey, as the road loops to the south and back again to the north beneath the huge peak of Zas. This is one of the many reputed birthplaces of Zeus, but one feels it would have been a softer nurse than Cretan Ida.

The country becomes more and more spectacular, though still green and beautiful below the heights. The sea seems a very long way away. Before the next village, Apirathos, you pass the isolated church of *Agios Ioannis Theologos*, perched dramatically on a conical peak to the right. It still has its annual festival in May, when a big procession climbs the many hundred feet of bare rock to the top.

Apirathos is the most beautiful village in Naxos. The clean narrow streets are actually paved in marble, and bordered by many old balconied houses of plain un-whitewashed stone, some with marble doorways. There is another 'Venetian' tower and a small carefully arranged museum. Apirathos owes its distinguished architecture to the Crispi Dukes, who rebuilt it in the late fourteenth century on an ancient site. More recently it was famous for its music and musicians. The violinist Manolis was known as the best exponent of popular music in all Greece, and an old recording of his has been reissued on cassette – he plays the old music with great verve and flourish.

Further north the scenery changes quickly to a bare and uncompromising mountain ridge. The underlying rock is volcanic, and it is the only place in Greece where emery is still mined. You can see the scars on the hillside, and piles of the shiny dark chippings waiting to be transported by lorry, or by the overhead conveyor line which connects with the little harbour of Moutsouna on the east coast. The main export market is Germany, where emery is used as an abrasive in heavy manufacturing, and most recently is being tried out as an anti-skid surface for motorways – which could be a growth industry. The workmen live in the villages of Koronas and Skado, plainer and poorer than any we have passed so far.

At **Koronida** everything changes again. This is a very pretty village, at the head of a deep and beautiful valley which falls steeply down to the sea at Apollonas. Before the real descent begins you see on your right two churches side by side on a small bluff. One is very early Byzantine in plain stone, tragically allowed to decay until a dull modern one was built in 1965, to which all the ancient ikons were transferred.

Now we are in the real Dionysus country. Vineyards are every-where, some properly cultivated, others with the vines straggling voluptuously and untended over steep terraces. High in the upper slopes of the valley is the cave – where else could it be? – where the god lived with Ariadne and where she bore him two sons. The tale has many variations, but it begins with Ariadne assisting Theseus first to kill the Minotaur in the labyrinth of Knossos and then to escape with the party of Athenian youths he had rescued by this deed. On reaching Naxos, Theseus abandoned Ariadne and sailed on to Athens, and her vocal recriminations have been the subject of musical extravaganzas from Haydn to Richard Strauss.

Dionysus (or Bacchus, God of Wine) now enters the story. While Ariadne slept, a shipload of pirates with Dionysus as their prisoner was nearing Naxos. Ignorant of their prisoner's divinity they were intending to sell him as a slave. But the god made a vine grow up from the deck, while ivy twined round the rigging, the oars became serpents and he himself was transformed into a lion. The pirates immediately jumped overboard, leaving the ship to Dionysus, restored to his normal graceful form, and to a phantom crew. The ship came on steadily over the water towards Naxos, while the air was filled with the sound of flutes. Stepping ashore on the island, the first person Dionysus saw was the sleeping Ariadne. The starry crown which Dionysus brought her as a wedding gift he later hung in the heavens, where it gleams for all to see – the *Corona Borealis*. Titian and Tintoretto both painted marvellous evocations of their meeting, with suggestions of a Naxian landscape in the background.

Where they first met can be argued about, but I like to think this lovely vine-wreathed valley was their home. The road clings dizzily to the right hand side – you can see the ribbon unfolding hundreds of feet below on its way down to the sea. Just before it reaches Apollonas there is a track to the left which in five minutes leads to something extraordinary. Out of an immense solid block of marble has been roughly carved the figure of a bearded giant, lying almost horizontal, ten metres long and weighing about thirty tons. Reversing the attributions of the temple on Cape Bacchus, this **Kouros**, as the archaeologists call it, was once thought to be Apollo but now is recognized as Dionysus. The carving of it was abandoned when the block of marble was found to be faulty, with seams which let in the weather. This is an archaic work, probably of the seventh century BC, but the slightly raised or forward position of one leg shows an early shift towards a more natural pose for sculptured figures.

Apollonas is a delightful fishing village with a sandy beach spreading round the head of a small bay. As a harbour it is exposed to northerly winds, and as a beauty spot it grows yearly more exposed to the tourist trade. Nevertheless it can still be a good place to stay. The best restaurant is under the trees to the right of the harbour – the more showy ones opposite prove less attractive when you get there.

This journey will not exhaust the attractions of inland Naxos, but there are only a few other short lengths of drivable road, and the distances are too great for other kinds of travel. If possible, you ought not to forgo an expedition to find the other **Kouros** of Naxos, better finished and more handsome than the one at Apollonas. A reliable car and map are needed, though there are signs pointing the way from the neighbourhood of a group of villages – Melanes, Kourounochori and Miloi – in the mountains east of the town. A new road is being built in that direction, but the final stages will still be rough. The site of the Kouros is marked on the map just east of Miloi; you will find him in a beautiful secret valley tucked in below the crag of Korakia. The final approach (after leaving your car in a safe place) is by a footpath through a glade of cypress, plane, olive and lemon trees. At the end of the path is a little stone hut in a flowery garden, set with tables and chairs where you can refresh yourself with necessary drink and simple food. The owners of this Garden of Eden are a couple who also own the land around, and they themselves dug out this *kouros* from a mass of rock and earth in 1945. By Greek law they own him, and he cannot be removed without their consent.

He lies in a quiet corner of the garden, a horizontal figure of Dionysus, complete but for the final process of raising him to stand upright. The head and body are finely modelled, the left leg

221

advanced, the right leg sadly broken below the knee. The hostess treats him as a favourite son, stroking his hair (dressed in the archaic mode) and pointing to his accurately placed *omphalos*. She will then make you a salad and cook you an omelette, if you wish.

While up in these hills you may like to visit the trio of villages, Mesi, Ano and Kato Potamia, at the head of the long fertile valley which descends to the coastal plain. The biggest of the three is **Ano Potamia**, a cool shady place with winding lanes between old houses. A handsome late Byzantine church is being restored here, and there is an accommodating café-restaurant opposite. Beware, however, of taking the road on further, which is signposted optimistically to Chalkio. Much of the surface is still bare rock, and you would be better to return direct to Naxia by the shorter route.

There are still more castles, towers, monasteries and two or three classical temples to be traced by the adventurous traveller. Naxians have a great pride in their history, and it would not be difficult to find someone to direct you to most of them. Wine is still made in quantity throughout the island, and sold either in bottles or from the wood (*bareli*). The best is from the *bareli*, white and unresinated with a slight golden tinge; it has a flowery essence and considerable strength. The wine of Naxos was in demand by connoisseurs in the seventeenth century, as Randolph tells us: 'A French merchant brought 5000 Barrels of wine, while I was there, which cost him but half a dollar per Barrel, which is about half a crown English for 15 Gallons of good wine.'

Apollo, Dionysus and Demeter are the divine patrons of Naxos, and they bring it the gifts of sun, wine and fertile earth, which have easily survived the Venetian Dukes and Turkish Pashas.

Access

Both islands are on several main ferry lines, and ships call frequently every day. There is a small airstrip on PAROS, but no regular air services.

Communications

Both islands have a good road system and regular bus services. 'Round the island' bus tours are organized by local travel agencies, and are good value. Taxis are freely available, cars and mopeds for hire. There are short sea crossings to Antiparos from Paroikia and Pounta on Paros. Day excursions by small boat to Delos and Mykonos.

Accommodation

PAROS   There are many hotels in Paroikia, especially beyond the harbour to the north. The best of these is PAROS (C), beautifully kept and run by a long-established island family. XENIA (B) has a good position but a poor restaurant. Most of the others have been built hurriedly for the tourist trade in the last few years. There are hotels, apartments and rooms to let in Naousa, Piso Livadi, Dryos and Alyki.

NAXOS   There are several C class hotels near the harbour, most of them noisy because of harbour traffic. Those on the outskirts are quieter, especially GROTTA (C) on the cliffs north of the harbour. In the harbour area the best small hotel is HERMES (C), discreetly run by a French-speaking lady of good family. There is a large holiday hotel complex at Pyrgaki in the south of the island, and rooms available at most holiday resorts.

Restaurants

PAROS   Two interesting restaurants in Paroikia are NISIOTISSA and ALIGARI. The others tend to be brash and noisy, especially on the waterfront south of the harbour. You can eat well at Piso Livadi, but Naousa is disappointing in this respect.

NAXOS   In the mass of pizzerias and 'fast food' establishments by the harbour, one restaurant is outstandingly good, APOLAVSIS, with a first floor balcony overlooking the harbour and the sunset; cooking and service are first-rate. Elsewhere in the island you can find good food in some of the villages inland, and at Apollonas in the far north.

Facilities

Banks: Branches of all Greek banks in Paroikia and Naxos town.

Yachts: Paroikia and Naxos harbours are well equipped in every respect. At Naousa a new yacht quay has been built alongside the cramped fishing harbour; the bay is exposed to the north and not a reliable anchorage. The little harbour of Antiparos can be crowded, but in good weather is a pleasant place to lie.

FOURTEEN

Amorgos, Irakleia, Schinoussa, Kouphonisi and Donoussa

Amorgos is one of the least visited of the larger Kyklades, lying as it does on their south-eastern fringes and with a great deal of open sea between it and the nearest of the Dodecanese. Yet it forms a short-sided and almost equilateral triangle with Naxos and Ios, both much busier islands. For communication it turns mainly to Naxos, having two harbours facing that way on the north-west coast. The principal one is at **Katapola**, where a small town has grown up on both sides of the bay – a very lovely bay, deeply indented, with steep headlands enclosing the entrance. The harbour front is one of the most natural and unspoilt in the Kyklades, and the same is true of the people – mostly fishermen and farmers – who live and work around it.

In times past it was the women of Amorgos who were famous for their beauty. Today they are warm and friendly, but the young men are more physically striking. Tall, with the typical straight back to the dark Greek head, they make one wonder whether this was not the type of *Kouros* realized in so many classical statues. That the ancient Greek was generally fair-haired could be a misconception based on the romantic ideas of the nineteenth century and perhaps fostered by German scholars. If you do meet light-haired islanders you could probably trace their ancestry to a much less distant past.

It might have been the women of Amorgos who gave rise to the only notable poem we have by Semonides, an iambic satirist who came from Samos to live in Amorgos in the seventh century BC. He likens at some length the wayward characteristics of women he knew to those of different species of animal. This can be unflattering,

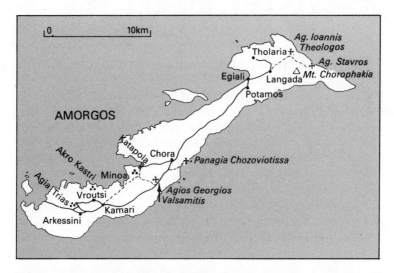

but he makes amends by concluding that the best kind of woman is like the queen bee:

> 'She makes life fertile and prosperous;
> bearing a noble and illustrious stock
> she reaches age in the love of a dear spouse.
> She grows in good repute among all women,
> and is invested with a heavenly grace.'*

Beekeepers may not recognize this portrait, but we hope that Semonides found one such in Amorgos – they are still there to find.

The finest scenery is in the far north, where the sheer magnificence of the precipitous cliffs takes the breath away if you sail close under them. Near Katapola the country is friendly rather than spectacular, though our old friend Mount Prophitis Ilias is stern and bare. On his flank is the earlier capital, or **Chora**, which you can reach by car or an occasional bus from Katapola – it is the only metalled road in the island. Failing a bus or a lift (there are no taxis) the walk is not severe. It takes little more than an hour and is well worth doing. Amorgos Chora has kept the remoteness and peace

---

* trans. Gilbert Highet. The author is not to be confused with Simonides of Kea, who wrote the famous epitaph on the Spartan dead at Thermopylae.

which is now lost to its equivalent in Ios. The streets are not steep, but they wind even more idiosyncratically round unexpected corners and up and down short flights of steps. It is easy but never distressing to lose your way. There are graceful white churches and two quite spacious *platéias* planted with cool rustling trees.

Off one *plateia* lives an unusual kind of artist, whose speciality is cutting out and painting the flat wooden figures associated with the Karaghiozi shadow plays. Karaghiozi is the Rabelaisian champion of the 'little man' involved in a series of brief triumphs and awful disasters as he pits his wits against a standard cast of typical Levantine characters. This satirical sequence probably originated in Asia Minor or elsewhere in the Levant, and reached the islands during the Turkish occupation – but Greek audiences took it to their hearts. Some features remind us of English mummers and Punch and Judy shows. Like Punch, Karaghiozi has a beaky nose and a humped back; like St George, Alexander the Great comes on to kill the dragon. Presentation is different, though, with the puppets manipulated behind a screen lit from the back. The best account of a full-dress performance is given by Lawrence Durrell, who was lucky enough to see one in Corfu in 1938.* We had thought they were extinct – there are only memories of them in Ios – but Kostas Ierakis of Amorgos still puts on shows in the summer and even travels with them to Athens. He sells his puppet figures to visitors from all over the world.

From the Chora a path leads out past a couple of ruined windmills and down in a steep zig-zag almost to the sea. To the left is a sheer cliff face of unscaleable rock, with just one narrow ledge half way down. On this ledge is stuck – the only word – the monastery of the **Panagia Chozoviotissa**, like a white cubist limpet fixed on the dark brown rock. A short traverse from the bottom of the path leads to the entrance, and visitors (provided they are decorously dressed and arrive before noon) are shown round the monastery.

This remarkable place was founded in the eleventh century, probably by Alexis Comnenus I of Byzantium. The chapel contains the holy ikon of the Panagia which reached Amorgos from Cyprus in one of those mysterious boats which seem to have been con-

* *Prospero's Cell* (Faber, 1945).

stantly errant on the face of the Mediterranean in the Middle Ages. The refectory is a touching survival, for the bare room has a long wooden table capable of seating at least thirty monks. Today there are only four, and how lost they must feel. If the inside is fascinating, the view from the upper terrace is blinding – bright blue sky, dazzling white walls and a sheer drop to the sea below. Further along the ledge the monks cultivate a herb garden and keep chickens. Where better to live a life of contemplation, as the senior brother has done here for fifty years?

Another short expedition from Katapola involves climbing the hill which overlooks the harbour from the south. A clearly marked path, stone-stepped in its early stages, leads up from the harbour to the site of an ancient settlement known as **Minoa** – a name which is bound to arouse interest. Nothing you see now can be identified as Minoan or even Mycenaean, and the solid masonry of the ruined walls is probably no older than Hellenistic. Even so, the foundations have been traced of a gymnasium (identified by a boy's footprint traced on the rock), a stadium and a small temple. Apollo was thought to be the likely dedicatee of the temple, but when they discovered the draped marble torso which is now set up there it seemed more likely to belong to a goddess, perhaps Athena. French archaeologists began to excavate in 1888, and in recent years they have come back regularly to reveal more and more of this intriguing town – for whatever its origin it was never less than a town in size.

The track which passes Minoa continues along the cliffs past the hamlets of Levkes and Thekla, then descends to the head of the deep bay of Agii Saranda. You are now on the old 'main road' which connected Katapola with the southern part of the island, known as Kato Meria. It is hardly a road in the modern sense, but a wide donkey track with the steeper sections built up in stone-lined steps. If you enjoy a strenuous walk, this is the way to reach Arkessini, one of the three early cities of Amorgos – the others being Minoa in the centre and Aegiale away to the north. There are several other villages in the area, and some ancient sites worth exploring.

Your track eventually joins a regular road between the villages of Kamari and Vroutsi – and if you need restoring after the walk there is a good little restaurant near the junction. There is nothing much to see in Vroutsi, though you would be a welcome curiosity in either of two small *kapheneia*. Theodore Bent came this way in the 1880s, and he quotes a local proverb which says 'Whoso goeth to Vroutsi and does not get drunk is like a pilgrim who goeth to the Holy Sepulchre and doth not worship'. However the water – fetched from the village well – is excellent and the best restorative for the walker. Passing on through the village you will see a sign directing you to the right, saying 'Archaia Arkessini'. This is the isolated headland known now as **Akro Kastri**, an obvious acropolis site you may have sighted earlier on your way. The track from Vroutsi passes the church of *Agios Ioannis*, while among the confused remains on the headland is another church, the *Panagia Kastriani*.

Straight on through Vroutsi runs the last section of the old 'main road' to the modern village of Arkessini. It makes a pleasant tramp round the contours of the hill – this is quite prosperous farming country – by way of **Rachidi** (village and church) from where you look down on what is said to have been a Mycenaean fortress. There are certainly walls, and the southern section stands several metres high in big dressed blocks. There is a gateway and a courtyard, and though the ground plan is confused after a good deal of plundering, it is a site well suited to the requirements of, say, 1500 to 1200 BC. Not an acropolis or a *kastro*, it nevertheless commands the countryside and the valley which falls to the sea at Limaniri Perivoli. In the Christian era it was taken over by the church of *Agia Trias*, the name by which it is generally known today.

Modern **Arkessini** has only a few houses, a big church and a hospitable *kapheneion*. A rough road continues through Kolophana to the very tip of the island, where the Ormos Kalotaritissa is both a secure anchorage and one of the loveliest spots on Amorgos – they call it *Paradissia*.

The topography of this part of Amorgos is confusingly presented in some of the maps on sale in Katapola – really because until quite recently few people have been there. The best authority on Amorgos is the German professor Dr Georg Perreiter, and the map he made (also on sale in Katapola) is both correct and informative about several other ancient sites in the area. Communications along the length of the island are still uncertain, but there is an unmetalled road all the way from the Chora to Arkessini and from the Chora to Egiali in the north – the problem being that there are no buses and only one taxi which can be persuaded to use it. This is why the walk from Katapola has much to recommend it, though one would prefer not to have to walk all the way back. It is a good idea to try to organize a lift back by private transport from Arkessini – ask at the *kapheneion*.

Still in the southern part of the island, a shorter walk from the harbour diverges left from the Arkessini 'road' soon after the turning to Minoa. The goal is the church of **Agios Georgios Valsamitis**, notable as the last place in Christendom where a heathen oracle was seriously consulted. Up to fifty years ago people would go there to consult the Pappas about the prospects for their various enterprises, and he would answer them by reference to the behaviour of holy water in a spring beneath the church floor. It was visited by Theodore Bent, who gives this description:

> 'On entering the narthex Papa Anatolios still demurred much about opening the oracle for me, fearing that I intended to scoff; but at length I prevailed upon him, and he put on his purple stole, and went hurriedly through the liturgy to St George before the altar. After this he took a tumbler, which he asked me carefully to inspect, and on my expressing my satisfaction as to its cleanness he proceeded to unlock a little chapel on the right side of the narthex with mysterious gratings all round, and adorned inside and out wth frescoes of the Byzantine School.
>
> Here was the sacred stream, the *agiasma*, which flows into a marble basin, carefully kept clean with a sponge at hand lest any extraneous matter should by chance get in. Thereupon he filled the tumbler and went to examine its contents in the sun's rays with a microscope, that he might read my destiny. He then returned to the steps of the altar and solemnly delivered his oracle.'*

In Brent's case the water was 'clear, with many white specks in it about the size of a small pearl'. The specks sank but rose again, which according to Anatolios signified 'health and success but much controversy'. Brent suggests that this was considered a suitable prophecy for a guest and a foreigner. Other manifestations such as

---

* *The Cyclades*, pp. 480–1.

black specks or hairs were supposed to indicate misfortunes in store – or, if they sank, that they had passed. Obviously a good deal of discretion was possible in replies to questioners, since only the Pappas operated the microscope.

The oracle is first mentioned in a work of 1651. In the 1820s Kapodistrias tried to close it, but popular support was too strong, and it was not until after the last war that the religious authorities decided to end this heathen practice. By that time the church had acquired as many rich *ex voto* offerings as an ancient Greek or Roman temple, if not quite rivalling Delphi itself. It is now kept closed, but plans are afoot to restore the fabric, though not its ancient mysteries.

The church is out of sight for most of the way along this narrow pleasant moorland track, but if you make for a large farm clearly visible on a bluff ahead, you will be hospitably received, offered a glass of fresh goats' milk, and shown the way to Agios Georgios – which by then is only two or three hundred yards further on round a corner of the hill.

As a change from walking, the north shore of Katapola bay has possibilities for a swim, and a sandy beach if you go far enough. If you prefer a splash off the rocks into a clear aquamarine sea, then keep to the south side. There is a path from the end of the quay, close to the shore line at first, but then it rises to cliff height and passes a series of little coves just right for the purpose. It also passes three small churches, each of which must be built on a classical or Byzantine site, judging from the bits of marble columns which have been incorporated here and there. This is a delectable coastline.

Up in the north is another deep westward-facing bay, which ends in a sheltered harbour capable of taking the larger ferries. The enclosing circle of hills contains three villages, Potamos, Tholaria and Langada, the last-named being the original Aegiale. Today it is the harbour village which is called **Egiali**. There is a good clean sandy beach round the head of the bay, so it is well suited to visitors who want a simple holiday base. All ferries call here as well as at Katapola.

There is a stirring walk from Langada which takes you to the crest of those beetling cliffs along the north-east coast. You come first to the derelict fifth-century church of *Agios Ioannis Theologos*, while further along the spine is *Agios Stavros*, from where if you wish you can climb by a spectacular path to the top of Mt Chorophakia, the highest point of the island at about 2500 feet. If you should be leaving Egiali on the way to Astypalaia or the Dodecanese, you will pass close under those mighty cliff faces which rise sheer out of the sea. There is nothing like them in the Kyklades, but then Amorgos is an exceptional island. Its outward appearance may be wild and rocky, but it has a gentle heart. Overall it has a quality and a dignity that is lacking in more famous islands.

North-west from Amorgos lies a string of lesser islands, like a necklace hanging below the throat of Naxos. Irakleia, Schinoussa and Kouphonisi are the principal ones, with Donoussa further to the north and due east of Naxos, and they are the least visited of all the Kyklades. During the season a small inter-island ferry runs through them once or twice a week to Naxos and back. This ship is based on Katapola, but two larger ferries from Piraeus come about as frequently via Naxos, though they are apt to arrive at awkward hours.

Disembarkation at these little islands is by small boats which come out when the ferry anchors offshore. This can be a hazardous process in bad weather, and always fascinating to watch from the safety of a large ship's rail. The speed and skill with which a mixed cargo of fish boxes, furniture, engine spare parts, household supplies and a few hardy tourists with their packs are transferred to the heaving tender seems a miracle. As in most Greek operations, ten minutes of din and confusion suddenly end, and the boat shoves off in good order and high good humour.

If you are coming from Naxos, the first and most interesting call is at **Irakleia**, which does have a harbour which can accommodate the smaller ferries. The Chora is an attractive sight from seaward, in a green setting with a blue-domed church above it. The road up from the harbour forks: straight on past the church you come quickly out into open country, and a stony track points into the hills beyond; to the left the road passes a welcoming bar-restaurant, its tables shaded by a huge spreading cedar, then climbs to a moorland ridge with a few scattered houses.

From the ridge a partly metalled track leads down to **Livadi Bay**, a lovely place with a long sandy beach at its head. The bay is favoured by campers, who far from being discouraged are served by a modern café-bar with showers and lavatories. On a spur which commands the bay are the substantial ruins of an ancient acropolis. You can make out a *kastro*, possibly Venetian, and the remains of many houses around its walls. A further stretch of metalled road continues for about two miles to a second Chora, about the same size as the harbour village, but it is a poor place without interest and has nowhere to stay.

Where to stay has for some time been the problem for visitors to Irakleia. The accommodation offered in private houses has been very primitive – sometimes with a privy-cum-washplace across a littered backyard, sometimes the only water supply a hosepipe or a bucket from a spring. However, an enterprising local family has completed a modern restaurant with a few well equipped rooms looking down over the harbour. The cooking is excellent, and from a table on the terrace you can look north to the grand mountains of Naxos, or watch the sun set over Paros.

Irakleia is in the awkward stage between a primitive simplicity and a dawning realization that tourists bring money. Cheap houses have been built on land bought by strangers from Athens who believe they can charge heavily for a bare room with little but a bed in it. The islanders have all too little to live on, and one hopes that progress will be gradual enough to allow the island economy to adjust fairly all round. Another thread in its life is a small army base, but the most notable single figure is the Pappas, whether he is meeting the ferries with a smart sunshade or casting his eye over new arrivals at the village restaurant. His two churches have both been restored recently, so some of the money which is beginning to come in has been used to advantage.

Given better accommodation, Irakleia is a good place for an unusual holiday. A swim in the clear blue water of Livadi bay – best of all in the early morning or evening, looking north to the softened outlines of Mt Zas on Naxos – is an experience not to miss if you are there.

Very close to the east is **Schinoussa**, or Echinoussa as it is sometimes called. This is an odd island, almost cut in two with a low sandy isthmus connecting the two halves. There are deep inlets on the west and south coasts, but the harbour in use is a deep sheltered bay to

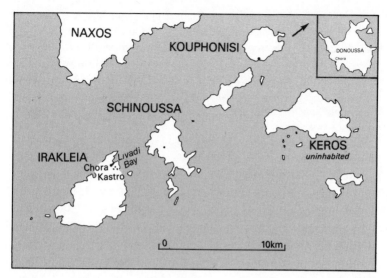

the south, with a vineyard reaching to the water's edge. Again the problem is where to stay, but camping sites and very simple rooms are available near the harbour, and the beaches are empty and inviting.

Further still to the east are two islands with the joint name of **Kouphonisi**. *Kouphos* means either 'deaf' or 'frivolous', according to the accent, but one likes to think that the 'frivolous islands' are a place to enjoy life. Indeed there is much more sophistication ashore, even a restaurant, and a number of acceptable places to stay. The harbour is on the south coast of the eastern island, and has been adapted rather more than its neighbours as a holiday base. Cornfields extend down to the edge of the bay, with a background of brown sculptured hills. The western island is long, low and almost uninhabited, as is **Keros** to the south of Kouphonisi – a barren bulk with little life on it and no harbour.

Donoussa is usually reached by ferries rounding the north cape of Naxos on their way to Egiali in Amorgos. There are two bays on the south coast, with a rocky headland in between. The main village is in the first you come to, and from there the small tenders put out to meet the ferry when it anchors. If there is a strong blow from the

233

west or south, the big ships prefer to anchor well inside the second bay, leaving the boats to weather the point as best they can. This is an ideal anchorage for small yachts; the immediate hinterland is pleasantly green and it has a lovely sandy beach at its head.

Donoussa appears briefly in historical records, though in periods far apart. An early classical fortified settlement was excavated for a few seasons after 1969; in 1914 it provided a respite for the German warships *Goeben* and *Breslau*, who were being hunted across the Mediterranean after the outbreak of war. They coaled off Donoussa (presumably by rendezvous with a collier) and made it safely to Constantinople. Camping sites, some fine empty beaches, and simple rooms near the harbour are all it can offer to the visitor today.

Access

AMORGOS has two harbours, Katapola and Egiali. Ferries call at both two or three times a week from Piraeus, but may visit the other islands only once. They are also served by a smaller ship which runs somewhat irregularly, and only in good weather, between Naxos and Katapola. The passage from Piraeus can take eleven hours or more; times of arrival are uncertain, and may be during the night or very early in the morning.

Communications

The only metalled road on AMORGOS connects Katapola with the Chora. It is used by one small bus whose timetable is unpredictable. Unmetalled roads, rough in places, connect the Chora (but not Katapola) with Arkessini in the south and Egiali in the north. On IRAKLEIA a metalled road connects the two Choras, but there is no public transport. There are no taxis or cars for hire on any of these islands, and no roads on SCHINOUSSA, KOUPHONISI or DONOUSSA.

Accommodation

AMORGOS   Katapola has no hotels, but one or two pleasantly run guest houses and individual rooms to let. The Chora has a few rooms too, but these get quickly booked during midsummer.

There are two hotels in Egiali. MIKES (C) is the older establishment, open only from June to September. LAKKI (C) is a modern hotel with private showers and WC, open for longer in the summer but closed in the winter.

IRAKLEIA   No hotels or guest houses. The only modern accommodation is in the few rooms attached to the restaurant owned by Anna and Niko KANTINI. Otherwise rooms are very primitive. There are good camping spots in Livadi bay, with showers and refreshments in a beach café during the summer.

SCHINOUSSA, KOUPHONISI and DONOUSSA   There are few facilities on Schinoussa or Donoussa, but some fairly comfortable rooms on Kouphonisi. Camping is possible and agreeable on all three.

Restaurants

AMORGOS   There are two good restaurants in Katapola, KAMARI and MOURAGIO, both on the harbour front, and simple eating places in the Chora.

IRAKLEIA   The KANTINI restaurant is good, and so is the older one half way up the hill leading to it.

SCHINOUSSA, KOUPHONISI and DONOUSSA   Very few facilities for eating. Kouphonisi has one bar-restaurant in the harbour village.

Facilities

Banks: Amorgos has exchange facilities at the ferry agency in Katapola harbour. Otherwise none.

Yachts: There are good berths and secure anchorages in Katapola and Egiali bays. Quiet anchorages in Irakleia, Schinoussa and Kouphonisi, but few shore facilities. The bay next to the harbour of Donoussa is a delightful place to lie.

FIFTEEN

Ios, Sikinos and Pholegandros

Ios has a good claim to be the most beautiful of all the Kyklades. It is more fertile than its 'dry' neighbours, and it has the most attractive harbour of them all. You enter it by a winding bay from the south, with the church of *Agia Irene* serving as a leading mark. Indeed, she presides over Ios harbour, keeping watch in all weathers. **Ormos Iou**, the port of Ios, lies to the right at the head of the bay, and has a fine new quay at which ships of all sizes can berth. An area beyond is kept for private yachts, but there is also a good safe anchorage out in the bay; you have only to make sure you are not obstructing the access of incoming ferries.

Ios is an island almost without history, though during the Middle Ages (when it was usually known as Nio) it was frequently used as a bargaining counter in dynastic exchanges under the overall rule of the Dukes of Naxos. When the Duchy broke up for practical purposes at the end of the fifteenth century, Ios was transferred with others of the Kyklades to Venice, and it was not until 1540 that it was surrendered to the all-conquering Turk.

Its chief link with the ancient world is its claim to be the burial place of Homer. Seven cities are recorded with a claim to be his birthplace, but 'Homer's Tomb' lies on the northern slopes of Mt Pyrgos, the main peak which dominates the harbour from the east. A certain Count Pasch van Krienen, a Dutchman who had read Herodotus, decided that Homer must have died in Ios on his way from Samos to Athens, and must necessarily have been buried somewhere on the island. Up on Mt Pyrgos he found several graves, and on opening one he found a coin with lettering that read something like the name OMIROS, as well as a clearer inscription on stone with the same letters. There could be few more suitable places for the poet's bones to lie than on the green side of this mountain, where the northerlies rustle the grass all summer, and where the eye turns instinctively north-eastwards towards Asia and the distant plains of windy Troy. It may be some Greek Patriarch, a Turkish warrior, or even a wandering crusader who lies there, but it matters little. Here is as suitable a place as anywhere in the Aegean.

Ios is rich in churches, and the brows of the hills and the green troughs of the valleys are encrusted with their domes. On a summer night they glow like moonstones. The church of *Agia Irene* at the entrance to the bay is a delightful example of the best in Greek island churches. This is not because it contains any fine ikons or other saintly relics, nor because of any architectural peculiarity – except perhaps for the projecting footholds around the dome which look just like almond kernels in the icing of a cake. What counts is the simple perfection of its dome and arched belfries.

In spite of, or perhaps because of, its obvious beauty, Ios is a place you have to know to get the best from. Any disadvantages arise from the island's popularity, especially with the nomadic throngs of young people who find access easy during the summer. The people of Ios are among the most friendly in the islands, and are very tolerant towards their often noisy and thoughtless visitors. At the same time they manage to live their own closely knit family lives. The hospitality due to the visitor at the gates is rarely forgotten in the Aegean, but here – though often abused – it seems to come most naturally.

Unwelcome visitors during the last war were the Italians. They were treated politely, but without respect or fear. There was traffic under their noses with the Allies, and even a visit from a British submarine. Later the Germans took over, and things were more difficult, but there were no ugly reprisals.

There are still memories in Ios of the Karaghiozi puppet plays for which Kostas Ierakis makes the wooden cut-outs in Amorgos. It is many years since those cracked voices sounded across the *Plateia Omirou* (as the wide harbour area is called), but the son of the last exponent still keeps a wholesale store by the quay and remembers helping his father to operate the puppets from the kiosk which stands there yet.

The high town, or **Chora**, dominates the harbour, a cascade of white houses almost to the summit of its hill, which is finally crowned by a white Kykladic church. It is in essence enchanting. A modern asphalt road leads up to it in a series of loops from the harbour, and buses go to and fro every half hour. The old way up on foot is more attractive, though it takes longer. The rough steps climb through a leafy cleft in the hillside, spattered with donkey droppings and at one point with ripe mulberries which fall from one particular tree during late May and early June. It can be a hot climb, but the view back over the harbour and across the straits to Sikinos grows more entrancing each time you stop for breath.

Early in the summer it is possible to enjoy the main streets of the Chora in comparative peace. By the end of June the little *plateia* becomes so crowded that you can hardly pick your way through, and the old men huddle together in the one corner café they can still call their own. But if you carry on up beyond the *plateia* into the higher alleys of the town, there is peace again. No bars, no restaurants, no 'clubs', no amplified squalling on tape – only the little houses crowding close together with flowery gardens, and a white church at almost every corner.

It was up here that early in the fourteenth century Domenico Schiavo of Venice was allowed by his feudal lord the Duke of Naxos to build a castle. It lasted intact only as long as the Schiavi family maintained it, for as soon of the islanders were left to themselves under the distant control of the Turks they quite naturally found better uses for such good building material. A few large stones from it can be seen around one of the bigger churches.

On the way up you can break away to the right, to climb a wide flight of steps to the bare ridge where once a double line of windmills whirled away to grind the corn brought in from the hills. Now they are sad ruins, the stone walls cracking, the thatched roofs fallen in, even the spokes of the sails gone from all but one. Barley is still grown on terraces throughout the island, but the old threshing floors are mostly overgrown with wild flowers, and the grain is used only for animal feeds. Flour for the excellent Greek bread comes in sacks from Athens – though it is put to good use in a few local bakeries.

The bus which brings you up from the port stops in a wide lower *plateia*, close by the handsome blue-domed principal church. On one side is the post office, and on the first floor of the adjoining building an excellent doctor's consulting room. The buses continue down the road beyond for about a mile to the long curving sandy beach of **Milopota**. Here again it would be lovelier without so many people, and without the cluttered backdrop of tavernas, discos and 'rent-rooms' which have sprung up to cater for them. But except in July and August there is plenty of room for a family to disport itself safely.

The beach at the head of the harbour is another safe spot for family bathing, and in the summer there is a wind-surfing base. As usual with beaches in that position a lot of plastic detritus gets washed up, but an irregular cleaning service keeps it reasonably pure. For better swimming within reach of the harbour, there are two beaches which can be reached on foot in about half an hour by a path which leads round the far side of the bay. Both have clean sand and clear water, and the further one (beyond the charming little rock-edge church of *Agios Nikolaos*) has a small bar-restaurant above it. The walk along the cliffs and over the intervening saddle is lovely in itself.

If you carry on over the rocks beyond Koubara beach (which is the second of the two) you reach a headland where you can wander along rocky paths among clumps of thyme and low-growing flowers. Here you may come across scattered flocks of grazing sheep and goats, which have come down in a black and white flood from the hill farm above, accompanied by a carillon of goat bells. If you look north from the high rocks you can make out the dim shapes of Naxos and Paros. Closer to the south-west is the big hump of Sikinos. This is what brings a sense of friendly unity – and rivalry – to all the Kyklades. From each you can see at least one other, and the surrounding seas are the common factor which bring food and livelihood to all.

There is another pleasant walk along the cliffs on the east side of the bay, beyond *Agia Irene*, and there are places where you can scramble down to swim in deep clear water off the rocks. The path leads eventually to a rather sultry anchorage and a narrow enclosed beach which – with its bar-restaurant behind – has not too good a reputation with the people of Ios.

There is only one other road, a new one still rough in places,

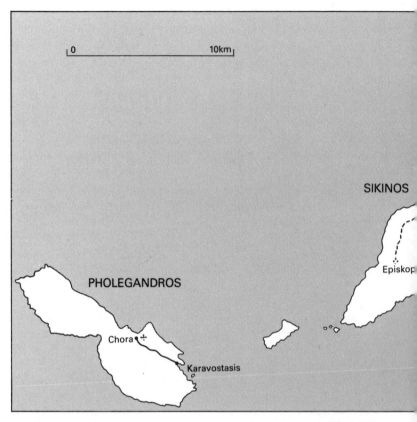

leading from the Chora across the width of the island, skirting Mount Pyrgos, to reach the sandy bay of **Agios Theodotos**. It has a small 'pension' hotel, with a group of holiday bungalows and thatched huts on the beach, all open only in the high season, and there is a delightful little family restaurant overlooking them. If you need exercise, the walk across gives you a sight of the real Ios and its lovely hinterland, but it will take you a couple of hours each way and can be very hot.

If the walk becomes too hot, you may be lucky enough to be hailed by the owner of a small house and barn by the side of the road to ask if you would like a drink of water. If so, accept promptly, because not only will you be given a glass of delicious cold water, but

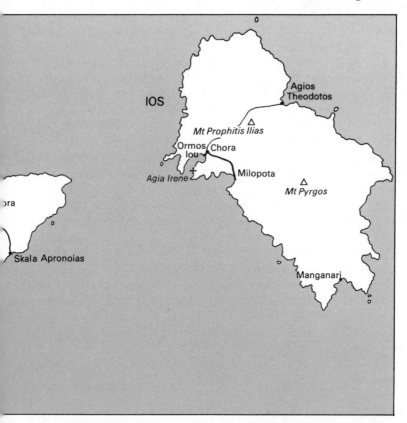

most likely a smaller glass of the colourless grape spirit, *tsikoudia*, which is the equivalent of the French *marc* or *eau-de-vie*. This man (his name is Kosta) is the only producer on the island, and he will show you his still in the outhouse, which would do credit to the cognac producers of the Charente. If you are on the way home, you will find the last few miles pass quickly.

Once the summer season has really begun in early June, there are several enterprising boat trips from the port of Ios. The most popular is down the length of the south coast to its eastern tip at **Manganari**, where a wide flat sweep of sandy beach can be an exhilarating place to swim from. Here too there is a 'pension' hotel open during the main season, and a little restaurant which lets

241

simple rooms alongside it. If you look to the south on a clear day, you can see the outline of Santorin, and you can pick up pieces of volcanic pumice on the beach.

In the other direction you can find a change of scene with an hour's run across to Sikinos, or an hour further to Pholegandros and back, picking up passengers from Sikinos on the way. Earlier in the year a *kaïki* may make the same trip, carrying a few passengers along with bags of cement to Sikinos, and returning with a flock of a hundred or so sheep in the hold.

Apart from the terraced strips of barley, which are harvested by the end of May, there is not much cultivation on Ios. Sheep and goats thrive in large numbers on the hills, and their milk provides a good soft fresh cheese not unlike the *brociou* of Corsica. But Ios is famous for its bulls, and probably always has been. In a field below the Chora I have seen two splendid animals taking their ease, surrounded by half a dozen obviously contented cows. I have seen a young bull calf being hoisted and lowered by derrick into the hold of a *kaïki*, so there is still an export trade. Were there perhaps bulls imported from Ios among those which provided sport for Minoan arenas in Crete? There are cattle too on the swampy ground at the head of Ios bay, and one year among the tufted grass I saw a pair of cattle egrets.

A familiar sound at night is a short plaintive cry on one note from a bird which is constantly changing position. This is the Skops owl, known to the Greeks as *Gkion* – the nearest you can get to the sound of this strange cry. Round it is built a local myth. Once there were two brothers tending their flocks on the edge of a cliff. They were separated at dusk, and one disappeared over the edge. Ever since, the survivor has roamed up and down, calling to his lost brother. Sympathetic gods have turned him into a bird, but still the cry comes as darkness falls: 'Gkion . . . Gkion . . . Gkion'.

The whole character of Ios is soft, friendly and welcoming. Few landfalls are more beautiful than its northern point as you sail south from Naxos, followed by the run down the softly swelling coastline, till you turn in past Agia Irene to anchor or berth in its lovely bay. Homer must have been happy to end his days here.

Sikinos is a baffling island. It looks so big and important when you look westward from Ios, yet when you cross the eight-mile channel between the two islands the nearest thing to a harbour is the bay at **Skala Apronoias**, which edges rather uncomfortably into the land halfway down the south-east coast. Although some of the big ferries now call there regularly, there seems no possibility yet of a quay being built there to receive them; instead, passengers still disembark into small boats from an offshore anchorage, sheltered only by the point on which the lighthouse stands. The north-west coast is even more uncompromising, with a sequence of mountainous capes which fall directly into the sea with no sign of life or habitation.

The little harbour is not unattractive, with a small beach at its head, and *kaïkis* and other lesser craft do come alongside below a range of solid if dilapidated buildings. The exchange of goods – import and export – can be revealing about the island economy: an inward cargo of cement for new building will be replaced by a flock of up to a hundred sheep, rounded up and dropped one by one into the hold, a performance assisted by most of the population. There are rooms to let beside the harbour, and visitors can be sure of a warm welcome and the freshest of fish to eat.

The most baffling feature of Sikinos is that there seems nowhere else to live. Where is the Chora? The answer lies four miles up a road from the harbour which follows a dry stream bed into the centre of the island. There are no taxis or buses, so failing a lift you can only walk – mule-hiring is not practicable these days. If not too burdened, and if the day is not too hot, you should take to your legs. The road is edged with olives and oleanders, and in spring and early summer there are wild flowers in the clefts of the rocks; birds sing and there is great peace over all.

You are almost across to the farther coast before you reach the ridge where the **Chora** stands. This is hidden by still higher ground on the seaward side, which explains why the Chora is invisible to ships passing below. There are two parts to it, village and *kastro*. The village is a simple place, with a few café-bars and rooms to let; the *kastro* is a mediaeval survival, with houses still crammed inside the defences which form their own back walls. On a nearby hill are the ruins of the fortified monastery of the *Zoodochos Pigi*, whose 'life-giving spring' indicates that there was always enough water for

243

the community even up here. This and their combined defences should have kept them secure from pirate attacks in this remote place.

Yet there was an older capital in an even more remote situation away to the south-west at a place called **Episkopi**. This curious site suggests that in late Roman times (AD 200–300) someone of importance lived here, for a building once supposed to be a temple of Pythian Apollo is now thought to have been a shrine incorporating a family vault, with a marble gateway leading to the crypt. There is hardly a mention of Sikinos in classical or mediaeval times. It was one of the minor possessions of the Duke of Naxos, but there is no evidence that any of the Sanudo family ever occupied it. According to Theodore Bent the *kastro* was built by refugees from Crete in the sixteenth century, whose descendants had lived there in seclusion ever since; so it seems that Episkopi must have been destroyed or abandoned very early on.

Bent was forced by bad weather to stay five days in the *kastro*, and had himself taken on mule-back to Episkopi. He found that the original 'temple' had been converted first to a church and then to a monastery, and was fascinated by the remains he saw of the town – which had been investigated by Ludwig Ross in 1837. This is how he describes its situation:

> 'It covered a precipitous height, fully one thousand eight hundred feet above the sea, and from the summit the rock goes down on the north side fully five hundred feet without a break. The rock is of blue marble, covered with a yellow lichen, which gives it an exceedingly rich appearance. Here and there out of crevices grow thick bunches of wild mastic; ravens rush out of their eyries and croak; quantities of partridges, too, disturbed by the unwonted noise of human voices, take flight.'

Without a mule the journey takes more than another hour's rough walking from the Chora, and the present writer has not attempted it. So we must rely on Theodore Bent, and we can leave him with the last word on Sikinos:

> 'The *demarch* had a capital repast for us on our return – partridges, pilaff, and local wine of the first quality – after which the inhabitants trooped in to see us, to laugh at our host's jokes, to drink wine, and to pick up any crumbs that might fall

from our table. Sikinos is as celebrated for its wine as for its honey, and the *demarch* had the best vineyards in the island. Even as far back as the days of Pliny and Strabo there was a report that the island in former days had been called *Oinoe* from the wine (*oinos*) which it produced.'

It would still not be disappointing or surprising to be weather-bound on Sikinos, for there is still wine and laughter to be found – and even the biggest ferries cannot take on passengers in all weathers.

The strange name **Pholegandros** is said to be derived from a Phoeni-cian word, *Phelegundam*, meaning a dry and rocky place. This reminds us that when sailing this sea we should never forget that long before the Greeks became rulers of the Aegean the Phoeni-cians, master mariners of antiquity, had penetrated all over it. Originating as an agricultural people they had made their home on the Syrian seaboard, and from there they began to trade throughout the Levant. The mediaeval name was Polykandros, whatever that signified; most of the names given to the islands by their Italian overlords show that they understood Greek as little as British soldiers have understood French place names.

From Skala Apronoias in Sikinos to the harbour of **Karavostasis** ('ship-station') is another long hour of often stormy sea-time. In between the two ports you pass strange rock pillars rising straight out of the sea, a reminder of what the landscape of the Aegean might have looked like before the sea swallowed all but its peaks. The harbour here is more sheltered and more welcoming, with a small church near the base of the mole and an increasing number of modern buildings at the head of the bay. However as yet not many people live down here, and the problem again is how to reach the Chora. There is a fine modern concrete highway leading to it, but no regular public transport and no taxis. The walk is shorter than in Sikinos – a steady uphill tramp of about forty minutes through treeless moorland scenery. The lack of trees is made up for by the low-growing red-foliaged shrubs which crowd the slopes on either side of the road.

The village itself is concealed over the brow of the final rise, but just before that you see on your right the conspicuous white shape of the *Panagia* monastery spreading along a ridge above the road. Its church, like all churches in Pholegandros, has an unusually flattened cupola. The monastery occupies a fine site, which as so often happened was taken over by the Christian church from the pagan goddess Artemis. Unfortunately to protect its treasures from theft its doors are no longer opened to visitors.

As in Sikinos there are two parts to the **Chora**, here known as *meso* ('inside') and *exo* ('outside'). Yet this is not like any other Kykladic capital. You have the immediate impression that here is a self-sufficient community, isolated from other island centres for centuries, which has kept up a serene standard of life owing nothing to any other source, least of all the tourist. The upland fields look fertile, with figs and vines and strips of arable land; the people you meet are civil and friendly but clearly content with their own ways.

You first come to *exo*, which has a number of good-looking houses grouped round three main squares, with several of these flat-domed churches intervening. Two of the squares are leafy and quiet. The larger one has a central plantation of flowering trees, where patient donkeys wait for their owners to leave the café tables. A smaller one has a paved area in the centre, shaded by several kinds of tree, with a well in the middle – a perfect place for children to play, or gravely watch their elders drawing water. Lastly you come to a busier *plateia*, with a café on one side and a civilized restaurant on the other. Here you will meet the discriminating visitors who have found rooms to stay in, and you can drink the local retsina by the carafe. The churches scattered all around are well kept and have each of them some special feature or shape, adornment or external carving, and always this curiously flattened dome – as though one architect had imposed a style on them all. Again their presence in such numbers argues prosperity as well as a communal spirit.

The *meso* part of the village is what is left of the old *kastro* – a main street unusually wide for the Kyklades, with white cubist houses rising irregularly on either side, some up steps, some down, but all with bright flowery balconies or tubs. Low arches lead to more secluded side streets, and at the far end you fetch up on a narrow terrace overlooking a glorious seascape – a drop of nearly a thousand feet to the waves which break on the rocks below, with even more precipitous headlands on either side. The blue Aegean horizon is clear to the north – or is there just a suspicion of solid land which could be Paros?

Pholegandros is an island for the connoisseur, and the Chora is not for the tourist who must have his hotel 'three minutes from the beach'. One look over that precipice disposes of such an idea, though there is a small and friendly hotel and some simple rooms to let. Down near Karavostasis harbour there are one or two pleasant if exposed beaches, but the Chora is the place to stay if you want to enjoy the best of the island. Perhaps two or three times a week there will be a flurry of hot and tired visitors up from the harbour demanding lunch, but there is peace before and after. Tracks over the inland hills lead either delightfully nowhere or to tinier isolated villages. Whatever its name means, Pholegandros appears seldom in history. The powerful peoples who came and went in the Aegean seem irrelevant to the confident simplicity of life here.

Access

ios is on the main ferry route through the eastern Kyklades, and the passage from Piraeus takes about ten hours. During the summer ships call every day from one direction or another. There is one service across to the western islands, leaving twice a week for Milos, Siphnos and Seriphos.

There is no airstrip, but helicopters can land in case of emergency or illness.

SIKINOS and PHOLEGANDROS can be reached twice a week from Piraeus, ferries calling at both islands after Ios. From June onwards there are frequent day excursions from Ios.

Communications

There are only two roads on ios. One goes from the harbour to the Chora and on to Milopota beach, the other from the Chora across the island to Agios Theodotos. Only the former has a regular bus service, and a taxi is hard to find. There are daily excursions by boat to Sikinos, Pholegandros, Paros, Delos and Mykonos, but these do not usually begin until late in May. The same applies to excursions down the coast to Manganari beach.

There are no metalled roads on SIKINOS, and only one on PHOLEGAN-DROS, between the harbour and the Chora. No regular transport is available.

247

Accommodation

IOS   There are several hotels close to the harbour. Of these CORALI (C) and PHLISVOS (C) are efficient, clean and comfortable. PHRAGAKIS (C) is an old-fashioned hotel of character overlooking the quay, where ACTAEON (D) is open all year. Not recommended are CHRYSSI AKTI (B) which is mainly a discotheque, and SEA BREEZE (C) on a noisy corner of the harbour. Of the others Armadoros and 'Homer's Inn' are much booked by travel agents. There are plenty of rooms and guest houses in and below the Chora and on the low ground at the head of the bay. Any rooms near the centre of the Chora will be very noisy at night. Camping is officially forbidden except in the enclosure near the church of Agia Irene.

SIKINOS   There are no hotels, but a few rooms in the harbour and up in the Chora.

PHOLEGANDROS   There is one friendly hotel, DANASSI (D) in the Chora, without private shower or WC. Rooms are available in the Chora and Karavostasis harbour.

Restaurants

IOS   Most of the restaurants here are aimed at the less discriminating tourist. Some of the best (all family run) are ANDREAS (small, good fish, expensive); PITHARI in the Chora (good local food and quiet surroundings); PAVLO in the upper Chora (the most real, with local clientele). You can also get a reasonable meal in the Plateia Omirou at open-air tables.

SIKINOS   There are no proper restaurants, but family cafés provide good simple meals.

PHOLEGANDROS   There is one good restaurant in the Chora, and a simple café at Karavostasis.

Facilities

Banks: Two banks have branches in Ios Chora. Travellers' cheques and currency can be exchanged at the tourist office behind the Hotel Actaeon on the Quay. There are no banks or exchange facilities on Sikinos or Pholegandros.

Yachts: Ios bay is a good safe anchorage, and there are berths stern-to in the inner harbour. Water, fuel and stores are available close by.

The harbour at Sikinos is undeveloped and exposed, and it would be difficult to get service ashore; there are no shops or stores there.

At Pholegandros there is a reasonably good anchorage in most weathers at Karavostasis, but little in the way of shore facilities.

SIXTEEN

Santorin and Anaphi

One comes to **Santorin** through a great circular bay whose shores are formed by Santorin itself and by the islands of Therasia and Aspronisi. The bay is a volcano's heart, and the water which glows like a sapphire beneath a boat's keel sinks down a thousand feet to the bottom of the ancient crater.

The earliest recorded name for the island is *Kalliste*, the 'Very Beautiful'. Beautiful it still is, but it is an exotic beauty which has more than a little of the monstrous in its nature. To say that it is different from the rest of the Kyklades (to which it geographically belongs) is an understatement. Santorin is not like anything or anywhere else in the world. The first sight of the bay's curving eastern rim is fantastic. The sheer cliffs, in places rising to a height of nearly a thousand feet above the sea, are striated in bands of coloured rock – red, purple, brown, black, with streaks of white and even green in places. Above the cliffs white houses straggle along the skyline, looking at first like snow, or icing on some rich and indigestible chocolate cake.

Once, as geologists agree, the whole of the bay (eighteen miles round its inner rim) was covered by a huge volcano. At some time during the Late Minoan age – perhaps between 1500 and 1450 BC – there was a tremendous eruption which blew to pieces the central massif. This explosion could have generated a tidal wave sufficient to destroy Knossos and the other Minoan cities of Crete. Such a fate overtook Krakatoa in the Pacific in 1883 – an inrush of sea water into a submarine cavity giving rise to explosions of superheated vapour. Krakatoa produced a wave fifty feet high which destroyed towns and villages hundreds of miles away. Santorin is only sixty miles from the northern coast of Crete.

In historical times there is plenty of evidence of volcanic activity. Strabo records that in 196 BC there was an eruption when flames and smoke rose out of the sea bed for four days. In AD 726 an island appeared in the middle of the bay. In 1570 the island of Mikra Kaumene arose, and in 1707 Nea Kaumene. Further activity in 1925–6 saw Mikra and Nea Kaumene merge. The last earthquake was in 1956, when parts of the main island – in particular the town of Pyrgos – were badly damaged.

As you approach from the north and enter the bay between Santorin and Therasia, you see ahead the dark, almost repulsive outlines of Palaia and Nea Kaumene, the old and the new 'Burnt Islands'. The Admiralty Pilot advises one not to navigate in their vicinity – and although excursion boats take tourists to land there it would be a brave stranger who took his own boat close in. The sea is charged with freshly minted pumice, and the water is warmer than you would expect even in the midsummer Aegean. Sinister bubbles like malignant boils break the smooth skin of the sea. To the seismologist they are as fascinating as a cancer to a surgeon.

The ancient Greeks called the island Thera, after the leader of a party of colonists from Sparta, and one theory has it that this was Plato's vanished paradise which he called Atlantis. It is still commonly called Thera by modern Greeks anxious to revive the classical name for their home, and they have adopted the spelling Phira for the principal town. It was not until the island became part of the Duchy of Naxos at the beginning of the thirteenth century that the modern name appeared – a corruption of Santa Irina, itself a Latinization of its Greek patron saint, Agia Irene.

The first of the Latin adventurers to rule Santorin were the Barozzi family from Venice, but in 1335 Duke Nicholas I drove them out and united it with the Sanudo family possessions, while handing over the principal castle of Akrotiri to their allies and feudal subjects the Gozzadini of Kythnos, later also masters of Siphnos. Four other castles were built on the island, and all five were still standing in 1577. Vines were intensively cultivated, and even cotton was planted on the volcanic soil. The Gozzadini castle remained intact long after the Turks had conquered the rest of the Aegean, finally falling with Siphnos in 1617 as almost the last strongholds of the Christian world there.

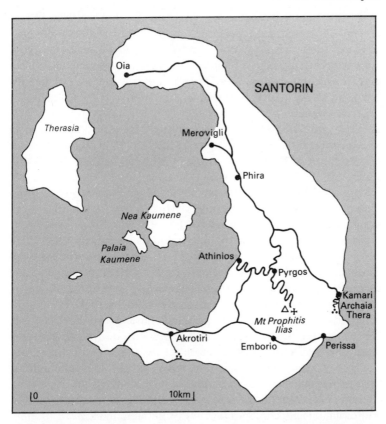

The objective of most travellers today will be **Phira**. Only small excursion boats and cruise liners now anchor below the town itself, leaving their passengers to tackle the six hundred or so steps which zig-zag all the way up to the top of the cliff. An army of mules and donkeys assembles down below when any big ship comes in, and this kind of transport remains one of the tourist attractions here. Nine hundred feet above the landing place, the town of Phira swings into the air. If you lean back on the jetty and crane your neck you can just make out the white towers and houses. The terraced path of steps winds backwards and forwards, and if you lean over carefully from your donkey's back and look down as you come to a bend, you will see the previous slope some thirty feet below.

251

A word here, for those unfamiliar with it, about the basic Greek saddle. A tent-shaped piece of wood, it is designed for riding side-saddle. You hoist yourself up by the wooden pommel, leaving both feet over the side (no matter which one), and slump your body over towards the centre for balance. In this way the ridge of wood is taken under the bend of the knees and the ride is not too agonizing for the beginner.

Most visitors to Santorin now arrive by ferry at the new port of **Athinios**, where a large landing stage has been built about two miles to the south of Phira. The journey up by bus or taxi takes about twenty minutes – the first part a spectacular climb in loops to the top of the cliff. When you reach the town you will find it internally not greatly different from other much visited island spots – apart from its incomparable situation.

Phira is a fairly modern foundation, built mostly during the mid-nineteenth century when the old mediaeval capital at **Skaros**, a little to the north, became untenable after several earthquakes and minor tremors. It has an unbelievable eagle's eye view of the world, and the air has all the rinsed taste of the wind. Along the bony spine that runs north from Phira, houses and churches clamber like goats on a mountain track. The narrow streets crackle with that intense light one finds only in the Aegean. So vivid is it that the moulding over a window a hundred yards away is like a detail under a magnifying glass.

In contrast around the bus stop, which may be your first view of the town, an ugly clutter of tourist offices, bars and ice-cream shops has grown up. The seaward streets are quieter and cleaner, but lined with shops selling the cheap (or not so cheap) jewellery and textiles which are turned out by mass production in Athens to feed the tourist trade. There is a handsome modern cathedral, though, and the view from the dizzy terraces over the deep blue sea-filled crater is unmatched anywhere.

From Phira you can walk a mile or so along the spine of the island to **Merovigli**, the old Catholic quarter. The best time is in the early evening when the light softens over the bay. If you return after dark, take a torch or try to pick a moonlit night. The streets and alleys are uneven and curiously unrecognizable in the dark. It is disconcerting to turn a corner and come upon a sharp drop to the sea, or walk down a flight of steps to find yourself in a ruined house which disappears in a crumbling slope.

Merovigli is sinking slowly into the stone from which its houses were quarried. Although a few sites have been cleared for new building or restoration, shadowed doorways still open upon empty courtyards, and the grass grows round the ring-bolts where once the mules were tethered. In the small *plateia*, so high that even Phira looks hundreds of feet below, a few trees grow, and there is a miniature promenade with iron railings through which one views the eastern sea.

Away from the great cliffs, the land slopes down in fields and vineyards, rich in volcanic earth that contrasts with the scarred sides of the ancient crater. Like the land around Vesuvius and Etna, the fields of Santorin are potent breeders of the vine. The vines are not trained on wires or regimented in rows, but grown low to the ground, the shoots trained in a circle like canes at the bottom of a basket. This is to help them to keep their heads down when the *meltemi* blow in from the north. The white wines of Santorin are among the best in the Aegean, and if you like a *rosé* you will like those too.

The bulk of the wine produced goes north in the big trucks which roll on and off the modern ferries. Another important export is the volcanic ash product, *pozzuolana*. This was the substance used by de Lesseps in 1866 to seal the walls of the Suez canal, and it is still quarried in quantity. You can see it pouring down the steep slopes above the jetties where the ships are loaded. As elsewhere, fish is no longer cheap in the restaurants, but vegetables of all kinds are plentiful. The tomatoes, lettuces, cucumbers and onions raised on those eastern slopes or in tiny plots behind the houses are first class.

The **Museum** in Phira must not be forgotten. There are some fine geometric vases, as well as a certain amount of 'Minoan' ware of rare quality. The wall decorations and other treasures found buried under the ash at Akrotiri have been taken to the National Museum in Athens, and will probably stay there. The Hellenistic and Roman periods are well represented, and there is a good collection of inscriptions. A weight-lifter's weight, perhaps used in some Greek Games (and therefore suggesting there was a champion in Thera), bears the inscription EUMASTES LIFTED ME. It weighs about half a ton. Despite its pleasantly hedonistic atmosphere, Thera could clearly build athletes.

An attractive alternative place to stay is in **Oia**, where most ferries call first on their way into the bay. This has a little harbour where the depth of water is as much as 1200 feet in places. The big ships cannot anchor, and as the quay can take only smaller vessels alongside, their passengers and luggage have to be ferried quickly in and out in local boats. Even if you are based in Phira it is worth taking the bus to visit it. The run takes about thirty minutes, and if you can manage to sit on the right going out or the left coming back it is a dramatic journey along the often dizzy elevation of the spinal road. Far down below, you see the cultivated slopes where the fingers of the lava flow spread out, subsided and finally congealed. Below again, the sea moves and sparkles as it never does in the landlocked western bay.

When you reach Oia, and the bus stops in a little open space – where as often as not an informal football kickabout is going on – wander down the old alleyways which crown the cliffs to the west. There is a good deal of recent development in Oia, but there are still ruinous old houses, with now and then a handsome classical façade. On a little headland jutting out to the south there is a ruined fort built in red stone, part of an extensive property which a notice warns you is private to the family of Leandros. On the seaward side below the fort are the ruins of a substantial three-aisled basilica church. The one column which survives is still faintly frescoed.

Below, the cliff face is honeycombed with caves, which form small houses or storerooms. The cliffs stoop down sheer to the sea, fascinating but frightening. The volcanic rocks assume the most fantastic shades of colour, especially at sunset. The cliff wall to the left is split by a vivid band of arsenic green. Above and below it, the rock is tinged with purple. Clumps of rose madder lift strangely out of screes of tufa, and the sea around can be full of pumice. Even the pumice of Santorin is strange, unlike those grey lumps we handle in our wash-basins at home. Some pieces are the softest shade of pink, others streaked with red. One picked out of the water had a bar of cobalt on a field of pale green.

There are two other places which no visitor to Santorin should miss. The ancient capital, **Archaia Thera**, stands on a broad headland on the south-east coast. At sea level, a thousand feet below, is the modern resort of **Kamari**, with a long beach of volcanic black sand and a great many hotels and tavernas. There is a good road all the way from Phira as far as Kamari, and the steep climb from there is also practicable for cars, taxis and coaches. The last few hundred feet can be done only on foot, and once you have passed the caretaker's hut (which is incorporated in the disused church of St Stephen) you can go back in imagination for two thousand years or more.

Archaic tombs found here date the town's origin before 900 BC, but the visible remains are of the Hellenistic period, when Thera was under the control of the Ptolemies of Egypt. This may explain the pervasive charm as well as the few signs of decadence which you find here.

A path leads seaward along the ridge, once the Sacred Way for all who lived or came here. The first thing you will notice is a walled enclosure on your right, the wall beautifully carved with the symbols of an eagle, a lion and a dolphin. The eagle is for Zeus, the lion for Apollo, the dolphin for Poseidon, and between them is a medallion with a head in profile which records that the enclosure was built in honour of Artemidorus, an admiral of the Ptolemies' fleet which was based in Thera.

A hundred yards further on you reach the centre of the town. Passing through the *agora* you have on your right the *Stoa Vasiliki*, or royal portico, a good forty yards long, with a row of column bases and two commemorative *steles* at the back. Beyond that on your right is the famous carving of a phallus with the surrounding inscription 'To my friends'. As you walk on your realize what a superb situation the town enjoyed, and it is no surprise to find one of the best sites occupied by a charming little theatre, with a quite capacious auditorium facing a backdrop of limitless sea and sky. Several large cisterns, with the long slabs which supported their roofs still in place, provided an elaborate water supply for Hellenistic lavatories and Roman baths.

The path now drops a little towards the headland, and you find yourself in older and more evocative surroundings. The sixth-century temple of the Dorian *Apollo Karneios*, a big rectangle with much of the west wall intact, lies below you to your left. To your

255

right is a terrace supported by a retaining wall built in massive blocks, best seen from below and further on. Here were celebrated the *Gymnopaidia*, displays of dancing and gymnastics in honour of Apollo, and beyond is the gymnasium itself, an area where the teenage boys lived a secluded life which suggests the parallel of the English Public School.

Their sleeping quarters centred on a grotto dedicated to Herakles and Hermes – suitable examples of the bodily strength and fleetness of foot for which they strove. All around, scratched on almost every available rock surface, are rough *graffiti* which have been dated as early as the seventh century BC, and deciphered as tributes to favourite boys from their admirers. Sometimes the outline of a boy's foot suggests a champion runner, while a different outlet appears in the elegant outline of a ship's prow with many oars. The boys would learn music here as well as dancing, for this was Apollo's world. What a place to go to school in!

If you come by taxi, your driver may be anxious to stop on the way to let you see the monastery of the **Prophitis Ilias**, finely placed on a shoulder of his eponymous mountain. The monastery dates from 1711, and the buildings are not notable. You will be received courteously, though, and the duty monk will show you an interesting collection of the original kitchen ware and implements used in the various trades.

To my mind the most vivid experience in Santorin is to visit the still only half excavated Bronze Age city of **Akrotiri**. This lies near the south coast of the long south-western peninsula, and is easily reached by bus from Phira. It was only in 1967 that Professor Spiridon Marinatos (who died in 1974) began to explore the thick layer of pumice and ash created by the volcanic eruption which probably also destroyed the Minoan cities of Crete. You can imagine the excitement with which he saw street after street and house after house emerging in a state of preservation equalled only in the Roman towns of Pompeii and Herculaneum.

Akrotiri is more exciting than either of those, not only because it was built and lived in perhaps two thousand years earlier, but because its creators, while almost as sophisticated in practical matters, were infinitely more aesthetically gifted than first century Romans. How can we judge this? In the area so far excavated there

Santorin. *Above,* the volcanic Kaumene Is;
below, the town of Phira

A dovecot on Tinos

are two large houses, both with walls and window spaces reaching to the third storey. In rooms on the first floor level were found intact some of the loveliest wall paintings to have come out of the ancient world. To quote Dr Christos Doumas, successor to Professor Marinatos:

> 'Their subjects, whether geometric or abstract motifs, whether idyllic landscapes or scenes from everyday life, are always chosen in a way which meets the requirements of the space for which they were intended. The diversity of themes is so great and their presentation so rich that the wall paintings, apart from their artistic merit, constitute a unique source of information about the society which created them. Costumes, jewellery, male and female hair styles, the men's armour, the craft of ship-building and sailing are immediately made known through these wall paintings.'

All these frescos (some of them executed in *fresco secco*, or tempera) can be seen in a special section of the National Archaeological Museum in Athens. There is a gorgeous young man with a stringful of lifelike fish in each outstretched hand. There is a graphic scene of a fight at sea. There are East African antelopes in black and white outline. There are blue monkeys (of a species found only in Ethiopia!) leaping from bough to bough. There are two boys squaring up to each other with boxing gloves. There is an elaborate sequence illustrating a long voyage up river in some distant land – probably the Egyptian Nile – with beautifully appointed and decorated boats, cities of departure and arrival, and the course of the river itself depicted with birds, beasts and flowers along its banks.

The most famous decoration was found in a small room on the ground floor. The walls were painted up to about fifteen feet with a design of waving lilies growing out of a rocky landscape, swallows darting in between the clumps – one pair beak to beak in a mating preliminary. The colours, as in most of the painting, are the deep browns, creams and ochres of the volcanic rocks, but most noticeable is a light sea blue which marks some of the special features like the boys' and women's hair, the monkeys and the fishes. It was outside this room that a double horn symbol was found, linking it with Cretan religious observances. It is a pity not to be able to see these marvels on the spot, but they are illustrated in a booklet by

257

Dr Doumas, available at the door where you buy your entry tickets.

Nor is the artistry confined to the wall decorations. Nowhere in Knossos or Phaistos can you see such beautifully coloured and decorated amphorae, cylindrical storage jars, jugs, ewers, and even a stone table standing on three short legs, decorated with dolphins and undersea life. The contrast with the vulgarity and crudeness of most of the Roman work at Pompeii could not be more marked. To live in such rooms, lit by large windows and cunning light wells, must have been a joy.

There are ground plans displayed at convenient points on your walk round the town. The endearing thing is that in contrast to the grid system of Roman streets you are following twisting alleyways on different levels between irregularly shaped houses. These open on to little *plateias* which may be only roughly square and in one case is triangular. A complete ground plan would be not unlike any you can find in a Kykladic village today.

There is an eerie, even a ghostly feeling now as you walk those deserted lanes. Stone and unexcavated earth are all reduced to the uniform grey of the volcanic ash which has preserved it for more than three thousand years. In spite of that, a charm lingers which is different from the heavy authority of the palace at Knossos. The excavations will continue between May and October each year, but tantalizingly slowly, because Dr Doumas will employ only a picked team of sixteen.

It was surely a grave setback for civilization when this and like communities were wiped out. There was a poignant twist to the ending when it came. Evidence found at Akrotiri shows that the inhabitants had had earlier warnings of disaster – probably severe earth tremors such as they or their ancestors had known in the past. On this occasion they were alarmed enough to leave the town and take to their ships. Meanwhile a certain amount of damage seems to have been done to the buildings, but when the tremors subsided they came back and set to work to repair it.

What finally happened is conjecture. The significant thing is that no human remains and very few personal belongings were found beneath the solid blanket of ash – not at all like the scenes uncovered at Pompeii. So – did the warning tremors come again? Did they once more take their possessions down the short distance to the beach where their ships lay, put off to sea and wait for the danger to pass? The force which must have hit them then was unimaginable. We know that no other shore received them, and indeed their ships could not have lived for a minute in that awesome upheaval.

About the fate of Knossos our feelings are ambivalent. There were features of that society which not many of us would regret. But at Akrotiri there seems to have been no form of dynastic or religious tyranny. The citizens apparently organized themselves on a communal basis. No public or official buildings have so far been discovered, let alone a palace. Yet they could construct efficient drainage and sewerage throughout the town, as well as perfectly effective toilet installations – one of the latter was found intact in the largest house complex. So far no tablets have been found in Linear A, as one might expect. Did they take their archives to sea with them?

We may be wrong about Akrotiri, but my feeling is that we lost more here than in Crete. If this was Plato's Atlantis, he could have agreed. But neither Ancient Thera nor Akrotiri, wonderful places as they are, compete in the mind's eye of memory with the astonishing physical framework of Santorin today. The moment one remembers best from a visit to the island is when the sunset flares along the rim of the cliffs, just before the sun dips below the backbone of Therasia, leaving the dark central islets sinister in the gathering twilight. Santorin and Delos are the two poles of this Kykladic world. On Mount Kynthos life begins with the birth of Apollo: the Burnt Islands of Santorin suggest how the world could end.

Away in the open sea, sixteen miles east of Santorin, is the lonely outpost of the Kyklades, **Anaphi**. In spite of its remote position it found favour with the noble Italian families who staked out domains in the Aegean during the Middle Ages. Its Italian name was Namphio, and for most of the fourteenth century the Gozzadini of Bologna occupied the castle whose remains can still be seen on a rocky hilltop in the north of the island. For a hundred years after that it was sufficiently favoured to attract and hold a junior branch of the Crispi, who had succeeded the Sanudi as Dukes of Naxos and the Archipelago. After being snapped up by Barbarossa in 1536 it reverted for a while to Venice, but disappeared into Turkish obscurity until Greek independence came in the nineteenth century.

Its popularity in the Middle Ages seems surprising today, for at first sight it looks an unpromising sea-girt rock in the middle of nowhere. The coastline is rocky all round, and the only harbour which now deserves the name is the small one on the south coast where the ferries call. The lack of a secure harbour in the past may explain why the inhabitants have tried several different sites in which to settle at different periods. The present population occupies a small Kykladic **Chora** built between the harbour of St Nicholas and a conical hill which in more dangerous times would have given them some protection if attacked by pirates.

At least Anaphi must have been a welcome sight to the Argonauts, who are said to have found refuge here from a storm on their way back to Colchis with the Golden Fleece. What they were doing in the southern Aegean is another story, but this story went that Apollo raised the island from the bed of the sea just in time to rescue them. The sudden appearance of an island in the middle of an empty sea would seem miraculous to any sailor in that situation.

Behind this misty tradition is the presence on the island in classical times of a famous temple to *Apollo Aiglites*, the 'shining Apollo'. It stood on a narrow isthmus between the main part of the island in the south-east, dominated as usual by Mt Prophitis Ilias, and a mountainous rock which projects into the sea there. As so often when Christianity came, the site was taken over by a monastery. This is the **Panagia Kalamiotissa**, which took to itself the name of the rock, Mt Kalamos; it has become the show place of Anaphi, and the inhabitants make much of its festivals of folk dancing.

The classical centre – and it seems to have been quite extensive – was about five miles east of the Chora at a place called **Katalimatsa**. There was an acropolis here, and there are traces of occupation in those times, as well as remains of a harbour mole on the shore below. The name is thought to derive from the rare classical word *kataluma*, meaning an inn or lodging. One reason why not many ancient artefacts have been found here or anywhere may be that a party of Russians from the fleet of Admiral Orloff landed here in the 1770s, and took what they found back with them to St Petersburg.

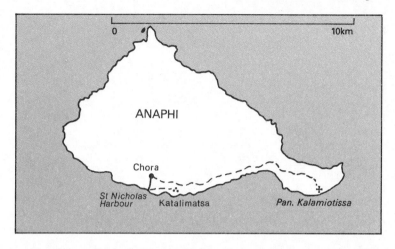

Another curious chapter in its history came before the last war, when during the Kondylis dictatorship Anaphi was used as a place of penal exile for communists who had opposed him; to be sent here was regarded as only slightly less harsh a fate than to be landed at Gavdo off the south coast of Crete. Here they won a reprieve only when several of their number went on a prolonged hunger strike.

Today the island has the advantages and disadvantages of being so remote. On the plus side, it remains one of the simplest and most natural of all, and even by Kykladic standards its people are wonderfully friendly. Its disadvantages follow naturally. You will look in vain for accommodation which is comfortable in the modern sense, though by no means in vain for the kind of meals any sensible traveller in the islands enjoys. With fish, young kids and even (if lucky) red-legged partridges on the menu you ought not to complain, though there is an understandable shortage of vegetables and fruit. A week here is an adventure, but could be worth it.

Access

SANTORIN is the southerly terminus of many ferry lines from Piraeus, and can also be reached by a regular service of smaller boats from Crete. There is an airfield with morning flights on most days from Heraklion, less frequently from Athens, but you need to book seats several days in advance during the summer and at Easter. The only regular call at ANAPHI is by a ferry from Piraeus which comes on here from Ios once a week, though smaller boats from Santorin come across during the summer at uncertain intervals.

Communications

The bus services on SANTORIN are frequent and well organized, connecting Phira with Oia and Akrotiri as well as with the modern tourist centres of Kamari, Perissa and Monolithos. A fleet of modern taxis lines up near the bus station, ready and anxious to take you anywhere in the island. It is as well to agree a price before you start. On ANAPHI there are no roads for traffic.

Accommodation

SANTORIN   The demand by travel agents from all countries ensures that there are a great many small hotels and guest houses. Easily the best hotel in Phira, and the most expensive, is ATLANTIS (A) which has a fine situation near the Orthodox cathedral. It is closed in winter and heavily booked during the summer and over Easter. More modest is KAVALARI (C) which also closes in winter. PANORAMA (C) is in theory open all year, but has not much else to recommend it. Outside Phira the seaside hotel below Akrotiri. ARVANITIS (B) is quiet, comfortable and obliging, with a resourceful family restaurant.

ANAPHI   There are no hotels. Rooms are let privately in the Chora.

Restaurants

SANTORIN   It would be foolish to pick out any particular venue, as managements are continually changing and favourite ones disappear.

ANAPHI   The village taverna is the only source of meals.

Facilities

Banks: There are branches of all Greek banks in Phira, none in Anaphi.

Yachts: For many reasons Phira is a difficult port of call, but the offshore moorings are safe, and most facilities can be found down by the quay. Yachtsmen would be well received in St Nicholas harbour in Anaphi, though it is exposed to the south.

Euboea

SEVENTEEN

Euboea

Euboea (in modern Greek 'Evia') can be reached from several places on the mainland, but before deciding your route it is wise to be sure exactly where you want to go. The largest Aegean island of all, bar Crete, it is ninety miles long, and it takes a long time to travel between the main centres. A journey by road from Athens to the principal city of **Chalkis** will be a good deal shorter than one from Chalkis to Edipsos in the north or Karystos in the south. Chalkis (now commonly called Halkida) stands on the Euripos, where the passage between Euboea and Attica is only 130 feet wide and is spanned by a retractable bridge.

Euripos, the narrowest point of a long winding channel, means 'swift current', and is rightly named, for the tidal streams can attain seven or eight knots, and even more after a bout of bad weather. Since there is a period of slack water lasting only about ten minutes between the north-going and south-going currents, and since these currents alternate as often as seven times a day, the passage is difficult even for steamships. Yachts and small boats are advised to look for a tow through the narrows.

Chalkis is only about twenty miles from Thebes, the chief city of ancient Boeotia, and as long as Boeotia controlled the narrows, the Athenian trade with the north depended on their good will. The first bridge over the Euripos was built by the Boeotians in 410 BC, and the Athenians were never able to challenge their authority in these waters.

During the early Christian and Byzantine periods not much is heard of Euboea, but after the Latin conquest of Byzantium in 1204 it was the scene of constant political bargaining and warfare. Lying where it does, it was a natural theatre for the ambitious adventurers who poured into the eastern Mediterranean with the Fourth

265

Crusade. The carving up of the Byzantine Empire between Venice and the various national groups from all over Europe left wide power in the hands of Boniface, Marquis of Montferrat, the military leader of the so-called Crusade. Balked by Baldwin, Count of Flanders, in his ambition to rule over the newly created Latin Empire of Romania, he accepted the nominally subservient position of King of Salonika, with licence to extend his kingdom over so far unconquered parts of the Archipelago.

Euboea was an early acquisition, and Boniface divided the island into three large fiefs, or baronies, with capitals at Negroponte (as Chalkis was then called), Oreos in the north and Karystos in the far south. This was in spite of a treaty agreement which gave Oreos and Karystos to Venice. However, Venice preferred the indirect power of her merchants, supported by a powerful fleet, to fighting on land for her rights, and this triarchy remained the basis for local rule for the next two centuries. Nevertheless Venice gradually established herself as *de facto* mistress of Euboea. She controlled most of its affairs through her 'bailie' in Negroponte, leaving a succession of Frankish or Lombard nobles to squabble and fight over tracts of land and the dozens of huge castles they built to protect themselves.

In the fifteenth century another force arrived in the eastern Mediterranean which was to bring its history to a full stop for over three hundred years – the Ottoman Turks. The still intermittently effective empire of Byzantium fell to them in 1453, and their armies swarmed to attack the outposts of Greece and the Balkans. In 1470 the Sultan Mohammed II arrived at the gates of Negroponte with 70,000 men and a fleet of 300 ships.

The name by which the city (and sometimes the whole island) was then called was once thought to derive from the 'black bridge' which crossed the narrows. First built by the Boeotians in 410 BC, it was constantly renewed and fortified during the Middle Ages. The Venetians built a fort half way across, and by the fourteenth century they had completed a strong circuit of walls, with the Lion of St Mark on guard over all the city gates. It is now accepted that Negroponte was an Italian corruption of the Greek 'Euripo', and there has never been anything black about the bridge.*

* It was common for foreigners to treat the Greek *upsilon* (written like an English 'y') as a *gamma*. The Turks called it Egriboz.

Mohammed took a long look at the fortified bridge and the tidal waters rushing through it, and he decided against trying to force a passage. Instead he built a bridge of boats at another point a little to the south, and his army crossed to invest the city. The garrison was outnumbered but defiant:

'On 25th June, when he had made all his preparations, the Sultan, through an Italian interpreter, summoned the bailie to surrender, saying he was resolved to have the city, but that, if the bailie would yield at once, he would exempt the inhabitants from all taxes for ten years, would give to every noble who had a house two, and would allow the bailie and *proveditore* to live in comfort at Negroponte, or else would assign them a liberal allowance at Constantinople. To this the bailie ordered his aide-de-camp to reply that Venice had made Negroponte her own, that ten or twelve days at the most would decide her fate, and that with God's help he would burn the Sultan's fleet and root up his tent, so that he would not know where to hide his diminished head. At this bold reply all the men on the walls shouted aloud, and the interpreter was bidden go tell his master to eat swine's flesh, and then try to storm the moat. The insult was faithfully reported to Mohammed, who from that moment resolved that the garrison should have no mercy.'*

In fact the defenders were relying on a Venetian fleet which they expected to arrive in the channel any day. Its commander, an un-military-minded lawyer called Nicolo da Canale, had already wasted time at Skiathos, and instead of intervening to protect the crossing had sailed off to Crete for reinforcements.

Now in the nick of time his advance squadron was sighted, and Mohammed was on the point of ordering a retreat. But instead of attacking at once to break up the bridge of boats and isolate the Turkish army, da Canale dithered too long and the fierce current turned against him. Seeing the Venetians anchor harmlessly in a bay six miles to the north, Mohammed made his final assault and captured the town. The bailie's earlier insult ensured that the men were massacred and the women and children carried off as slaves. Only in 1833 did the then Sultan give up the keys of Chalkis to the new Greek government in exchange for the island of Lemnos, which had just been liberated.

* William Miller, *op. cit.*, pp. 472–3.

Nowadays you will probably have crossed the bridge and passed within the Venetian walls without realizing it. There is hardly a break in the buildings, and the fort which stood in the middle of the bridge has been pulled down. There is not a lot to be seen in Chalkis today. From the Turkish period a mosque survives in the old town, though now it serves only as storage for the museum. Of more interest is the church of *Agia Paraskevi* on your right after crossing the bridge. It was built as a Byzantine basilica but converted to the Gothic style in the fourteenth century – an oddity in this part of the world.

From Chalkis you must decide whether you want to go north or south. The long road to the north at first follows the coastal plain, but then climbs into the wooded hillsides between Mt Pixaria and the Kandili range – both rising to nearly 4000 feet. The woods are almost all of the Aleppo pine (*Pinus halepensis*), and leave enough light and air for flowers and herbs by the roadside – which means that beekeepers can set out their hives in thousands all along this part of the route. It is a most beautiful drive.

Once over the col, the road drops to the village of **Prokopi**, where the chief interest for visitors from Britain may be the estate maintained by the Noel-Baker family, descended over several generations from the Noels – who were themselves descendants of Byron. It was originally a Turkish-owned enclave, and is still known by the Turkish name of Achmetaga. The present owners have had difficulties with recent Greek governments, but the house which is the centre of the property takes in students from all over the world to learn arts such as weaving and pottery in a simple but beautiful and traditional setting. The estate is a good example of what you find in this part of Euboea – sensible afforestation, good irrigation schemes and a well conducted agricultural system. The pine forests are softened by many walnut, plane and other deciduous trees.

In the village the church of *Agios Ioannis Rossos* (St John the Russian), which figures in most guide books, is a disappointment. Money has clearly been spent on it, but the result is a harsh exterior and garish painting within. The most interesting feature is an elaborate entombment of a carved wooden figure which represents its patron saint – whose story illustrates the confused events in the northern Aegean during the last few centuries. This was a soldier from Tsarist Russia who was captured by the Turks and carried off as a slave to Ürgüp (Greek 'Prokopion') in Turkey. He died there in 1730, but when Greek refugees returned to Euboea in 1923 they brought his relics with them, and substituted the Greek name of their village of exile for the Turkish contraction of Achmet Aga. The last bizarre touch came when their hero was canonized by the Russian Orthodox Church in 1962, and a yearly pilgrimage instituted on 27 May.

From the wide central *plateia* in Prokopi a bus will take you by way of the main road junction at Strophilia to the fishing harbour of **Limni** on the west coast. This is an attractive place. There are two or three sensible small hotels, and although the beaches nearby are pebbled a few days here could be very pleasant. This would give you a chance to visit the convent of Agios Nikolaos, or the **Moni Galataki**, at a place of that name about four miles down the coast to the south. The road along the shore is easy walking, but good enough too for a taxi ride – worth it for one way, at least, to save your legs. There is an excellent restaurant at almost exactly the half-way mark.

The convent stands on a green headland above a rocky shore – just the place for a classical temple to Poseidon. In the seventh or eighth century the sailors' god was replaced as usual by the Christian St Nicholas, a basilica church was built on the same site, and substantial monastic buildings grew up around it under the Byzantine system. Then in the confused period after the Fourth Crusade the place was frequently damaged either by pirates or by marauding followers of the various factions disputing sovereignty in the island. Total destruction followed the Turkish conquest in 1470, and the monastery was deserted.

Now comes a time when chance and a touch of the supernatural intervenes. In the sixteenth century the captain and owner of a large ship trading out of Constantinople was sailing down the tricky north Euboean channel bound for Chalkis when he was caught by a sudden squall off the mountains of Kandili:

> 'Being in danger of foundering any minute he called on St Nicholas to rescue him. Quickly the storm abated, and his ship came ashore on the beach below the ruins of the monastery. Galatakes (so called because he came from Galatia in Asia

Cape Artemision

Pevki

Orei

Loutra Edipsou

Strophilia

EUBOE

Limni

△ Kandili Mts.

Prokopi

Moni Galataki

△ Mt. Pexaria
(4165 ft)

Northern Gulf of Euboea

Chalkis

0   50km

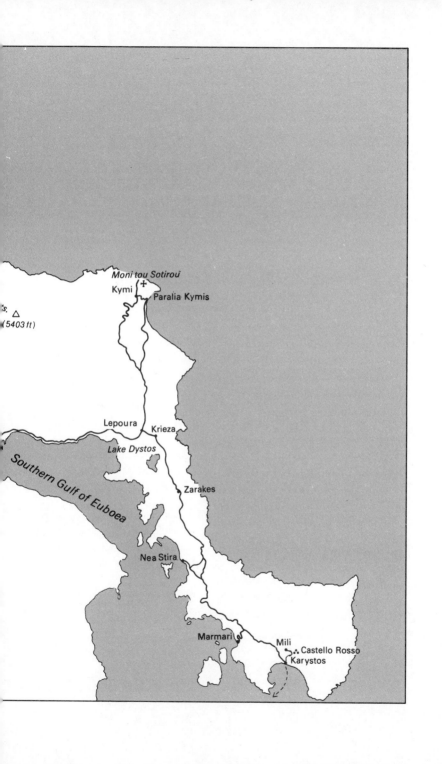

Moni tou Sotirou
Kymi ✛
Paralia Kymis

's. △
(5403 ft)

Lepoura   Krieza

Lake Dystos

Southern Gulf of Euboea

Zarakes

Nea Stira

Marmari   Mili
Castello Rosso
Karystos

> Minor) climbed up and knelt before the ruins of the church and undertook to rebuild the monastery.'*

That he was as good as his word is testified to by an inscription over the church door, giving the date it was finished as December 1547.

It must be said that the name of the monastery has been otherwise explained, given that *gala* is the Greek for 'milk':

> 'According to another tradition the monastery once possessed a vast number of sheep, from which they made quantities of cheese. So great was the supply of milk that they constructed a Galaktagogeion to bring it by artificial channels from the sheepfolds to the monastery, where there were underground cisterns to receive it.'*

No doubt the Romans would have called it a Lactiduct.

There must have been many shipwrecks along this dangerous coast, and many fervent prayers to St Nicholas. After another rescue twenty years later the grateful skipper undertook to decorate the still bare walls of the church with the proper wall paintings. Both he and Galatakes were rewarded by having their portraits included in the decoration, with an inscribed date of 1567. Although most of the paintings were destroyed in a later visitation by the Turks during the war of liberation, there is a little chapel to the south of the nave which is covered on walls and ceiling with unusually fine frescos. There has also survived a graphic Last Judgment at the west end, with a ladder to heaven and a splendid dragon waiting below for the rejects. All these are in the style of the sixteenth century.

Fate had not finished with Galataki even then. In 1896 a rich seam of magnesite was discovered on the property. Mining was undertaken by a European company, and the revenues from this made it one of the richest communities of the region. In spite of this it became more difficult to recruit monks after the last war, and by an ecclesiastical decree of 15 November 1946 it was converted to a nunnery.

The convent buildings are simple and pleasant, set in a flowery courtyard. A substantial stone tower rises from the south wall, first

---

* Translated from a booklet written by the Prioress Maria and published in Chalkis, 1976.

* *ibid.*

built by the monks as a refuge from attacks by pirates. Now the sisters have fitted out bedrooms on three of its floors for visitors and pilgrims. Their simple furnishings only underline the beauty of the views to seaward on every floor – and at least one of the sisters makes an excellent walnut liqueur.

From Strophilia the road continues northward, but it is a long haul. The big holiday complex at **Loutra Edipsou** is more easily reached by ship from Agios Konstantinos or Kamena Voula on the mainland. It was originally, as the name implies, a fashionable 'watering place' for Greek valetudinarians, with warm sulphur-impregnated springs. Now the tourist industry has taken over and nearly a hundred hotels are listed in the current brochures.

It is all a lovely coastline, and one can understand why holidaymakers flock there – not only to Edipsos but to other beaches like Orei and Pevki on the north coast. Pevki (the Greek word for pines) is not far from Cape Artemision, off which the first naval action of the Persian campaign of 480 BC was fought. It was inconclusive, but as in later actions the Greeks scored by knowing the tides and weather conditions better than the Persians, who outnumbered them. Istiaea, the largest town in the area, has a fine position but is now an untidy industrial sprawl.

Should you be bound only for the southern part of Euboea, then it will likewise save you time to take the ferry from Rafina on the east coast of Attica – a much shorter bus ride from Athens than it is to Chalkis, and then only an hour by sea. These little ships cross to three different ports on the west coast, Nea Stira, Marmari and Karystos. All three have pleasant holiday developments and good beaches, but Karystos is a town of character in its own right. The visitor who lands on the long quayside will find everything and everybody more relaxed than elsewhere in Euboea. There are beaches at either end of what is really a broad promenade, with attractive stretches of soft sand.

The line of bars and restaurants which extends for a hundred yards at the back of the quay is shaded all along by the thick leaves of as many mulberry trees. Their trunks are painted white and their lower branches are often padded to protect the head of a diner if he rises too suddenly. The cooking is good, and it is a very civilized scene, especially when on a Sunday evening the inhabitants turn out for the family *volta* – the slow parade up and down the front by all generations in their best clothes. Only in midsummer do the restaurants get so overcrowded that you have to queue for tables, and even then the good humour of the Greek waiter keeps most people happy.

The history of Karystos crops up literally as you walk about the town. In a street running parallel to the front a kiosk attendant will show you the remains of a classical temple at his feet. Next to the pleasing gardens which border the sea at the quieter end is a massive foursquare mediaeval keep. Above all – and this is literal too – the town is dominated by the huge and spendidly situated **Castello Rosso** which crowns the bare hill behind.

This hill was probably the ancient acropolis, but the modern history of Karystos begins as usual with the aftermath of the Fourth Crusade. We have seen that it was the capital of one of the three baronies instituted by Boniface of Montferrat, and a succession of Frankish, Lombardic and Catalan nobles held both the title and the castle during the thirteenth and fourteenth centuries. Overall power gradually passed into the hands of Venice, and in 1365 she bought the whole barony – castle, serfs and all – from the Catalan Bonifacio Fadrique. For once Venice made a bad bargain, for the land and its revenues deteriorated quickly, but it remained in the gift of Venice until the Turks took over after the fall of Negroponte.

The huge castle and the rock on which it stands blend together in the reddish-brown mass which gives it its name. You see it long before you enter the town by the road from the north. The proper approach to the entrance is from the village of Grabia in the hills to the north-west of the town, though so vast is the enclosure that another entrance overlooks Mili, a village several miles to the east. It is not so well preserved as other Crusader castles further east, but it is an awesome place. With its ring of defensive walls on many levels it must have been as nearly impregnable as military architecture could make it, and huge underground cisterns ensured an endless supply of water.

Inside the dramatic eastern battlements are the tumbled ruins of houses built for servants of the Turkish rulers, instantly pulled down when freedom came. The Beys were harsh overlords, none more so than the last of them, Omar Bey, who compelled the villages around to contribute a heavy load of wood every week – to be carried up to the castle on the backs of the women if they had no donkeys. Today the Castello seems a massive irrelevance, and perhaps it always was. It protected nothing except its masters against their rivals of the same race and breed – whereas the eastern Crusader castles were at least first built to defend the Christian against the infidel.

The hill villages to the north are lovely, the pick of them being **Mili**. Its scattered houses are perched above leafy depths, fed by streams running down all year from outlets in the village. Wine is made locally, and drunk under the vine trellis of a little bar-restaurant.

There is more evidence of an unfailing supply of water at the shrine of **Agia Triada**, a little to the west of Grabia. It is a stunningly lovely place. As you come to the end of a dusty track (a taxi will take you there) you pass into a cool Arcadian world of ancient plane trees and gushing water. Facing you at the foot of a narrow ravine is the very small church of the Holy Trinity, nicely restored in 1960 by a local man in memory of his two young grandchildren.

The source of water is a cavern in the rocks above, which must surely have been a place for benign nymphs, or later for a hermit. Under the spreading and twisting trunks of the planes you may see a great company of black and tan goats enjoying the shade. The goatherd will be doing the same, sitting on the low wall outside the church. He told the writer that there were five hundred in his flock, and that the tiniest had been born that morning. It was hard to leave such peace behind.

The nearest neighbour to Karystos along the coast is **Marmari**, to which there is a direct ferry from Rafina. A genuine fishing harbour, it lies in a pretty bay sheltered by offshore islands to the west. Small holiday houses are being built on the eastern arm of the bay by Greeks from the mainland, but on the whole Marmari is natural and unspoilt. This strikes you most if you walk round the harbour to the right, where little houses with bright terraces border the path above the sea.

From Karystos an excellent road leads north, keeping to the spine of the narrowest part of Euboea. After Zarakes the road drops down to an enclosed plain with **Lake Dystos** in its centre. On a low hill to the east of the lake are the remains of a fifth-century city –

not today an attractive site, but more fertile than the bare hillsides which surround it.

A mile or so further on is the village of Krieza, the birthplace of Nikolaos Kriezotis, who commanded the strong Euboean contingent in the War of Independence. Then you come to the dusty road junction at Lepoura. The left turn will take you on to Chalkis by way of the coastal road, along which the most interesting place is **Eretria**, in classical times an equal and rival city to Chalkis. Their rivalry came to a head in the sixth century BC over the fertile Lelantine plain which lies between them, and Chalkis prevailed. Although Eretria played an important part in the Persian wars, her position on an open coast never matched the advantages of Chalkis, who controlled the straits. When the Romans arrived in 198 BC they promptly sacked the town, and a hundred years later it was completely destroyed during Sulla's campaign against Mithridates.

The modern town is built on the classical site, but fortunately (unlike Chalkis) it never grew big enough to hide the important features. This has left it the best preserved classical site in Euboea. In the open spaces of the town you can see the foundations of a Doric temple of Apollo, and of a *tholos* in the neighbourhood of the *agora*. More accessible remains are up in the north-west quarter, where new building has stopped short of them. At the foot of the slope is a good small museum, above which are the excavated remains of a residential district which includes a fourth-century palace, with a very practical-looking clay bath. This area lies close to the western gate, which has some good intact masonry, while above that you find the *cavea* of a big Hellenistic theatre. The main interest is in the elaborate arrangements for the *scena*, as the seating has mostly been plundered to build the later town. It never rose very high, as it was built well down the eastern slopes of the hill which formed the earliest acropolis – little to see there except the marvellous view of the historic mountains of Attica across the Euboean straits.

Your last call in Euboea may be to Kymi, because its harbour, the Paralia Kymis, is the starting point for the only ferry line which serves the island of Skyros. There is no difficulty in getting to Kymi, but it is a long journey by bus, whether from Chalkis or Karystos. If you come from Karystos you may have to change buses at Lepoura.

Twelve miles north along the road from Lepoura it forks again, and the bus takes the left hand branch through a series of mountain villages, eventually reaching Kymi by following the contours of the wooded lower slopes of the Mavrovouni (Black Mountains). Behind the Mavrovouni are the immense bare summits of the Dirphi mountains, which dominate the coastline of Euboea on this side. With the sun setting to the north-west behind them, and clouds swirling around the tops, it is one of the most dramatic mountain scenes in the Aegean.

Kymi itself is a pleasant if featureless little red-roofed town, lying high up on a hillside facing east. It was thoroughly sacked by Omar Bey after the 1821 rising, so that both the principal churches have modern exteriors. The more interesting is the *Panagia* of the Dormition (*Koimisis*) of the Virgin – really the best thing in the town. In spite of its treatment by Omar Bey, a sensible nineteenth-century restoration has left it a lot of charm. You see it first below you from the road, blue domes nestling among cypresses and flowering trees. A wide paved courtyard looks down over the sea, and swallows nest in the scaffolding holes of the surrounding wall. Inside is one of the loveliest Virgin and Child ikons, which must date from the seventeenth century. The Dormition next to it is probably later, but still painted with skill and feeling.

While in Kymi it is worth taking a short taxi ride to the **Moni tou Sotirou**, the convent of Christ the Saviour, about six miles to the north in a fine situation overlooking the coast. This is a cheerful and prosperous place, with the thirteen sisters all lending a hand in a well organized plan to turn part of the old buildings into new living quarters. Before going into the church women visitors not wearing a skirt will be most politely proffered one from a stock kept at hand, which can be put on over the offending trousers. The dedication of the church is to the *Metamorphosis*, or Transfiguration, but the outstanding painting is an ikon of the *Panagia Odegetria*, Our Lady the Guide. A date for the foundation of about 1600 is suggested, though the church is a complete basilica, and there is a tradition that it replaced an early hermit's cell. Until desecrated by the Turks it must have been a holy and peaceful place.

In 1821 the monks of the Sotiros monastery were among the first to join the Euboean revolt, and between 1941 and 1944 they again defied an invader, housing and protecting refugees from the forces of their allies. The necessary restoration of 1847 was more gentle than elsewhere, and now there are gentle nuns to guard it. The beauty of the flowers and trees around is entirely natural, and it is again both holy and peaceful.

To take advantage of the ferry service to Skyros or the other northern Sporades you have to descend to the **Paralia**, or harbour of Kymi. This is a soulless place, which seems to resent being used only as a convenient annexe to the town. But whether you sail away eastward or northward, the last sight will be of the huge and frightening masses of the Dirphi mountains. The memory will be of an island of strong scenic contrasts, with a history as varied as its landscape and as confused as the seas around it. Euboea is on the eastern frontier of Europe, and though she has often paid the penalty for that there is a character rooted in her soil and people which seems to defy the threats of modern life.

Access

To an island of this size so close to the Greek mainland, several approaches are possible:

To CHALKIS: by road from Athens.
To KARYSTOS, MARMARI and NEA STIRA: by ferry from Rafina.
To ERETRIA: by ferry from Skala Oripou.
To EDIPSOS and the north: by ferry from Kamena Voula or Arkitsa. The shortest crossing (30 minutes) is from Glipha to Agiokampos.

A longer route is from Agios Konstantinos on the mainland to Kymi, by way of Skiathos, Skopelos and Alonnisos.

Communications

Long distance buses connect Chalkis with other centres and villages on the main roads, some coming right through from the Athens bus centre at Tris Gephyres.

Taxis are available in Chalkis and other main towns. The long distances make them expensive compared with the buses, but they save time and fatigue.

Cars and mopeds can be hired in any large town.

278

Accommodation

For the many hotels in Chalkis and Loutra Edipsou (more than a hundred in the latter) it is best to consult the tourist brochures or road maps. In Gregolimano, on the coast to the west of Edipsos, ROI SOLEIL (A) is deservedly in the top class. Karystos has two good hotels: APOLLON RESORT (B) caters for both agency and private visitors and has a good restaurant; KARYSTION (C) is smaller and more elegantly run. Both are in good positions close to a sandy beach. Kymi has no modern hotels, but KRINEIO, though only in category D and without private plumbing, is clean and pleasant, with quiet rooms facing away from the main *plateia*. If you have to stay in Paralia Kymis, then BEIS (C) has modern comforts but a surly management. Many more hotels all over Euboea are listed in the brochures and tourist maps.

Restaurants

The field is too wide for individual recommendations.

Facilities

Banks: Branches of the usual banks will be found in any sizeable town.

Yachts: Navigation is tricky all round the coast, and the best harbours will be found on the mainland coast across the Euboean narrows.

The Northern
Sporades

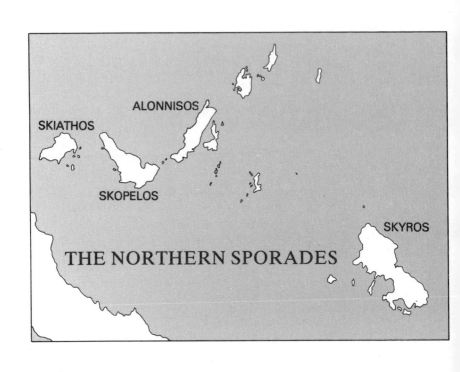

SKIATHOS

ALONNISOS

SKOPELOS

SKYROS

THE NORTHERN SPORADES

THE NORTHERN SPORADES

The Sporades, the 'scattered islands' of the Archipelago, fall into two main groups – the northern Sporades lying a little to the north-east of Euboea and the eastern Sporades off the western shores of Asia Minor. The name of 'southern Sporades' is confusingly given sometimes to the northern Kyklades and sometimes to the Dodecanese.

The northern group comprises the four main islands of **Skiathos**, **Skopelos**, **Alonnisos** and **Skyros**, with a number of small islets which are hardly inhabited, if at all. The group has become popular with Greek holidaymakers now that Skiathos is connected by air with Athens – a flight of little more than half an hour. These islands have one thing in common which distinguishes them from most of the Kyklades – they are well wooded. Coming upon them after a visit to the sun-tawny 'dry' islands further south, one's first feeling may be one of relief, if not of amazement, at the sight of the wooded slopes, dark green even in summer.

The main part of the group, with the extension of a few islets, runs out like a sickle from the long peninsula below Mount Pelion. It curves towards the north, so that the outermost islet is less than thirty miles from the southern peninsula of Chalkidiki. Mount Athos is less than forty miles away, due north across one of the windiest stretches of sea in the Aegean. If the weather is clear, and you come down by sea from the north, the views are magnificent. Pelion and Ossa (those mountains piled one on the other by rebellious Titans in an attempt to dislodge Zeus from Olympus) thrust their shoulders against the western skyline, with craggy Euboea to the south and the islands marching out in shadows of green and blue towards the open sea. Further up the coast, in the waters between

283

Olympus and Chalkidiki, the humidity and the airlessness can be oppressive, but in the Sporades the air is fresher, cooled by the *meltemi* in summer; at all times the violence of sudden storms is notorious.

EIGHTEEN

Skiathos, Skopelos, Alonnisos and Skyros

The modern town of **Skiathos** – the only one on the island – lies towards the eastern end of an undramatic south coast, and its large harbour is one of the safest in the northern sea. The town straddles a low headland at the entrance to a deep inlet which extends northwards almost to the end of the airport runway, and the two arms of the harbour are divided by a curious wooded promontory. The ferries berth at a big new quay in the eastern section, where the waterfront is disappointing, backed by a line of undistinguished buildings concerned mainly with tourist interests.

Round the corner to the west is another series of quays facing south, where you will find more of the traditional features of a Greek fishing port – the fishing boats themselves, with their nets spread out to dry on the quay or unloading their catch in the early morning, and at the far end a splendid old fish market. The rocky **Bourtzi** peninsula which divides the two parts of the harbour is softened by pine trees; at the end of its connecting causeway you come first to the town's *Gymnasion*, or High School, on the site of a mediaeval fortress, and then to a secluded restaurant overlooking the harbour.

The ship-building trade, once as busy here as anywhere in the islands, was based on a lagoon at the northern end of the bay. Now it has almost disappeared, faced with the competition from the nearby mainland, and the airport has cut off the lagoon from the life of the town. Instead, Skiathos harbour has become a base for the flotilla boat hirers, whose one-design yachts line a hundred yards of the eastern quay.

285

The town of Skiathos was built in the early and mid-nineteenth century, when increasing trade and the liberation of Greece had coaxed islanders all over the Aegean to come down from their hilltop *kastros* and to build again at the water's edge where the classical capitals had always been. They were there not only because the inhabitants were inveterate seafarers, but because a certain security obtained in classical times. In the Middle Ages, however, the Italian-born nobles lording it in their castles were unable to control the seas around them, and the pirates of the Aegean became a byword in Europe. Life in the islands retreated from the shores and went up inland to fortified places in the hills. The ancient harbours decayed and silted up, becoming no more than havens for coastal fishermen, or even bases for pirates. In the case of Skiathos they held out by the sea until the sixteenth century, when the arrival of the Turks finally drove them inland. When they returned in 1829 they built their town on the two low hills which overlook the harbour.

Not all the Skiathot families are native to the island, many having come as refugees from Asia Minor after the Greco-Turkish war of 1921. The convention which ended the war arranged for the compulsory exchange of Moslem and Greek minorities, and something like a million and a half Greeks from Asia Minor were settled in the islands and on the mainland of Greece.

Of the two higher points of the town, the eastern one is crowned by a rocky outcrop and the little church of *Agios Nikolaos* – modern, but in a quiet shady setting with a view over the harbour. The other and larger hill has many quiet alleyways, and much of the peaceful atmosphere of an island Chora. It would be unfair to blame the Skiathots for the dullness of the building round the harbour, for in 1944 the Germans burned down the whole area before retiring. The Chora has much more character. A feature of its alleyways is the central couloir of stones laid in herringbone pattern, making a natural duct for surplus water. There is peace and quiet here, and you can see the old ladies of Skiathos walking abroad with their distinctive long twists of hair hanging over their shoulders below black headscarves.

Kastro, the place to which the islanders retreated before the Turkish corsairs and invaders, is far away on the mountainous north

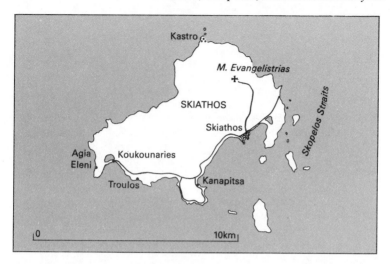

coast. It is still virtually inaccessible by any overland route. During the summer, however (but only in calm weather), a small boat leaves the fishing harbour for a day trip round the coast to Kastro and back. Below the now deserted site, tourists will find a place for swimming and for lunch, and are promised ten minutes in a 'Cyclops cave'. The main objective is the ruined town on a rocky promontory, once joined to the island only by a drawbridge. It includes the church of *Christos Sotiros*, still reasonably well preserved, with a late seventeenth-century *templo* and some frescos of about the same date. Once there were three hundred houses and twenty-two churches, but the only other recognizable churches are an *Agia Marina* and an *Agios Nikolaos* – though there is an abandoned monastery overlooking the bay to the east of the promontory. It is an eerie and spectacular place, where it would be rewarding to be able to spend time on one's own.

It must have been here or not far away that the Greeks had a lookout post to keep watch on the Persian fleet advancing down the opposite coast in 480 BC. It was keeping pace with the army of Xerxes, which was making its way south along the traditional invasion route between the mountains and the sea. The Persian ships had to negotiate the unfriendly coast of Magnesia between Mt Pelion and Cape Sepias – the point immediately opposite Skiathos –

287

while the outnumbered Greek squadron was stationed off Cape Artemision in the north of Euboea to bar the way through the Euripos narrows. The lookouts in Skiathos had a grandstand view of what Herodotus tells us happened to the Persians:

> 'The vessels of the fleet, after their arrival on the coast of Magnesia, betwixt the town of Castanea and the shores of Sepias, there stationed themselves, the foremost drawing close to land, the others lying on their anchors behind. As the shore was of no great extent, the fleet was ranged in eight regular divisions, with their heads towards the main sea, in which situation they passed the night. On the approach of day, the sky and the sea, which had before been serene, were violently disturbed; a furious storm arose, attended by a violent squall of wind from the east, which the inhabitants of these parts call an Hellespontian wind. They who foresaw that the tempest would still increase, and whose situation was favourable, prevented the effects of the storm by drawing their vessels ashore; of those whom the hurricane surprised farther out at sea, some were dashed against the promontory of Sepias, others were carried to Meliboea and Castanea, so severe was the tempest.'*

Four hundred enemy ships were destroyed in this way, with the loss of their stores and most of the soldiers on board. This disaster, followed by another to a squadron wrecked on the coast of Euboea, probably prevented the Persians from outflanking the three hundred Spartans under Leonidas who held up the invaders for a crucial week.

Kastro found a place in history again during the last war, when Skiathos was a staging post for Allied troops cut off by the German advance through Greece – which of necessity followed the same route as the army of Xerxes. Again, it has been argued, the brief but determined defence put up by the rearguard delayed the enemy advance for a crucial few days. Survivors of this action were secretly ferried across to Skiathos to wait for boats to take them to Turkey, from where most of them were able to rejoin their units in Egypt. Leonidas and his men had not been so lucky.

More New Zealanders than any others seem to have used the Skiathos escape route, and it was in Kastro that they were often

* *Histories* 188, trans. Beloe (London 1812).

An olive grove on Lesbos

The *Chozoviotissa* monastery on Amorgos

concealed. A key figure in the escape system was a woman in her forties called Kaliarina, who arranged their hiding places till a caique was ready to take them off. When the Italians finally ran her to ground she wounded one of their soldiers before being forced to surrender. To their credit they did not shoot her but sent her to Italy as a prisoner-of-war, with fifteen New Zealanders she had been sheltering in her cottage. In the town hall of Skiathos there is a framed letter of thanks from General Freyberg to the people of the island, who had in the end to suffer the revengeful burning of their capital by the retreating Germans – though Kaliarina returned in triumph.

An easier expedition than to Kastro is to the monastery of the **Evangelistria** – an hour's walk or a short taxi drive into the hills to the north of the town. It enjoys the usual lovely situation on a tree-clad hillside, but as usual it shows signs of dilapidation, and those who serve it have dwindled to three. The church is tucked away behind the high walls of the monastery, but it proves to be a charming building of a much earlier date than its eighteenth-century surroundings. It has a grey slate hat to its little round tower, and it is approached (once you are inside the main gates) through a garden courtyard with welcoming seats. It seems now an unlikely scene for dramatic events, but here as early as 1807 the Greek flag was hoisted when Theodore Kolokotronis and other leaders of the national revolt took the oath to liberate Greece.

The map of Skiathos reveals a remarkable contrast. Most of the island is impenetrable mountain terrain, yet along the south-eastern coastline are strung out some of the finest beaches in Greece, and the modern road with its regular bus service connects them all with the capital. You can take your pick of a fresh one every day by getting off the bus at the right stop, or you can spend all your holiday at one of the big hotels which dominate the most popular beaches. Most popular of all is the one at **Koukounaries**, which must be illustrated in every travel brochure for the Sporades, with its long sweep of sand and sheltering pine trees close behind. It does however pay the penalty for its popularity by overcrowding in summer, and many will find a quieter scene and just as good swimming at the beach of **Agia Eleni**, only ten minutes' walk from a bus stop a mile before Koukounaries. One simple café-bar provides refreshments at the nearer end, and the rocks beyond allow more privacy if the beach fills up with more bodies.

The shortest crossing from Skiathos to **Skopelos** is to the harbour of **Loutraki** on the north-west coast. It takes only an hour, and the regular ferries have a bus connection which brings the main town of Skopelos within half an hour's drive. This is a saving in time and money over the all-sea route, which involves rounding the northern cape and following the long rugged north-east coast down to Ormos Skopelou.

Whichever way you come, you will find Skopelos a brighter and more natural island than Skiathos. It is even more attractively wooded, mostly with pines, though there are plenty of olives, figs and some deciduous fruit trees in the valleys. The road which follows the south-west coast is exceptionally beautiful, and it passes beaches – in particular those at **Milia**, **Limnonari** and **Agnodas** –hardly inferior to those on Skiathos, though there are not so many of them.

If you come from the sea, the first thing to catch the eye on entering the harbour is the town itself. This is a true Chora, which climbs steeply up round an amphitheatre of rock, and it is one of the most beautiful and unspoilt towns in the islands. The houses are not only whitewashed (much though one loves the stark cleanliness of the Kyklades, it can be monotonous) but often washed in pinks and blues and even rich terra cotta, reminiscent of some of the eastern Sicilian villages. The woodwork is left a stained dark oak. The narrow alleys and stepped streets are clean and flowery, and you will have a friendly answer to your greeting or request for direction.

What distinguishes Skopelos Chora from any other is that a large proportion of the houses are roofed in heavy irregular blue-grey slates, and a further refinement is that the coping on the ridges is picked out in white. This is true too of many of the churches – said to number over a hundred – and the effect is cool and graceful even in the hottest sunshine.

These heavy slates are not unlike the massive ones which come from the Horsham area of west Sussex. Like them they come straight from the quarries and are impossible to cut into rectangles; but their place of origin is very different. These come from the

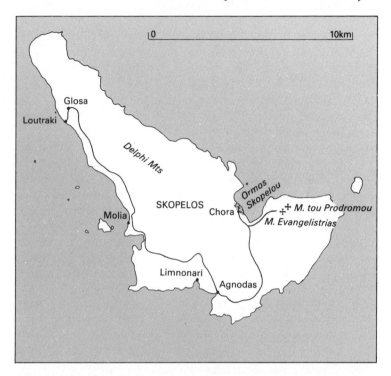

craggy sides of Mount Pelion above the Magnesian coast, and there was a time when you could find them in Skiathos too. Already in Skopelos these roofs are becoming fewer as the cost of quarrying and ferrying them across from the mainland grows heavier. What may save them for a time is their indestructible strength and resistance to weather, but factory-made tiles will inevitably take over, as they did on Skiathos when post-war building had to be done as cheaply as possible. It is said that a new slate roof costs as much as the rest of the house.

The town avoids the formal shape of an amphitheatre, as it rises to three separate points with two slight dips in between. The southern district is the least interesting, but it contains the cathedral church of the *Koimisis tou Theotokou* (the Dormition of the Mother of God), with the Italianate semi-detached campanile you see a lot of in these northern islands.

291

On the northern summit, overlooking the harbour entrance, are the remains of the mediaeval **Kastro**. To call the site mediaeval would be misleading, for although the centre is occupied by the church of *Agios Athanasios*, probably Byzantine in origin in spite of a *templo* dated 1669, local historians say that it replaced a temple of Athena such as is often found on a classical acropolis. From a small *plateia* outside you look down on an enchanting little whitewashed church with a dumpy octagonal tower, all roofed in crazy patterns of weathered grey slate. Framed by trees it perches above the deep blue bay with all the grace of a living creature. Its dedication to the *Evangelismos* makes one think of the angel of the Annunciation. As you wind slowly down to the harbour there seems to be an ancient church round every corner, ranging from the very early single nave of *Agios Georgios* to the handsome basilica of *Christos Sotiros*.

The long harbour front you will find more attractive than the one at Skiathos. Inevitably some of the bars and restaurants whose tables spill out over the quay grow rather tatty during the summer, and the food and its service varies in quality. The northern end, where the ferries berth, is cleaner and better than the rest. Also at this end is the distinguished and recently restored building which houses the *Limenarcheion*, or Port Police. In the proper tradition of Skopelos it has dark oak door and window frames set off by whitewashed walls, with a long roof of blue-grey tiles.

As you sit at your table on the quayside in the thick shade of the carefully trimmed mulberry trees, you look across the lovely bay at a steep green hillside on which you can make out the lighter outlines of one or two buildings. Almost at the top is the monastery of the **Evangelistria**, which is a convent for nuns. There is a good road up to it, though you could walk up in little more than an hour. The position is beautiful, but it is a sad place and the three remaining sisters are very poor – desperately anxious to sell you something from their little shop counter. The church is dull, except for some good seventeenth-century woodwork, but they keep the garden round it bright and flowery. The best feature of the convent buildings is the kitchen, with scrubbed wooden tables and a huge bread oven. One fears that little food finds its way up here to be cooked, and the only refreshment they can offer to the visitor is a glass of water – but it is very good water.

Just before you reach the Evangelistria a sign points the way up a rocky path to your left which leads to another convent, the **Moni tou Prodromou**, dedicated to John the Baptist. After half an hour's not difficult scrambling you come out on to an open plateau with lovely views over fresh parts of the island. The first building you see as you turn to your left is a monastery in miniature – a little grey-slated church surrounded by white walls which look welcoming. The gate, however, is rustily padlocked and the courtyard overgrown, and it is the now deserted 'Moni' of *Agia Varvara*.

The Prodromou monastery is a far grander place built into the hillside further on. At once it appears to be a more prosperous place than the Evangelistria, and several cheerful and well-nourished nuns can be seen scurrying about. It is difficult to say whether it is the choice of the sisters to live poorly or comfortably, or whether it is a question of a richer foundation or a better patron. The garden is well kept, and the nuns' quarters look attractive in an arcaded terrace above the church, mantled in vines. The church too is more interesting, though it carries the same date of 1640, and it has a richly carved *templo* with the gilded figures of stags, horses and hounds running along over the ritual doorways. Perhaps this gives a hint of the tastes of some powerful patron? One ikon, which looks earlier than the seventeenth century, shows the twelve apostles grouped round a window whose two shutters actually open to show a Virgin and Child – just like a once popular form of Christmas card.

Skopelos teems with churches. Apart from the hundred or so in the Chora, there must be nearly two hundred scattered about in the mountainous hinterland, including several more monasteries. As they all appear to date in their present form from the sixteenth or seventeenth centuries, it would seem that if the people built far enough away from the harbours which were the administrative centres their Turkish masters never interfered. Few of them are accessible except by rough ways on foot or donkey, but with such a varied company of saints to protect it Skopelos seems naturally an island of the blest.

At the end of the ferry line through the northern Sporades from Volos or Agios Konstantinos lies **Alonnisos**. This attractive island can also be visited before the others by taking ship direct from Kymi in Euboea, after which you can travel back to the mainland in the reverse direction. There is also a daily sailing in the summer by small boat from Skopelos, which leaves the quay opposite the bus stop in the early morning and returns in the afternoon. This gives you about five hours to look around the only immediately accessible part, which consists of the harbour of Patatiri and the inland Chora which now carries the name of the island.

There are two confusing things about the name Alonnisos. One is that few sources agree on how to spell it. Different versions appear even in the official tourist brochures, but the Greek word clearly has two 'n's and one 's' (as in Peloponnisos) so that must be the one to follow. What is certain is that the stress accent in both cases falls on the last syllable but two.

The other difficulty is to know whether the name belongs to this island at all, or whether it should still be Ikos, as Strabo called it, or Chelidromi, as it was known in the last century. An eighteenth-century map (printed in London and 'Designed for the Use of Schools and of Gentlemen who make the Antient Writers their Delight or Study'), for all the fanciful shapes and position it gives these islands, clearly marks one of the larger ones 'Alonesus' and places it next to 'Skopelus'.

Furthermore it is the central and almost the largest island of the group (with its attendant island of Peristera it covers the largest area), and it was the subject of a wrangle about ownership between Athens and Philip of Macedon in 344 BC. A speech before the Athenian assembly called 'On the subject of Alonnisos' may have been wrongly attributed to Demosthenes, but it was obviously about a place important enough to be used as a bargaining counter after Philip's forces had cleared the harbour of a nest of pirates.

Whatever the truth is, the modern harbour is properly called **Patatiri**. Here all visiting ships berth, yet it is still a genuine fishing harbour, with boats being repaired along the foreshore and a line of bars and restaurants behind. The small town which has grown up in the background has little character, simply because it hardly existed before 1970. In 1965 the Chora above was badly damaged by an earthquake, and the Athens military government (as it was in the time of the 'Colonels') not only discouraged any attempt to rebuild it but pulled down any building which looked at all unsafe. The

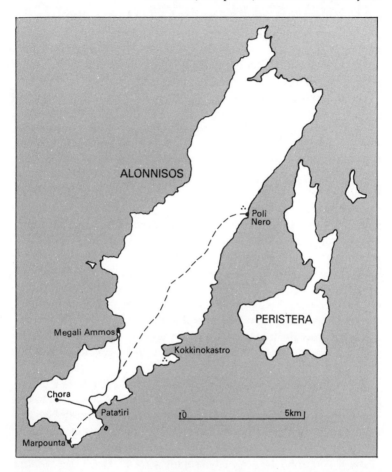

people whose home it had been for centuries at first refused to move, but when in 1973 the government moved the school to new buildings in Patatiri they had to give in. The houses built for them there proved shabbily designed and constructed, far worse than the ones they could have reoccupied or rebuilt for themselves in the Chora, where the damage was far from universal.

To reach the old Chora from the harbour is a long and dusty walk, and if there is a taxi it is habitually elusive. However, the enterprising manager of the Ikos Travel Agency at the harbour runs a small

295

bus between there and the Chora which takes on board the morning crop of arrivals for an hour's conducted visit. Born in the island, Mr Athanassios is very well educated and knows its history thoroughly, so this is an opportunity not to miss. His must be the only bus in Greece which has Vivaldi on tape instead of *bouzouki*.

There is an elusive beauty up there. Perhaps the process of desertion leaves something intangible behind, but Alonnisos has not only regained its name but enjoys new life. Those Greeks who can afford it have joined with a handful of visitors – mostly from Germany – in a project to rebuild the village in its original style. This has meant whenever possible bringing in the blue-grey slates of Pelion to roof some modest cottages of one or two storeys. Gardens are difficult, because the water supply is so meagre that it can only be used for drinking. But they have preserved all the trees they can, and with all the wild flowers and the glorious views in all directions you hardly need gardens.

So far they have not managed to reconstitute any of the old churches, which are now locked and deserted. Another sad result of the enforced evacuation was that some precious ikons were stolen during the confusion. As one inhabitant ruefully said, nobody realized they were precious until they were stolen. The waterless Chora is not a place to stay, though a simple taverna and general store open during the summer.

The long bony spine of Alonnisos runs on for another ten miles to the north, but no road yet reaches further than the two miles to the beach of **Megali Ammos**. Yet there are dozens of unspoilt beaches on both the west and the east coasts, as well as on its close neighbour, Peristera. There are ancient sites at **Kokkinokastro** ('Red-castle'), said to be the original acropolis of Ikos, and further up the coast at **Poli Nero** ('Much Water'). All these places can be reached during the summer by day boat trips from Patatiri, so just five hours in the island can never do it justice.

A holiday on Alonnisos could be fascinating, but you would have to accept that there is practically no road transport and little village life. One of the simplest of Greek islands, it seems to have survived fairly unscathed on fishing and on the tending of sheep and goats, though there are two modern hotels and a daily influx of tourists on excursions from neighbouring islands.

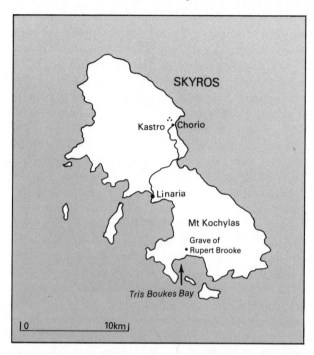

Skyros differs from the other northern Sporades in being a bare and classical island. Geographically too it is the odd one out, for it lies a good forty miles south-east of Skopelos across a windswept sea. This may be why the only ferry line which serves it sails the much shorter distance from Kymi in Euboea. It can be tiresome not to have direct communication with the other islands, but the new airfield puts it within about the same flying time from Athens as Skiathos.

The port of arrival, **Linaria**, lies at the head of a deep bay on the west coast. It is still only a fishing village, though there are probably rooms to let if you arrive late by boat. The capital, which is officially called Skyros, though locally often known as Chorio or just 'the Chora', is on the opposite coast. A bus runs between there and Linaria, a journey of about half an hour which takes you right through the narrow waist of the island (sometimes with detours to reach villages which lie off the route) and across to the east coast.

297

The Chora is built on a high terrace which faces inland, but is itself dominated by the steeply rising hill which was the site of the now ruined **Kastro**. It was also the acropolis of the ancient city, and was probably the site of the palace of King Lykomedes.

For this is the island of Achilles, and here 'what song the Sirens sang, or what name Achilles assumed when he hid among women, though puzzling questions, are not beyond all conjecture'. At the plea of his mother Thetis, the future Greek hero was hidden by the king in the palace, disguised as a girl. Thetis had learned from the fates that her son was destined never to return from Troy if he went on the expedition, but that if he could be induced to stay at home he would enjoy a long life – 'a short life, with eternal fame, or a long but inglorious existence'. Thetis, being rational and life-loving, like all women, decided that the latter would be better for her son.

Unfortunately her concealment of Achilles was foiled by Odysseus, another reluctant hero who had himself tried a rather similar ploy without success in Ithaka. Arriving in Skyros, Odysseus was given permission by the king to search his palace for the supposedly hidden young man. The wily Odysseus had brought armfuls of gifts for the ladies of the court, including jewellery and dresses (he reckoned perhaps that even if he did not find Achilles he might profit from his generosity). At a given moment Odysseus retired from the palace and ordered his trumpeter to sound the alarm. The inevitable happened. While the ladies rushed to make sure of their clothes and gems, Achilles stripped himself to the waist and seized a sword and buckler – which Odysseus had thoughtfully placed among the gifts. He re-entered the palace in the midst of the panic, and Achilles was forced to accept the glories of war and a short life.

Although the supposed dates hardly tally, this was the same Lykomedes (or was it his grandfather?) who is reputed to have killed Theseus by hurling him 'headlong from the top of the rocks', according to Plutarch. It is easy to imagine that Theseus may have become a bit of a bore by then, endlessly relating all his exploits to the court. After the battle of Marathon, when Theseus was seen to appear in the Athenian ranks, they sent to Skyros and had his bones removed for burial in Attic earth. This was done by Cimon in 469 BC, and his festival the Theseia was celebrated annually in Athens on 21 October.

The encircling walls of the Kastro are Venetian, though traces of earlier ones can be seen in the foundations. The principal gateway remains, with a lion of St Mark lording it above. Inside the walls and linking these two periods are the crumbling remains of a convent dedicated to *Agios Georgios Skirianos* (a St George who was said to have Arab origins), founded in AD 962.

The town itself follows the architectural pattern of the Kyklades, with geometric houses, flat-roofed and brilliant with whitewash, built up on varying levels of the hillsides. Once inside any of the houses one finds the evidence of a native tradition of craftsmanship in wood which is rare in the Aegean. Some element of Byzantium perhaps lingered on here through all the centuries. It is to be seen in the embroidered textiles, the carved wooden coffers and in the furniture itself. The folklore section of the town's museum confirms that the people of Skyros have for many centuries been artists and craftsmen. It is a tradition that has not died.

At the same time it may be the only place in the Aegean where one finds woodcarving in the Victorian-Swiss style. The interiors of the houses are often quite un-Aegean, with rounded and arched fireplaces, plates hanging on the walls or supported on special plate ledges, and even chairs with barley-twist legs. The thing that hits you as really incongruous – so distant in time and taste from the nature of the island – is the memorial statue to Rupert Brooke, who died of fever not on Skyros but in a hospital ship on the way to Gallipoli. It is a bronze figure of a naked youth in the Greco-German manner, which stands on a bastion overlooking the sea, symbolizing 'Immortal Poetry'. Brooke, as is clear from his letters and poems, had a sense of humour. The man who reverenced Webster and whose own favourite poet was Donne would have been delighted to hear that in the words of a Mayor of Skyros 'it is popularly considered rather indecent'.

The beach here is of fine golden sand, and stretches for about half a mile between Magazia and Molos, with a few fishermen's cottages at the far end. There are other good beaches at different points around the island, but it is wise to consult the most recent source of information about how to get there. The state of island roads can alter radically within a few months, so powerful an instrument for change is the modern bulldozer.

299

You can swim too in the bay of **Tris Boukes**, or Trebuki, far down on the south coast, a large but uninspiring anchorage with its mouth half sealed by two islands – hence the name Tris Boukes, meaning 'three mouths'. This is where Rupert Brooke's hospital ship put in when he died in April 1915. He is buried in an olive grove about a mile from the shore. A white cross surmounts the grave, and a small plot of ground is fenced off by iron railings. A visit just after the last war found the railings bent and broken, the grass growing high over the mound and the surrounding stones chiselled with the names of Greek visitors. It was not until 1960 that a fleet chaplain from Malta led a naval expedition to the grave and restored it. The railings were renovated, a blacksmith straightening them out over a fire of olive wood. The tomb was cleaned and re-whitewashed, and the initials R.B. etched at the base of the cross. The poet has found a pleasant resting place.

Access

SKIATHOS, SKOPELOS and ALONNISOS are served by daily ferries from Volos and Agios Konstantinos on the mainland, and less frequently from Kymi on Euboea. Skiathos has an airport, with daily flights from Athens. So has SKYROS, but the only connection by sea is from Kymi.

Communications

Bus services, mainly coastal, connect principal towns and holiday centres. Taxis are usually available, though rare on ALONNISOS.

Accommodation

For a full list of hotels in the main categories consult the tourist brochure for the Northern Sporades. There are also rooms to let in the main towns, especially in guest houses in Skiathos.

SKIATHOS There are big holiday hotels near most of the popular beaches. In the harbour area SAN REMO (C) is comfortable and well run, ALKYON (B) is huge, unattractive and badly sited, MELTEMI is a pleasant guest house facing the yacht station.

SKOPELOS Most hotels are some distance from the harbour, very few in the town. A good choice there would be CAPTAIN (C) – enquire at the

Tourist Office – which is small, quiet and comfortable, three minutes' walk from the quay.

ALONNISOS   Of the listed hotels GALAXY (C) has the best position overlooking the harbour and a small beach. MARPOUNTA (C, 200 beds) is more impersonal, and overlooks a pebbly beach a few miles from the harbour.

SKYROS   Only one hotel is listed, XENIA (B) on the beach below the Chora, typical of its class. Others are being built and there are rooms to let.

Restaurants

SKIATHOS   Selection is difficult, but you probably eat best in the streets behind the harbour

SKOPELOS   The best of the harbour-side restaurants are near the landing quay.

ALONNISOS   There is little choice, and in the few places round the harbour of Patatiri standards vary considerably.

SKYROS   There are several attractive places in the Chora.

Facilities

Banks: The usual banks can be found in Skiathos, Skopelos and Skyros towns. For exchange facilities in Alonnisos enquire at the tourist office in Patatiri – which is by no means always open.

Yachts: Skiathos has an extensive small yacht quay and facilities. Skopelos has berths available and is a safe anchorage except in a northerly blow, when the bay of Staphylos is better. Alonnisos has a safe and attractive anchorage at Patatiri, with reasonable facilities ashore. Limenaria in Skyros is a very sheltered harbour with good facilities ashore.

The
Northern Aegean

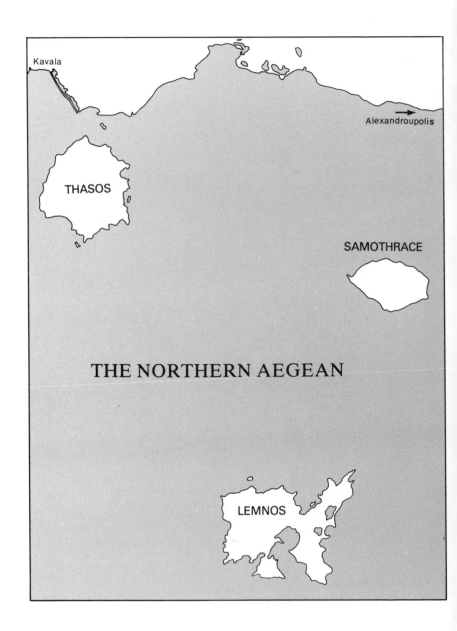

Kavala

Alexandroupolis

THASOS

SAMOTHRACE

THE NORTHERN AEGEAN

LEMNOS

THE NORTHERN AEGEAN

The three fascinating islands described in this chapter appeal very differently to the modern visitor. The physical contrasts are striking. Thasos is thickly covered with pine forests, and its core is marble. The trees which line the mountain gorges of Samothrace are many of them deciduous; maize and tobacco grow in the coastal plain. In Lemnos the hills are low and bare, the interior fertile, the shores sandy and hospitable. Rarely does natural beauty and visible history combine so harmoniously as in Thasos, or religious mystery and spectacular scenery meet so dramatically as in Samothrace. Lemnos is a less obvious draw, but it has the remains of a city older than the first to be built at Troy, and evidence of civilized occupation in uninterrupted sequence ever since.

Faraway islands they may seem from Athens or the Kyklades, but two of them lie close under the southern coast of what is still the Greek mainland, while the third guards the narrow channel which separates Europe from Asia. Between them they cover the approaches to the ancient trade route from the Mediterranean to the Black Sea, and for different reasons they have attracted colonists, adventurers and important visitors throughout their history. Merchants came to Thasos for gold, wine and marble, to Lemnos for gold too and other metals, while Samothrace was the scene of elaborate religious mysteries which attracted kings and queens from Sparta, Macedonia and Egypt, statesmen and even an emperor from Rome. The few tourists who find their way here with some difficulty today would be astonished to see the crowds that assembled to celebrate the Great Gods of Samothrace two thousand years ago – brought here in ships undeterred by some of the stormiest waters in the Mediterranean.

305

NINETEEN

Thasos, Samothrace and Lemnos

Northernmost of all the Aegean islands, **Thasos** has a beauty which eclipses many of the better known ones. It does have some remarkable ancient remains, but it also possesses that rarest and most pleasant advantage in a hot climate – the sound of streams running through pine-forested hills and even through the streets of mountain villages.

Lying so far to the north it is not easy to come at by sea from ports further south, except in a cruise liner – which is unsatisfactory because you need at least a week to understand and relish its beauty – or in your own boat, which can involve long and stormy passages. The key lies in the busy but well ordered city of **Kavala**, just across the narrow strait from Limena, the island's only large harbour. The quickest and most painless approach is by the daily morning flight from Athens to Kavala airport. From there it is best to take a taxi to the little port of **Keramoti**, about twelve miles east of Kavala, because from there an hourly (sometimes half-hourly) ferry service runs straight across to Limena. There is a longer and less frequent daily service from Kavala itself which lands you not at Limena but at Skala Prinou on the north-east coast. The ships used for these crossings will be familiar to wartime servicemen, for they are converted from the tank landing craft used by Allied navies.

The landing place at **Limena** is a big modern quay. Immediately behind it is the departure point for the island's buses, and across the wide promenade are the modern buildings – banks, restaurants and hotels – which have grown up since the war. You should have no difficulty in finding a hotel room here, though there are more obviously holiday hotels which overlook the beaches out to the west of the town. The charm of Limena is that the town is built on the site of the ancient city, and that the remains of the old capital exist side by side with the modern buildings – some of the most important being not more than a hundred yards from the waterfront. Behind them, encircling both modern and ancient structures, the old city walls rise from a natural bastion of rock.

You will quickly realize why landing craft are used here when you see that their principal cargo is not tourists but lorries carrying huge blocks of marble or piles of pine trunks. All day they line up on the quay waiting for the next ferry, and they come back with machinery and supplies for the island's building and quarrying industry. Marble has been quarried and exported for more than two thousand years – a trade which was highly organized under the Roman empire, but never so intensively as it is now. Modern methods of quarrying and transport take full advantage of the fact that a great part of the island's rock formation is pure marble, while the demand for it in Athens, the provinces and the islands is insatiable for use in all kinds of building. The vast pine forests (mostly of *Pinus halepensis*, the Aleppo pine) are another source of export wealth, but it is also satisfying to see that ships are still built here in the traditional way from Thasian pine.

Not that in classical times these were the only reasons for the wealth and reputation of Thasos. Although Herodotus writes of previous occupation by Phoenician traders, the earliest records, supported by archaeology, tell us that it was colonized from Paros between 710 and 680 BC, and that the colonists prospered by working the gold mines they found here. With them came the satirical poet Archilochus. During his stay in Thasos he fought alongside the islanders against Thracian invaders. He ran away from the battlefield 'incurring the disgrace of losing his shield' – no Spartan he – and far from being ashamed he recorded the event in one of his poems. He did live to fight another day, though his eventual fate is unknown.

Thasian marble has not always been mainly for export. You have only to walk fifty yards back from the old harbour to find yourself in the *agora*, the civic centre of the classical town, crowded with the remains of substantial monuments. The earliest is of the seventh century BC and the latest from the first century AD – not counting a few from the Byzantine age. Other buildings, chiefly sanctuaries of gods and heroes, can be identified as you walk about the town. Your first sight of them can be misleading, for what was built in great blocks of gleaming white marble now looks dark and a little forbidding. The effect of weathering over the centuries has given them almost the appearance of basalt, yet where there is the slightest chip you can see the pure marble underneath, and suddenly you get the revelation of what the city must have looked like in its glory.

The *agora* today is a broad open space, pleasant to wander through, with grass and flowers growing almost unchecked among the ruins, trees to give shade here and there, and convenient blocks or marble where you can sit unrebuked to study the plan of the site – or just to drink in the atmosphere. Most of the buildings have been identified after a careful study of inscriptions by the French School of Archaeology, which is still in charge of excavation on the island. The earliest seems to be a monument to Glaucus, an associate of Archilochus and one of the original colonists from Paros. Then there is the base of a monument to a more famous citizen, the boxer Theogenes who was said by Pausanias to have won 1400 medals in Greek athletic games. An all-rounder of the fifth century BC, it may have been partly his work as a local politician which won him this honour; perhaps more important was his claim to be a descendant of Herakles, to whom a large sanctuary was dedicated in the western part of the town.

The most extensive remains in the *agora* are of the first century AD, when it was replanned on a huge scale with colonnades surrounding it on four sides. Of this date is an altar erected in honour of Caius and Lucius Caesar, the young sons of Augustus's daughter Julia by Marcus Agrippa. They both died before their grandfather, a tragedy which spoiled his plans for the succession and led to much unseemly and murderous intrigue. Their memorial here shows the importance of Thasos in the Roman world, and suggests that Caius the elder son may have used it as a base for the campaign in Asia Minor in AD 1. They both died within the next three years.

Although the main buildings are named on signs put there by the French School, the ground plan of the *agora* is hard to follow, and you would be wise at some point to look in at the **Museum** just outside its western (and only) entrance. Here they have a well organized collection which includes some remarkable finds from all over the island, and from the curator you can buy a copy of the comprehensive guide published by the French School in 1974. Even if he has only a copy with the Greek text it is worth buying for the clear and detailed plans of all the main sites.

One thing the 1974 edition does not show is a new area of excavation beyond the *agora* to the south-east. It does show a marble-paved passageway, on the walls of which a frieze of lively sculpture and the names of important visitors were carved. This led to it being called the *Diodos ton Theoron*, or 'Corridor of the Ambassadors'. The panels of marble reliefs were removed to the Louvre – without apparently any protest from the Greek government!

Until recently it was not clear where the passage led, except in the general direction of the **Sanctuary of Dionysus**, a hefty monument which can be seen on the far side of a modern roadway. Now a fresh complex of buildings has come to light in the intervening space. Probably the earliest lies to the right as you emerge from the passage, where a few steps lead up to the base of a small sanctuary. There is a niche in the wall to the left of the steps, of a shape associated with cults of Dionysus or Pan, possibly to contain a vessel of sanctified wine; the obvious parallel – *piscina*! Further on you see a big circular water cistern, and beyond that the unmistakable foundations of a Roman bath system, complete with hypocaust. It is clear that the water supply for the *agora* came in here through a roofed conduit, and was distributed along stone couloirs to refresh the town.

Above this area, to the south, is a site identified as a **Sanctuary of Artemis**, now an olive grove; in ancient Thasos you could pay your respects to a comforting number of deities, just as in most Greek islands you find a multiplicity of saints. There is nothing much to see above ground, but in the Museum is the carved ivory head of a lioness, tiny and exquisite, which came from the Artemision; near it you can see an elegant bronze figurine of the goddess herself, which formed the handle of a polished bronze mirror.

Better perhaps than walking studiously around the *agora* with nose in guidebook is to sit for half an hour in this shady, green, evocative spot and imagine life here during those centuries of peaceful and prosperous sanity. If you face seaward, there close ahead is one of the most attractive of small harbours, once the naval base for the triremes and galleys which protected the coast. Since then there has been some silting, but fishing boats and small yachts are still sheltered by its protective moles. Beneath the silt the bed of the harbour is natural marble (no anchoring here) and a fringe of ancient plane trees shades two waterside cafés.

If you turn and look inland to the south you see a ring of pine-clad hills, with (on a clear day) the peak of Mount Ipsarion soaring behind them. Through gaps in the encircling trees you can make out what must be masonry as well as rocks. There in fact was built the ring of walls which defended the city from the landward side – walls with gates in them which still stand to almost full height. The circuit is not difficult to walk, and steep in only a few places. Moreover it is an experience which no reasonably active visitor ought to miss.

It is best to begin at the north-eastern end, where a substantial section climbs southwards from the headland known as Ebraiokastro. First, though, you can follow the line of the seaward-facing wall from the point where it joins the extension of the harbour's eastern mole. A path runs inside it, and almost at once you come to the sea gate which led to the enclosed harbour, where one of the massive vertical pillars has a vivid carving in relief of the goddess Artemis, riding in a chariot behind a horse led by a male figure – probably Hermes.

Next, behind an orchard on your right, is the **Sanctuary of Poseidon**. Here was found an altar to Hera in her capacity as 'Protectress of Harbours'; on one stone of it was inscribed a law forbidding people to sacrifice she-goats to her. You will probably find one of them munching gratefully nearby. On your left further on is another gate which led to the old 'commercial' harbour, where trading vessels were anchored or beached. It is now thoroughly silted up, though from above you can see the line of its eastern mole.

As you approach the headland you may be lucky enough to see a big ship being built under its cliffs – at a traditional place by traditional methods. It is a beautiful sight, the lovely curves of the timbers outlining a shape which has not changed in a thousand years. The men who work on it – never more than three – will come from a family which has been building ships here for generations. The timber for the ribs and planking comes from the woods above,

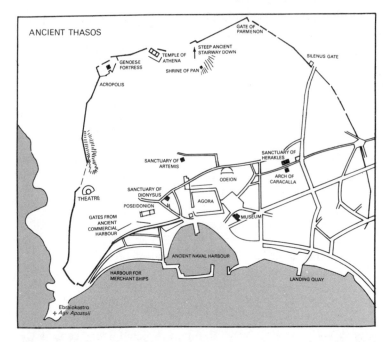

and it is of pine used when still green. An island shipbuilder will never use weathered timber – it is too stiff and hard to work – and the curves are allowed for by eye when they fell the trees and saw the planks. No blueprint drawings are used on the site, but modern electrically-powered tools have at last superseded the rhythmical swing of the adze. Whether champagne has replaced the blood of a freshly killed cockerel to give life to the ship could not be determined – local answers were evasive, and the writer has not seen a recent launching.

The mediaeval **Ebraiokastro** (its Jewish origin is not explained) crowned the final headland. Above it is a site which neatly illustrates a religious sequence often found in Greece. First there was a classical temple, dated by its scattered tiles to the end of the sixth century BC. Then came an early Christian basilica church of the fifth or sixth century AD, which can be traced on the ground, and finally the little modern church of *Agii Apostoli*.

From here the path climbs easily up outside the walls through pine woods till you reach the **Theatre**. It lies below you at a point where the pines give way to a clump of ilex, which surrounds and invades the *cavea*. First built in the fifth century BC on the usual plan of the time, it was given a more elaborate *scena* in the Hellenistic period, and finally adapted in the first century AD for the cruder taste of Romans who enjoyed wild beast shows. This explains why the three lowest rows of seats were removed and a five-foot stone barrier erected to protect the VIPs. Now it is a peaceful and shady resting place, though for a few days in the summer classical Greek is heard again – usually in the plays of Aristophanes.

Another easy climb over soft pine needles and between low clumps of cistus brings you to the first buildings which mark the ancient **Acropolis**. Most prominent now are the two guard towers of the mediaeval castle, built, or at least completed, by the Gattilusi family from Genoa who held both Thasos and Samothrace as fiefs during the fourteenth and fifteenth centuries.

The second of the towers has been excavated to a lower level than the first, and on the far side you can see a charming relief carving of a family at dinner in the classical style. The master of the house reclines by the table, his wife sits at the head of it and a slave boy waits at his master's elbow. Benignly watching the scene is the owner's horse. This was probably a funeral *stele* of the fifth or fourth century, re-used and built into the later walls – in the same way as the outstanding exhibit in the Thasos museum. This is an unfinished statue of *Apollo Kriophoros*, so called because the god is holding a young ram in his arms. It stands over ten feet high, and the archaic style of sculpture puts it at about 600 BC. The two halves of this colossal figure ('nothing beside remains') were found built into a mediaeval wall on the acropolis close to the site of a temple to Pythian Apollo. In classical times this was the chief building there, but now its foundations are overgrown and dwarfed by the mediaeval towers.

The path dips to a saddle before climbing to the second high point of the acropolis. Here stood the most impressive of all the Greek structures on Thasos, the great fifth-century **Temple of Athena**. Enough of the foundations and supporting walls survive to show the scale and beauty of its formal classical plan. Seen from the town below, or from out to sea, it would have been a superb sight.

The third and last crest is a rocky one with no building on it. However, before the path begins its short climb to the top you come face to face with a unique manifestation of a religion older than Athena's. A smooth shoulder of rock has been sliced into, to form a roughly triangular vertical surface. On this has been carved the unmistakable figure of **Pan**, with a wicked little face and jaunty horns, playing his multi-reed pipe while his goats crowd round to listen. By his side stands an amphora of wine, and on a pointed niche over his head is carved a wine cup – and the shape of the niche is the same we have seen in the wall of the sanctuary beyond the *agora*. Although the cult of Pan is older than the Olympian gods, there is something about it which will take far longer to die out. His presence here must have been recorded by an artist of the Hellenistic age, with a subtly decadent menace that still sends a *frisson* down your spine as you look at it. The soft earth around is pitted by the pointed hooves of modern goats – who knows what goes on up there under the stars after dark?

The rocky peak is marked by a stubby concrete pillar, and there is a wonderful view all around – to the south Ipsarion rises from the attendant green hills, to the north and far below a toy ship is entering one of the town's toy harbours, now seen from a goat's-eye view. The way down on the far side of the peak is not easy to find, for it follows a 'secret' stairway cut into the southern rock face. Look for the metal handrail which begins about half way down (to your left as you face Pan), and in no time you will have descended fifty feet to a point where the city walls begin again. They still fall steeply, with a rough path outside them, till you reach the massive **Gate of Parmenon**, built in the fifth century BC and named after the master builder who carved his name on one of the stones. Looking back at that point you will see above you two enormous circular eyes carved on a block of stone – concentric rings which were probably drawn by compass. This is an *apotropaion*, a sinister device to put the evil eye on a would-be invader.

After the gate the slope is gentler, and just before you strike a main road leading out of Limena to the south you come to another gateway, the base of which stands below the modern road. This is the **Gate of Silenus**, best known for the figure with rampant phallus carved in relief on a huge block of marble. That it is marble and not

313

basalt is proved by the efforts of puritans to chip away the offending member.

Two more gates pierce the last section of the wall before it disappears in the flat and cultivated ground to the south-west of the town; the wall was plundered long ago for house building. The road running in from the last gate takes you past the **Herakleion** and the Roman **Arch of Caracalla**, along a section of the Roman road below the **Odeion**, until it reaches the southern edge of the *agora*. The whole circuit will have taken you a little over two hours, with intervals for reflection or refreshment, and it is worth every minute.

A continuous modern road makes the circuit of the island, running most of the way close to the sea. The inland roads are rougher, making connections with the few villages for which space has been found among the mountains, or used to bring timber down from distant hillsides. The buses which leave the quayside at Limena take schoolchildren and villagers as near as they can to their homes, and two or three times a day, according to the season, they make the whole circuit.

Two pretty villages lie directly on the east coast route not far from Limena. First comes **Panagia**, where narrow streets lead up to and from a shady *plateia* towards the church of the *Koimisis* (Dormition), which in spite of being a nineteenth-century reproduction basilica does contain some things of interest. One big seventeenth-century ikon panel has above it the eye symbol (here a more life-like oval) which wards off the evil one. Superstition keeps vandals away from Christian shrines just as it kept enemies from Pagan walls. Below the church runs a stream which combines three spring-fed channels – the *Tris Pigi* – and waters the village below.

Two miles further on is **Potamia**, a village without the charm of Panagia, but with a character of its own. It has a number of small rectangular houses with old slate roofs and eccentric chimneys, said to be a Turkish (more likely Macedonian) style of building. Towering over both these places is the mighty peak of Ipsarion, while they in turn look down over the fine beach of **Chrysi Ammoudia**, one of many which can be reached from this side of the 'ring' road. The most popular, **Makryammos**, is only half an hour's walk or a very short drive out of Limena, and is almost the private property of the hotel of the same name.

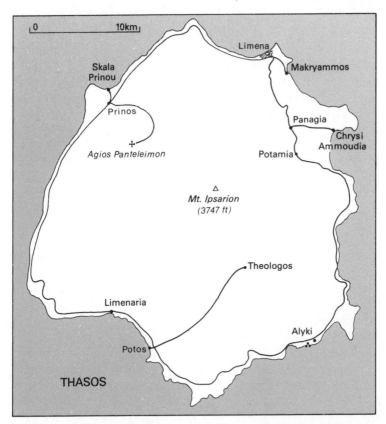

The road to the west follows a flatter coastline, and the beaches beside it are pebbly. This is the nearest way to the second main town, **Limenaria**. (Both names are only variations of the Greek word for harbour.) Limenaria is smaller and quieter, with the air of an English seaside town in the west country. The hotels look pleasant, and the generally friendly atmosphere suggests a good place for a holiday.

From whichever direction, you should try to reach **Alyki** on the south-east coast, where a low headland separates two little sandy bays. There is no modern building there except a few fishermen's cottages above the eastern bay. Yet within a hundred yards' radius you can see two seventh-century BC temples, two very early Christ-

315

ian basilicas, a series of marble quarries at the water's edge which were operative from the seventh century BC to the seventh century AD, and two caves where many archaic votive offerings were found.

The temples are practically twins, with clearly outlined foundations lying alongside each other. Prayers for the safe passage of ships in the marble trade were found carved on the stylobates and on fallen stones; a later thanksgiving to the Dioskouroi (Castor and Pollux) suggests a dedication for the temples, and perhaps a connection with the Kabeiroi cult of Samothrace and Lemnos. The two basilicas further up the headland are also a pair, a kind of Christian retort to the twin temples below. They must have been lovely buildings, with a cluster of small columns at their east ends, some of which are still standing. The date of both is certainly as early as the second half of the fifth century AD, and they were known as important shrines in the time of the emperor Justinian.

The quarries were in continuous production from the arrival of the Parian colonists, and reached a peak of activity in Roman times. They were abandoned only when the sea began to eat them away, and you can still see blocks of marble with marks of tooling on them standing ready for shipment.

In the heart of Limena there was another marble Christian basilica from the early Byzantine epoch. You find it at the south end of the only real *plateia*, a peaceful square behind the modern landing quay, with its original columns neatly stacked beside the east end. In the far corner the twisted trunk of a plane tree looks almost coeval, and I suspect that there would have been a tavern on the west side where now tables from the best restaurant stand on the pavement. 'Best', that is, for the people of Thasos, for it is open all the year to feed with the best Greek food the workmen, the bank officials, the ships' crews and the local families, whose children play in and out of the ruins and round the trunk of the ancient plane tree.

There is nowhere like Thasos, with its antiquity, its eloquent remains and its physical beauty today. As you look back from the deck of your ship, and Mount Ipsarion disappears in the haze, you will remember green trees against blue depths, and the sound of the wind in the pines. The Greek physician Hippocrates was happy here, and judged it healthy for body and mind.

If Thasos is the most beautiful, **Samothrace** is the most mysterious of the islands in the northern sea. For a thousand years or more it has been considered almost inaccessible, and so preserved from the ships of the traders and the war galleys of the invader. Today it is slightly more accessible, but the most convenient approach is from Alexandroupolis on the Thracian mainland – and, pleasant small town though it is, not many people go there for its own sake.

As we saw in Thasos, the key is to be found in Kavala. From there buses run to Alexandroupolis, which has a regular morning ferry service across to Kamariotissa on the west coast of Samothrace. However, that means spending an awkward night on the mainland, so it may be better to wait for a weekly ship which leaves Kavala early in the morning and reaches Kamariotissa four hours later.

The approach by sea from the west can be mystifying in itself if, as often happens, the island is wrapped in a sea fog. Until almost there you may see nothing at all, and then only a low coastline, difficult to recognize as mountainous Samothrace. You may be alongside before you see Mount Phengari towering into the clouds, far higher than is reasonable from so small a base. *'Phengari'* is the popular Greek word for moon, so perhaps the inhabitants have the same trouble.

Kamariotissa is hardly more than a line of buildings behind a long and undistinguished harbour front. There are a few cafés and travel offices, but the atmosphere is unfamiliar. You miss at once the lively feeling of a Greek seaport, the arguments and gestures, the rapid fire of conversation. Round the café tables people sit almost in silence, and – most unusual in the Greek world – there are few friendly words for the visitor. Taxi drivers are curt, even surly.

There are two explanations, both possibly true. One is the large number of non-Greeks ('barbarians' as they used to call them) in the population; you are close to Bulgaria here, and it was to the Bulgarians that the Nazis handed over Samothrace after their conquest of Greece in 1941. The other is the feeling they may have that nobody comes here except to see 'the ruins', and they long to escape to mainland Alexandroupolis, even for a day. This is a pity from both points of view, for the island they live in has some of the grandest scenery to be found anywhere, and it would not be difficult to make it more welcoming and accessible.

The land behind the harbour, though fertile, is not inspiring. Once the summer crops of maize have been cut it is a brown and dusty desert, but the soaring skyline beyond is a different matter. **Palaiopolis**, the ancient capital on the north coast, is dominated by Mount Phengari, over 5000 feet high and, after Mount Athos, the highest in the Thracian sea. From its summit you look west to Athos and east to Phrygian Ida, and on that summit Poseidon sat to monitor the siege of his own city of Troy.

For many centuries Palaiopolis was the home of an eastern fertility cult, whose central figure was a Mother Goddess, most easily identified in classical times as Demeter. The city itself was built on a rocky ridge extending northwards to the sea from the main mountain range, but nothing remains of it but parts of the massive wall which protected it from the west, and two mediaeval towers built by the Genoese Gattilusi as a guard to seaward.

The city thrived from the sixth century BC to the second century AD almost entirely because of the **Sanctuary of the Great Gods**, which lies athwart a ravine to the west of the walls. The Great Gods of Samothrace were a family group, perhaps of Phrygian origin, and their cult existed before the first Greek-speaking people arrived about 700 BC. The language spoken then has not been identified, but it seems to have been an Aeolian dialect from Asia Minor, and it was still used for the rituals of the cult in the first century BC. In it the name of the Mother Goddess was Axieros, and she had a subordinate husband called Kadmilos whose speciality is known in polite archaeological circles as 'ithyphallic'. They were later identified with Demeter and Hermes.

Making up a formidable quartet was a pair of twin 'spirits', or *daimones*, called Kabeiroi, and it was with these that the cult became chiefly identified in the public mind. When the Greeks arrived they adopted them as the *Dioskouroi* (Castor and Pollux), the twin sons of Zeus who among their other functions were particularly invoked by those in peril on the sea. Successful initiates were presented with an amulet of purple cloth to protect them at such times. St Paul actually called at Samothrace on his way 'over to Macedonia' (his destination was Kavala, then known as Neapolis) and although he was an unlikely initiate he was later to be memorably saved from shipwreck. Pilgrimages to the island continued into

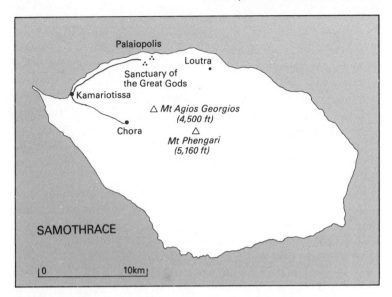

Palaiopolis

Loutra

Sanctuary of
the Great Gods

Kamariotissa

△ *Mt Agios Georgios*
(4,500 ft)

Chora

△
Mt Phengari
(5,160 ft)

SAMOTHRACE

0   10km

the late Roman period, for the Romans claimed the Kabeiroi as a legacy from their Trojan ancestors.

In essence the cult of the Great Gods was an early 'mystery' religion, involving initiation, revelation and probably baptism in blood – by its nature a matter of secret rituals about which we can only guess. In importance it at least equalled the Eleusinian mysteries of Attica, and in a sense it was more popular because it admitted initiates without distinction of sex or social status. This popularity did not deter the Spartan King Lysander, the historian Herodotus, the royal house of Macedon or the Roman emperor Hadrian from taking part. It was just the scene which would have attracted that restless and impressionable ruler, and if you add the Egyptian Ptolemies the list gives an idea of the fame and richness of Palaiopolis for most of its history.

We can imagine some of the procedure most easily by visiting the site, which was first thoroughly excavated by an American team with a research fund from New York University. They began work in 1938, and it was continued after the war under the leadership of Karl Lehmann until his death in 1960. Apart from the excavations he was also responsible for building the museum close by, which is a

319

necessary first call, if only because the road ends just outside it. (Although buses go that way in the summer, the most reliable way of getting there is by taxi.) Since Lehmann's death his widow Phyllis Williams Lehmann has seen to the orderly development of both site and museum.

It is not primarily a museum for *objets trouvés*, but rather laid out to illustrate the nature and architecture of the various buildings discovered, with the help of some dramatic restorations. Lehmann's illustrated *Guide*, now in its fifth edition of 1983, is on sale there and well worth buying. A stony path leads uphill from the museum to the main part of the site.

You may well catch your breath as you come out on to the shelf which follows the north-to-south line of the excavations. Clearly marked foundations, with walls which sometimes rise to ten feet or more, fill a flattened ridge between two stream beds, but first the head lifts high to the south, where jagged mountain shoulders jostle each other among the clouds, and a final gap is filled by the peak of Phengari. Streams run all year long down those mighty gorges to keep the lower stretches green in summer, and in autumn the leaves of the plane trees turn golden.

At the lowest point of the site is the **Anaktoron**, a building where the lesser and preliminary mysteries were enacted; it is about a hundred yards long and probably dates from the Roman period. Most of the wall on the east side still stands, and there is a libation pit in the south-east corner. Next towards the south is an impressive circular building known as the **Rotunda of Queen Arsinoë**, probably used as a gathering place for overseas dignitaries at the annual summer festival. This is the biggest enclosed circular structure known in Greek architecture, and judging from the restoration portrayed in the museum it must have been the most elegant.

That it was built at the orders of a queen, the wife of King Lysimachus of Thrace, is only one sign of the interest in Samothrace shown by the royals of the Macedonian, Ptolemaic and Seleucid dynasties which succeeded Alexander the Great. It was here that Alexander's mother, the princess Olympias of Epirus, first met his father Philip, founder of the Macedonian empire. They were fellow initiates, and it would be hard to think of a more romantic and emotional setting for the encounter.

Further along is a less well defined rectangular space, the **Temenos** (meaning 'enclosure') where people gathered in the open air for organized feasts. Stones around it were pierced to hold torches, which suggests that possibly all the initiation ceremonies were held at night. The Temenos was entered through a *propylon* with an Ionic portico which has a lovely frieze of girls dancing to a lute – some of its slabs are preserved in the museum.

The last group of buildings in the sequence was approached only by initiates who had passed through the Anaktoron in the first stage of revelation. The great temple, or **Hieron**, now with five columns of the *pronaos* re-erected, was the place of final revelation and acceptance, but we know that before the candidates could enter they had to go through something like the confessional of the Roman church. Standing or kneeling on a particular stone before a sacred flame – the socket for the torch is still there – the initiate had to convince a priest that he was clean from sin and worthy to take part. This was not quite the moral or psychological sanction of the confessional, as it was intended to ensure that the sanctity of the temple was not profaned by the entry of a technically 'unclean' person. We can only guess at the nature of the ceremonies and revelation: the word 'mysteries' comes from the Greek *muein*, 'to whisper in secret', and no one, as far as we know, ever broke the code of secrecy in writing.

Two other regular features of the classical world can be traced nearby. The stonework of the **Theatre** has disappeared, but the semicircle hollowed out for the seats can be seen above the path to the south of the Hieron. Behind it was built a vast **Stoa**, a good hundred yards long, to shelter visitors during times of leisure. Several other large buildings have been excavated round about, all concerned in some way with the mysteries. The most notable lies across the bed of the eastern stream, a majestic **Propylon**, or ceremonial gateway, commissioned by Ptolemy II and built in the Corinthian order early in the third century BC to provide a direct entry from the city of Palaiopolis.

We come last to the most evocative place, the site of the **Nike Fountain**, above and to the left of the theatre. Here in 1863 the French Consul at Adrianople, a M. Champoiseau, discovered what was left of the marble figure of the **Winged Victory**, represented as standing on the prow of a ship – the ship seeming to float in a marble basin filled with running water. With no more inhibitions than Lord Elgin he sent the pieces home to Paris, where Nike was reconstituted to stand at the head of the Louvre stairway. 'Stand' is hardly the word, for she seems at that moment to have landed, her wings still half spread. Who the sculptor was, and who designed that magical setting to commemorate an unidentified naval victory in the second century BC, no one knows. In 1950 Nike's right hand was discovered near the fountain, and the Louvre authorities quickly offered to exchange for it three valuable exhibits to go on permanent loan to the museum. Swift as usual off the diplomatic mark, the French seem to have forestalled any call for the body to be repatriated to join the hand.

Nothing else you see in Samothrace compares for excitement or even interest. A small village occupies the site of the inland **Chora**, for which the last inhabitants of Palaiopolis deserted their city during the pirate-infested fifteenth century. Long before that the harbour had begun to silt up, and the source of their wealth had dwindled as Christianity spread. In the ninth century a Byzantine castle was built to protect the new self-supporting community, and this was converted into a much stronger fortress by the Gattilusi. It is still the only ancient place on Samothrace with a modern identity.

A much smaller village at **Loutra** on the north coast marks a rising of thermal springs, but on the whole the coastline is grand and harsh. At one point on the south coast a waterfall drops sheer out of a cliff face into the sea. It is the grandeur and isolation which distinguish Samothrace, to which man has added an extraordinary witness to the power of ancient religion. Although there is no one left to initiate the visitor into the mysteries of the Great Gods, if he stays long enough he should be entitled to wear the purple amulet and be spared the dangers of shipwreck.

Lemnos is one of the most strategically placed of the Greek islands. Lying off the entrance to the Dardanelles, it played an important part in wars as far apart as the siege of Troy and the Gallipoli campaign of 1915. It also saw the decisive sea battle in the last fight for independence from Turkey in 1912. Today it is an important military outpost for a Greece which is still suspicious of Turkish intentions.

After the Latin conquests of 1204 it was for a time exploited by Venetian merchants, but being so close to Constantinople it was one of the first islands to be retaken in the brief Byzantine revival. In 1355 it was taken by the Genoese, and for over a hundred years it was the headquarters of the Gattilusi, who also controlled Thasos and Samothrace. The Turks came early to Lemnos, and after a year's heroic resistance they overran the island in 1479. The Greek revolt won it back in 1829, but they had to exchange it by treaty for Euboea, and it was not until 1912 that success in the Balkan War secured it finally for Greece. Until 1924, when the Greco-Turkish exchange of populations took place, Lemnos had quite a large Turkish element. Now no Turkish *hodjas* call the faithful to prayer and divide the worship of God with their Orthodox brethren. Instead Greek army bugles call the soldiers to their drill or their meals.

At least three places have been rated in their time as the principal city of Lemnos. Today it is **Mirina**, which has a fine harbour on the western coast, protected from the prevailing winds and with a wonderful view over the sea from its higher ground. It is at the end of the long ferry run out of Agios Konstantinos, which connects it with Kavala and the northern Sporades, and in the other direction with Mytilene on Lesbos and Kymi on Euboea. Dominating the town is a formidable castle, built on a craggy headland by the Gattilusi in the fourteenth century, though much of the fortification now visible was contributed by the Turks later on. It is a strenuous climb in hot weather, but from the top you can make out Mount Athos, thirty-five miles away to the west.

The quay where the ferries and cargo ships berth is featureless and noisy, and the hotel overlooking it would be tolerable only for a night if you arrive late. Yet the little enclosed harbour for fishing boats is both natural and colourful. Between the two a narrow winding street leads up through a scene you would not at first associate with a Greek island – not a bucket of whitewash nor a tubful of geraniums to be seen. When the shops are open and the wares spill out on to the pavements you might be in an eastern *souk*. Yet when evening comes and the traffic stops this is where the young people and families of Mirina come out for the *volta*, rather than along the harbour front. Traditional craftsmen like tailors, carpenters, shoemakers, metal-workers and even barbers go on working in their dens well into the night.

You will discover a different face of Mirina if you take any side street on your left as you reach the upper town. In a couple of minutes you will emerge on a fine esplanade which follows the line of a wide beach of soft sand, and behind it there is a long row of dignified nineteenth- or early twentieth-century houses. Some of them are now public buildings, but many were built by prosperous shipowners and are still in private hands. Recently a well designed new hotel has arrived, and looks not at all out of place. Beyond this are three very important buildings: the Museum, the High School and the residence of the Metropolitan Bishop of Lemnos. The public beach stretches a long way further on, and right at the end of the bay is a good-looking 'luxury' hotel complex – bungalows, tennis courts, swimming pool and other amenities discreetly laid out on a series of well kept garden terraces. The beach below is beautifully sheltered, but inevitably crowded when the hotel is full.

Should you arrive by air from Athens (by far the quickest method) you will find the airport occupying a low-lying isthmus, central between two distinct halves of the island. On the southern side is the great harbour of Mudros, where the British fleet lay during the Gallipoli campaign. The Gulf of Bournia takes another bite out from the north, so that Lemnos is almost cut in half at this point.

Travelling from the airport to Mirina you will have a good view of the western half, as the road passes from wide tracts of arable land into the sterile brown hills which surround the bald peak of Prophitis Ilias. It is a volcanic landscape, and was probably never as well wooded as either the northern or the eastern Sporades. Although there is no volcanic activity today, ancient myth claims Lemnos as the home of Hephaistos (or Vulcan, to give him his Latin name), who was the patron of smiths, metal-workers and jewellers. The story goes that Hephaistos was rash enough one day to berate Zeus about the way he treated Hera – whereupon Zeus hurled him out of Olympus. The smith-god fell upon Lemnos, breaking both his legs, with the result that ever afterwards he could only walk with special gold leg-braces he had made for himself.

It was probably not only the volcanic nature of Lemnos which made the Greeks consider the island sacred to Hephaistos. Metal-working first reached continental Greece from the Aegean islands, and it is likely that Lemnos had an early tradition of ironwork and metallurgy. In the workshops of Mirina you will find that it still has that tradition.

The eastern parts of Lemnos are fed by streams which water more fruitful valleys. Citrus fruits and plums are grown, and prune-drying is one of the local industries. The true home-dried Aegean prune, with its delicate aroma and its lovely dark blue colour, is a far call from those dark withered things long associated with institutional meals in England. Sadly, though, you may ask in vain for *damaskina* at the supermarket or general store, where local products have given way to continental imports of packaged foods.

The oldest known site for a capital city was at **Poliochni** on the far eastern coast, a few miles south of the village of Kaminia. This was the most advanced neolithic centre in the Aegean, as can be seen when you visit the museum in Mirina, and it remained an outpost of civilized life well into the late Bronze Age. The most ancient city, which stood on a steep cliff close to the sea, was excavated with three later ones by the Italian School in the 1930s, and ascribed to the fourth millennium BC – considerably antedating the first city of Troy. Walls, towers and gates of a later date still stand as high as sixteen feet in places, and built as they were about 2000 BC they still predate Homeric Troy by several centuries. When the Greek fleet passed on its way to attack the seventh city of Troy the artistic standards of Poliochni were already in decline, and eventually it was destroyed by an earthquake.

It was probably Poliochni that saw one act of the 'Lemnian deeds' – atrocities often referred to by later writers. There are two stories which gave the island such a bad reputation. In this one the women of the island, loyal followers of Hephaistos, neglected the service of Aphrodite when she deserted him for Ares, god of war. Her revenge was to visit them with an evil-smelling complaint which in turn made their husbands neglect them for sweeter companions – whereupon each wife save one murdered her husband. The exception was the king, who was saved by his daughter Hypsipyle, and when the Argonauts called on their way to Colchis Jason picked her out of the many who were ready for male consolation. The Argonauts stayed for two years and successfully repopulated the island.

It could have been near Poliochni too that Philoctetes was marooned by his shipmates on the way to Troy. This was because of the insufferable smell of a leg made gangrenous by a snakebite. The play of *Philoctetes* by Sophocles describes how the Greek leaders, realizing that because he carried the bow and arrows of Herakles he was essential to the war, sent an embassy to Lemnos to persuade the now resigned castaway to return with them. With Odysseus as the chief persuader, and a doctor on hand to cure him, they prevailed – and it was Philoctetes who killed Paris with an arrow-shot in front of the walls of Troy.

It seems that there must be some connection between the legendary hero suffering from – and being cured of – gangrene, and the famous 'Lemnian earth', the *terra sigillata* of antiquity. This 'stamped earth' was impressed with the head of Artemis in classical times, and was considered a cure for snakebite and festering wounds. The earth was dug up by a priestess, on one day of each year, from a barren mound near the modern village of Kotsinos on the eastern side of the island. This Lemnian earth continued to have a wide sale throughout eastern Europe, and you may be able to find it still on sale in the island. Galen went to see the digging of the earth, and recorded that it was considered so valuable that only one waggon-load was allowed to be removed every year. Until recently the tradition was still observed on 6 August, the feast of Christ the Saviour, under the surveillance of a priest.

The role of leading city next passed to **Hephaistia**, where the Italian School excavated a north coast site on the promontory which divides the Gulf of Bournia from the smaller bay of Tigani. They found an eighth-century BC necropolis and evidence of earlier occupation going back to late Minoan and Mycenaean times. The pottery was unusual in showing an uninterrupted development into the Archaic and Geometric styles. From the sixth century BC onwards, if not before, it was the main seaport of Lemnos, though the harbour gradually began to silt up.

Hephaistia would have been the scene of the second tale of atrocities which Herodotus couples with the earlier example of 'Lemnian deeds'. He is explaining how Lemnos became subject to Athens early in the fifth century BC, but the story begins hundreds of

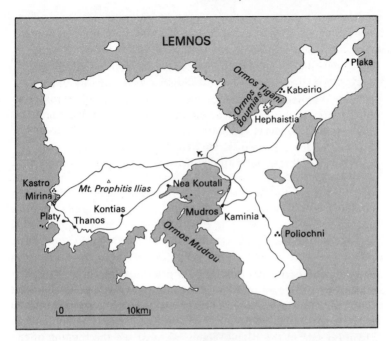

years before when the Pelasgian population of Attica was dislodged by the Achaians and found a new home on Lemnos. By way of revenge they raided the Attic coast near Brauron and carried off a number of women taking part in a religious festival. These women, treated as concubines, bore children to their captors. Later the Lemnians of legitimate birth took exception to the arrogant and aggressive manners of the half-Athenian bastards, and massacred them and their mothers. Such behaviour in the Greek world nearly always brought *nemesis* in its train, and when not only the married women but even the animals in the fields became barren, representatives were sent to Delphi to ask how they could purge the island from this crime.

The answer was simple: they were to go to Athens and offer to make whatever reparation the Athenians asked for. The Athenian answer was equally simple: they must cede their country and all its goods to Athens. The Lemnians retorted that they would do this but only 'if a ship can reach our country from yours in one day with a north wind blowing' – another version of the Greek Kalends, given the relative positions of Lemnos and Athens. However, 'very many years later', as Herodotus says, Miltiades the Athenian general found himself after the Marathon campaign of 490 BC in control of the Thracian Chersonese, at a time when the *meltemi* were blowing strongly from the north:

> 'When the Etesian winds were well established, Miltiades son of Kimon arrived in Lemnos by ship from Elaios in the Chersonese, and published an order for the Pelasgians to quit the island, reminding them of the oracle – something which the Pelasgians had never expected to be fulfilled. The Hephaistians promptly gave in, but the people of Mirina, refusing to admit that the Chersonese was the same thing as Attica, had to endure a siege before they too capitulated.' *

We see that by now Mirina was on an equal footing with Hephaistia, and perhaps felt more secure in their redoubtable acropolis. The ancients would have even better cause than we have to know the inevitability of those 'Etesian winds' in the Aegean during the sailing season. As for Miltiades, he was a ruthless character and eventually came to a bad end on Paros.

On the other side of the pleasant bay of Tigani is **Kabeirio**, a site whose name suggests that the mysteries connected with the Kabeiroi may have begun here rather than in Samothrace. They do seem to have been less refined than what went on in Samothrace – *orgia* rather than *musteria* – and were connected not with sailing and shipwreck but with drinking and metal-working, so more appropriate to the island of Hephaistos. The Italians discovered the foundations of an *Anaktoron* and a *Stoa*, and of a huge building which they identified as a Hellenistic *Telesterion*, or Hall of Celebration, with a façade of twelve Doric columns.

The scenery of these northern bays is the most attractive in the island, and with two such important archaeological sites it is a pity they are so difficult to reach – and the same applies to Poliochni on the east coast. The road system is extensive, but the buses which use it are scheduled primarily for the transport of schoolchildren into Mirina from distant villages and back. The bus going to Plaka in the

* *Histories* VI, 138–40.

far north-east passes within five miles of Hephaistia, and another stops at Kaminia, about two and a half miles short of Poliochni, but in neither case does it return the same day. It is probably worth while to hire a car for a few days if you want to explore the island properly.

Most people will think of going to **Mudros**, the second largest town, which overlooks the great land-locked bay. It is a magnificent natural harbour, about twice the size of Kalamitsa in Skyros. It is curious to compare these empty acres of water today with the old photographs which show hundreds of transports, battleships, cruisers and destroyers at anchor. The sea keeps no records, and only the Allied war graves at Mudros and a few place names like 'The Pier of the Australians' serve to remind that it was from here that the vast and ill-fated expedition to the Dardanelles was launched. Mudros itself is nothing to look at, and has no amenities, while even the village of Nea Koutali across the bay – dubbed 'picturesque' in the guide books because it has a few trees – has little to offer.

The most attractive villages are Kontias, Thanos and Platy, on hillsides facing the southern sea not far from Mirina. The first two on closer inspection have a deserted air, being too big for a depleted population, but **Platy** overlooks a very long sandy beach, easily reached on foot from Mirina. At the far end of the beach a big restaurant and entertainment complex shows how popular it is in the season, but as the beach is over a mile long there should be a bit of room for all. The road passes a large and obviously efficient military encampment.

Whether or not you succeed in reaching Poliochni, Hephaistia or Kabeirio, you must on no account miss the **Museum** in Mirina. Although the most valuable finds have inevitably gone to Athens, this is a fascinating collection of objects from the Neolithic to the Hellenistic and Roman ages. In particular insist on seeing the rooms on an upper floor, where finds from Poliochni are displayed in a most illuminating sequence which compares its development with that of the first six cities of Troy.

There is so much more than can be described here, but look on the first floor for the archaic red clay figures of Sirens and Sphinxes from Hephaistia, and the classical bronze figurines from Kabeirio – a snail (edible snails are found both here and on Thasos), a snake, a

329

bull's head, an Eros, and most surprising of all a flamingo sitting on its nest. The curator will tell you it is an eagle, but the long sinuous neck and the curious overlapping beak could only belong to a flamingo. Perhaps they once bred or fed on the salt marshes of the eastern coast, or was it an offering by a visitor from the Egypt of the Ptolemies?

From Poliochni (on the upper floor) comes a marvellous assembly of finely made implements in bone and polished stone, including a trayful of obsidian – produced here as on Milos by volcanic action, though not in such quantity. The whole collection is labelled in Greek and Italian only, but a new guide book is being prepared which should supplement the information which has rather to be dug out of the curators.

Not one of the most beautiful islands, Lemnos grows on one during even a short stay, and its characteristic outlines persist in the memory. It has an appendage in the island of **Agios Evstratios**, about twenty miles to the south, which has sometimes been used as a place of exile or detention for political offenders – more recently as a base for NATO exercises. It is quite unspoilt, and its Chora has traces of a history stretching back from Byzantine to Mycenaean times. The ferry calls here on the way to Euboea.

Access

These are the most difficult of the Aegean islands to reach by sea. An infrequent ferry service from Agios Konstantinos in the Euboean Gulf eventually reaches KAVALA, from where there is an hourly local ferry service across to Limena on THASOS. From Kavala it is a four-hour run to SAMOTHRACE, which can also be reached by local ferry from Alexandroupolis on the Thracian coast near the Turkish border. LEMNOS can be reached by sea from Kavala, from Mytilene on Lesbos and from Kymi on Euboea. The ferry schedules concerned are complicated and unreliable, but there are airfields at Kavala and Alexandroupolis, and on Lemnos. Flights from Athens to any of these will save time and tedium.

Communications

THASOS   There is a bus service from Limena round the island two or three times a day, and separate services to individual villages. Plenty of taxis are available near the modern harbour. Cars and mopeds can be hired from the tourist office.

SAMOTHRACE   A daily bus connects Kamariotissa with the Chora, but with Palaiopolis only in the summer season. There are usually two or three taxis on station by the harbour, though drivers are not anxious to please the tourist.

LEMNOS   Buses run to most of the inhabited villages from the big *plateia* in Mirina, but they are not intended for tourists and rarely return the same day. During the holiday season there are tourist buses, whose destinations and times can only be learned from the office next the bus stop, which is not always very helpful. Taxis can be found in the smaller *plateia* in the town centre, and there is a taxi office in Mudros. Cars for hire are advertised in Mirina. Olympic Airways have an office in Mirina, and a bus from there takes passengers and luggage to the airport.

Accommodation

KAVALA   In a long list of hotels it may be useful to know of NEFELI (C) at 50 Leoforos Erithrou Stavrou, which is convenient and well run, though rooms at the back are quieter than in front.

THASOS   For a full list of hotels consult the tourist brochures. In Limena the smartest is TIMOLEON (B); it has a restaurant and faces the harbour. ANGELIKA (C) is roomy and comfortable; its position between the old and new harbours is interesting, but it has no restaurant. Most of the holiday hotels lie in the west of the town, but MAKRYAMMOS (A), a typical new 'bungalow' complex with a private beach, is two miles out to the east. There are several attractively placed hotels in Limenaria.

SAMOTHRACE   The only two hotels on the island are the very small XENIA close to the Museum at Palaiopolis, and NIKE on the pebble beach to the north of Kamariotissa.

LEMNOS   Reliable accommodation is to be found only in the capital, Mirina. There AKTI MIRINA (A) is a well placed and attractive 'bungalow' complex, with every imaginable amenity and an enclosed beach. CASTRO (B) is modern, spacious and well designed. Of the lesser hotels SEVDALI (C), in a quiet street off the town centre, is well run, with an English-speaking manager. LEMNOS (C), in spite of its convenient position on the quay, is to be avoided as noisy and not very clean.

331

The Greek Islands

Restaurants

KAVALA   If staying in Kavala overnight try VRACHOS (The Rock), above the beach about a mile west of the harbour. There are also busier places near where the ferries berth.

THASOS   The harbour front at Limena has a number of the familiar kind of holiday eating places. MON CHERI is more civilized than some, but really only a *crêperie*. For the best food and service at night go to the well organized restaurant beside the main *plateia*, which is open all year and patronized by Greek families and businessmen.

SAMOTHRACE   The little bar-restaurants along the harbour front are not bad, if rather cheerless.

LEMNOS   The best local food is at the far end of the quay, near the office of the Port Police. There are two 'fish tavernas' beyond the fishing harbour, which are good value, though the nearer one is usually crowded with soldiers. The café-bars by the quay are for tourists in quantity.

Facilities

Banks: In Thasos, Limena and Limenaria have the usual branches. There are no banks in Samothrace. In Lemnos there are branches in or near the main street of Mirina, but not elsewhere.

Yachts: In Thasos yachts can berth near the Port Police office on the new quay at Limena, and at Skala Prinou. There is an open anchorage off Limenaria.

No anchorages can be recommended as secure in Samothrace, but there are berths alongside at Kamariotissa.

Mirina in Lemnos has very limited berthing for private yachts, but the fishermen are friendly to visitors. There are sheltered anchorages in Mudros Bay and the Gulf of Bournia, but few facilities ashore.

The
Eastern Sporades

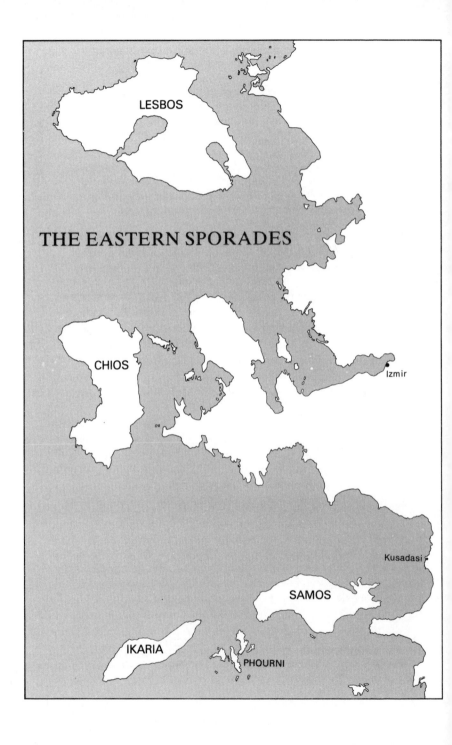

THE EASTERN SPORADES

LESBOS

CHIOS

Izmir

Kusadasi

SAMOS

IKARIA

PHOURNI

THE EASTERN SPORADES

This is a convenient as well as the correct term for the chain of
islands which hug the Turkish coast from Cape Baba in the north to
Cape Kanapitza in the south, sometimes leaving a strait less than
five miles wide between them and the Asian mainland. The islands
great and small which make up the group have an atmosphere and a
physical character quite distinct from other groups. Physically their
rock formations are a continuation of the mountain ranges of Asia
Minor, though their land is greener and more fertile than the
opposite shores. Of all the Aegean islands their scenery is the most
varied and often the most beautiful, and there is a poise about their
way of life which derives from a common fund of culture and
experience.

Given their position it is natural that much of their history has
been shared with the peoples of the mainland, but it was their
basically Greek population which brought civilized values to the
Asian coast rather than the other way round. In the centuries after
the fall of Troy to a Greek army there was a constant movement of
population eastwards across the Aegean, prompted partly by pressure from northern invaders, partly by an adventurous wish to
expand on the part of a sea-going people. Two main groups have
been identified in this process, the Aeolians and the Ionians, though
it has never been clear exactly where on the Greek mainland they
came from. Lesbos was in the Aeolian, Chios and Samos in the
Ionian sphere.

Herodotus, in the long prelude to his history of the Persian wars
in the fifth century BC, constantly refers to these islands, or at least
their principal cities, as sharing Greek characteristics with other
cities on the mainland of Asia such as Phocaea, Priene and Miletus.

We read that Solon the Athenian lawgiver was a guest at the court of King Croesus of Lydia when he gave his famous opinion that no man could be said to have had a happy life until after his death. When the cities of the Ionian coast joined in an unsuccessful revolt against the Persian kingdom, it was an excuse for Darius in 490 BC and for Xerxes ten years later to attack Greece itself for having supported the revolt. Thereafter the island cities had an uneasy time, having to choose first between the new Aegean power of Athens and the still powerful Persian empire, and then between Athens and Sparta during the long see-saw struggle of the Peloponnesian war.

United under the Macedonian, Roman and early Byzantine empires, the islands prospered in proportion to their fertility and commercial skills. After the Latin conquest of 1204 they fell into the hands of Genoese rather than Venetian overlords, and were out of range of the Knights of St John in Rhodes.

Lesbos and Samos were captured by the Turks soon after the fall of Byzantium in 1453, but Chios was left undisturbed until 1566, partly because its export trade was valuable to the mainland – especially in mastic gum for the Sultans' harems – but also thanks to the authority and diplomacy of the Genoese family who ruled it. None of these islands regained their liberty or were united with Greece until 1912. When the War of Independence broke out in 1821 they were far too close to the mainland power, as their ancestors had been more than two thousand years before, to avoid savage acts of repression.

Of the three principal islands Samos has been the most subject to tourist development, Lesbos less so, while Chios has been affected least of all. Of the smaller islands Psara and Phourni are unknown, Ikaria has been barely touched by foreign tourists.

TWENTY

Lesbos and Chios

Lesbos is the most northerly of the eastern Sporades, and one of the largest islands in the Aegean. It is separated from Turkey by the narrow Mytilene channel to the east and by the Muselim channel to the north, the latter no more than five miles across at its widest point. The only deep-water harbour is at Mytilene, on the east coast of a peninsula separated from the southern part of the island by the Gulf of Geras. This is the smaller of the two gulfs which bite deep into the land from the south, both forming almost totally enclosed sea-lochs with very narrow entrances.

As the airport is only a mile or so to the south, Mytilene will be your point of arrival whether by sea or by air. As the principal town it has so dominated Lesbos since classical times that its name has often been used synonymously for the whole island, though the authorities now tend to distinguish between the two. The modern harbour is large, usually with a few warships of the Greek navy berthed there. There is a busy if undistinguished air about it, but on the high projecting point to the north the buildings suddenly stop, and the walls of a big mediaeval castle rise out of thick green pine woods.

Lesbos was always a rich island, and its prosperity was based then as now on its agriculture and its good harbour. Its position off the Asian coast added to its importance, for Mytilene must have been able to trade with the mainland even in winter. Even today, when there is so much suspicion and hostility between the governments of Greece and Turkey, a good deal of friendly local trade goes on across the narrow straits. Every now and then the authorities on either side try to check this, and not long ago some Greek fishermen were arrested in their traditional fishing waters close to the Turkish coast. Almost immediately a bewildered Turk was rounded up in a Mytilene bar where he had been a regular customer for years. Honours were considered even, and the prisoners were released on both sides after amicable negotiations.

Rather further back, there was probably a trade connection with Homeric Troy, and Homer says that during the ten years of siege by the Greeks Lesbos was attacked by Achilles and Odysseus. There is evidence that Mytilene was destroyed by fire at the end of the Mycenaean period, perhaps as a punishment for taking the wrong side, as she did several times later. In the tenth century BC Aeolian colonists, mainly from Thessaly, joined their neighbours the Achaeans in founding new settlements on the eastern shores of the Aegean. Herodotus lists six cities which they developed in Lesbos, and their names can still be read on the map – Mytilene, Methymna, Eressos, Antissa, Arisbe and Pyrrha.

The last two have little to tell us now, but in the seventh century Antissa produced Terpander, called the father of Greek music, while Arion of Methymna was the first to write personal lyric poetry instead of long epic or descriptive works. It was their influence which inspired the two great lyric poets of the sixth century, Alcaeus of Mytilene, and Sappho, reputedly born at Eressos. This was a time when Lesbos was also at the height of its material prosperity. The architect of that was Pittacus, a citizen who was chosen as dictator to settle a period of internal strife. His wise and liberal administration secured peace and prosperity for the island, and for himself a place among the Seven Sages of Greece.

It was under his influence that schools of many kinds flourished, with a high standard of education – notably involving freedom for women to participate. In the fourth century a school of philosophy was established, where both Aristotle and Epicurus came to teach. Aristotle's most famous pupil Theophrastus was born in Eressos, and later succeeded him at the Lyceum in Athens. He was said to have died at the age of a hundred and seven, lamenting the shortness of human life.

The arts necessarily require a soil of prosperity and culture in which to flourish, and one can easily understand how this rich and gracious island provided it. With its olives and its vines, and a large and flourishing commercial port, Lesbos has an economic balance rare in the Aegean. The olive trees seem to grow thicker and more luxuriantly than in any other island, and it was calculated a few years ago that they produced twenty per cent of the whole commercial crop of the Aegean. They still produce a massive crop, but to pick and market the innumerable small holdings is growing less and less profitable, so that thousands of trees are left to shed their fruit ungathered on the ground. Nevertheless they are a fine sight as the wind runs through them like the waves of the sea, with the blue-grey mountains behind them.

The ancient city occupied mostly the neck of land between its acropolis, where the castle now stands, and the area covered by the modern harbour and the streets behind it. It depended more on an older harbour to the north of the acropolis, now largely silted up, but whose southern mole still shows above water. To the north of that was the theatre, excavated in 1958 and partially restored ten years later. The old quarter is still more interesting than the new town which grew up round the southern harbour, which is a hodge-podge of twentieth-century nondescript and nineteenth-century Ottoman. It spreads in an aimless sort of way, with churches and mosques, *ouzo* exporters' warehouses and olive refineries around the bay. The tall brick chimneys of the olive refineries are a feature of many parts of Lesbos – they were designed to draw off the fumes when the residue after the crushing process was baked to produce a solid fuel, which was understandably popular as a cheap product of the principal industry.

A curious and individual feature of domestic architecture in the neighbourhood of Mytilene is a kind of defensible home. Its lower storeys were built foursquare like a tower, while the upper storeys overhung their walls on all four sides. Normally the inhabitants would live and store their goods down below, but if there was danger of attack they could retire to the top and shower all kinds of unpleasantness on enemies below. These *pirgi*, as they are called, date from the unsettled times of the nineteenth century, and are being eagerly bought up for restoration and reoccupation.

There are not many signs of Roman or Byzantine occupation in this part of Lesbos, probably because it was repeatedly devastated by Saracen invasions between AD 800 and 1100. Only such arts survived as could be developed by monastic foundations outside the

339

capital. Prosperity and security returned when in 1354 the Byzantine emperor John Palaiologos gave Lesbos as a dowry for his sister Maria when she married Francesco Gattilusio of Genoa – a reward for having helped him to regain the throne.

Their first act was to build on the site of the ancient acropolis the enormous fortress whose outer walls we see so clearly from below. It was finished by 1373, and the area enclosed even within the upper bailey was enough to hold a small town, complete with markets, churches and places of entertainment, overlooked by the ruling family's keep, or *phrourio*, at the south-east corner. This replaced an earlier Byzantine castle which they incorporated in the western *enceinte*. High up between the towers of the keep is a decorative marble slab, featuring the Gattilusi monogram between figures of Crusader soldiers, puzzling scenes of men confronting lions, and the Gattilusi arms – in which the displayed eagle of the Palaiologi joined the curious pattern of overlapping scales which represented the Genoese family. The same markings can be seen on a large marble sarcophagus which stands Ozymandias-like in the middle of a vast space – empty now but for fragments of buildings from different periods and a stage set for *son et lumière* productions.

The western defences are an imposing system of inner and outer walls and moats, but it was the Turks who extended the fortifications to link up with the northern harbour below. Within them has survived a tiny ruined early Byzantine church, standing low with a typical group of flattened domes over a Greek cross plan. You can see it clearly from the walls above, but access from below is prevented by a wire fence. The Turks arrived in 1462, shortly before the fall of Negroponte in Euboea to Sultan Mehmet II, and they held the island until it was freed by treaty in 1912. Ironical that Khair-ed-din 'Barbarossa', the dreaded corsair who ravaged the Aegean coasts in the early sixteenth century, should have been born here of Greek parentage.

The harbour to the north of the castle seems to have been preferred in mediaeval times, but we cannot be sure where the two triremes from Athens put in at the climax of a dramatic episode early in the Peloponnesian War. In 428 BC the oligarchs who ruled Mytilene had engineered a revolt against the Athenian alliance, while the second city, Methymna, remained loyal and revealed the conspiracy to Athens. After a long siege the city surrendered, and in the assembly at Athens the demagogue Cleon proposed a terrible vengeance – to put to death the entire male population and enslave the women and children. The assembly agreed, and a trireme was despatched to instruct the army to carry out its orders. Next day a more sober and less vengeful mood prevailed, and the assembly heard a carefully reasoned speech by one Demodotus which urged clemency, not as the juster but as the wiser course.

They decided to reverse their decision, and immediately sent a second trireme after the first. The first ship had a day and a night's start; could it be overtaken? Envoys from Mytilene supplied the crew with wine and barley and offered rewards if they got there in time. They slept and rowed in shifts, while the earlier ship sailed slowly on its unpleasant errand. Nevertheless the Athenian general already had the decree in his hand when the second ship entered harbour and the city was saved. The ringleaders had already been deported to Athens and were executed there.*

Lesbos is almost split in two by the deep Gulf of Kalloni, which means that Mytilene and Methymna, rivals all through history, are each the principal city of a distinct area. The larger area lies south of the gulf, and can be easily explored from the capital by hired transport, or within narrower limits by bus. The main road leading westward skirts the head of the smaller Gulf of Geras, where it diverges from the principal route to the north. It crosses the northern flank of Mt Olympus, thick with pine woods, and continues to Polychnitos, a small town of no interest in itself, but providing access to holiday resorts at **Vatera** on the south coast and **Skala Polychnitou**, just inside the sheltered waters of the Gulf of Kalloni.

It makes a more interesting expedition to turn south off the main road after about twelve miles for **Agiassos**, an unusual village higher still up the side of Mt Olympus. The streets are cobbled and shaded with climbing plants as well as trees. The centre of a bright and cheerful scene is the big monastery church of the *Koimisis*, or Assumption of the Virgin Mary. It was a Byzantine foundation, but nineteenth-century restoration has not left much of interest inside. The courtyard around it is attractive, though, and gates in each of its

* Thucydides III, 36–49, and Bury, *History of Greece*, Chapter 8.

sides connect it with the life of the village, which is vaguely Italianate in feeling.

There is supposed to be a ring road round the village, but at
present the only way you can carry on south in the direction of
Plomari on the coast is by driving bravely up the narrow central
street past tethered donkeys and gesticulating villagers. A good
road continues south through hills green with pines, planes, chest-
nuts and small oaks. **Plomari** is a comfortable and relaxed seaside
town with a small harbour. It has some dignity, with good modern
buildings and tree-lined streets, but the islanders respect it most as
the producer of the best *ouzo* in Lesbos. There are no signs of
fortification in the neighbourhood, and with rather more grudging
respect the other towns put this down to the fact that it needed no
defences against pirates because it was for a long time their headquarters.

A rewarding round journey can be completed by taking the road
eastward out of Plomari, which later turns north through a varied
countryside past the villages of Skopelos, Messagros and Pappados.
The short turning left to **Skopelos** is the one to pick. It looks and is an
ordinary hill village with one narrow street and a fairly large church
at the top of it, with two towers. Past this and to the left you come to
the smaller church of *Agia Magdalena*, where in a paved courtyard
there is a little stuccoed building with a miniature cupola. If you
apply to the nearest house a lady will let you in and unlock an iron
gate at the top of a flight of steps, which lead to a genuine and
extensive system of catacombs – used for Christian services and
burials during the early years of persecution. There are many
ramifications and side-issues, sometimes only four feet high. Unique in the islands, as far as we know, this is a creepy and claus-
trophobic experience, totally unexpected. Christianity was
accepted in Lesbos by the beginning of the second century, which
suggests a very early date for the catacombs. St Paul spent a night in
Mytilene on his way back to Jerusalem in AD 52.

A little further on you strike the western shore of the Gulf of
Geras, planted with olives, poplars and cypresses, much cultivated
but so far undeveloped; there you can rejoin the main road back to
Mytilene. The Gulf seems not to have been used much commercially until modern times, perhaps because there were no unloading

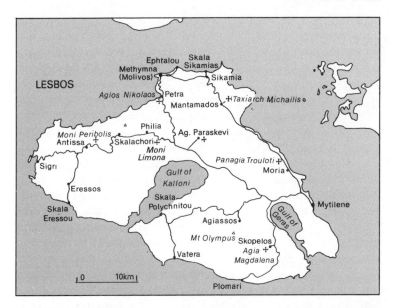

facilities. It was however used as an anchorage for British warships during the Dardanelles campaign in 1915. The Admiralty thought they had found a secure hide-out, but the Turks spotted it, and brought up a German 'Big Bertha' gun to the mainland coast – the same weapon which was able to lob shells across the Channel from the Belgian coast. From a much closer range the fire became so accurate that the Navy had to pull out.

There are two routes north to Methymna, which may have been your objective in the first place, as it is a good deal more popular as a holiday resort than Mytilene. Most Greeks have abandoned the old classical name and call it Molivos, but all agree on its superior attractions. The easiest road is by way of Kalloni at the head of its gulf, but a more interesting one follows the east coast as far as the bay of Aspropotamos, and then crosses behind the north-western headlands through Mantamados to Sikamia. From Sikamia a some-times rough but drivable road goes west to Molivos.

Leaving Mytilene by the eastern route you soon come to the village of **Moria**, where are the remains of a Roman aqueduct which was once the city's main water supply. Moria is to the left of the

343

main road, and you have to go a little way past it to see several of the dark stone uprights still standing, with a few impressive arches. Just beyond the roadside village of Pirgi Thermis a short path leads left to one of the most delightful of small country churches, the **Panagia Trouloti** (Our Lady of the Cupola). There is no whitewash; the round roughly-tiled central tower, the high eastern apse and the squared-off transepts make a harmonious picture. Inside there is a small intricate *templo* in dark wood, and some substantial arches spring from square pillars – all on a very small scale.

On the outside of the south wall facing the road are two stone tablets carved with hunting scenes: in one what looks like a bear is pulling down a stag; in the other a man lies prone on the branch of a tree waving something to attract the same animal's attention, while another figure is waiting to kill it. The church is probably no later than the fifteenth century, but we could find nobody to explain or put a date on the carvings.

The road continues close to the sea for another ten miles, and then cuts inland through the village of **Mantamados**. Here a minor road turns off right to the monastery of the *Taxiarch Michailis*, which is a great centre of pilgrimage because of its 'black ikon' of St Michael. This is a bust portrait carved in strong relief in very dark wood, and in its silver trappings it is prominent to the right of the main entrance to the sanctuary. On a Sunday or feast day many people bring *ex voto* offerings to be blessed by the priest (and to be photographed while he does it), while the sick or injured come hobbling, hopping or even crawling up the aisle to touch the ikon and bow low before it. Great emotion is shown as they wipe the face with fresh flowers, or touch it with their fingers and afterwards stroke their own face – a flowery fragrance is said to emanate from the ikon. Meanwhile metal bowls of water from a holy spring are brought for invalids to bathe their arms, faces, or other limbs. The scene is a strange mixture of a family day out and primitive superstition. The superstitious element is also present in the eyes painted above the side entrances to the sanctuary – the *apotropaia* which ward off the evil one.

There is other evidence that the 'old religion' survives here as strongly as anywhere in Greece, and that on the doorstep of a Christian monastery. Mantamados is one of two places in Lesbos where the feast day of Agios Charalambos soon after Easter is celebrated by a ritual slaughter of young bulls which are subsequently eaten at a public festivity. Several promising candidates can be seen in the fields round about. The same far from Christian kind of festivity happens at the same time of year at the village of **Agia Paraskevi**, a more sophisticated religious centre set in farmland a mile or two out of Kalloni, to the north of the main road between there and Mytilene. In the middle of the village there is a large ornate neo-classical church, in shape a basilica with tall Corinthian columns. Being more accessible than Mantamados it attracts even more local people, and on the feast of Agios Charalambos the ritual bull-slaughter is followed by parades and horse-races. As we saw at Skopelos, Christianity came early to Lesbos, and could well have taken a garbled form from the beginning. St Paul would certainly not have approved, and his stopover at Mytilene in AD 52 seems to have had little effect in the long run.

Beyond Mantamados the road rounds the eastern flank of Mt Lepetimnos to Sikamia, and from there continues in a steep descent to **Skala Sikamias**, a delicious little harbour bright with fishing boats and watched over by a neat church which perches on an isolated rock at the entrance to the harbour. Sikamia itself is no more than a road junction where the cross-country road to Molivos begins. At the time of writing it was a rough ride through an arid countryside, but with fine views over the rocky north-east coast. The final approach to Molivos is over a well cultivated plain with a clear view ahead of this historic hill town, built on a headland facing Cape Baba on the Turkish coast. The channel at this point is only five miles wide, running deep and blue with white flecks of broken water where the current swirls into the Gulf of Adramyti.

Molivos is the most exhilarating place in the island. Land and sea breezes blow back and forth across the strait even in midsummer, when Mytilene can be humid and enervating. If by any chance the visitor should be awake at dawn – and Lesbos is a cheerful place where parties can last all night – then is the time to enjoy one of the great moments of the Aegean. The sky lightens behind Mount Ida, thirty miles away in Asia Minor, as the sea begins to take on colour all the way down the gulf. The night fishing boats are coming in, and there is usually a *kaïki* or coastal trader engraving a deep scroll through the silver of the strait.

345

A classic island Chora, its narrow dark-paved streets criss-cross below a ruined *kastro* – the original acropolis. The houses are solid, distinct and well kept. Since 1965 Molivos has been declared a protected national site, and care has been taken to save town and harbour from unsightly development. The final drop to the sea is arrested by a kind of walled promenade which slants down to a tidy little harbour.

The *kastro* is another Gattilusi stronghold, more impressive seen from outside and below than from inside. The formidable walls enclose a mostly empty space from which all stonework has been plundered. Yet the southern entrance is impressive, and you can follow a parapet walk most of the way to the great tower at the north-west corner. Two periods of building can be distinguished, as the lower courses of the walls are built of large blocks of dressed stone, while the upper levels are of smaller and more irregular stonework, bonded with mortar and brick tile fragments. Apart from the castle fortifications, sections have survived of the city walls – particularly where they support the terrace road leading to the harbour. Their pattern of closely fitting polygonal stones without mortar has become known as the 'Lesbian method', and it continued into Hellenistic times.

Molivos attracts the visitor because it is a neat, colourful and picturesque survival. For the more usual tourist lures of sandy beaches in the sun you have to go some distance. To the south it is quite a way before the unfriendly pebbles give place to sand in the bay of Petra, and if you take the road to **Ephtalou** you will find two big modern hotels and a long curving beach, but this is still uncomfortably stony with a few patches of grey sand.

At a serious level there is an artistic tradition which has encouraged both Greek and foreign artists and writers to settle here permanently. Over the past decade there have been several international conferences and symposia, and a Gallery of Fine Arts was opened in 1981. You will not be allowed to forget that Arion was a native of Methymna, though he lived mainly in Corinth under the lucrative patronage of its ruler Periander. Greek story-tellers described his return to Lesbos on the back of a dolphin: the crew of his ship had robbed and threatened to kill him, but Arion attracted the dolphin by playing his lyre and then jumped overboard to ride home on the friendly creature.* In fact he was no romantic troubadour, but a serious poet whose experiments with metre led to some of the choral elements of Greek drama. Greeks have always loved a good story, though, and one of the oldest of the Molivos hotels (now easily the best and largest) is called the 'Delphinia' after Arion's friend and rescuer.

Petra is a long village spread beside about half a mile of waterfront, within easy reach (even on foot) from Molivos. Its outstanding feature is an isolated outcrop of rock, high on which stands the monastery church of the *Panagia Glykyphilosa*, an attribute which means 'sweetly affectionate' rather than implying that Our Lady had a sweet tooth. To reach it you have to climb several flights of steps, but the eighteenth-century interior is not remarkable except for another superstitious eye painted over the centre of the *templo*. So superstition lives on here too, and outside the church people can be seen filling plastic bottles from a well of holy water.

The much more remarkable church of *Agios Nikolaos* can be found near the foot of the rock. The present church is said to date from 1600 and contains many frescos of different periods – the later ones are rather crude, but there are some good examples inside the sanctuary. The small gilded *templo* has a very fine early panel of St John the Baptist, with fluid lines and a naturalistic landscape. In front stand two slender pillars, probably from an earlier basilica church on the same site.

Most visitors to Molivos will sooner or later want to make the longer excursion to the far west of the island which ends at **Sigri**, a holiday village near the much publicized phenomenon of its 'petrified forest'. We should say at once that though Sigri itself is a good if isolated place for a holiday the famous 'forest' is not in itself worth the journey. Apart from a few other fragments of this coniferous wood, which was buried in volcanic ash, and later turned to stone by the action of a thermal spring containing silicic acid, only one 'tree' now remains. Even that has been reduced in size as bits were chipped off as mementos, and it is rough going to reach it by way of a track going south from the village.

---

* Herodotus says he was carried only to Taenarus, on the southernmost cape of the Peolponnese, and from there returned to Corinth, but Lesbians believe otherwise. (*Histories* I, 24.)

The journey west is worth making for its own sake, both for the extraordinary variety of scenery it encompasses and for the places (with their associations) you pass on the way. From Petra there is a ten-mile drive round the pine-clad shoulder of Mt Skoteino and down to the Kalloni plain – really a delta fed by at least four rivers coming down from the ring of mountains round the gulf. Kalloni itself has no place to stop, unless for petrol; though at Skala Kallonis, surrounded by salt pans, they bring in a delicious variety of fresh sardines which you will find on the menus of local restaurants.

Your road turns right just short of Kalloni, and as it begins to climb towards the village of Philia you will see below you the huge red brick rectangles of the **Moni Limona**. This is said to be a foundation of 1523, but what you see now is mostly of the eighteenth century with modern extensions and a good deal of rebuilding still going on. It is important today because of its library of over 450 valuable manuscripts, which attracts scholars and researchers from many countries.

Its religious function has declined to a strength of nine monks, though they take in novice pupils, which is unusual in island monasteries. There are nests of ill-kept little churches and a *katholikon* basilica, majestic but overdecorated with inferior wall paintings. The lay arrangements are more interesting. They include a splendid wine vault, with huge amphorae sunk up to their necks, and ladles and jugs handy (though one fears that all are now empty). There is a big bakery with the remains of a wood-fired oven, and in the second of the two courtyards there are cages full of lively-looking peacocks – the birds which featured so much in Byzantine church decoration.

The main courtyard has galleries for monastic quarters, and there are notices everywhere warning that women must keep to the covered passages at ground level. It turns out that they are now restricted only from entering the main church – which can be seen by men if they apply to the agreeable young *igoumenos*, or Father Superior.

Philia proves to be a small town on a fertile plateau at about 1500 feet, after which comes **Skalachori**, looking north to the sea past the peak of Mt Prophitis Ilias. The road circles round some lovely valleys, in which pines give way suddenly to planes and oaks. One of the loveliest valleys is formed by the bed of the river Voulgaris, which virtually connects the modern inland village of Antissa with the ancient site of the same name on the coast. On the eastern slope of the valley, in a beautiful sheltered glen below the road to the north, is the miniature gem of the **Moni Peribolis**, or 'garden monastery'.

A little walled courtyard, full of fruit trees and flowers, encloses a small church. Outside the walls are olive and vegetable patches worked by two part-time gardeners. Inside lives one dear old sister who will let you go in between 8 a.m. and 12.30, or between 3 p.m. and 7.30, though she is wary of visitors since they began to plunder her walnut trees. The church is dated 1590, and has some notable frescos. They are not in good condition, but the west end has some clear scenes of the 'Second Coming', with a quite startling picture of the sea giving up its dead. There are two striking ikons of Christ and the Virgin Mary – he is dark-bearded, straight-nosed and formidable, she has a face of great dignity, and both heads are set off by a glowing golden background. A lovely and peaceful place.

Antissa is the best of the villages on this route, almost a small town, with glorious views down the steep romantic valley to the sea. At its foot lay the ancient city, which lasted from the Bronze Age to 168 BC when the Romans destroyed it during the Macedonian wars. It has a special place in the island's folk-lore, for it was here that the head of Orpheus was washed ashore after his dismemberment in a jealous frenzy by the women of Thrace:

> 'When by the rout that made the hideous roar
> His gory visage down the stream was sent,
> Down the swift Hebrus to the Lesbian shore.'*

The sand soon covered his head, but the lyre which came ashore with it was rescued by the inhabitants, and it played by itself when the wind blew through its strings – the first 'Aeolian harp'. There are no better illustrations of the Greek genius for myth and story-telling than the tales of Orpheus and Arion, which suggest an origin for the musical and poetic life for which Lesbos became famous – of which the first exponent was Terpander of Antissa.

Just beyond Antissa the road divides – straight on for Sigri and its lone stone tree, left for **Eressos**, birthplace, it is said, of Sappho.

* Milton, *Lycidas*, 61–63.

Before the junction you will have entered a landscape which contrasts utterly with everything you have seen so far in Lesbos. The hills are bare, the mountains naked rock, and everywhere fantastic rock formations shoot out of the barren earth. It is of course a volcanic area, but that the gentle Sappho should have been born or brought up as a child here seems an anomaly in nature. Perhaps it was the contrast of bitter and sweet in the landscape hereabouts which brought out the contradictions in the little we know of her life and work, but it was probably not here but in Mytilene that she chiefly lived and wrote. The idea that she kept a kind of finishing school for girls of good family is only a guess; she obviously lived among the young of her own sex and delighted in their company – and women in Lesbos were allowed more freedom to live and develop their own lives than anywhere else in Greece.

In view of the many misconceptions about Sappho, and the universal modern use of the word 'Lesbian' to describe female homosexuality, it is worth reading the words of a distinguished classical historian:

> 'Sappho, no great beauty – she was little and dark, typically Greek in fact, whereas the ideal was to be tall and fair – enjoyed fame for her poetic genius, and parents even from Ionia would send their daughters to be taught by her. They left, normally, to be married; Sappho herself was married and had a daughter of her own; music was considered a desirable accomplishment for a lady and mistress of a household. . . . But it must be added that a later tradition, which made Sappho nothing more than a pervert, is probably a piece of literary silliness, a caricature of Sappho, produced by solemn scholars in late antiquity.' *

Eressos itself is just another pleasant little town, with an open *plateia* shaded by plane trees. Below it the road continues in an almost straight line down the course of the river Chalandra to **Skala Eressou**. This is an old-established village with a little rock-girt harbour below the remains of a mediaeval *kastro*. Now it has been developed as a holiday village to take advantage of a long stretch of good grey sandy beach – there must be nearly a mile of it. There are

* A. R. Burn, *The Pelican History of Greece.*

rooms to let and cafés and restaurants close to the sea – a good place for a family holiday.

Lesbos is more than a holiday island. With its poets, musicians and philosophers it was one of the cultural centres of the Greek world. We shall always connect it with the enigmatic Sappho, and it matters little what her sexual preferences were. What does matter is the irrevocable and tragic loss of nearly all her poetry. There is no doubt from the small amount that remains that she was a poetic genius and possessed one of those unique voices which occur too rarely in the history of the human race. She wrote in the Aeolian dialect of Greek, and the fragments which have come down to us read like so many petals of spring flowers blown away by the wind, and defy translation. Sappho's island too has a quality which is hard to analyse.

The town of **Chios** makes no great impression when first seen from the sea. It has for so long been of commercial importance that it has assumed the nondescript appearance of a busy port in any part of the world – though not nearly such a busy one as it was fifty years ago. Even the harbour has been reduced in size by encroaching modern buildings and quays. As for the architecture, there was a vicious earthquake in 1881 which demolished any building of character, and the redevelopment then and in this century has been haphazard and unimaginative. The approach from the airport – only a mile away to the south – takes you through more attractive suburbs which have kept their greenery intact, and the *parko* (or municipal gardens) beyond the *Plateia Vounakiou* is a relief from drabness.

It is some time before you realize that the slightly higher ground to the north of the harbour is occupied by a large *kastro*, mainly because the walls have been reduced to a height little more than that of the surrounding houses. Unlike the fortress at Mytilene, its central space still encloses the remains of the old Turkish quarter, with typically narrow and disorderly streets. The ring of walls, though, is still distinct, and so are the lower courses of towers and gates built by the Giustiniani family in the fourteenth century – their arms can be seen at several of the gates. Like most of the Aegean islands Chios had Venetian masters for a time after 1204, but the

Giustiniani captured it for Genoa in 1261. Their first occupation was brief, but after some vicissitudes they returned in 1344 to found a chartered company to exploit its trade. The family and the company prospered until the Turks ejected them in 1566, and even then the island remained untroubled and prosperous for nearly two hundred and fifty years.

If the town of Chios is dull, that is not true of the rest of the island. Scenically it is magnificent. The rock formations are basically volcanic, and the tops are bare, but the deep green valleys which lace the crags are a continual excitement to the traveller. Chios has one of the best road systems in the islands, and there are buses from the centre of the town to the main outlying villages – though to see them and the countryside properly you need to hire a car or moped.

Twelve miles out of the town to the west is one of the most famous establishments of the Greek Orthodox Church, the **Nea Moni**, or 'New Monastery', founded by royal decree of the Emperor Constantine Monomachos in the middle of the eleventh century. The short journey there illustrates at once the special excitements of Chian scenery. In what seems a few minutes the road whisks you from sea level to something like two thousand feet up in the Provation mountains, to find the monastery buildings at the head of a deep pine-clad ravine, with a stunning view down to the eastern sea.

The story of its founding is one of those lovely Greek fairy-tales which live on and deserve retelling in full. Briefly though, there were three hermits living in these mountains who came in mysterious circumstances upon an ikon of the Virgin Mary, round which they built their cells and a small church (the 'old monastery'). In a vision she prophesied to one of the hermits that Constantine would shortly regain the throne of Byzantium for his family. As he happened to be in exile on Lesbos at the time, the hermits visited him and extracted a promise that if the prophecy came true he would build a new church on the site of their discovery. It did come true, and as Constantine IX he set about fulfilling his promise. He sent one of his best architects to Chios with authority to employ the finest artists and materials available. The church was begun in 1042 and took twelve years to build, though the emperor died before it was finished. His original decree, sealed with a golden seal, is in the monastery library.

352

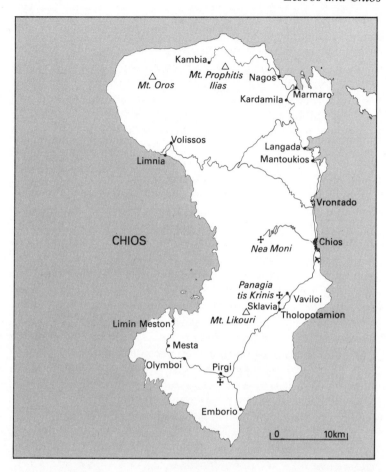

The church we see today has survived many disasters, from plunder by Saracens in the thirteenth century to a savage ransacking by the Turks in 1822 and the final catastrophe of the 1881 earthquake. Time and destruction have spoilt the impact of the exterior. The western tower, originally detached, was added in 1502; though its proportions are good, the upper levels had to be rebuilt after the earthquake. The church itself is disappointing from the outside: the walls are covered with a dull stucco, and the reconstituted central tower is lifeless.

Inside much has been lost, especially in the outer narthex, which was added by Constantine's sister-in-law the Empress Theodora after his death. Once the vaulting was covered with brightly coloured frescos, but most of these and the upper parts of the rich purple stonework were wrecked by the Turks. The domed inner narthex is a different matter. It was part of Constantine's original building, and there are some striking mosaic decorations to lift the spirit. The most vivid scene stretches across the top of the north wall, a fluid and animated picture of Christ washing his disciples' feet. Opposite it to the south is the Betrayal in the Garden, while Lazarus is resurrected over the entrance to the main church.

Even these mosaics do not compare with what meets the eye as you pass through into this splendid chamber. You have to remember that practically the whole of the central tower collapsed in 1881 and was rebuilt in 1900. Yet you can still see the masterly way the central dome was erected on an octagonal base, and the whole set in the stone framework dictated by the outer walls. The figure of Christ Pantocrator has disappeared from the centre of the dome, but all the way round its lower parts the mosaics have been restored to an astonishing brilliance in gold, blues, browns and reds. They are all scenes from the life of Christ, and none is more telling than the Baptism, an imaginative conception with Christ's body showing through rippling water as he stands shoulder-deep in the river. The Crucifixion has a wonderful group of mourning women, while the Deposition from the Cross is a representation unique in Greece; the face of St John alone is profoundly moving. These are the original mosaics commissioned by Constantine and executed by experts from Byzantium. That so much has survived is astonishing, and we owe a lot to Bishop Phostinos of Chios, who soon after the last war preserved and restored what remained.

In front of the triple eastern apse stands an unusually small *templo*, built in Pentelic marble. This was happily installed by the Archaeological Foundation of Greece to replace a more ornate one built in 1907, and it is simple enough not to compete for attention with the mosaics. Nor does it overpower the holy and historic ikon which occupies the traditional position to the right of the main sanctuary entrance. Of the original painting you can see only the tiny head of the Virgin, though the beaten silver sheath which covers the rest reproduces the eloquent position of the hands – empty, but seemingly looking for a Child to hold.

Since its miraculous discovery, the ikon has had many miraculous adventures, being rescued from the attention of the iconoclasts in the ninth century, surviving impious arrows and disastrous fires, or hidden in the roof of the tower during a Turkish attack. Our Lady is now a part of the monastery family, and it is most endearing to hear one of the nuns having what sounds like a morning gossip with the Mother of God.

Of the monastery buildings the most evocative is the Refectory, built in the seventeenth century to accommodate eighty monks. A great stone table with fixed stone benches extends the whole length of the room, and as in the monastery on Patmos there are pigeon-holes down both sides for the monks to store their platters and cutlery. Now there are only six nuns in residence, for as part of the reorganization after the war the Nea Moni was declared a convent under the supervision of an Abbess.

The most impressive secular building is the underground water cistern, with a roof supported on fifteen arches springing from a double row of columns. It is contemporary with the church, and imitates the one attached to Santa Sophia in Constantinople. The oddest place is the Chapel of the Holy Cross, just inside the present entrance to the monastery. It was built in the Middle Ages for the use of women, who were not otherwise allowed within the precincts; the nuns today keep it fresh and sweet-smelling with flowers and herbs, but at the west end there is a rather gruesome display in a glass case of the bones of people killed here in the Turkish massacre of 1822.

The year 1822 is a date you cannot avoid in any account of the history of Chios. In 1821 the men of Samos persuaded their neighbours the Chians to join them at the outbreak of the War of Independence. Although on the whole they had prospered under Turkish rule they agreed to rise, but the campaign misfired. In revenge the Turks massacred 25,000 Chians and enslaved nearly twice as many, as well as wrecking many of the finest monuments of the Orthodox Church. The island of Psara nearby was treated just as ruthlessly, and survivors from both islands – industrious and well educated people – sailed across to Syros and built the new city of

Ermoupolis below its mediaeval acropolis. The immediate riposte by Admiral Kanaris, who blew up the Turkish flagship inside Chios harbour, was little comfort, but Turkish brutality caused such a stir in Europe that most countries for the first time took the Greek cause seriously. Delacroix's picture 'The Massacre of Chios' had something of the same effect as the war paintings of Goya, and though the original is in the Louvre there is a copy in the Chios museum – ironically now housed in a Turkish mosque near the Plateia Vounakiou.

The southern parts of Chios are on the whole less rugged and more fertile than the north, though no less beautiful. It was here that in earlier days the chief wealth of the island was produced – from the growth and export of citrus fruit and mastic resin. A network of roads leads south from Chios town, and the long fertile plain, or *Kampos*, through which they pass was once the home of rich Chians who built their comfortable and ornamental houses in the centre of their estates of olive, lemon and orange groves. Most of these estates have been cleared away to make room for the airport, but you can still see a few crumbling mansions behind high stone walls, and in early summer the pervasive scent of the blossom spreads on the breeze.

Beyond the Kampos you reach a more rolling landscape of farms and small villages. One of these is **Vaviloi**, and you should not miss a short detour from here along the byroad which leads to Sklavia. About a mile out of Vaviloi a sign directs you to the church of the **Panagia tis Krinis** (Our Lady of the Fountain). This is a lovely surprise at the end of a sandy lane – a low building in warm pinkish stone with 'romanesque' arches picked out in decorative brick tiling. It was a daughter foundation of the Nea Moni and not many years later in date. Like Nea Moni it lost its central tower in 1881, but here it has been more sensitively restored. The Greek Arts Ministry has taken the church under its wing, and the series of magnificent but dilapidated frescos inside are being carefully and painstakingly examined and classified before restoration. These are mostly thirteenth-century paintings, though there are a few eighteenth-century additions in a typically allegorical vein. The interior is officially closed to visitors for the time being, though you may be lucky enough to find the presiding archaeologist at work there. If so, you should be careful to treat both him and the church with the respect they so much deserve.

You rejoin the main road just before Tholopotamion, and it crosses the southern slopes of Mt Likouri before reaching more fertile farmland around the small town of Pirgi. Already you will have noticed beside the road specimens of the Chian 'mastic tree' – actually an evergreen bush rising to about six feet in height. It is grown commercially for its resin, or gum, which is collected and brought into centres like Pirgi from surrounding farms. The plant is botanically identified as *Pistacia lentiscus*, 'a dense aromatic shrub of 1–3 metres, with dark green leaves of two to six pairs of elliptic leaflets'.* Both flowers and fruit are initially red, and make quite a show in spring and autumn.

The resin is collected from incisions made in the bark, and solidifies into what look like crystal teardrops. For an unknown reason this solidifying process occurs only when the shrub is grown in Chios – it has been tried elsewhere without success. It has had manifold uses, of which the most general has been in the making of chewing gum – something as popular in classical times and with the odalisques of the Sultan's harem as it has been throughout the modern world. It has been used in medicine to treat rheumatism, toothache and gout, and as an ingredient in picture varnish. Unluckily for Chios synthetic varnishes and whatever American manufacturers put in their chewing gum have largely ruined the trade. Locally it is still the basis of a popular sweet and a liqueur, but the *ouzo*-like *mastika* is rarely drunk and hard to come by – only the rather sticky liqueur is sold.

Pirgi is more than a mastic centre. Its unique character derives from the style of exterior house decoration known as *sgraffito*. Naturalistic designs are scratched on the stucco, and a geometric pattern of white and grey paint applied to the surface – often the whole front wall of a house. The larger houses surround a central *plateia*, dominated by a large and uninteresting 'metropolitan' church. At the east end of the square is the narrow entrance to the ancient church of *Agii Apostoli*, another gem of the twelfth century, with brick tile decoration similar to that at the *Panagia tis Krinis*.

* Huxley and Taylor, *Flowers of Greece and the Aegean* (Chatto & Windus 1977).

The Apostles were Peter and Paul, so several panels of frescos show scenes from their lives – including a nice view of Paul and Silas in the stocks. Most of the frescos were done in 1665 by a master of the Cretan school called Domestikos, but there are some much earlier fragments of a twelfth-century ikon of the two saints, restored and mounted on canvas. They were casualties of the Turkish savagery in 1822, though the 'mastic villages' were spared the worst effects because the harems wanted to preserve their sources of the gum. At the highest point of the town the central keep of a Genoese castle has been partly converted to domestic use.

The defensive character of these southern villages is more obvious when you come to **Olymboi**, which also has a central keep and houses which have been incorporated in an outer ring of walls. Another striking example is **Mesta**, a few miles further along the road to the west. You can enter it through several arched gateways in the outer wall, but you can only reach the central *plateia* by following narrow alleyways which often tunnel their way under three-storey houses. It is an extraordinary survival, built when pirate attacks on the south coast could be expected at any time. Both Olymboi and Mesta are built on plateaux raised above the coastal plain, but invisible from the sea. Mesta too has a church worth discovering, that of the *Taxiarchis*, with a fourteenth-century east end and more brick tilework, though its west end is a modern extension. The *templo* inside is a delight – small but high, and of intricately carved fifteenth-century woodwork. Some of the mediaeval houses have been converted into accommodation for visitors, and it would be a wonderful place to stay in an authentic Greek island atmosphere.

You would also have a pleasant outlet to the sea at **Limin Meston**, or Limani as it is usually called. Here there is a substantial harbour, big enough to take small freighters for repair. There are fishing boats too, of course, and just a few houses round the waterfront with rooms to let. Beside the approach road to the harbour there is an excellent little restaurant with a few tables set on a shady terrace above the road.

As a diversion from the main road you can reach the ancient port of **Emborio** by a turn-off to the left just before Pirgi. This was an important Bronze Age settlement, a rival perhaps of Troy.

Between the eighth and sixth centuries BC there was a Greek city with an acropolis on the hill of Prophitis Ilias north of the harbour. The whole site was excavated by the British School from 1951 to 1954, including an archaic temple of the sixth century near the harbour. Underwater exploration revealed its importance in the wine trade, at least, when amphorae were found with origins as far apart as Attica, Rhodes, Kos and Thasos.

Only two roads penetrate the mountainous north, where the landscape is dominated by the two great peaks of Mt Oros, at 3500 feet, and Mt Prophitis Ilias at just on 4000 feet. South of the main massif a twenty-five-mile drive takes you through wildish country to **Volissos**, a small hill town which curls round another ruined *kastro*, and to the harbour below at **Limnia**. This is a simple place with one taverna, frequented by Greek families from Volissos, and with rooms to let. It is useful too as the starting point for a local ferry service to **Psara**, a passage of seventeen miles. This island has always been closely linked to Chios, and has some claims on history – beginning with Mycenaean tombs of the thirteenth century BC, but mostly arising from the eighteenth and nineteenth centuries AD, when the Psariots took every opportunity of harrying the Turks. Like the Chiots they were fine seamen, with an excellent harbour on the south coast, and they sided with the Russian fleet under Admiral Orloff in the Russo-Turkish war of 1770–5 – an adventure they got away with because Turkish reprisals were thwarted by stormy weather. Admiral Kanaris, hero of the later Greek resistance, was born here in 1785.

They finally overreached themselves when the War of Independence broke out in 1821. The Turks were infuriated by their raids on the mainland coast, and in 1824 they suffered the same fate as the Chians had two years earlier. Fourteen thousand Janissaries landed to deal with a population of about the same number, whereupon the islanders blew up their own powder magazines and only 3000 escaped – many of whom joined the Chians in founding the city of Ermoupolis in Syros. Today you find little life and few comforts on Psara, but the southern anchorage is a safe and peaceful place to lie up for a day or two.

The other main route to the north is aimed at Kardamila, a sizeable town close to several harbours in a conveniently indented coastline. It is the reputed birthplace of Homer, and of all the seven cities who have claimed the honour it seems to be the general favourite. The classic support for the claim is in the anonymous *Hymn to Apollo*, written probably during the archaic period to introduce a recitation from the Iliad or the Odyssey:

> 'Tell me, maidens, of poets that visit here
> who sings to you the sweetest, whom do you hold most dear?
> Remember me then, one answer, one only giving:
> "A man that is blind, in scarry Chios living,
> supreme in song, both now and in times to come".' *

Byron's line in 'The Bride of Abydos' picks up the tradition:

> 'The blind old man of Scio's rocky isle'.

It may be too easy to imagine a relationship between scenery and poetry, but the sweeping grandeur of Homer's hexameters reminds us, however, illogically, of the mighty mountains and winding valleys of Chios.

This is not to say it is sensible to connect particular scenes of objects visible today with famous figures of the past – the 'plane tree of Hippocrates' in Kos, or the 'house of Sappho' in Mytilene. So when you read that a massive block of stone, on an outcrop beside the road out of Chios to the north, was where Homer sat to teach his pupils, you will probably (if reluctantly) accept the modern view that it was the base of a temple to Cybele.

The original town of Chios has now spread to join its northern neighbour **Vrontado**, and the two form a sprawling community stretching some three miles along the coast. Vrontado itself, now a residential suburb of Chios, has a small yacht harbour and some popular beaches. Beyond it the road follows the corniche between Mt Kenavros and the sea to reach two villages of character. First comes **Mantoukios**, the simplest of fishing harbours with a huge plane tree which has its feet almost in the water. Then **Langada**, a bigger place with a fleet of brightly painted boats bobbing alongside the quay. Most of them have a little lugsail furled round a flimsy gaff which they clearly use when weather allows, and just a pair of oars – no engine or outboard motor.

---

* *Homeric Hymns* III, 169–73, trans. T. F. Higham.

From Langada you have a good view of the **Oinousses Islands**, which are served by a daily boat from Chios harbour. This arrangement is largely for the convenience of the staff and pupils of the *Navtiko Gymnasio*, the only nautical boarding school in Greece – similar as an idea to the San Giorgio training school in Venice. Apart from the school there are various conveniences in the main harbour of Oinoussae, and it makes an interesting day's excursion.

At **Kardamila** you will find no Homeric clues, but a pleasant small town, popular with the Greeks for holiday houses and commanding the seaside village of Marmaro. It is worth exploring the upper part of the town, where modern houses give way to a ruined mediaeval quarter. **Marmaro** is disappointingly plain after Mantoukios and Langada, but beyond the next headland you come to **Nagos**, which is quite natural and unspoilt. There is no harbour but a long sandy beach overlooked by a very good little restaurant.

That is the last of the coastal villages, but it would be a mistake to turn back now. A new road has been built along the northern flanks of the highest mountain range in Chios, and even without an objective it makes a glorious drive. The road crosses valleys which run from high in the mountains right down to the sea, and the views either way are superb. At four thousand feet (probably two thousand feet above you) this Prophitis Ilias is the handsomest of his kind. Before reaching the present end of the road at Kambia you pass a couple of other villages, but for most of the way you will see nothing but mountains, trees and the sea far below. Somewhere above you was a sanctuary of Apollo, and that is company enough.

An Ionian rather than an Aeolian origin and background seems to have directed the culture of Chios to more practical, or at least tangible, ends. Sculpture rather than poetry was its main interest, and a school of that very Greek art flourished there in the sixth and fifth centuries BC, while a local artisan called Glaucus was the first to discover how to weld iron.* This practical bent was also put to commercial uses: Chios was the first Greek city to enter the slave trade, even before Delos, and by the end of the Peloponnesian War only Sparta had more domestic slaves.

The verdict of Thucydides was that 'of all others, only the people

---

* Herodotus, *Histories* I, 25.

of Chios seem to me happy and full of common sense'. This is as true today as it was in the fifth century BC. They are also a vigorous people, swift of response and quick to offer help to strangers. To come to Chios and to live among its people even for a short time is a vivid experience.

Access

Overnight ferries from Piraeus call on most days of the week, first at CHIOS (the advertised passage time is ten hours) and then four hours later at Mytilene on LESBOS. Once a week a ferry comes down from Kavala in the north to Mytilene by way of Lemnos, and twice a week a smaller ship comes across to CHIOS from Samos.

Both islands have well established airfields, and the forty-minute flight from Athens saves a great deal of sea time.

Communications

The roads are excellent where the terrain allows, and bus services are frequent between all main centres. There are many taxis and car hire firms in Mytilene and Chios town. There is a small ferry service from Limena on CHIOS to the neighbouring island of PSARA on three days a week.

Accommodation

LESBOS   There is little peace in the Mytilene harbour area, but one mile to the south on the coast road leading from the airport is XENIA (B), a quiet and comfortable hotel with a swimming pool. Further out still is KOUDOUROUDIA (C), a small modern hotel on the shore of the Gulf of Geras. This is just what an unassuming holiday hotel should be, spotless and friendly, with all conveniences.

Molivos (Methymna) in the north has plenty of rooms to let, but the only hotel of distinction is DELPHINIA (B) on the coast a mile to the south of the town. This has only pension terms, but there is a large restaurant and 'club' facilities in a discreetly separate building with a swimming pool – an outstanding hotel in its class.

CHIOS   The fashionable hotel in Chios town is CHANDRIS (B), which is comfortable and well run, but as it overlooks the harbour is apt to be noisy. XENIA (B) on the southern exit road has the same disadvantage in the front rooms, but is also very comfortable and has a most obliging management.

Restaurants

LESBOS   The most interesting restaurant in Mytilene is the NAVTIKOS OMILOS (or Yacht Club), a surprisingly simple place with tables on a sandy expanse near the yacht berths, and patronized mainly by the families of the local boat-owners. The environs of the harbour are less inviting, but there are a few pleasant eating-places in the residential suburbs on the way to Agia Marina, inland from the airport road.

CHIOS   Again the harbour area is to be avoided, but there are two good restaurants close to the Xenia Hotel. TASSO is the more conventionally attractive, with tables set in a garden beside the road, but in the side street immediately alongside the Xenia is the PSISTARIA where all the Chiot families go, especially at weekends; it has Chian wine by the carafe. Elsewhere in the island a good simple meal can be had at most fishing villages, notably at Nagos in the north and Limin Meston in the south.

Facilities

Banks: There are branches of the main banks in all the principal centres.

Yachts: Mytilene harbour is busy and crowded, but there are peaceful anchorages in the Kolpos Geras and elsewhere around the coast. Molivos (Methymna) harbour is picturesque, but small and crowded. There are berths at the Yacht Club south of Chios harbour, and at Vrontados to the north, with good shore facilities. There should be good anchorages at Mantoukios and Limin Meston in Chios, and on the south coast of Psara.

TWENTY-ONE

Samos, Ikaria and Phourni

Samos lies nearest of all the Greek islands to the continent of Asia, being separated from it by a strait less than two miles wide. It is seen at its grandest if you come by sea through the channel between Ikaria and Phourni. A great mountain chain runs along the island from west to east, rising to two main peaks. Mt Kerketeus at the western end, nearly 5000 feet high, spins up out of the sea like a fantastic top, while away to the east the head of Mt Karvouni dominates the fertile plains.

Ferries from Piraeus call first as a rule at Karlovasi on the north-west coast and continue eastward to the harbour of Vathy, which serves the modern capital – now called Samos like the island. The airport is conveniently close to the most popular holiday centre at Pithagorio.

In ancient times the beauty and fertility of the island led to many flattering epithets. Homer called it *hydrili*, the 'watery place', because of its many streams and springs. It was known to other poets as *anthemoessa* for its flowers, *phylia* for its wild olive trees, *pityoessa* for its pines and *dryoessa* for its oaks. It was also called *parthenia gaia*, the 'maiden land', though this can hardly have been a tribute to Hera, whose birthplace it claims to be. Menander, originator of the Athenian 'new comedy', declared that Samos was so fertile that even its fowls gave milk as well as eggs. It is still beautiful, and fertile enough for its own needs, but the tourist industry has soured it a little around the edges: crowded beaches mean crowded hotels and restaurants. Only among its magnificent central mountains, with the pines, the oaks, the streams and the flowers, does the old *persona* survive.

Vathy harbour too is magnificent at all times. Well sheltered, except very narrowly from the north-west, it forms an almost perfect horseshoe. A summer evening is its best time, the sun just setting beyond the entrance and maybe a new moon ready to follow it behind the dark mountains to the west. Then all round the bay the lights come on – still a restrained spectacle, with very little neon vulgarity. The old town of Vathy still rises on the southern slopes, but it has been thrust aside by the modern development which extends around the remaining shores, and continues for miles beyond the northern mole. Samos is the most sophisticated island capital outside Crete, Rhodes and perhaps Kos, with a broad dual-carriageway road serving half a mile of the waterfront.

In Samos town there is little of interest, for the classical city was not here but almost directly opposite on the south coast. Its mediaeval name was Tigani, but this was changed as recently as 1955 to Pithagorio in honour of the philosopher Pythagoras. This man was one of the great practical philosophers of antiquity, and though his doctrine of the transmigration of souls may not have gone down well with western Christians (*pace* Polonius in *Hamlet*), generations have tried to learn his proof that the square on the hypotenuse of a right-angled triangle is equal to the sum of the squares on the other two sides – the basis of the system of logarithms which dominated our higher calculations until the coming of the computer.

His skills extended to music and medicine, and as an astronomer he has been credited with the first theory that the sun was the centre of the universe. The same conclusion was reached by Aristarchus, born in Samos three hundred years later, though it was not revived until Copernicus restated it convincingly in the fifteenth century. Neither Pythagoras nor Aristarchus stayed long in Samos, the latter living and teaching mainly in Alexandria, the former moving to Croton in southern Italy, where he had an immense reputation and following; but one likes to think that it was in the clear night sky above Samos that they both first began to examine the heavenly bodies.

As a young man of eighteen, Pythagoras won the prize for wrestling at the Olympic Games, which must have impressed his later pupils. Mentally and physically tough, he decided early on that there was not enough room in Samos for himself and Polycrates, its

365

autocratic ruler during the second half of the sixth century BC who made it a major Mediterranean power. Herodotus gives us a vivid account of this man's achievements, saying that he was the first Greek since Minos of Knossos to develop sea power as an instrument of policy. With his 'fleet of a hundred and fifty oared galleys and a force of a thousand bowmen' he won command of the eastern Aegean. Among his decisive victories was one over the Lesbian fleet, when the prisoners he took 'were forced to dig, in chains, the whole of the moat which surrounds the walls of the city of Samos'.* He was also responsible, says Herodotus, for three of the greatest building and engineering feats in the Greek world. The first was the long mole which protected the harbour, the second was a tunnel through the hills north of the town, and the third was the temple of Hera, the largest known to Herodotus in Greece.

Of the city ruled by Polycrates practically nothing remains after repeated sackings and plunderings in later centuries. The modern mole is certainly founded on the one he built, and the ruins of the temple of Hera are not far away. The most extraordinary feat was the tunnel, designed by his chief engineer Evpalinos, and therefore known as the **Evpalinion Origma**; it was possibly dug by the same Lesbian prisoners, or others taken at sea. A mile long and measuring eight feet high by eight feet wide, its primary use was to bring water by an underground channel to the city from beyond the northern hills, but it could also be used as a way of escape in times of danger. This actually happened during an attack on the city by King Darius of Persia.

The road from Samos takes only a short time to cross the low intervening ridge and reach **Pithagorio**. It must be said that whatever charm survived here from mediaeval Tigani has been trampled on by the tourist trade, which has turned the colourful harbour front into one of the flashiest promenades of cafés, bars and restaurants you will find in the islands. This is a shame, because the narrow streets which descend to the harbour deserve a better issue, and so do the inhabitants, who are defenceless against the hordes who fill their hotels and lodging houses throughout the summer – except through the charges they make.

* *Histories* III, 39 seq.

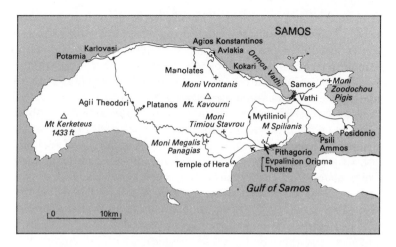

If you decide to retreat, go back to the main road above, and take a byroad off it which is signposted to the Evpalinion Origma. This will take you not only to the southern entrance of the tunnel, but also close to the ancient **Theatre**. Difficult to see from below because of the embankment, it occupies a terrace on the right just before a fork in the road. No seating is left, only a rough semicircle of rock and earth facing the sea, but the roofed-in passage behind the *orchestra* reveals that Roman residents and tourists preferred wild beast shows to classical drama.

A hundred yards further on you reach the end of the road and a gate in a wire fence – a gate which is open for a few hours on Mondays, Thursdays and Saturdays, and leads to a plain square building. This covers the entrance to the tunnel, a flight of steps only just shoulder-width which descend into this extraordinary subterranean passage. No wider at first than the steps, it widens after about twenty yards to the full eight feet and forms a level pathway beside the water channel for which it was built, stretching ahead farther than you can see. The pathway is dry and there are lights for quite a distance, but then notices discourage you from going farther – how can the curator check there is no one left in the tunnel when the time comes to lock up?

Beyond the tunnel entrance a rough track (no motors) leads round to the right and to a point where you can see the western

367

abutment of the northern city walls built by Polycrates. The masonry is massive, and you can see the line of it climbing straight up the hillside. Then it turns east, and well preserved sections of it, with the bases of over thirty towers, extend for about another three miles along the crest before turning south and downhill towards the city. The eastern section has mostly disappeared.

Enclosed in the north-eastern corner is the mediaeval **Moni Spilianis** (Monastery of the Cave) which you reach by taking the right-hand fork just beyond the theatre. A small, well kept but homely place, with a population mostly of cats, it has a lovely view over Pithagorio to the Turkish coast. The church is a modest one, with a double dedication to the Panagia and St Nicholas, but the chief draw for visitors (if claustrophobia is not a problem after the tunnel) is a natural underground rock chamber which includes a hermit's cell. This is not at all like the scientifically dug tunnel of Evpalinos, but a low-lidded cave with an entrance like the jaws of a monster. Water drips from the roof, and there are cisterns to collect it to right and left. It was used as a refuge when Turkish rulers became violent, and by those resisting the Germans in the last war.

Back on the main road which leads towards the airport you will see beyond the western limits of the town the ruins of a big square tower. Disappointingly this turns out to be an early nineteenth-century building, the *Phrourio Logathetis*, but further on the road passes close to a large excavated area with the remains of classical-looking buildings. This is no part of the original city of Polycrates, but a western extension built chiefly in the Hellenistic, Roman and early Byzantine eras. Each period is represented, the Roman by a large bath complex, the Byzantine by a Christian basilica church with an early baptistry.

Samos had been a part of the Roman province of Asia since 129 BC, one of the last territories to be prised from the successors of Alexander. Its capital at that time still contained some of the finest treasures in the Greek world remaining after the destruction and pillage of Corinth twenty years earlier. Roman provincial governors had a quick eye for loot – they had to have, with only a year to make the most out of their office – and in 82 BC the notorious Caius Verres helped himself from Samos before going on to worse depredations in Sicily. There he was brought to book by Cicero in a famous legal prosecution; Cicero also befriended Samos when proconsul of Cilicia. Antony and Cleopatra lifted more treasures during a riotous holiday here in 39 BC. How many tourists, one wonders, think of those two as their predecessors? They would certainly have eaten better, and what would they think of the discos?

The third great achievement of Polycrates was the temple of Hera. The temple itself was only part of a sanctuary known still as the **Heraion**, which lies near the coast three miles beyond the airport, at the mouth of the river Imvrasos. To be the birthplace of the consort of Zeus is a grandiose claim, and everything built on this site has more than a touch of the grandiose. Quite how much of it we owe to Polycrates is not clear. There were buildings on the site in the Bronze Age, and two major temples were put up between 800 and 600 BC. A third, the one attributed to Polycrates, was begun early in the sixth century under the direction of a Samian architect, Rhoikos. This however was burnt to the ground about 525 BC, only three years before Polycrates was lured across to the mainland by a jealous Persian satrap and foully done to death. He had probably already put in hand the rebuilding of the even larger temple whose ground plan we see today, but it was never finished.

The scale is vast. The single incomplete column left standing gives you some idea of it, if you imagine a hundred and sixty-six others like it standing in row upon row in this huge rectangle. The style was a Samian version of the Ionic order, with larger and more elaborate column bases and capitals than the more refined Athenian taste allowed. The temple was surrounded at a lower level by other buildings of various dates. There were Greek temples to Apollo and to a combination of Hermes and Aphrodite. There was a Hellenistic Stoa, two smaller Roman temples to Hera, a Roman baths and an early Christian basilica. The whole site is still being thoroughly and discreetly investigated by the German Archaeological Institute, who have been at it with necessary intervals since 1910. They emphasize how much is still to be revealed.

As you might expect, the best beaches are on the south coast, some of them at the foot of a rocky peninsula to the south-east of Vathy. One road leads to **Psili Ammos**, a general favourite, and the other crosses the Dendrias headland, thick with pines, to reach a deeply sheltered bay at **Posidonio**, well supplied with tavernas. One of the most accessible of the island's monasteries is the **Moni Zoodochou Pigis**, whose life-giving spring emerges from another rocky headland a few miles north-east of Vathy. It was founded in 1756 – a friendly place, but not remarkable except for some fine contemporary carving in local wood.

So far we have explored only the eastern tip of Samos. A not too laborious day's expedition farther west begins along the northern coast road, which gives you some marvellous prospects up a series of wooded valleys to the high central peaks. Between the villages of Kokari and Avlakia there are some exposed and shingly beaches. From the latter you can take a mountain road up to the **Moni Vrontanis**. This is the oldest monastery in Samos, founded in 1566, and surrounded by pines and cypresses. Very high walls, whitewashed within and with wooden galleries all round, enclose a peaceful courtyard. The church is a small and narrow *Panagia*, with a lovely ikon of the Virgin. Outside it there are conveniently shaded seats round a circular fountain – altogether a very sane and understandable place of God.

The next valley opens up just before the more sophisticated and flowery town of **Agios Konstantinos**, and a lovely road winds sharply up it through the deep shade of plane trees, with a stream tumbling past you, to end at **Manolates**, an idyllic village which climbs in stages further up the hill. There are gardens bright with flowers on every hand, two or three cafés and a warm welcome to be had from the villagers.

Prosperity has reached these mountain villages indirectly from tourist development on the coast. The men work down there during the summer, supporting their families above. Good roads connect the two worlds, and a happy atmosphere results. This end of Samos is a great wine-producing area, once the mountains flatten out a bit, and the vineyards are as thick as anywhere in France, if not so well organized. Figs are abundant, but as in Lesbos the olives often drop neglected from the trees. The scenery is marked by an abundance of pencil-like cypresses, stiff dark verticals among the silvery fluttering olives.

The end of the road comes at **Karlovasi** – actually three distinct communities. Neo Karlovasi is an ugly commercial sprawl and the centre of the wine-producing trade; Meso and Palaio Karlovasi are more attractive but have been much developed to take advantage of good beaches at **Potami**, further to the west. The road back to the south begins in between these two, a wide, well surfaced highway up the side of a valley and over the watershed at Agii Theodori. The village of **Platanos** lies just off it to the east near the highest point, a sensible place with a restaurant to provide a welcome half-way meal.

The return journey, in sight now of the southern sea, takes you through more pine woods – some of them sadly ruined by fire – but villages are rare. At Koumaradeoi a roughish road goes south to the **Moni Megalis Panagias**, built on the site of a shrine to Artemis and reputed to be the most interesting in Samos. It has been the wealthiest, too, and monks came from the monasteries on Mt Athos to decorate the church walls with frescos. Unfortunately visitors are not now admitted, ostensibly for fear of damage or theft. There seems to be a political struggle involved here between the civic authorities and the Orthodox Church. The church everywhere objects to the lax attitude of the present Greek government to divorce and abortion, and refuses in some parts to co-operate in tourist activity – which is how they view inconvenient visits by foreigners.

The same situation obtains at the Monastery of the Holy Cross, **Timiou Stavrou**, a handsome eighteenth-century foundation a little further along the road. It must also be remembered that many of these places have just one old monk or two or three frail nuns to look after them, and they only open their doors when the *pappas* from a distant town comes up in his car for a service or a visit to the sick. One should be more than ever grateful for the warm welcome which can be forthcoming in the most remote places.

At the next large village, Chora, you have a choice of two roads back to Vathy. One goes the way you came, through Pithagorio, but for variety you can take the slightly longer route through Mytilinioi – in spite of its name a dull place with one long main street. The approach from this direction gives you another lovely view over Vathy bay as you come down off the hills in the evening light.

Samos suffers from overcrowding. This is absurd, of course, when you consider the gloriously unspoilt interior of the island, but in Samos town and Pithagorio it is almost impossible between May and November to find a hotel room unless you have booked a holiday through a travel agency several months ahead. This seems to wear off on the hotel staff, the waiters and the taxi-drivers; certainly you find a warmer welcome in Lesbos and readier one in Chios. As for food and drink there is little variety or temptation. A lot of wine is produced, but by the time it is bottled you will find it no different from similar products all over Greece. If you ask for a bottle of the traditional red *moschato*, back will go the head, the eyes will lift and a barely audible *'ochi'* will be your answer. In vain to echo Byron: 'Fill high the bowl with Samian wine.'

The hot sandy beaches are the draw, but others have learned to enjoy a different kind of holiday here – walking among the mountain villages. You can still take a bus or get a lift down to the sea if you feel like it, but if you are content to take what accommodation you find (and it will always be clean and welcoming) there are many natural pleasures up there – not least to drop in for a genuine Greek country meal in the evening and – who knows? – there may be a litre or two of the real Samian left in the *bareli*.

Ikaria is a strange island. Its long and rugged mountain backbone leaves little room for life along the south coast, though towards its northern end the mountains withdraw just enough to admit the small harbour of **Agios Kirikos**, which is where the ferries call daily on their way to Samos and back. This is a business-like harbour, backed by little more than a friendly village where everybody knows everybody and tourists are for once outnumbered.

At the end of the quay stands a thirty-foot-high piece of modern bronze sculpture – between two huge pointed wings the forlorn body of Icarus plunges downwards. Commissioned a few years ago by an Ikarian family, it illustrates the overwhelming local belief that it was into the *Ikario Pelagos*, the sea enclosed by Ikaria, Patmos and the Phourni islands, that the son of the inventor Daedalus fell as they were escaping from the service of King Minos of Crete – the wax hinges of his wings melting as he flew too near the sun. Why bother to derive the island's name from a Phoenician word for 'fish' when you have a myth like that to call upon?

Behind the harbour a green valley rises in a series of terraces as the mountains tail off towards the north, white houses and churches

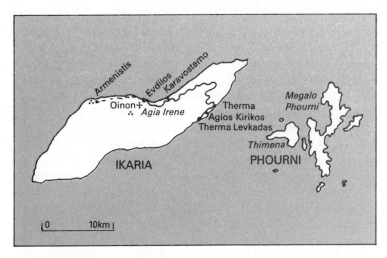

peering through the screen of cypress, fig and olive. Here you would think is a place to enjoy simple rural Greek life, away from the crowds of Samos or Mytilene. You would not be altogether wrong, but that is not what Greek visitors come for in their thousands from all over the Aegean. Just round the point from Agios Kirikos is another bay with a gravelly beach and a busy village behind. Tiers of modern houses climb the steep hillside to the south; thronged café terraces overlook the beach and the little wooden pier which projects into the harbour.

This is **Therma**, where warm 'radio-active' mountain springs would flow naturally into the sea, but are now channelled and piped through the public thermal baths which men and women come to enjoy from as far away as Crete. It makes an extraordinary sight, and 'enjoy' seems not really the right word as you watch the daily processions of mournful invalids from their hotels and rooms and back again, muffled even in the hottest weather in woollen dressing gowns with towels over their heads. Those not directly involved, mainly husbands who have brought their wives for treatment, congregate endlessly at the café tables, where even the Greek capacity for gossip and argument is pushed to the limits. From morning to evening the more active patients swim slowly around like captive whales in the warm pool below.

373

There is a road connection between Agios Kirikos and Therma, from which the few taxis profit, but in good weather the quickest and cheapest way is to take the small boats which leave and arrive at the pier every half hour. They spend less than ten minutes in transit between the two harbours, and when a ferry is due they will take passengers and their piled-up luggage right to the main departure quay at Agios Kirikos.

In the other direction a good road continues along the coast, but at present only as far as **Therma Levkadas**, a smaller but socially superior outlet for the same kind of thermal springs. There is no village. The social centre is a large modern hotel set back from the cliffs among pine woods; the attraction for bathers is a rock-lined sea pool where the water can be so hot that steam rises even on a warm day. This will not be everybody's idea for a summer swim, and a little farther on there is a lovely quiet beach between outcrops of rock – though it needs a scramble down the cliffs or over boulders on the foreshore to reach it.

To complete the pleasure of your swim, either before or after it, look around for a well hidden little restaurant just below the road where it comes nearest to the sea. This would be a joy just for its position, but it is kept by a fisherman and his wife, in whose tiny kitchen she cooks the fish he brings in – usually timing it for about one o'clock in the afternoon. Should he be late, there will be fish soup and fresh vegetables.

From here the road goes further down the coast to the scattered village of Xilosyrtis and the convent of the Evangelismos. It will go further still as long as it has room between the mountains and the sea; the good surface is being gradually extended, but it is a long and barren way to the few isolated villages at the south-western end of Ikaria.

As well as this so far incomplete route, there is one fully maintained road which runs from Agios Kirikos up through the green combes, round the tip of the mountains, then down in wide sweeps to the north coast. The views are splendid all the way, and if you stop among the heathery slopes of the watershed you can see the head of Mt Kerketeus on Samos towering across the sea. At this point you will notice that the rock formation has changed to horizontal strata of flat schist slabs showing very near the surface, and nearly all the older houses on this side of the island are roofed in heavy slates which are quarried here. The Greeks call them *plakes*, and they are even bigger and heavier than you find on Skopelos in the northern Sporades – immovably secure in wind and rain, but heavy to fix or replace.

You first make contact again with the coast at **Karavostamo**, which is being not very convincingly developed as a holiday base. This northern coast is more amenable to development, particularly when you reach the town and harbour of **Evdilos**. There is more here for the visitor than at Agios Kirikos, so far without spoiling its character as a major fishing harbour – though the big ships berth here too twice a week during the season.

Evdilos lies at the foot of the only fertile valley which penetrates any distance into the central mountains, and between here and **Armenistis** on the far north-western promontory the country is lovely. You could wander for days among the inland villages, and a reasonable road takes buses as far as Armenistis. This was where one of the island's few classical sites was discovered, a fifth-century sanctuary of *Artemis Tavropolos*. This attribute does not connect the goddess directly with the rearing of bulls, but links her sanctuary and temple with the one at Tauris in the Crimea where Iphigeneia was transported after the attempted sacrifice at Aulis. However, coins discovered here do show a bull on the reverse side to the head of Artemis, together with the name OINOI.

The name Ikaria does not appear in any form on the coins, but two miles inland from Evdilos is a place called **Oinon**, once the most important town in the island. Now Oinoe or Oenoe is a common name in the Aegean, but *oinos* is the ancient Greek word for wine, and vines grow abundantly in this part of Ikaria. Indeed, it was once almost as famous for its wines as Samos, and the head of Dionysus appears on another of the coins found near Armenistis.

The acropolis of Oinon is easy to find beside the road about a mile beyond the village of Kambos. There are no fortifications to be seen, though there are the remains of a small *odeion* which was later incorporated within the *Palatia*, or mediaeval governor's residence. Today there is more interest in the eleventh-century church of *Agia Irene* and its surroundings. It was built on the site of a very early Byzantine church of the fourth century, of which the mosaic floor is

375

said to be preserved under the present courtyard. You enter this unusual and charming place through a Roman gateway, and beside it there is an excellent little museum with finds from neolithic to Roman and Byzantine times. There are some quite undamaged small jars with both geometric and red-figure decoration, but the best thing there is a slim, delicately moulded hermaphrodite torso in marble, probably Hellenistic. It seems extraordinary to find such feeling in a limbless trunk.

Ikaria could never be sultry. The air of the mountains is exhilarating, and the seas around are constantly refreshing to mind and spirit – even without the radio-active springs. If you should want to explore further, an excursion boat leaves Agios Kirikos on one or two mornings a week (regularly on Sundays when the weather is fine) for **Phourni**, an intriguing group of islands between Ikaria and Samos. The passage takes about an hour, and the same boat will bring you back in the afternoon.

This is a favourite Sunday outing for residents and visitors, and must be a relief from the valetudinarian atmosphere of Therma. There are two main islands in the group, and you come first to the smaller of the two, Thimena, which is virtually uninhabited. Megalo Phourni is the name of the larger one, an irregular straggling island with a deep bay facing towards and sheltered by Thimena. The harbour is always busy about its main business, which is fishing, though all supplies from whatever source have to be landed here. On Sundays the three restaurants are even busier serving lunch to the visitors, and there is no doubt that the fish they cook are as delicious, as fresh and as cheap as you will find anywhere. Lobster and prawns are advertised on their placards, but recently these delights have been restricted to conserve stocks, and the port police are supposed to enforce a ban on their sale at certain seasons – especially on Sundays.

The feeling of the Phourni islands is more akin to the Kyklades than anything you find elsewhere in the eastern Sporades. There are no natural woods, and the hills are bare, empty and aloof. It is a surprise to find that the village behind the harbour has a long, straight and nicely paved avenue between rows of mulberry trees which runs for about a hundred yards inland to end at the village church – a kind of 'sacred way' from port to sanctuary where local families can enjoy their *volta*. There are beaches each side of the harbour, and many remoter swimming spots. A stay here with the use of a small boat would be an idyllic holiday, though few yachtsmen seem to have discovered this.

Access

The daily ferries from Piraeus call first at Agios Kirikos (occasionally at Evdilos) on IKARIA, and then proceed to Karlovasi and Vathy on SAMOS. They are mostly daytime passages, taking an advertised eight hours to Ikaria and twelve to the end of the run in Vathy. From Chios a smaller ship arrives at Vathy twice a week. The large airfield on the south coast of Samos takes daily flights from Athens, but there is no airfield on Ikaria.

Communications

The interior of SAMOS is mountainous, but there is a good coast road running west to Karlovasi, and a very busy one across to Pithagorio on the south coast. From there the road continues across the southern foothills to the resort of Marathokampos, and also branches north to Karlovasi, so that a circuit of the island by road is fairly easy. There are regular bus services between these centres. Taxis are much in demand for the shorter journeys, but cars and mopeds can readily be hired in Vathy, Karlovasi and Pithagorio.

IKARIA has only one completed road, by which buses run from Agios Kirikos (though infrequently) to Evdilos and a few villages beyond. Between Agios Kirikos and Therma it is quicker and cheaper to take the half-hourly small boat service than look for a rare taxi. Boats also leave Agios Kirikos and Therma two or three times a week for the PHOURNI islands – the only way of getting there.

Accommodation

SAMOS   More hotels are built every year in Vathy, but they can hardly keep pace with the demand for rooms. The pleasantest is XENIA (B) at the quieter end of the harbour front. In Kalami, a heavily developed suburb north of the harbour, ANDROMEDA (C) stands out as the most sensible and friendly, with a lovely prospect over Vathy bay. At Pithagorio during the summer and autumn it is almost impossible to find accommodation except

377

through travel agents. For a quiet life or a walking holiday you can be sure of finding a simple room and a warm welcome in one of the mountain villages such as Manolates, overlooking the north coast.

IKARIA   There is not much to recommend in Agios Kirikos. At Therma Leukadas, a little way out to the west, TOULA (A) is a large spa hotel with all comforts and facilities, in a secluded setting. In the more populous medicinal centre of Therma itself APOLLON (C) has a good position facing the sea, though the arrangement of balconies makes privacy difficult. In Evdilos on the north coast EUDOXIA (C) is modern and comfortable.

PHOURNI   There are simple rooms to let in the attractive harbour village of Megalo Phourni.

Restaurants

SAMOS   In Vathy the most popular restaurant with tourists is GRIGORI'S, but it tends to be crowded and noisy. More discreet is SAMION, next door to the Xenia hotel, where tables are set in a big garden under huge palm trees, and the cooking and service are professionally good. In Pithagorio there are the standard harbour tourist places, but you can eat simply and well in the mountain villages, and there is a good restaurant in Platanos.

IKARIA   Good food is hard to find in Agios Kirikos or Therma, but Evdilos has one good restaurant run by a well-known local family beside the harbour. The choicest spot is SPIRO'S at Therma Levkada, hidden away on the cliffs below the big hotel. Run by a fisherman and his family, it has a delightful position and a cheerful atmosphere.

PHOURNI   The fish restaurants by the harbour are deservedly popular with Greek visitors from Ikaria, in spite of a seasonal ban on lobster sales by the port police.

Facilities

Banks: In Samos there are branches in all the main centres; in Ikaria only in Agios Kirikos and Evdilos. There are no exchange facilities in Phourni.

Yachts: There are berths on Samos quay beside a busy thoroughfare, and a fine anchorage in Vathy bay. The berths in Pithagorio harbour are more cheerful, with good shore facilities, but the scene is very crowded. There are very few harbours along the northern coast until you come to Karlovasi. There are quiet berths in Agios Kirikos and Evdilos on Ikaria; Megalo Phourni is even quieter, with a delightful place to anchor, and good facilities ashore.

The Dodecanese

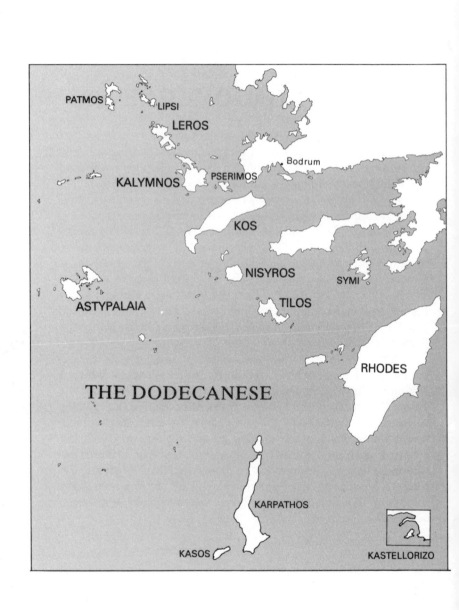

PATMOS

LIPSI

LEROS

Bodrum

KALYMNOS   PSERIMOS

KOS

NISYROS

SYMI

ASTYPALAIA

TILOS

RHODES

THE DODECANESE

KARPATHOS

KASOS

KASTELLORIZO

THE DODECANESE

The Dodecanese, the Twelve Islands, lie down the western coast of Asia Minor like a cable linking Samos to Rhodes. The Turks always referred to them as 'The Privileged Islands', since they enjoyed special privileges and tax exemptions granted them in the sixteenth century by Suleiman the Magnificent. These privileges they retained until 1908, when the twelve islands so designated united in protest against their removal. Italy took advantage of this during her war with Turkey in 1911–12 and ended by occupying them, though with a promise they would eventually be returned to Greece. This promise was conveniently forgotten at the Treaty of Sèvres after the First World War, when they were awarded to Italy for her share in the Allied victory, and they were not formally united with Greece until 1948 after Italy had been on the losing side in the Second World War.

Although the term Dodecanese was not publicly applied to them until 1908, Theophanes, a Byzantine chronicler writing between AD 758 and 818, refers to them in his *Chronography* as the 'Dodeka Nisoï'. For literalists there is a problem in the name. Which are now considered to be the twelve? In the chapters which follow we have listed fifteen which were claimed by the Italians in 1912 and awarded to Greece in 1948. Fourteen of these (the exception is Pserimos) have an independent local government. No matter: the name is convenient and euphonious, and all these islands have something about them which distinguishes them from their neighbours in the Kyklades.

TWENTY-TWO

Patmos, Lipsi, Leros, Kalymnos and Pserimos

The most northerly of the group is **Patmos**, and apart from Rhodes it is the most regularly visited by cruise liners. The island where St John the Divine (*Agios Ioannis Theologos*) wrote or dictated the *Apocalypse* is to the modern world what Delos was to the ancient – the most sacred island in the sea.

It is mainly a barren island, formed by three large volcanic masses, the central mass being joined to the northern and much smaller southern section by narrow isthmuses. The harbour of **Skala** is really a fjord-like channel which almost cuts the island in two. The first thing you notice, coming here after Samos and Chios, is the predominantly Kykladic character of the buildings. This is especially true of the Chora, the upper town, which is a blinding surgical white. Gone are the red tiles and the Levantine muddle of Chios, and in their place we find once more the cubist pattern of light and shade, the square flat-roofed houses, and the patches of green vineyards vivid against a mainly bare landscape.

Skala harbour is not an attractive place today, largely because it has been overrun by the quick 'in-and-out' tourist trade. **Chora**, on the other hand, which is built on a ridge just south of the port, is a small town where it would be pleasant to spend a few days. It replaced as the capital the ancient town which occupied the isthmus at the head of the gulf.

The best known reference in antiquity to Patmos is in the prologue to the *Book of the Revelation*, where the Authorized Version has these words:

'I, John, who am also your brother and companion in tribula-
tion, and in the kingdom and patience of Jesus Christ, was in
the isle that is called Patmos for the word of God and for the
testimony of Jesus Christ. I was in the spirit on the Lord's Day,
and heard behind me a great voice, as of a trumpet, saying "I
am Alpha and Omega, the first and the last", and "What thou
seest, write in a book and send it to the seven churches which
are in Asia . . .".'

Traditionally St John was exiled here by the Emperor Domitian
in AD 95, but there is no certainty that he actually wrote the
Apocalypse here. (The Greek word is often misused today to mean
'cataclysm', but it properly means 'uncovering' or 'revelation'.) The
Acts of St John, written by his disciple Prochorus, describe the
miracles performed by the saint while he was in Patmos, but make
no mention of the Revelation having been written or dictated here.

Half way between Skala and the Chora, to the left and below the
road, is the **Monastery of the Revelation**. This is a complex of
buildings, the heart of which is the Sacred Grotto, sometimes called
the **Cave of St Anne**. In fact the chapel of St Anne is separate, and
the Grotto is cut about twelve feet further down into the rock at the
lowest level of the monastery. A monk is always on duty here, and
he will point out a triple fissure in the rock from which came the
voice of God. A ledge of rock served Prochorus as a desk, and a
silver halo marks the place where St John's head rested in sleep. In
the chapel above there is a delicate ikon representing St Anne, the
mother of Mary.

The site was neglected for centuries, and it was not until 1088 that
the Emperor Alexis Comnenus made a grant of Patmos and the
surrounding islets to St Christodoulos so that he could found a
monastery to commemorate the Evangelist and author of the
Apocalypse. Christodoulos was an outstanding figure in the early
church, once a hermit, who had already founded monasteries in
Caria, on Leros and on Kos. The site which he chose was the most
commanding possible. It dominates the town, the bay and the whole
island, and with the tremendous battlements added later it became a
true fortress of God. Viewed from the outside it is awe-inspiring
rather than beautiful, and it reached its present proportions when
the waters of the Ikarian sea were infested by pirates. One feels that

its thick frowning walls were designed to repel sea-rovers as much as the legions of the Evil One.

The winding climb to the monastery was not so long ago a matter of either foot-slogging or mule-riding, but now a modern road takes cars, taxis and buses almost to the gate. Buses leave every two hours from Skala, but more visitors arrive in coaches laid on for cruise tours. Even so, an early morning visit will often win you a conducted tour in a small party by a relaxed father of the Church.

There is a discreet approach to the entrance courtyard, which is a harmonious blending of some very mixed architecture. Its completion date is displayed as 1698, but the east side incorporates the outer porch of the chief monastery church, or *Katholikon*, which has elements derived from a classical temple of artemis. The *Katholikon* is on a simple Greek cross plan and dates back to the eleventh-century foundation of Christodoulos. His marble sarcophagus is in a side chapel, and on top of it a silver-gilt reliquary displays a skeleton hand for the faithful to kiss.

Of more interest is the **Chapel of the Theotokos** (the Mother of Christ) on the south side of the main church. This was added as early as the twelfth century, and the frescos are said to be contemporary. They include a typical Byzantine group of the Virgin with an archangel on each side wearing imperial robes. We owe the discovery of these frescos to an earthquake in 1956, when a later layer was dislodged and careful treatment revealed the original painting. On the other hand the ancient marble *templo* was replaced in 1607 by the present one elaborately carved in wood.

An inner courtyard leads to the **Refectory**, which is a remarkable room in itself, but at the time of writing was housing the most precious items from both the Library and the Treasury, which are being thoroughly restored. There is a long stone table down the centre, with spaces at intervals under each side for stowing plates and other utensils. There are more twelfth-century frescos on the walls, showing very suitable scenes like the miracle of the loaves and fishes.

You could wish for no better temporary home for some of the greatest treasures from the magnificent monastic library. Here you can see thirty-three pages from the *Codex Porphyrios*, a fifth or sixth-century manuscript of the Gospel of St Mark, of which the

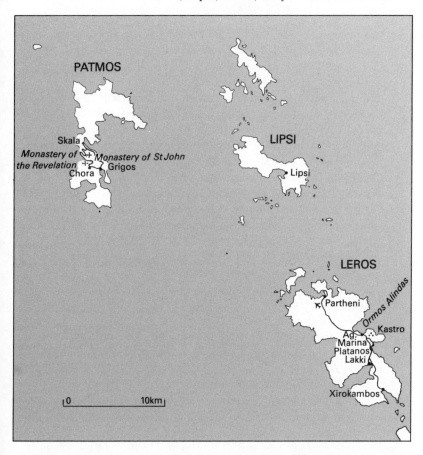

major part is in Leningrad, though the British Museum has a few
more leaves. There is a complete seventh-century illuminated *Book
of Job*; there is a twelfth-century illuminated text of all four Gospels, a miniature gem measuring only eight inches by six. A reminder of ancient library practice is a parchment scroll still on its
wooden spindle. Housed in a gilt frame is the eleventh-century deed
(now unrolled from its spindle) which ceded the monastery site to St
Christodoulos.

The pieces which represent the Treasury are mostly silver-gilt
vessels made in the sixteenth and seventeenth centuries, ornate and

385

valuable; there are some marvellous copes and other ecclesiastical finery worked in gold and silver thread; the ikons displayed are mostly of the same date, with the exception of a twelfth-century figure of St Theodore in military uniform. None of these things approach the manuscripts in interest or beauty.

The ramifications of the monastery are too great to allow the visitor to see much more, but if you are lucky enough to be in a small party and not being hurried through, you should ask to see the **Bakery**, a room concealed within the monastic quarters which is said to date from the original foundation. At one end a ten foot long hollowed-out boat was used as a kneading trough, at the other end is a wood-fired bread oven. Around are the quarters of the seventeen surviving monks, attended by a few women servants. One curious refinement of monastic life is a bar suspended in an upper gallery with one side of iron and the other of wood. This enables the duty monk to sound the regular signals for offices or prayers with a resounding clang or a discreet thump.

All visitors are taken up to the battlements, from which you have a magnificent view of the whole island. You can see how narrow is the peninsula on which the ancient capital was built – an excellent site, with the two anchorages of Merika and Skala on either side to give shelter at all times of year. It was recorded by the French traveller Thévenot in 1664 that the harbour of Patmos was much favoured by corsairs, who used it as a place to lie up and refit their ships. It is still a good anchorage, dangerous only during south-easterly winds, but subject to strong squalls which whip down the surrounding slopes when the northerlies are blowing hard. There are a few other villages and some beaches to the north and south, but the latter are shingly or pebbly, and not inviting. Looking east from the battlements you can see the islets of Lipsi and Arki, to the south-east Leros, and far to the north the trident-shaped head of Mt Kerketeus on Samos shows white against the windwashed Aegean sky.

Lipsi is the smallest of the Dodecanese group which can be said to be separately inhabited. There is a fine sheltered harbour in the middle of the south coast, with a small hotel and a good beach. Another attractive inlet to the south-east has a restaurant and a quiet dreamlike beach for swimming or lying about on. The local wine – if you can find it – is fresh and mildly sparkling.

No regular ferry service calls at Lipsi, and to get there you have to rely on day trips or small boats from Skala or from **Leros**, which is the next major island to the south. Its principal port is **Lakki**, a big natural harbour, one of the biggest in the Mediterranean. Today it is a lifeless place: the long quays are almost empty, and the Italianate buildings behind suggest an importance they no longer have. Also discouraging is more than a hint of imperfect drains. The better part of the town lies behind the farther end of the quay, and from there a road leads up to the Chora, sometimes called **Platanos**, two miles inland.

The Chora is less pretentious than Lakki, but noisier and no cleaner. To find fresher air the quickest way is to climb up to the magnificently sited **Kastro**. There is a roundabout road there, and the long flights of steps can seem interminable in the heat, but the advantage of walking is that each time you stop for breath you have an ever finer view over all quarters of Leros, until at the top you realize that the castle commands every one of the six bays which eat into the coastline, and so every possible line of attack by sea. The Turkish coast is clear to the east, and to the south the backbone of Kos rises behind the blue bulk of Kalymnos.

It began as a Byzantine stronghold, but when the Knights of St John established themselves at Rhodes in the fourteenth century they needed strong defensible positions and look-out posts for their operations against the enemies of the Cross. The castle on Leros was the most distant choice, but it was one of the strongest. The lower sections of wall are early and rough, with an occasional marble block inserted, but once inside the main gate you are in the world of the Knights.

A low vaulted passage leads to a series of battlemented enclosures built out to the limits of the space available; immediately to the left of the passage is the most typical feature of their architecture, the chapel built under the main fortifications. This is a fine chamber, high and wide, and it is good to find it is being restored. The smaller and older Byzantine church can be traced alongside, and a well-head did double duty as a font.

There are several potentially agreeable holiday centres on Leros, not so far over-developed. From Platanos you can walk comfortably down to the well-established resort of **Agia Marina**, a pleasant little waterfront with a fishing harbour and a few tavernas. The road beyond leads to the bay of **Alinda** on the same east-facing coast, and passes the British war cemetery – still carefully maintained after the disastrous 1943 campaign which gave rise to it.

Leros, probably because of its many harbours, was the island picked as the first objective when the High Command attempted to take over the islands of the eastern Aegean after the surrender of Italy. Leros and its neighbours Kalymnos and Kos were occupied by British troops brought there and supported by the Royal Navy, but the usual lack of air cover meant they were defenceless in the face of a strong German counter-attack. Faced with heavy casualties and an ultimatum that the Germans would obliterate the town of Rhodes from the air, the British commander surrendered. Afterwards special units of the allied forces – including many Greek supporters from the islands – carried out a very successful campaign of harassment against German communications. These narrow waters saw many hair-raising exploits by camouflaged *kaïkis* with naval officers or Greek skippers in command.

The road continues beyond Alinda to the far northern bay of **Partheni**, a quiet land-locked anchorage – quiet, that is, except when the big new airfield is in operation close by. It will be a pity if this makes ordinary access difficult, for the countryside here is pleasantly rural and there is one small but evocative site. The name Partheni was given to the bay in honour of Artemis, maiden goddess or *parthenos*, who had a sanctuary close to the bay. This was no fifth-century Parthenon, like Athena's in Athens, but a little shrine on a hillock where the priestesses kept the sacred quails which were strangely associated in mythology with Artemis. You can find the hillock still, on the far side of the airfield, but the only sign that it was a holy place is the little church of *Agios Michailis* – a pretty interior with wall-paintings, and marble slabs dividing the nave from the sanctuary. No quails are visible.

Lying close to the south-east of Leros, with a mile-wide channel dividing the islands, is **Kalymnos**, mountainous and imposing. Its shape on the map is that of a bunched fist with a long finger pointing northwards; viewed from the sea it has an individual grandeur and beauty unmatched in the Dodecanese. The mountain slopes seem almost sculptured in a violet-toned rock. Ovid in the *Ars Amatoria* described it as 'shaded with woods and fruitful in honey'. The woods have all gone, sacrificed to centuries of ship-building or eliminated by forest fires, but the bees and their honey are still important here after two thousand years. Though the mountains are bare and bald, the hidden valleys are flowery, and the beekeepers of Kos send hives over to enjoy them at certain times of year. They say the bees of Kalymnos resent this, and warfare results between the colonies. They add that the war sometimes extends to the rival beekeepers themselves.

The principal port and capital is at **Pothia**, facing towards Kos at the head of a wide bay in the south. The harbour is sheltered and crowded with fishing boats and *kaïkis*, the waterfront welcoming as well as busy. The town is comparatively modern, but one of the largest outside Rhodes and Crete – almost comparable with Ermoupolis in Syros. It spreads out round the head of the bay, on both sides of the valley which ascends to the old capital or **Chorio**, and across to the tourist developments of the west coast.

Two castles, both ruined, command this valley. The first is to the left of the road, crowning a small hill with three distinctive windmill towers on its slopes. This was adapted by the Knights as their principal stronghold on the island, and they managed to incorporate within the exceptionally thick walls a tiny thirteenth-century church. The second castle is higher up the valley overlooking Chorio; there is more left of it because it was used as a refuge from pirates until late in the Middle Ages, but it has no great interest. Nor has the village below, but a little further up the road there are some surprises.

In the village of **Damos** you can see a group of Hellenistic graves sunk about ten feet down near a tree on a corner of the road; one is recorded as belonging to a local *archon* (or 'mayor') of the third century BC. If you turn past the graves to your right, and scramble for five or ten minutes up a rough hillside and stream-bed, you come to a much bigger 'monolithic' tomb – that is to say it is carved out of a solid piece of rock. It is a very large vault with a single opening;

they say it is Hellenistic too, but it is likely to be very much older and made for more than a mere *archon*.

On the left of the road as you approach Damos is the ruined Byzantine church dedicated to *Christos of Jerusalem*. It owes this dedication to the Emperor Arcadius, who stopped here on his return from the Holy Land. Only the apse survives to roof height, but it contains the usual concentric steps and had three small window openings to the east. It was built on the site of a Hellenistic temple to Apollo, using a lot of marble material derived from it. Part of one of the columns supporting the arch is a marble slab taken from the architrave of the temple. It has an inscription which you read sideways now, including the beautifully carved name of the god. Another block of marble has a closely carved insciption recording the terms of an alliance made between Athens and Kalymnos during the Peloponnesian War – unlike her neighbours, Kalymnos was always on the Athenian side. A third slab must be of the fourth century or later, as it contains the names of Plato and Aristotle.

Whereas the church was aligned east and west, with its west end now a back garden full of chickens, the temple ran north to south, and more of its foundations have survived. Yet a little further on, past some overgrown enclosures, is the church of *Agia Anastasia*, smaller but on the very early Byzantine plan of the fifth or sixth century. It too has marble columns as well as some Byzantine mosaics featuring the Cross and the Christian symbol of the fishes. Traces of other pavements can be seen nearby, though much overgrown, and there is a possible theatre site – though this needs the eye of faith.

Even with so little evidence to go on, this must have been an important site – a conclusion arrived at by the English archaeologist Sir Charles Newton, who came here to dig in 1852 and took some of his finds back to the British Museum. A large number of *pithoi* (clay storage jars) were also found, which suggests at least a Mycenaean settlement. Probably unconnected, but none the less fascinating, is the village of **Argos**, down a track no more than a mile to the south of Chorio. Who will argue with the tradition that it was first settled by Argive troops returning from Troy who found in Kalymnos a nearer and more welcoming home than stony faraway Mycenae? None of these places are easy to find, but some of the taxi drivers in Pothia are very knowledgeable and all would be helpful.

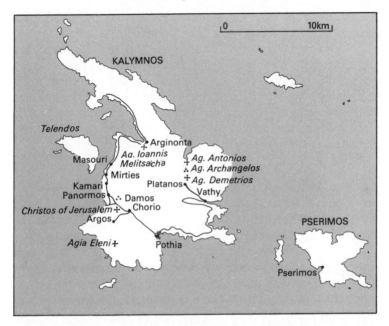

The Kalymniots are in fact a proud and cheerful people, proud of their lovely and historic island and anxious to preserve its ancient sites and customs from the encroaching tourist industry. The island's *Lykeion*, or High School, took first prize in 1984 in a national competition for native costume dancing – a recently revived art – and the costumes were all made on the island.

The reader or the visitor will always associate Kalymnos with sponge-fishing, and in spite of reports it is good to find that the industry is still flourishing in a number of islands. In Pothia you can see a warehouse and factory which handles thousands of sponges at all stages. The sponge fleets no longer go off to north Africa every year – Colonel Quadafi has declared them unwelcome – but they have obviously found new sources accessible on the sea bed, and modern diving techniques make the process quicker and safer.

The history of sponge fishing is as old as the history of civilization in this sea. In the *Odyssey* we find the servants of Odysseus using sponges to wash down the tables in the dining hall on Ithaka, while in the *Iliad* there is a reference to Hephaistos cleaning himself from the dirt of his smithy with a sponge. Sponges were used as padding

391

inside classical armour. This 'very fine, very dense and very strong' sponge, as Aristotle describes it, was known as the *Achilleon*, and was almost certainly the shallow cup-like sponge nowadays called 'elephant's ear'. The 'honeycomb' and the 'cup' are the two main types which still find a market, the honeycomb being the familiar bath sponge, while the cup has a harsher surface and is used in industry. During the Middle Ages the Venetians gained a monopoly of the sponge trade, so that a sponge became known as a 'Venetia'. The honeycomb sponge is still called a 'Venise' in France.

If you have found a friendly taxi-driver it is worth continuing along the road which leads down to the west coast resorts of **Panormos**, **Kamari**, **Mirties** and **Masouri**. In fact, the main road skirts the cliff edge above these not unattractive developments (there are so far no monstrous hotels, and the grey sand beaches are not over-run). From the road you have a fine view of the distinctive island of **Telendos**, a huge high hump once joined to Kalymnos. The great earthquake of AD 554 broke up the intervening neck of land and let in the sea. There are said to be sunken houses half way across, but we have found no one to confirm this. Clearly visible, though, on a lower neck of land protruding to the south of Telendos, is a group of Roman or Byzantine tomb chambers which show up well on the skyline.

The road continues at a high level round the promontory which juts into the bay of **Arginonta**. To your left is a wholly ruinous Byzantine castle which looks like an eagle's eyrie commanding the sea lanes to the north; to your right the church of *Agios Ioannis Melitsacha*, another remarkable early Byzantine building with finely carved Christian symbols in marble, neglected mosaic floors, and re-used pillars from a Greek temple – all features one associates with the period.

There is another expedition to make in Kalymnos which leaves an even more vivid memory. If you come in your own boat, be sure to put in to the narrow inlet of **Vathy** on the east coast. If you have landed in Pothia, be sure you take a taxi (the bus is not to be relied on) by the coast road to Vathy. Perhaps this is the better approach, for the view from the last bend of the road as it turns inland is astonishingly beautiful.

Below to your right is the tiny bay entered between high walls of

rock; ahead and still below is the lovely green valley which continues almost out of sight into the bare hills of its origin. The
greenness is the foliage of every kind of fruit tree – orange, lemon,
almond, plum, peach – which fill the floor of the valley for a good
three miles. The road winds down to the harbour, **Rhina**, a simple
quay with fishing boats and a nice little restaurant set back from the
waterfront. On the far side is a sensible pulling-out place and
workshop for boats, and in the rocks above that a space about eight
feet high has been hewn out – a 'rock throne', they say, for a king to
review his ships, and why not?

A pleasant walk of about a mile and a half brings you to the village
of **Platanos**, based on a rectangular *plateia* with a huge old plane tree
and made up of neat houses with pretty gardens. Two hundred yards
beyond the village a narrow path to the right leads to three churches
on a higher level – *Agios Antonios*, *Archangelos*, and *Agios Demet-
rius*. All three are interesting, but *Archangelos* is unique for its
setting alone.

From *Agios Antonios* a narrow, level path leads on past orchards,
till you have a sudden startling view of a line of walls – ten feet high
in places – of massive masonry. Built into this is the apse of the
church, which now proves to be surrounded by the walls of what
looks like a palace, complete with doorways with huge lintels and
big square window openings. In the middle is an area carpeted in the
spring with blue irises, while the outer walls continue to the west,
making a very large enclosure. Similar masonry can be seen in the
fields beyond, extending into the hillside and suggesting the dimensions of a considerable city. How old this is remains for archaeologists to decide, but there are features which suggest a very early, even
a Mycenaean, origin.

There has been no attempt at excavation, though a pit at the west
end of the church shows there has been a visit from treasure-
hunters. There is not much to see in the church, though there have
been extensive frescos at the east end, and it looks like early
Byzantine – with the ruins of an earlier one alongside. The tiny
church of *Agios Demetrios* stands a little higher and further on, a
square chamber with a blue roof and a narrow doorway leading to
the sanctuary. Although in a way it is an anticlimax it has the best
view of the three churches – across to the soaring hills opposite and

all the way down the valley with a glimpse of Rhina harbour in the far distance.

The main site can be reached or left by an ancient stepped path cut through the rocks from the road below – probably the original approach to the palace. Once down on the road again you can look back and see how the city took advantage of the long escarpment to the north of the valley. It is certainly one of the most exciting places in the islands for the visitor to find for himself. In the village there is a wonderfully muddled general store which sells locally woven goods and the local Kalymniot honey – stored in a big cylindrical container and drawn off by a tap at the bottom to order. The proprietor is an educated man and will be delighted to direct you to the three churches and their surroundings.

Some of the woven products he sells are the work of a community of nuns at the remote convent of **Agia Eleni**, close to the sea on the deserted south-west coast. They also do much finer work, including the traditional 'Kalimniko' dress known as *Karavadi* which is used in the dancing competitions.

Neatly dividing the eastern end of the Kos–Kalymnos channel, and close to the Turkish coast, is the pleasant low-lying island of **Pserimos**. The only buildings are around the little harbour, and there are no roads. There is more vegetation, though, than appears from out at sea, and walking inland along a goat track is better than taking a bus on a bumpy road. Already an agency offers holidays at the one 'pension', which is almost in the sea, and there are day trips from Kos to enjoy the swimming. If the beach near where you land is occupied, half an hour's walk brings you to another which you will probably have to yourself. If you are staying, there are few better places to swim, walk, eat, drink and sleep, but there are very few rooms and only two showers between them.

Access

There is a daily ferry service from Piraeus to PATMOS, LEROS and KALYMNOS, in that order, and in the reverse order from Rhodes. Hydrofoils run from Rhodes to Patmos three days a week. A slow ship from Rhodes reaches LIPSI once a week, but it is easier to get there from Leros or Patmos. There are day excursions from Kos to PSERIMOS. Access by air is to Leros only, but the new airport will take flights from Rhodes as well as Athens.

Communications

The three larger islands have taxis and local buses, but the bus services in LEROS and KALYMNOS are unreliable.

Accommodation

PATMOS In Skala the quietest hotel is KASTELI (B), a small pension. The new SKALA (B) is pretentious, and the two hotels on the harbour front are very noisy at night. In Grigos XENIA (B) is better, and there are others around the coast.

LEROS On the quay at Lakki, LEROS PALACE (C) is a soulless place. At the back of the town XENON ANGELOU (B) is secluded but very small; PANTELI (C) is on the main road, but ARTEMIS (C), though also very small, is plain and quiet. There are holiday hotels at Agia Marina and Alinda.

KALYMNOS In Pothia OLYMPIC (C) is in the best position and efficiently run. THERMAE (C) is above a busy restaurant. There are several good hotels in the west coast resorts.

There is one small hotel in Lipsi, and a taverna with rooms in Pserimos.

Restaurants

PATMOS One can make no recommendation in Skala. In the Chora *plateia* there is one tiny bar-restaurant which serves good local food.

LEROS Lakki and Platanos are both unpromising. There are better places to eat near the quay at Agia Marina.

KALYMNOS You can eat well at a number of restaurants around the harbour of Pothia. The little bar-restaurant on the quay at Rhina (Vathy) is fun and good value.

You will have to take pot luck in Lipsi and Pserimos, but there is likely to be good fish.

Facilities

Banks: On Patmos there are the usual branches in Skala, but none in the

Chora. On Leros you will find them in Lakki, Platanos and Agia Marina. On Kalymnos they are in Pothia only.

Yachts: Skala harbour on Patmos is crowded, but shore facilities are good. There is plenty of space at Lakki on Leros, but shore attention is grudging. There are good if crowded berths and facilities at Pothia on Kalymnos, and a quiet anchorage, berths and pulling-out yard at Rhina (Vathy). Of the two smaller islands Lipsi has the more sheltered and peaceful harbour, but Pserimos is very pleasant too.

TWENTY-THREE

Kos and Astypalaia

The largest and most celebrated of the original twelve 'privileged' islands is **Kos**. Only in this century have Rhodes and her smaller neighbours been reckoned among the Dodecanese; in the Middle Ages there was no question but that the power of the Rhodian Knights extended at least as far north as Leros, and Kos was the most important of their outposts.

There are many similarities of character and of history between Kos and Rhodes. Both have their capitals and principal harbours at their most northerly point, close to the rugged Turkish coast, and in either case the principal town was founded late in the Classical period and enjoyed its greatest prosperity during the succeeding Hellenistic age. The same popular name, *Mandraki* (meaning a sheepfold), was given to their harbours, and the entrance to both of them was guarded by a fifteenth-century castle built by the Knights of St John. Like Rhodes, Kos today has a busy airport, but as with Rhodes the approach from the sea is far more memorable. Few harbours are more welcoming than Mandraki on Kos when you have been beating up the coast in a gale of wind and can put the solid walls of the castle between you and the elements.

The castle occupies the whole width of the spit of land to the south of the harbour entrance. It was purely a fortress, built by the Knights between 1450 and 1514, when the outer *enceinte* was completed in the face of constant Turkish threats. The long eastern wall needed no protection but the sea, and to the west the fortifications drop straight into the harbour. Only on the south side was a moat needed, and the entrance today is by a drawbridge over it and a gateway in the curtain wall. The angle towers and battlements are impressive as fortifications, but there is little to see within the walls except a litter of marble fragments and monuments lifted from other sites in the town. The inhabited city of the Knights, later known as the Chora, partly overlaid the classical city to the south of the castle.

The usual toll taken by the Knights when they built one of their fortresses was to pillage the classical sites they found nearby. At Kos, however, the damage had been done a thousand years earlier when in AD 554 an earthquake buried the city completely. The 'whirligig of time' brought its compensation in 1933 when another severe earthquake demolished the mediaeval town and gave the enterprising Italian archaeologists the chance to excavate, and to a certain extent recreate, the city known to Alexander and the Ptolemies, to Theocritus the poet and Apelles the sculptor – though perhaps not to Hippocrates the doctor.

It should be said at once that the modern town of Kos is a more relaxed and gracious place than its equivalent in Rhodes. One reason is that open spaces have been kept open, not only around the harbour, but in the shape of tree-lined avenues and parks, and most effectively in the excavated areas of the ancient city. Like Rhodes it was a comparatively late foundation, built in 366 BC to replace an earlier capital, and like Rhodes it was carefully laid out. The first-century historian Diodorus of Sicily described the arrival of the inhabitants at their new home:

> 'The people of Kos at that time settled themselves in the town they now enjoy, adorning it with the gardens it now has. It became very populous and a very costly wall was constructed right round it, and a harbour built. From this time onwards it grew apace, both in public revenues and private fortunes, and in general it rivalled the most celebrated cities of the world.'

The nucleus of the new city was the *agora* with the adjoining harbour quarter, the first site to be excavated in the 1930s. It can be freely visited, and has remains of a fourth-century *stoa* with re-erected columns and the foundations of a temple of Aphrodite. Between here and the castle is the enormous but rather self-consciously enclosed trunk of a tree of very great age. This is the '**Plane Tree of Hippocrates**', to which direction signs point from the harbour area. Sceptics say that the tree cannot be more than five hundred years old, and that in any case Hippocrates would have

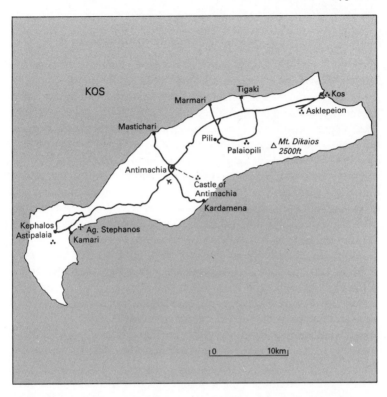

been nearly a hundred by the time the new city was built. However he is said to have lived to be at least a hundred and four, and this tree is only a few miles from where he is known to have taught in the sanctuary of Asklepios – and the origin of that goes back to the Trojan War. Let us say that under just such a plane tree. . . .

A smaller area with a Roman bath system was excavated further round to the west, beyond the *Plateia Elevtherias.* This fine square is bounded on the south by an arcaded market, on the north by the pompous Italian-built Museum, and on the east by the Deftedar Mosque, but there is enough space for such different features not to clash. From here the long straight *Odos Vasileos Pavlou* runs out to meet the *Odos Grigoriou V*, which marks the southern boundary of the town.

This is a valuable thoroughfare to know, because it not only provides an easy exit route to the rest of the island but also passes some important and useful places. First on your left you come to what has become known as the **Casa Romana**, or simply the 'Roman House'. This was a private villa of the third century AD, of which the three inner courtyards, or *atria*, were restored and given their present appearance by the Italian archaeologist who discovered it in 1933. Very sensibly the house has been walled in all round, but not so sensibly the fine mosaic floors have been left open to the weather. The best of them, a delightful scene of sea life in various forms – dolphins, fishes and a Nereid riding on a seahorse – has deteriorated badly in the last ten years. All the same the restoration, which in the largest atrium goes up to the second storey, gives a very clear idea of prosperous domestic life, including conveniently placed kitchen and laundry areas.

Almost at once on the other side of the road you see the beginning of a big L-shaped area of excavation. You enter it (free) down a short flight of steps and you will be struck at once by the amount which has been revealed and by the neglect which the authorities have again allowed of such an important site. There are both Hellenistic and Roman elements, and central to this longer arm of the L is a long paved street, the *Decumanus maximus* of the Roman town. To the right of it are the foundations of several houses with fragments of tesselated floors, almost the last of which – set well back from the street – is the extensive **House of Europa**, so called because of a lively third-century AD mosaic of a naked Europa entangled with a frisky and lecherous bull – Zeus in disguise, as usual. Not great art, but technically admirable – obviously one of the more expensive items in the pavement supplier's catalogue.

At the end of its run the *Decumanus* meets at right angles the *Cardo*, the town-planner's 'axial' street, which is fully paved in marble and follows the short side of the L. Overlooking both streets is a low hill crowned by a minaret, which surprisingly was the acropolis of the ancient city. Most of Kos is low-lying, and the town rises very little above sea level.

There is a lot to see on each side of the *Cardo*, but again the unrestricted feet of sightseers have been allowed to wear away far too much, and the serious visitor is given little help to identify the buildings. The larger area is to the left, or west side of the street, incorporating a very big Roman bath system. The *frigidarium* of this was converted in early Byzantine times to a Christian basilica, of which the cross-shaped baptismal trough survives and the marble entry door has been re-erected. Behind all this the long colonnade of a second-century BC gymnasium displays a row of seventeen Doric columns, put together from the original eighty.

The most unusual building is further on to the right of the street, and at first sight it looks like an elegant shrine – slender Ionic columns support arcading on three sides of a shady courtyard, the fourth side taken up with three large stone basins. A *Nymphaeum* was the earliest guess by those who uncovered it, but the truth dawned later that it was a splendid combination of *lavabo* and latrine – the public *forica* of the baths – with drainage channels all round the base of the walls. This is better preserved behind high protective walls, but its immediate surroundings have been allowed to get very messy. Finally at the end of the street on the left is another fine pavement of gladiatorial scenes which for once has been given a proper roof to protect it.

There is one more thing not to miss in these parts, the small theatre or **Odeion**, reached through a short avenue of cypresses on the further side of *Grigoriou V*. Like all these intimate little theatres, it makes a charming picture, with seven of its original marble rows of seating, and the remaining seven decently restored.

An important place in this southern quarter of Kos town is the bus centre, to the right of the end of *Vasileos Pavlou* street. The bus services are excellent and reliable, though it is a little difficult to spot the destinations of the buses scattered rather casually round an irregular square, and the office which controls them is not always occupied. Apart from the buses this is a useful guiding mark to reach what is probably the best restaurant in Kos, half way between here and the end of *Vasileos Pavlou*, always full of Greek families and friends.

The continuation of *Grigoriou V* brings you to the main exit route from the town to the south-west. After a mile it forks, and the left-hand fork leads into an avenue of dark green cypresses which ends at the most famous place in the history of Kos, the **Asklepieion**. One would not want to quarrel with the tradition that Podalirios,

401

son of the divine Asklepios, was wrecked on the coast of Kos when returning from Troy and established here the worship and practices of his father.

The three wide terraces we see today were built not earlier than the fourth century BC, and most of the monuments are of the Hellenistic or Roman period. This was a place which had not only a great religious and social part to play, but was actually a centre for medical teaching, research and practice. Again there is no need to argue with the tradition that the school was founded by Hippocrates, the island's most famous son.

The lowest terrace, reached by way of a familiar complex of Roman baths, had pillared porticos on three sides. It was the centre of the medical school, with a museum of anatomy and pathology, and into here flowed the mineral springs which were essential to the treatment centre. The middle terrace is the oldest, with an altar to Apollo the healer (not his son Asklepios) as the centrepiece at the head of a ceremonial flight of steps; there is a graceful Ionic temple of the fourth century BC to the right and a clumsy Roman Corinthian one to the left. The third and highest terrace was concerned more clearly with ceremony, and an even grander marble stairway leads to the massive second-century BC temple of Asklepios, where even today the ceremony of taking the Hippocratic oath* survives.

Today all this gives you a fascinating glimpse of a period of high civilization, before the crudities of the early Roman empire began to spoil things. Not the least pleasure here is to overlook so much of this green and fertile island. The view to seaward and across to Turkey is magnificent, but all around is a landscape which justifies the claim of the French traveller Tocqueville: 'Viewing its lovely scented gardens you would say that it is a terrestrial paradise.' One only hopes that the authorities will not be so preoccupied with the tourist industry that they allow development to spread unrestricted. To be fair they have not yet done that. Here is Theocritus on a country walk in Kos :

> 'Many poplars and elm-trees were waving over our heads, and not far off the running of sacred water from the cave of the nymphs warbled to us; in the shimmering branches the sun-

* See pp. 410–11.

burnt grasshoppers were busy with their talk, and from afar the
little owl cried softly, out of the tangled thorns of the blackberry;
the larks were singing and the hedgebirds, and the turtledove
moaned, murmuring softly; the scent of late summer and of the
fall of the year was everywhere; the pears fell from the trees at
our feet, and apples in number rolled down at our sides, and the
young plum trees were bent to the earth with the weight of their
fruit.'*

Idealized, no doubt, and I question whether little owls lurk in
blackberry bushes, but it does remind one of Andrew Marvell, who
'stumbled on melons' as he passed.

It is time now to take account of the many visitors who arrive by
air. The airfield is two-thirds of the way down the island near the
small town of Antimachia, and it is quite likely that arrivals here will
be whisked straight away by coaches to seaside resorts like Kardamena or Mastichari, very close to the airport on opposite coasts,
or even further up the northern coast to Marmari or Tingaki. Not
long ago all these were quiet fishing villages, but in the past few
years they have been taken over by tourist hotels and all that goes
with them. They do have good beaches nearby, and these, with the
lovely climate and country which surround them, probably explain
the popularity of the island as a holiday place today. Its interest and
most of its beauty lie elsewhere.

There is only one really main road in Kos, which runs down the
centre of the island almost to its southern tip and is so well served by
buses that taxi rides are hardly necessary. The main geographical
feature of Kos is the mountain ridge of Dikaios, with a rocky spine
rising to about 2500 feet. A few villages are lodged on its northern
slopes, and near one of them is the most surprising place in the
whole island.

If you take the bus to Pili and ask to be put down as near as
possible to **Palaiopili**, you will have an easy walk up a metalled
stretch of road and then a delightful climb up a steep rocky path
which brings you out on to a green and flowery shelf underneath a
fantastic rocky pinnacle. You look up and see that the pinnacle is
crowned by an even more fantastic ruined castle – apparently
unreachable except by the ravens which wheel around the crags.

---

* *Idyll* vii, 135–146, trans. Walter Pater.

You look at the gentle slopes around you and you see the remains of a village or small town surrounded by grass, flowers, orange trees and bird song. Everywhere there are crumbling walls, and you keep coming upon deserted churches, mostly with frescos still discernible. There is no sign of human life, only lovely mountain scenery and a view right down to the northern sea and across to Kalymnos.

Of the many churches one alone shows signs of present use – perhaps only a feast-day visit at that – and it is worth a long look. The western entrance has pillars which support a triple arch, and it leads into a handsome basilica with six columns on each side supporting a high vault on semicircular arches. The apse has a concentric flight of steps which must have ended in a *kathedra*, and there is a wall painting of Christ *Pantokrator* above. The exterior walls are well preserved, and on the south side they contain layers of bonding tiles in the Roman manner. These details suggest strongly that the church could have been built as early as the sixth or seventh centuries – which suggests an equally early origin for the deserted village which surrounds it. The smallest of the churches is a minute building composed of two domed chambers with shallow cupolas perforated to let in the only light. Empty, but not ruinous, it is almost sunk into the hillside above, and the signs are of something even earlier than the basilica. One can wander happily round here for an hour or more and still find things to marvel at.

The main road keeps clear of Mount Dikaios and carries on to the largish village of **Antimachia**. Half a mile before that, a byroad to the left leads to a well preserved castle built by the Knights. It stands on no great height, but it has an unusual triangular plan and is big enough to contain houses, water cisterns, and the church of *Agia Paraskevi*. You can see it from the main road, but it you are staying at Kardamena you will find it an easy walk of a mile or so.

Beyond Antimachia the sea has squeezed the neck of Kos to a width of little more than a mile, after which the ground rises steeply and the road winds with it to **Kephalos**. This is another sizeable village, on or near the site of the earliest capital, **Astipalaia** (this name, which you meet elsewhere in the Aegean, means simply 'ancient city'). It was only after it had been sacked by the Spartans at the end of the Peloponnesian War and later devastated by an earthquake that its inhabitants decided to abandon it. Some of them are said to have sailed west to the island which is called Astypalaia, while others moved north and eventually founded the new city of Kos. There is not a great deal to see in Kephalos itself, but to reach it the bus first takes a loop down by the coast to the fishing harbour of **Kamari**. This gives you an opportunity to leave the bus at a place called **Agios Stephanos**, where on a low headland opposite an off-shore rock there are the remains of two very early Byzantine churches, complete with mosaic floors and some re-erected columns. It was probably also the site of a classical temple, but the freshness and beauty of it would suit any religion. It even manages to preserve its peace in the face of a monstrous holiday agglomeration which occupies several hundred yards of the adjoining coastline and provides every imaginable kind of diversion for holiday-makers – including amplified announcements which assault the ear in three languages (none of them Greek).

Yet Kos can still be enjoyed by visitors with very different tastes. The Knights' castle is the best mediaeval building in this part of the Aegean outside Rhodes, the city revealed by classical excavations has an interest surpassed only in Thasos, Dikaios is a noble mountain with some delightful villages on its slopes, the countryside is pleasant and fertile, and the holiday attractions are as good as you will find in any large island. If your taste is for melons, then Kos has the best in the Aegean.

Like Karpathos, **Astypalaia** may be a long way from her sisters in the Dodecanese, but there is no doubt she belongs in their company. Admittedly the island was never an outpost of the Knights of St John, and briefly during the thirteenth century it owed allegiance to the Duchy of Naxos, but under its Italian name Stampalia it was held by the Quirini family for Venice from 1310 until its capture by Barbarossa in 1536. It was finally consolidated with the other Dodecanese in 1912, when the Italians made it their first objective in the war with Turkey and used it as a base for the recapture of Rhodes. In 1948 it passed to Greece and resumed its ancient name – of which there are many variants in both spelling and pronunciation.

There is also the historical connection with the city of the same name on Kos, but the real evidence is visual as you come into **Skala** harbour on the deeply indented east coast. What you see ahead of

405

you is the huge ruined castle of the Quirini standing high above the untidy muddle of small buildings and church domes which make up the Chora – the only settlement of any size in the island.

Down below, the old fishing harbour has been extended by a long concrete quay to receive the big modern car ferries which connect it with the rest of the Dodecanese and with Amorgos, its nearest neighbour in the Kyklades – at present a spasmodic and unreliable service. The inner semicircle of the decaying waterfront speaks of Italy still rather than Greece. A long balustraded terrace, with a row of arcaded buildings behind, looks attractive from a distance, but paint has flaked from the ironwork and the stucco looks Venetian in its decay.

The houses of the **Chora** straggle down to merge with the harbour buildings. The road leading upwards is steep, and it skirts a ridge with the remains of eight stumpy windmills before reaching the Chora proper. Here things are cleaner, though you miss the Kykladic purity and the friendly white outlining of paved streets. Instead these upper alleyways wander rather dispiritedly in a decreasing circle round and under the daunting walls of the fortress. Every now and then you come across a nest of two or three whitewashed churches, but otherwise it is a desolate place.

In contrast with the general dinginess is the well kept precinct and rich interior of the monastery church of the *Panagia Portaitissa*, which occupies the most easterly outcrop of rock. Its layout is basically of the eighteenth century, with a gallery at the west end, but the mural decorations are modern and crude – why has Greek religious art stayed fixedly banal since the nineteenth century?

No grand stairway leads up into the citadel, only an obscure flight of uneven steps which break into the south-western curtain and end before a genuinely imposing entrance gateway. From there the usual low vaulted passage of Latin military architecture should lead to the kind of inner fortifications we find in the castles of Rhodes, Kos or Leros. Instead you emerge on to a deserted plateau with wild flowers and weeds growing between piles of rubble. The walls which looked so immense from below rise only at a few points to more than head height, though on the northern escarpment the shells of a tower and some spacious domestic apartments have window spaces up to a second storey.

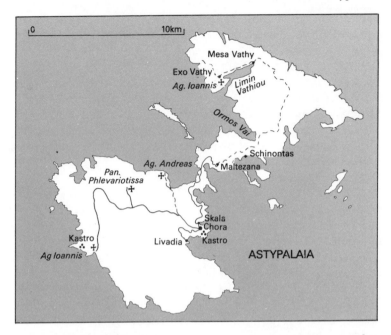

It is here that you can see the only remaining evidence that this now hollow grandeur was for two centuries the almost impregnable stronghold and valued family property of the most distinguished of the Venetian clans to penetrate the Aegean in the wake of the Fourth Crusade.

In 1207 John Quirini took possession of Astypalaia under the suzerainty of Marco Sanudo, newly established Duke of Naxos and the Greek Archipelago, and began to build a castle on the old acropolis. At the same time similar fortresses were shooting up on a dozen other Aegean islands. What was the fascination of these remote and rugged kingdoms for sophisticated urban Italians, one wonders. Later on, in the other islands of the Dodecanese, we can more easily understand why the Knights of the Cross needed military and commercial bases for their continuous conflict with the followers of Mohammed, but what brought the Quirini of Venice here? Standing inside their castle walls and looking over the barren hillsides of their modest island, and all that empty sea with no other

407

land in sight, one's guess would be that they wanted simply to get away from it all – and especially from the swamps and mists and unhealthy summer heat of the Veneto.

Whatever their motives the Quirini were proud of their island. They gave it the Italianized name of Stampalia, and adopted it as part of their family title. Today in Venice the *palazzo* Quirini-Stampalia houses a fine collection of Venetian art and furnishings. The Quirini arms – three fleur-de-lys quartered with nine 'counters' – appear only on a slab of marble fixed disrespectfully sideways to support the lintel of a window in a ruined wall.

At opposite ends of the *enceinte* are two churches, the *Panagia Kastelli* and *Agios Georgios*, both of seventeenth or eighteenth-century origin, later modernized but showing little sign of present use. The Panagia has an unusual bell tower, with a stairway leading to a railed terrace, and from here you look down, as the Quirini would have done, on the only fertile ground they could easily command. A green valley slopes down to **Livadia**, the bay which opens on the south side of the Chora peninsula. Here at least water flowed and there were crops to harvest, while in all other directions there is only low scrub and bare rock to be seen. Today the shoreline of Livadia (no longer a harbour) is fringed with a double row of tamarisks, and two restaurants offer refreshment at all hours during the summer. The beach, though, is messy, and for a clean swim there are beaches or rocks further down the coast, most easily reached by boat from Skala.

Looking north over the castle walls you see what a strange shape the island has – almost two separate islands joined by a narrow, deeply indented isthmus, so that arms of the sea appear everywhere between the grey-brown hills. A regular if infrequent bus service runs from the Chora *plateia* along the central isthmus as far as the village of **Maltezana**, which has a nice little fishing harbour and a few quiet if pebbly beaches. The road beyond, whatever the official map pretends, is so far rough and only practicable for about a mile further.

A short walk from Maltezana brings you to the coast between there and the next village of Schinontas. Beside a beach not far from a strange pillared monument you come suddenly upon a large tesselated pavement, surprisingly well preserved, which was undoubtedly the floor of a large Christian basilica of the early

Byzantine period – a site whose position and plan recall Agios Stephanos on Kos. One marble column base in the sea beyond is all that otherwise remains unplundered.

The same official map shows an airport just to the north of Maltezana, and though this is so far only a joke for the inhabitants it will surely come before long – perhaps to spoil the charm of the island's isolation; for it has a charm and an interest in spite of the seedy and dilapidated air one first encounters at Skala. To find it you need the help of one of the island's taxis and a friendly driver. Westward from the Chora an un-made-up road leads through dry and featureless country to a little oasis in the hills, the monastery of the *Panagia Phlevariotissa* – the elaborate-sounding epithet means simply that the Virgin's principal celebration here comes in February. Greek scholars might be forgiven for suspecting a case of swollen veins. As usual its position and unsophisticated outside have more charm than the inside, and the six monastic cells now have only one occupant. Almost collapsed into a ravine to the west of the church are the still distinguishable remains of the east end of a much earlier one.

The road continues past the few houses of Mesaria to the tiny monastic church of *Agios Ioannis*. It lies at the foot of a great crag on which are a few remnants of another castle – but it would be a fearsome climb to reach them. Almost as fearsome is the drop of nearly a thousand feet down a well watered valley to the sea. The path is rough and hard to find, but the empty little beach at its foot offers a welcome swim. The most remarkable feature of the valley is a sequence of cascades which carry a considerable force of water even in summer, but to follow it down, let alone up, is really for the young and agile.

Another more distant expedition is to the delightful landlocked anchorage of **Exo Vathy** away in the northernmost parts and at the end of a so far imaginary road. In the summer season a *kaïki* will take you there from a landing stage below the church of *Agios Andreas*, about five miles north of the Chora. When there is less custom in the spring or autumn a taxi will leave you at the head of the inlet of *Ormos Vai* beyond Maltezana, when in response to an earlier telephone call a fisherman's boat will chug down to pick you up for a thirty-minute run to his home village.

Either way it is a visit not to miss. You enter the *Limin Vathiou*, an almost enclosed sea loch, by the narrowest of entrances from seaward, and only when well inside do you see tucked away to your left a welcoming line of small houses and the white dome of another monastery church in a patch of green beyond. Between church and bay there are green trees surrounded by cornfields. The boat will land you right outside a well equipped restaurant, and opposite it a little concrete platform has been rigged up on the rocks for diving and swimming in these warm sheltered waters.

The church (another *Agios Ioannis*) is empty of monks, but the low ground at the head of the inlet will delight ornithologists. I have seen there within half an hour a purple heron, a white cattle egret, a nesting pair of golden orioles, and a glimpse of another pair with such a flash of blue that they must have been the Aegean kingfisher – the *alkyon* itself.

On the slopes behind the line of modern houses are the remains of a considerable earlier settlement. Indeed at one point you can distinguish courses of a much heavier dressed masonry which suggest something earlier still. Nothing of the kind is recorded, but it would not be surprising if this beautifully placed village has survived from Mycenaean times.

In any case the boat for your return may leave too soon for you – here is the choicest place in Astypalaia.

The Hippocratic Oath

I swear by Apollo the Physician, by Aesculapius, by Hygeia, by Panacea and by all the gods and goddesses, making them my witnesses, that I will carry out, according to my ability and judgment, this oath and this indenture. To hold my teacher in this art equal to my own parents; to make him partner in my livelihood; when he is in need of money to share mine with him; to consider his family as my own brothers and to teach them this art, if they want to learn it, without fee or indenture; to impart precept, oral instruction, and all other instruction to my own sons, the sons of my teacher and to indentured pupils who have taken the physician's oath, but to nobody else. I will use treatment or help the sick according to my ability and judgment, but never with a view to injury and wrong-doing. Neither will I administer a poison to any body when asked to do so, nor will I suggest such a course. Similarly I will not give to a woman a pessary to cause abortion. But I will keep pure and holy both my life and my art. I will not use the knife, not even, verily, on sufferers from the stone, but I will give place to such as are craftsmen therein. Into whatever houses I enter, I will enter to help the sick, and I will abstain from all intentional wrong-doing or harm, especially from abusing the bodies of man or woman, bond or free. And whatsoever I shall see or hear in the course of my profession, as well as outside my profession in my intercourse with men, if it be what should not be published abroad, I will never divulge, holding such things to be holy secrets. Now if I carry out this oath, and break it not, may I gain for ever reputation among all men for my life and for my art; but if I transgress it and foreswear myself, may the opposite befall me.

Access

There are daily ferries to KOS from Piraeus via Patmos, which return next day from Rhodes. During the summer hydrofoils run between Rhodes and Kos. There are daily air flights from Athens, and connections with Rhodes.

Ferries from Piraeus call at ASTYPALAIA twice a week via Amorgos, returning from Rhodes via Kos; days and times of arrival are uncertain. When the airfield is built there will be flights from Athens and connections with Kos.

Communications

There are taxis and buses in both islands, but the bus service in ASTYPALAIA is very limited – as is the road system.

Accommodation

KOS   The tourist brochures have an enormous and baffling list of hotels in Kos town and the outlying resorts. All those near Kos harbour tend to be noisy at night. Quieter possibilities are OSCAR (C) which is very large (300 beds) and has a swimming pool, but stands in a quiet side street, and PARITSA (C), smaller and in another tree-lined side street.

ASTYPALAIA   The only recognized hotels are in the harbour area. Of these PARADISOS (C) is in the best position, with balconies looking out to sea; AEGEAN (C) is modern and clean, but ASTYNEA (D) on the front is neither; an interesting one on the way up to the Chora is GALLIA (C) where the French host bakes his own croissants and his Greek wife runs the place efficiently.

411

Restaurants

KOS (town)   None can be recommended near the quayside. In the Plateia Eleutherias the LESCHIS establishment is well run but expensive. The OLYMPIADES is an excellent Greek family restaurant between the top of Vas. Pavlou street and the bus centre.

ASTYPALAIA   The best is the bar-restaurant attached to the Paradisos hotel. The waterside restaurant at Exo Vathy, up in Limni Vathiou, is also very good; the proprietress is a character.

Facilities

Banks: There are several in Kos town. In Astypalaia there is just the one small branch behind the main harbour.

Yachts: Kos harbour is always crowded, but there are some good ship chandlers ashore; at Kamari there is a small fishing harbour, exposed in bad weather. In Astypalaia there is a safe anchorage in the main harbour, clear of the ferry berth, but the berths for small yachts are awkward. There are better facilities at Maltezana, and a lovely sheltered anchorage in Limni Vathiou.

TWENTY-FOUR

Nisyros, Tilos and Symi

Nisyros is the strangest of the Dodecanese, being little more than the crater of a huge volcano, in the centre of which an uncompromising rock rises to nearly three thousand feet. Island life is concentrated in the few settlements which have found space along the northern coastline, and in two nearly deserted villages which perch on the lip of the crater.

The old fishing harbour (another **Mandraki**) has been developed sufficiently to take the bigger ships, but it remains dangerously exposed to weather from the north-west. In spite of its forbidding appearance from seaward there is much of interest in Nisyros. The biggest place – hardly a town – has been built on the headland overlooking the harbour, and it is itself overlooked by a ruined castle, another of the outlying strongholds of the Knights of St John. The unusual feature of this one is that the former mediaeval chapel (built as usual inside and below the fortifications) has been restored and transformed into the *Panagia Spiliani* – Our Lady of the Cave.

Ships and day trips from Kos pass along the north coast, and before reaching Mandraki you can make out first a group of large industrial buildings which were once the centre of an export trade in *choma*, the widely used building material derived from volcanic rock – visitors to Santorin or Kimolos will be familiar with the steep grey and white slopes reaching right down to the sea. The settlement is shown on the map as **Skala**, but the rusting iron piers show that the trade is dead.

Next you see some better preserved and almost grandiose buildings at **Loutra**, which as its name implies was a nineteenth-century centre of thermal baths based on volcanic and sulphurous springs, while high on the crater wall above you can make out some of the

413

surviving houses of **Emborio**, one of the only two inland villages.

In fact the flanks of the crater have a good deal of vegetation, and if you are lucky enough to find a taxi in Mandraki you can make an exciting trip round its eastern lip which takes in first Emborio, which is in a dramatic enough position, and then over on the southern side the fantastically placed village of **Nikia**, stuck like a limpet to the very rim of the crater. Day excursions from Kos engage coaches to follow this route, and allow passengers to disembark and walk down to the bed of the crater itself. This is a disconcerting experience, because there is still activity down below and the sea of yellow earth heaves and even bubbles in places.

More readily accessible from Mandraki – a walk of about half a mile – is the site of the ancient acropolis, with substantial sections of the walling preserved. Several bits and pieces from various periods were discovered here and can be seen in a museum housed in the town hall.

Close to the north-west of Nisyros is the small oddly shaped island of **Giali**. The land rises to high cliffs on its western coast which have also been quarried for *choma*. Today there is hardly a building and very little vegetation to be seen.

Tilos comes at the end of the slanting chain of islands which began with Patmos, and it lies far enough to the west to escape the rough encircling mountains of the Turkish mainland. Strabo accurately if dismissively describes it as 'long, high, and narrow', but for the visitor today it has a lot to offer of character and interest, and a remoteness which has so far kept the tourist hordes at bay.

The only harbour is at **Livadia** on the east coast, which serves as an entry port with one functional bar-restaurant on the quay and a handful of rooms to let. The best of these are along the southern shore-line of the bay – a long sweep of shingly beach with a strip of fertile farm land behind.

A walk this way, past a modern church of little interest, is rewarding if after a quarter of a mile you turn inland across a couple of fields to look at one of the familiar little low whitewashed churches, for outside it someone has uncovered about forty square feet of tesselated pavement. This is a sure sign that a larger and earlier Byzantine church occupied this peaceful site, and one suspects that a

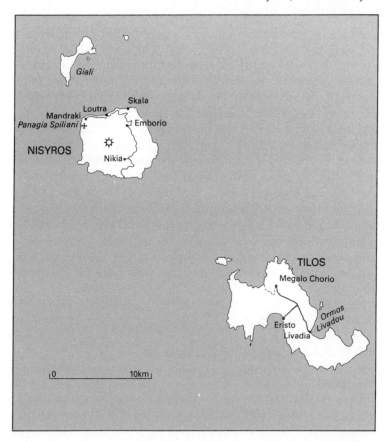

good deal more lies covered by the light dry soil.

The problem in Tilos is communications, for there is no bus or taxi to take you up the four and a half miles to the main village, Megalo Chorio. There are friendly people round the harbour, though, and you may find someone willing to take you up in his truck. There is a small military establishment on the island, and soldiers off duty rely on this kind of transport.

There is only this one road, but it is serviceable and there is quite a lot to see by the way. On the left after a couple of miles is a very ruinous castle perched on a rock, and below it an obviously early

415

domed church. It was here, so local historians say, that a burial spot was found containing the bones of a quantity of small mammals. It is believed they were a small species of mastodon – a kind of mini-mammoth. Initial scepticism is met by the possible theory that all these islands of the Dodecanese were in pre-history joined to the mainland of Asia, and that the animals trooped over a land bridge to their last resting place. It is a fact that the elephant tribe do go long distances to seek a communal place to die, but one has never heard this extraordinary tale before in the islands.

Next on your left the now deserted village of Mikro Chorio (still marked on the map) occupies rising ground above the road, but the road ends at **Megalo Chorio**. The village itself is ordinary, but it contains the very interesting church of the *Taxiarch Michailis*, which is built on the site of a classical temple. This is very often the case, but here you can see alongside the church the original wall of the temple, built of massive dressed stone blocks, and preserved as a retaining wall for the rising ground above. Inside there is an unusually fine carved *templo*, the work of an artist in this *genre* who created only two such examples in his life – here and in Smyrna. It is worth finding the key from a house nearby to study it. The space round the church is pleasant and peaceful, with an attractive belfry tower. In the village you may be offered a drink of white sweet liquor made from almonds – made only, they say, here and in Nisyros.

On a rock at least a thousand feet above Megalo Chorio are the remains of a huge castle said to be Venetian, but probably another outpost of the Knights. It would have been this feature which won Tilos the earlier name of Piskopi.

You will still not have seen the best of Tilos unless your driver will take you down a dirt road which turns off westward about halfway between Livadia and Megalo Chorio. It leads through a beautifully green and flowery valley to the pretty seaside hamlet of **Eristo**. This can also be reached by boat from Livadia, and you can camp here or hire rooms near the beach, and eat at a very good family restaurant.

All around are fields where fruit trees grow in well irrigated soil, with patches of market gardening between. The largest estate here belongs to a warm character called Antonios, who may well have been your driver. He will happily show you round, and on the way back may describe how the last of the German troops in the Dodecanese were winkled out of foxholes beside the road above Livadia – he was there to see it. Kestrels and golden orioles now join the friendly islanders in welcoming the visitor.

In **Symi** you are only twenty miles from the harbour of Rhodes, and even closer to Turkey. So close does it lie to the shores of Asia Minor that at first sight it looks not like an island but like a peninsula running out from the mainland into the Gulf of Doris. One can reach it by ship either from Rhodes or from Kos, or by the longer route all the way from Piraeus. The principal harbour is at **Egialo**, at the head of a deep gulf on the north coast.

This is the centre of tourist activity, but the beauty of the harbour stands up well to the pressures. The town rises steeply to the south, with dignified flights of steps and a number of well proportioned neo-classical houses. Some of these have fallen empty and derelict, but quite a few are being rebuilt in an obvious revival of prosperity. The island capital **Chorio** straddles the ridge above, merging with Egialo on the harbour side and looking over beyond the ridge towards **Ormos Pediou**, or Pedi Bay – just as beautiful a harbour but much quieter and so far not developed. A good road and bus service links Pedi to Egialo.

It is important to remind ourselves that all these islands to the north of Rhodes, scattered as they are like a necklace across the Aegean, were the outer defences of Christian Rhodes in the Middle Ages. Nearly all were fertile and all had useful small harbours. In much the same way as the Knights in the Holy Land and in Syria had built their defensive castles, so they now acquired these islands to serve the same purpose for their new home in Rhodes. Like the towers on the outer perimeter of a castle wall, they also provided excellent look-out points – Piskopi, the earlier name for Tilos, means exactly this. Their purpose was not only defensive either, because a beacon lit on a high point could alert the galleys in Rhodes harbour to fall upon a convoy of slow-moving Turkish merchant-men.

Now one of the more rocky and bare of the Dodecanese, Symi was once well wooded and its boat builders were famous. Along with the natives of Rhodes, the Symiots themselves manned galleys

417

for the Knights of St John. Their *skaphai*, light fast sailing galleys, were as active as hawks along the trading routes of the Ottoman empire. They still turn out *kaïkis* of distinctive design, and the sponge-fishing industry has revived sufficiently to keep them in business. Even today, when the boats are all motor-powered, the lines of those from Symi are finer and more graceful.

In modern times the Symiots distinguished themselves by being among the first to revolt against the Turks in 1912, and took an active part in the battle of Psinthos. Michael Volonakis, in his book *The Island of Roses and her Eleven Sisters* (a fanciful title on several counts), describes them as 'worthy of their earliest ancestors, the best divers and the boldest seamen in the Aegean'.

From the upper part of Chorio you can walk along the flank of the ridge overlooking Pedi Bay to reach two monastery churches, both worth a visit. You come first to the **Moni Panteleimon**, just a small and simple building with an unusual ikon of the Virgin and Child, the Child held on the right arm and looking about six or seven years old. Half a mile further on is the **Moni Vrissi**, a little whitewashed cluster nestling in a fold of the hillside. There are just a few rooms or cells and a tiny church of no great interest, but there is great peace here, with a lovely view down to the harbour and across to the distant hills. In spring you can pick up the sound of the nightingale as well as the friendly tinkle of goat bells.

There is a third excellent harbour at **Panormitis** on the south coast, and though there is no road to connect it with the northern ports there are frequent, sometimes daily, sailings across from Rhodes. Panormitis has a character all its own, as well as being comprehensively sheltered from all points of the compass. There is a long and well paved harbour front, dominated by the very large monastery buildings of the *Taxiarch Michailis*. This is a genuine sixteenth-century foundation, though the façade is in overpowering nineteenth-century style and capped by a campanile worthy of Albert's Kensington. The lines of the waterfront are saved by three long residential blocks, built in a discreetly Italianate style with agreeable balconies.

The chief interest comes when you pass through the ornate doorway of the monastery into the informal courtyard which surrounds the church – almost like a galleried cloister on two of its sides. The

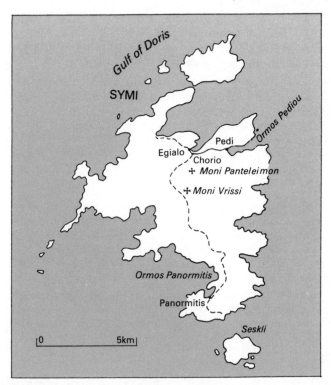

church contains a lot of dark-toned frescos with contrasting
silvery-white detail – not easy to appreciate. The fine sixteenth-
century *templo* is carved from local walnut wood.

Behind the church is a museum, with a mixed bag of exhibits.
Many are labelled as 'gifts' from overseas donors, or objects mys-
teriously recovered from the sea coast or the harbour, but the belief
has gained ground that they represent a tithe of the loot won by
island freebooters. There is a collection of ship models, including
one in ivory of a 'prehistoric' boat with figures on board carrying
spears. One item which must have been honestly come by is a big
longcase clock dated 1780, which is known to have been going
continuously since 1880 and keeps good time. The community is
presided over by a genial and prosperous-looking Abbot, who
offers some of the former cells as holiday rooms for poor or under-

419

privileged visitors. It would be a privilege in itself to occupy one.

Almost like a footnote to Symi – for it lies close to the south of Panormitis and its enclosing cape – is the islet of **Seskli**, one of several which are scattered around the coast. Seskli is the best known, for it is a breeding-ground for the Mediterranean monk seal and the Manx shearwater. Pairs of these birds are a lovely sight in these waters, as they bank and skim with their long sword-like wings close to the waves. The seals are more retiring, and you would have to stalk them in a small boat to find one.

Access

There are ferries twice a week from Piraeus to all three islands by way of Amorgos, returning from Rhodes via Symi. A smaller ferry operates to and from Rhodes twice a week. There are day trips to NISYROS and TILOS from Kos, and a small boat service to SYMI daily from Rhodes.

Communications

Each island has only one metalled road, and the only bus service is between Egialo and Pedi on SYMI. There are taxis here too, but very few on NISYROS and none at all on TILOS. Eristo on Tilos can be reached by small boat from Livadia, or by a rough inland road.

Accommodation

NISYROS   No hotels are listed, but ROMANTZO and THREE BROTHERS are restaurants with rooms near the harbour of Mandraki.

TILOS   No hotels are listed, but there are a few well furnished bungalows beside the beach at Livadia, and rooms and a camping site at Eristo.

SYMI   ALIKI (A) and NIREUS (B) are sophisticated hotels on the north side of Egialo harbour, and there is plenty of other accommodation available there.

Restaurants

NISYROS   The TAVERNA NISYROS at Mandraki is the best.

TILOS   There is a sensible bar-restaurant on Livadia quay, and a friendly family restaurant at Eristo.

SYMI   There are several undistinguished places in Egialo, and two more original ones on the road up from Pedi bay – the higher one is better, with an outdoor terrace and a view down the valley.

Facilities

Banks: There are no banks on Nisyros or Tilos, but the usual branches at Egialo on Symi.

Yachts: On Nisyros, Mandraki has two harbours, one modern for ferries, one for smaller boats below Mandraki village. Neither are sheltered anchorages. There are good berths and facilities at Livadia on Tilos. On Symi, Egialo harbour is crowded but well served; Pedi bay is quieter, also with good facilities; Panormitis has plenty of room and a very sheltered anchorage.

TWENTY-FIVE

Rhodes

The only proper first view of **Rhodes** is from the sea. Every day in the summer thousands of tourists may touch down at the island airport, ten miles away to the south-west, but sooner or later they will find their way to the two historic harbours which have sustained the city of Rhodes since its foundation. It is these harbours which challenge the imagination at once.

In the smaller harbour, now called **Mandraki**, lay the Rhodian fleets which held the balance of power between Athens and Sparta after the end of the Peloponnesian War, and afterwards between the successors of Alexander; they went on to assist Rome in the Macedonian wars of the second century BC. Here stood the Colossus of Rhodes, one of the seven wonders of the ancient world. Here in mediaeval times rode the galleys of the Knights of St John of Jerusalem, and their headquarters ship the Great Carrack herself. Into the 'commercial' harbour to the south came the trading ships from all quarters of the Mediterranean, from Sicily and Cyprus, from Africa, Macedonia and Asia Minor.

Today Mandraki (the word means simply a small enclosure or fold) is crammed with private yachts all the year round, often double-banked round three of its sides. Ten years ago there was room for a line of fishing boats and their nets along the eastern mole, but now they are banished to a section of the larger harbour. On the mole itself, which separates the two harbours, there still stand three disused windmill towers, relics of the days when grain could be unloaded and ground on the spot; right at the end is the fifteenth-century fortress tower of St Nicholas, capped by a modern lighthouse.

The trade which reaches the commercial harbour today is almost all tourist. A succession of summer cruise liners queue up to berth at its long modern quays, disgorging their passengers for what is usually only a stay of twenty-four hours at the most – hardly long enough for more than a glimpse of the standard attractions. As they step ashore they are immediately faced by the seaward stretch of the formidable city walls which guard the old town and were the outer fortifications of the city of the Knights. They are pierced by five gates altogether, four of them entered from the harbour, while above them to the right rises the citadel, or Collachium, which was once the headquarters of the Order.

Although they occupied Rhodes for only just over two hundred years, the Knights of the Order of St John of Jerusalem have left their mark indelibly on the city we see today. The Order stemmed from a Benedictine hospital for pilgrims which was established in Jerusalem in the eleventh century. In 1113, in gratitude for the services which the hospital had rendered to the Crusaders, Pope Paschal II took the Order and its possessions under his protection. In 1291, after the fall of the last Christian stronghold in Palestine, the Knights of St John emigrated to Cyprus. At that time Rhodes was under the control of the Genoese, who had fortified the port to some extent, but who felt incapable of holding the island against the depredations of Turkish corsairs. In 1309, at the instigation of the Pope and with the connivance of the Genoese, the Knights of St John took over Rhodes together with the neighbouring islands of Kos and Leros.

For two centuries the Knights Hospitaller, as they were usually called to distinguish them from the Knights Templar, held Rhodes against the Turks. From being hospitallers first and fighting soldiers second, they became seamen first and hospitallers second. Unable to prosecute the Holy War against the Moslem by land, they now turned themselves into Christian corsairs. They became the finest fighting seamen the Mediterranean had seen, and Rhodes was the ideal base from which to harry and sink the shipping of the Sublime Porte. It is to these centuries that we owe the formidable defences of Rhodes. Here too they perfected the form of their Order – 'the most remarkable body of religious soldiers the world has ever seen', as W. H. Prescott described them.*

* *History of the Reign of Philip II*, London 1855.

Divided into eight national languages or 'tongues', those of Auvergne, Provence, France, Aragon, Castile, England, Germany and Italy, they were an aristocratic foreign legion of militant Christians. United by their vows of obedience and chastity (often taken lightly), they were divided into five groups: Military Knights, Conventual Chaplains, Serving Brothers, Magistral Knights and Knights of Grace. The last two were honorary knights nominated by the Grand Master. He himself was elected by the Grand Council after he had served in all the major positions of the Order. The Serving Brothers were soldiers, required only to be of 'respectable birth', while the Chaplains, apart from their religious duties, were mostly employed in the Grand Hopsital.

It was the Military Knights who gave the Order its distinctive characteristics, and from whom the Grand Masters were chosen. The sons of the great houses of Europe, they were required to prove noble birth on both sides of their families for at least four generations before they could be admitted to the Order. It was not surprising that with such a constitution the Knights of St John should have been both aristocratic and arrogant in their manner. They were also brave and ruthless against their hereditary enemy. Gibbon said with some accuracy: 'The Knights neglected to live, but were prepared to die, in the service of Christ.'

The Knights lived inside the **Collachium**, or citadel which occupies the northern sector of the old city. Here were the Auberges, or Inns, of the national Langues, the Great Hospital (which now contains the Museum), the Palace of the Grand Master, and the Arsenal. In the Street of the Knights one finds the finest Gothic in Rhodes, and it is still one of the grandest sights of the Mediterranean. The Palace was entirely rebuilt by the Italian Governor in the 1940s in a state which could house if required his Duce or his King. It has come in for harsh criticism, describing it as 'Hollywood Baronial' or 'Mussolini Gothic'. Pompous the building and its interior appointments certainly are, but time has tempered its vulgarity. At night it blends with the true Gothic, and is a moving and imposing silhouette. Then vivid exhibitions of *son et lumière* depict the last and most famous siege of Rhodes.

In the days of the Knights the smaller harbour of Mandraki was the Port of the Galleys, where they kept those long lean war-craft

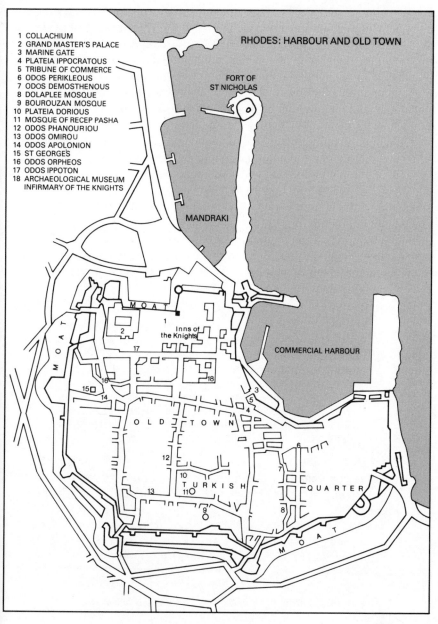

RHODES: HARBOUR AND OLD TOWN

1 COLLACHIUM
2 GRAND MASTER'S PALACE
3 MARINE GATE
4 PLATEIA IPPOCRATOUS
5 TRIBUNE OF COMMERCE
6 ODOS PERIKLEOUS
7 ODOS DEMOSTHENOUS
8 DOLAPLEE MOSQUE
9 BOUROUZAN MOSQUE
10 PLATEIA DORIOUS
11 MOSQUE OF RECEP PASHA
12 ODOS PHANOURIOU
13 ODOS OMIROU
14 ODOS APOLONION
15 ST GEORGE'S
16 ODOS ORPHEOS
17 ODOS IPPOTON
18 ARCHAEOLOGICAL MUSEUM
   INFIRMARY OF THE KNIGHTS

FORT OF
ST NICHOLAS

MANDRAKI

MOAT

Inns of
the Knights

COMMERCIAL HARBOUR

OLD TOWN

TURKISH QUARTER

MOAT

which proved so ill-omened to the masters of Turkish ships. Not only the galleys were moored in Mandraki. There too could be seen the Knights' flagship, the Great Carrack of Rhodes, one of the largest and most extraordinary vessels of the Middle Ages. One can never look at Mandraki without seeing the Great Carrack at rest there, with the tower of St Nicholas behind her, and the wolfish galleys idling in her shadow. She has been vividly described by a nineteenth-century writer:

'It had eight decks or floors, and such space for warehouses and stores that it could keep at sea for six months without once having occasion to touch land for any sort of provisions, not even water; for it had a monstrous supply for all that time of water, the freshest and most limpid; nor did the crew eat biscuit, but excellent white bread, baked every day, the corn being ground by a multitude of handmills, and it had an oven so capacious that it baked two thousand loaves at a time.

'The ship was sheathed with six several sheathings of metal, two of which underwater were of lead with bronze screws (which do not consume the lead like iron screws), and with such consummate art was it built that it could never sink, no human power could submerge it.

'There were magnificent rooms, an armoury for five hundred men; but of the quantity of cannon no need to say anything, save that fifty of them were of extraordinary dimensions; but what crowned all is that the enormous vessel was of incomparable swiftness and agility, and that its sails were astonishingly manageable; that it required little toil to reef or veer, and to preform all nautical evolutions; not to speak of fighting people, but the mere mariners amounted to three hundred.' *

One suspects that a layman was being carried away by what he had read in contemporary descriptions, often prone to hyperbole, but she was not so far away in time from the galleons of the Spanish Armada.

For the student of military architecture Rhodes is eternally interesting, and the evidence of our eyes rules out exaggeration in describing it. The curtain walls are as much as forty feet thick,

* J. Taafe, *History of the Order of St John of Jerusalem*, London 1852.

defended by huge towers – proof that when they were reconstructed under the direction of Pierre d'Abusson, Grand Master at the time of the Turkish attack in 1480, the age of cannon had begun. Before this a thickness of about twelve feet was considered adequate against the rams and siege engines which had changed little since Roman times.

The city walls still stand, restored to a level which allows the Museum authorities to open them for tours on two or three days a week. You can cover about half their total circuit of two and a half miles – a well-spent three-quarters of an hour today. Looking down on the city they enclose, you can see not only the tidily restored streets and Inns of the Knights, with the Grand Master's Palace rising close to the northern bastion, but also the old irregular Turkish quarter to the south. From the walls you can see little of this but an untidy muddle of roofs and dilapidated outhouses, broken by the domes and minarets of a few deserted mosques. You do have a fine view of the harbours and the open sea beyond, and the tour would be worth it just for the sight of the massive fortification system on the landward side.

To appreciate the Turkish quarter you need to penetrate it at ground level. Once you have left behind the worst of the tourist shops which line the outer walls, it is a pleasant place to wander on a sunny morning. If you enter by the Marine Gate and turn left, you come first to the *Plateia Ippokratous*, dominated by the handsome early fifteenth-century Tribune of Commerce, sometimes called the Palace of the Castellan. Its ground floor is, somehow appropriately, given over to a flourishing fish market. A little further on try a right-hand turn down the *Odos Perikleous*, a narrow street which gives you the first sight of a typical feature of the quarter. Many of these paved or cobbled alleys are crossed at intervals by flying buttresses – an arrangement which has served to protect the houses from the earthquakes to which Rhodes, like many parts of the Aegean, has been subject.

At the far end of *Perikleous*, where it joins the *Odos Demosthenous* (how these Athenian worthies jostle each other here!), you will see the 'Dolaplee Mosque', a harmonious building standing on its own in a patch of waste land. There is more to these relics of the Turkish occupation than you expect, for in almost every case they were originally Christian churches. The dome, or cupola, was after all a Byzantine feature, and all the Turks had to do was to rid the church of its Christian decorations and build a minaret alongside. When they were finally driven out by the Italians in 1912 these buildings resumed their Christian identity, and today outside each one is a brass plate which names its patron saint or other dedication. Ironically, though, few of them are in use as churches: some are empty and derelict, others converted into private houses or offices.

The published town plans still name them all as mosques, and several have minarets standing beside them. The brass plate outside the Dolaplee Mosque says it is the fifteenth-century church of *Agios Trias*, and its minaret has lost its top storey. From there you can work your way through twisting alleys into the long *Odos Omirou*, running parallel to the southern walls. Halfway along it on your left is a short passage leading to what the plan calls the 'Bourouzan Mosque'. This turns out to be another fifteenth-century church called *Agios Kyriaki*, standing with its delightful and intact little minaret in a quiet leafy corner.

Further on to the right is the peaceful *Plateia Dorious*, on the far corner of which stands the huge and ruinous Mosque of Recep Pasha, which was in fact built as a mosque after the capture of the city. On the nearer left-hand corner of the square you can see the apse of a very small church marked on the plan as *Agios Phanourios*, but when you turn the corner you discover that the west end has been turned into a municipal office.

Nevertheless St Phanourios has given his name to the most attractive street in the old quarter, the *Odos Phanouriou*. The old houses on each side enclose little courtyards, and every twenty yards or so a flying archway spans the quiet street. It comes as a shock when it finally debouches at its northern end into the *Odos Socratous* and a different world of tourist shops and bars.

Never mind. If you turn left and persist to the end past the huge Mosque of Suleiman (built immediately after the Turkish conquest) the *Odos Apolonion* will take you to the best of the earlier Byzantine churches, *Agios Georgios* (more commonly called 'St George's). It is sadly deserted, and the little portico at its west end stands in an untidy garden, but the cupola above is set on a tall cylindrical tower, decorated with three tiers of blind arches – a conspicuous sight from the walkway on the walls close by.

If the morning is now getting uncomfortably hot, you can walk a little way up the *Odos Orpheos* and enter the vast courtyard of the **Palace of the Grand Master**. On the whole this building deserves the charges so often made of vulgar ostentation. An appalling row of statues in the Roman style faces you across the courtyard, and having climbed the first-floor terrace you pass through one grand and characterless state room after another, whose only merit shows in some fine oak stalls and panelling purloined by the *fascisti* from sixteenth-century churches, and a series of remarkable late Roman and early Byzantine mosaic pavements lifted from sites in Kos.

The original building dates from the fourteenth century and served the knights in wartime as a fortress within a fortress, and in peace as the residence of the Grand Master. It must have been a superb piece of mediaeval architecture, and it survived more or less intact until the nineteenth century, when it was wrecked by an earthquake in 1851 and an explosion a few years later. Then in 1939 the Italians began to restore it in a style they thought suitable either as a summer palace for King Victor Emanuel or as a strutting place for Mussolini, though they based the work honestly enough on original plans. Greek irony saw to it that it was completed only in 1943, the year when the Italian forces surrendered, Mussolini was lynched by his own people and his puppet king abdicated.

It is not a place to linger, even on a hot day. Far better value is to stroll down the marvellous mediaeval *Odos Ippoton* – 'Street of the Knights' to every English-speaking visitor – and spend an hour in the **Archaeological Museum** at the bottom end on the right. The Greeks are good at museums. This is small in terms of content, but one of their best – beautifully arranged, with not too much to see at once, and a lot of space to sit and think about what you have seen. It is incorporated in the **Infirmary of the Knights**, or the Great Hospital, a splendid building with a severe arcaded courtyard and a wide flight of steps leading to a gallery which runs round three sides of the square. Almost the whole of the east side is occupied by the Infirmary Hall, surely one of the most wonderful rooms in Europe. Nearly a hundred yards long, it has a vaulted roof supported by arches springing from the seven pillars which divide the hall lengthwise. In this cool and airy chamber there was room for thirty-two canopied beds for sick or wounded knights, attended night and day by surgeons and orderlies. Discreet little cubicles down each long wall could have served as dispensaries, washplaces or *garde-robes*. The care of the sick, after all, was the first reason for the existence of the Hospitallers.

At the south end of the hall a door leads into a smaller room which was conveniently placed as the hospital refectory, and this in turn into three rooms which house the museum's small collection of statuary. The first contains only a few portrait busts, but in the second we find a cool glistening marble Aphrodite of the first century BC, crouching in the most natural of poses to comb and arrange her hair. Famous and lovely as she is, an earlier headless and anonymous 'Nymph on a Rock' has even better lines of body and drapery.

As you move on to the third room you will see on your left an unusual group of figures against the wall, including the Goddess Hygieia, who is feeding a snake from a ritual saucer, and the God Asklepios himself, who has a snake twined round his staff – the now universal symbol of the medical profession.

In the third room you will turn at once to the tall figure of *Aphrodite Pudica*, the 'Marine Venus', found in the sea by fishermen early this century. The marble flesh has an almost ghostly patina, as though one was still seeing it through a screen of sea water, but the body is firm and beautifully modelled, as are the folds of drapery which fall away below the hips to justify her Latin title. She was born in the third century BC, an example of the best of Hellenistic art. In contrast, and not to be overlooked, is a remarkable composite statue of the archaic period, a 'Hekateion' of the seventh or sixth century, in which the goddess Hekate is represented in triplicate by figures which originally supported a lustral basin. One's mind turns to Macbeth, but this is a classical not a Gothic conception. Like most of the other statuary here, apart from Aphrodite, it came from the early Greek settlement at Kameiros.

From here you come out on to a pleasant gallery planted with flowers and shrubs which looks down on a small courtyard with a sixth-century mosaic pavement brought from Karpathos. On the north side of the gallery are two rooms with more things of interest. There is another archaic piece, again perhaps a Hekateion, where the three goddess figures stand on the backs of lions to support their basin, and two athletic but headless Kouroi of the same period from Kameiros. Finest of all is a beautifully executed and preserved fifth-century funerary *stele* showing a daughter (Timarista) taking farewell of her dead mother (Crito). Both are clearly named, their dresses are delicately carved, and the expressions and postures are deeply touching.

By now we may have forgotten about the Turkish quarter of the old town, where the morning began, but it is a reminder that the Knights could not hold on to their island for ever. It had become too great an irritant, these Christian seamen plying in the Sultan's seas. The defences of Rhodes were twice within fifty years put to the test by the Ottoman Turks in their counter-crusade to rid the Aegean of the infidel enemies of Mohammed. In 1480 the Knights fought off a sustained attack by the Sultan Mehmet II, a story told in a magnificently illuminated contemporary text by Caoursin, now to be seen in Paris, but in 1522 Sultan Suleiman I, Suleiman the Magnificent, invested the city with a force of about 200,000 men. The siege lasted for six months and ended in the capitulation of the Order. But before the Knights were forced to yield to the almost unlimited manpower of the Turks they had put up a resistance that was unequalled until the famous Great Siege of Malta in 1565, when they drove off the Turks in utter defeat.

Both sieges have been brilliantly researched and described by Eric Brockman*, himself a Knight of Malta, and have also been recalled elsewhere by the original author of this book**. In 1522 the Turkish strategy was to invest the city from landward in a great crescent following the lines of the walls. They brought up huge cannon to bombard the upper works, and even built an earthwork opposite the tower of Aragon from the top of which they hoped to fire into the helpless town. At the same time they began extensive mining under the walls, only to be thwarted by the ingenuity of Tadini, a brilliant engineer in the service of the Knights, whose sophisticated listening devices detected the mining and whose countermines could be used to blow up the operators.

---

* *The Two Sieges of Rhodes: 1480–1522* (London 1969).

** Ernle Bradford, *The Shield and the Sword* (Hodder & Stoughton 1972).

All attempts to storm the defences failed, but finally the privations of the siege and the onset of winter without any prospect of relief from outside led the Knights and their Rhodian allies to accept generous terms of surrender from Suleiman. On a cold December day the seventy-year-old Villiers de l'Isle Adam, Grand Master of the Order, together with the remaining Knights, servants-at-arms and followers (including some native Rhodians loath to stay behind) embarked aboard their galleys and the Great Carrack of Rhodes. It is said that the Sultan, contemplating the departure of the Grand Master, remarked to his staff: 'It is not without some pain that I oblige this Christian at his age to leave his home.'

'Nothing in the world was ever so well lost as was Rhodes!' These were the words of the Emperor Charles V on hearing the story of the siege. It remains one of the epics of war, and it is still the shadow of the Knights which falls across this island. They have left their imprint so clearly on the town that their armoured feet still seem to ring down the alleys. The sandalled shuffle of the ancient Rhodians has become no more than a faint lisp, and the chatter and clatter of millions of tourists fail to vulgarize the memory of the Knights Hospitaller of St John.

Yet the naval traditions which enabled them to build and man their galleys were native to the Rhodians, a maritime power which was effective a thousand years before the Crusaders arrived in the eastern Mediterranean. They too came off best in a famous siege, when in 305 BC they beat off the Macedonian prince Demetrios Poliorketes – a feat which clinched their reputation and gave rise to one of the most famous works of art ever erected, the **Colossus of Rhodes**.

Demetrios, 'compulsive besieger of cities', as the name Poliorketes implies, was so impressed by the defenders' spirit that when he withdrew he left behind for their use the vast siege engines he had used against the city. No doubt it would have been more trouble to take them with him, but the resourceful Rhodians sold them to defray the cost of erecting a statue in gratitude to the Sun God who (in partnership, it must be said, with Ptolemy I of Egypt) had preserved them. The bronze statue stood a hundred feet high at the entrance to Mandraki harbour, most likely where the fort of

St Nicholas stands today. Apollo Helios was shown with his head framed in sunrays, holding a torch in his right hand, but whether he actually bestrode the entrance, leaving ships to pass beneath, has been a matter of controversy since ancient times.

The trouble was that the statue, listed as it were Grade I among the historic buildings of the world, stood for only sixty-five years before it was overthrown in 225 BC by the kind of earthquake which has always plagued the islands and coasts of the Aegean. 'Its enormous fragments continued to excite wonder at the time of Pliny, and were not removed till AD 656 when Rhodes was conquered by the Saracens, who sold the remains for old metal to a dealer, who employed 900 camels to carry them away. The notion that the Colossus once stood astride the entrance to the harbour is a mediaeval fiction.'*

This last sentence has been convincingly challenged, at least as regards physical possibility. Arguing from the established dimensions of classical triremes, and their practice of entering harbour under tow with lowered masts, it has been calculated that with a statue of this overall height there would have been ample clearance between legs planted firmly each side of the entrance. What is not clear either is whether the Colossus was actually cast wholly in bronze (which from the *Treatises* of Benvenuto Cellini would seem impossible at the time) or constructed of separate plates bolted together round an iron core. In either case one feels that, however physically possible the feat of straddling may have been, it would have been an aesthetic oddity at the height of the Hellenistic age – more in the Roman than the Greek spirit. Like Sir Thomas Browne's 'song the sirens sang' we shall never know what it was.

What we do know is that from the fourth century BC into imperial Roman times the city of Rhodes rivalled Athens as a university town. One reason why it attracted both the intellectual and social world was that it was literally a 'new town'. In 408 BC the three earlier cities of Lindos, Ialyssos and Kameiros (all mentioned in Homer) agreed to join forces and build a common capital on a site exceptionally well qualified for international trade. To design it they commissioned Hippodamos of Miletus, an architect and town

* *Encyclopaedia Britannica*, Fourteenth Edition.

planner much in demand at the time. He is known to have been responsible for a smart residential suburb at Olynthos in Macedonia, and he was the first to lay out a city on the grid system – though it would be hard to trace his ground plan today.

Aeschines the orator, after his unsuccessful brush with Demosthenes in Athens, founded a breakaway school of rhetoric here. In the third century a professor there was Apollonius, who though by birth an Alexandrian was adopted as an honorary citizen with the *cognomen* Rhodius. In the first century Cicero, Cato and even Julius Caesar attended the school, but the climate and the ambience must have been just as big an attraction, for Tiberius spent one of his happier periods of exile here during the reign of his stepfather Augustus. Even Nero is said to have thought of abandoning his hectic life in Rome to pursue the arts in Rhodes.

Lamartine in his *Voyage en Orient* of 1835 wrote of Rhodes: 'I do not know in the whole world a more excellent strategic position, nor a more beautiful sky, nor a more smiling and fecund soil.' Every one of his individual statements might be questioned: Malta (as the Knights were later to find out) is in a better strategic position; the sky above the Kyklades is more beautiful; there are other islands with just as good a soil.

Taken generally there is much to support Lamartine's enthusiasm. Rhodes has some of the finest military architecture in the world, delightful small villages, grand mountains and gracious valleys. Yet the visitor today – if he stays within the overcrowded northern tip of the island – cannot fail to be appalled at what the tourist industry has made of it outside the walls of the old city. North of Mandraki sanity survives for a time, with a long range of restored buildings in the Venetian style looking out to sea; if you turn left up the broad *Odos Vasileos Konstantinou* you will find an extensive Turkish cemetery on your right – an untidy but endearing garden with turbaned headstones inscribed in Turkish lettering, little round family mausoleums and a large deserted mosque. A peaceful place, where a smell of herbs and eucalyptus hangs on the air.

The new town beyond is a sad example of what man can do to a beautiful environment, and it is difficult to see what enjoyment can be had on the 'beaches' round the northern coastline, with rank upon rank of beach umbrellas projecting from the shingle – sometimes used as a protection against the northerly winds as much as from the sun. There are a few quiet corners where you can find a sensible hotel and a good restaurant, but you have to search for them. No blame attaches to the tourist authorities; there are just too many people to cope with in the summer, and it is the visitors' standards which prevail.

To appreciate the real value of Rhodes (the island) you need to hire a car or a moped – neither difficult nor expensive – and keep out of town for three or four days. The tourist incubus continues for five miles down the west coast road leading south – as far in fact as the virtual suburb of Trianda. Before going on further south there is a chance to visit the site of the nearest of the three classical cities, **Ialyssos**. A left-hand turn in Trianda takes you quickly into more attractive country and uphill to the commanding summit of **Mount Philerimos**, where stand two major monuments from the past.

The older one is little more than the massive foundations of a third-century temple to Athena, built after the exodus to the new city below. Of the remains of the classical city there is little to be seen, but the site itself proclaims its importance: the twin harbours of Rhodes are clearly in view six miles away and eight hundred feet below, and the sea horizons are clear to west, north and south. No wonder Suleiman I chose Philerimos as his headquarters to watch the progress of his siege.

Next to the temple the Knights built their church to Our Lady of Philerimos, on the site of an earlier Byzantine basilica (you can trace its baptistry close beside the later church). Being the Knights of St John they used the idioms of military architecture, with vaulted chambers side by side looking more like the guardrooms of a castle. There are two altars in adjacent shapels, one for Catholic, the other for Orthodox worship, but only the latter is used today. Beyond the church are the attractively laid out buildings of a monastery, some-what heavily restored this century and no longer a religious centre. Over the crest of the hill to the right of the entrance a flight of steps leads down to a delightful little classical fountain of the fourth century, screened by a row of Doric columns.

If you continue beyond Trianda, the road south runs past the airport and through a pleasant coastal plain from which another turn to the left will bring you into the **Valley of the Petaloudes**.

435

This lusher green area cuts into the dry slopes of Mount Psinthos, and is much visited by coachloads of tourists hoping to see the clouds of butterflies (*Callimorpha quadripuncta*) which feed on the resinous bush or small tree known as *Styrax officinalis* which grows in the valley. Not only butterflies enjoy this species of gum, because it is widely used in the preparation of religious incense. The common practice of guides is to dislodge the insects by blowing a whistle – a curious sight, but take heed if an advance notice warns you that they have not yet arrived, or it will be a wasted journey. A further curiosity is that entomologists are not all agreed whether this rare variety is properly butterfly or moth.

Of more constant and lasting interest is a visit to **Kameiros**, the second of the three ancient cities of Rhodes, which is reached by a short side road another ten miles down the coast, just as you pass below the jagged ridge of Mount Prophitis Ilias – second highest in Rhodes. Kameiros is a very special place, not only because it is one of the best preserved of classical Greek towns, but because of the great charm of its position. On a gentle slope looking down over the western sea the houses rise each side of a central street which leads upwards from a newly excavated area, mainly of third-century buildings. The house foundations are clearly marked, and one has a little peristyle courtyard with columns still standing. There are no fortifications or strong points – it could have been defended only by sea power, like the Minoan cities of Crete, and it has an air of undisturbed peace. So has the countryside it looks down on from a modest 400 feet above sea level.

Kameiros was only rediscovered in 1859, and it was not until 1929 that Italian archaeologists began to excavate. The work they did was first class, but it stopped after the war. Now digging is being extended at the lower levels, and there should be much more to be discovered – where for instance is the theatre without which a Greek town seems empty? The excavators have been in two minds about what structures occupied the upper terraces. These seem to culminate in a very long row (at least three hundred yards) of buildings, possibly shops, but whether there was a formal Doric *stoa* beneath is in doubt. The six columns speculatively re-erected there have been removed, leaving uncovered a huge underground water cistern. This seems to have held the main water supply before a line

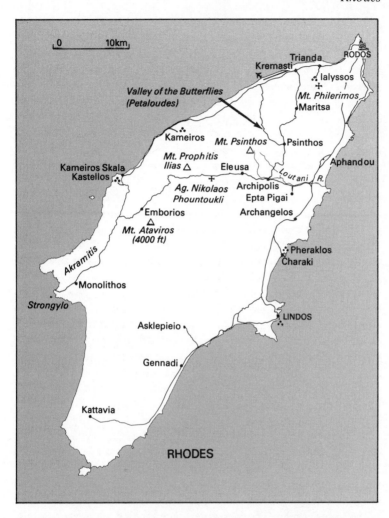

of wells was sunk on the next level above – in both cases the water was channelled conveniently down the centre of the town.

The harbour associated with Kameiros is called **Kameiros Skala**, another seven miles to the south. This is a nice little place – not really an anchorage – with fishing boats and a couple of friendly bar-restaurants. In the summer a *kaïki* takes passengers through a

437

group of offshore islands to **Chalki**, whose harbour and seaside capital are rightly beginning to attract visitors from Rhodes.

Close to Skala is the impressive ruined fortress of **Kastellos**, reached by a loop off the main road. Its strategic position obviously attracted the Knights, for it commands nearly fifty miles of the western coastline, and they built it on their grandest scale with the escutcheons of Grand Masters carved high on the landward walls. The masonry is well preserved, but the roof of the chapel (a large underground vaulted chamber) has fallen in. The views all round are marvellous, even to landward, where the great bare hump of Mount Ataviros fills the skyline at a height of almost 4000 feet, and the swallows enjoy their summer lodgings in the castle walls.

The name Kastellos has also been given to an even more spectacular site at the end of the south-westerly spur which completes the craggy range of Akramytis. It is close to **Monolithos**, a village at the end of the presently navigable coastal road, and it was the obvious place for another castle which could take over surveillance of the coast right down to the southern tip of the island. This one perches on an isolated hill-crest, smaller in scale but exciting to come upon. Not a lot of masonry survives, but you can trace a small chapel beside which a modern church has been built. Goat bells resound across the valleys, and the castle overlooks the round islet of **Strongylo**, where Eleanora's falcon is said to breed.

Another all-day journey will take you down the east coast, which has become a more established highway chiefly because it leads to Lindos, a place now bursting at the seams with a daily torrent of visitors by car and coach. However, if you slow down enough on the way to spot the turn-offs, there are several interesting preliminaries to enjoy. To begin with, the turns are mostly towards the coast, where a spattering of hotels continues as far as the **Aphandou** resort, but a few miles further on a right-hand turn leads up the valley of the Loutani river, a sudden and welcome relief after the scorching tarmac of the main road. Here there is moorland scenery, and after less than two miles a track to the left disappears up a leafy cleft to a place called **Epta Pigi**, or 'seven springs'. This is a delightful shady spot with swift-running streams and a restaurant with inviting tables set on a terrace under the trees. There is bird song all round, and ducks splash in deep-water pools.

Back on the main road it is worth stopping briefly in the pleasant village of **Archangelos**, with a ruined castle and a church with a detached 'wedding-cake' tower. Further on, a worthwhile detour takes you to the coast at **Charaki**. The most prominent thing there is the castle of **Pheraklos**, now ruinous, but occupying an extensive flat area on a hill-top which overlooks the long sweep of coast between Archangelos and Lindos – an important link in the chain of military defences. The castle may have the commanding position, but if you wander through the flowery fields below towards the cliffs you will find a line of marble blocks which indicate that a classical temple once stood on a more serene and peaceful site. The village of Charaki has a small unfrequented beach, an attractive waterfront and some clean-looking rooming establishments. A regular bus service connects it with the capital.

Now to **Lindos**, one of the great monuments of the Greek islands. You first see the huge castle crowning its hill with the little white town spread round its rocky neck like a cravat. It stands on a steep promontory, the land falling sheer into the sea with two islets guarding the entrance to the harbour. This, one feels, is what a fortress should look like, remote and powerful, on a height with a port lying in a fold of land beneath it. In Lindos one finds a microcosm of the island's history.

The town, with houses dating from the fifteenth to the eighteenth century, is interesting but in summer impossible to appreciate. You can catch a glimpse of carved armorial doorways and pebbled courtyards, but it is almost impossible to negotiate, so great is the press of people who seek they know not what.

The acropolis is everybody's main objective, and no one can deny it is a noble sight. The long flight of approach steps can be testing in the heat, but just before the final flight you are justified in resting to look at a unique carving in relief, above and to the right of an *exedra* cut into the rock for that very purpose. Originally designed as part of the base for a statue of a priest of Poseidon, it represents the almost life-size stern of a ship complete with poop and steering paddles, and it has helped many maritime historians in their researches.

The steps from here climb steeply to the first level of the citadel, reached through a gateway and a vaulted passage. These were built

439

by the Knights, but from here on you are faced with remains from widely spaced periods of ancient history. The most prominent at first are the ruins of the Byzantine church of *Agios Ioannis*, but you have by now entered both the *enceinte* of the castle of the Knights and the Sanctuary of *Athena Lindia*, which goes back at least to the fifth century BC.

On this level there are few classical remains, only a waste area of tumbled blocks of stone, column drums and statue bases, but the wide flight of ceremonial steps leading to the upper level is dominated by a huge double-winged Hellenistic *stoa* built in 208 BC. Many of the surviving columns are being crudely restored with artificial stone drums; these and the inevitable scaffolding involved deprive the architecture of its essential dignity. Perhaps we can hope this is a temporary stage in a sensible programme of restoration.

Finally you come to the best part of the whole acropolis today, the very small temple of Athena which has the topmost level all to itself. It is said to have been rebuilt after a fire in 345 BC, and though not much remains to be seen its lines are simple and its position superb. To the south you look down over the tiny, tightly enclosed 'harbour of St Paul'*; to the north over the larger bay with its guardian islets and its now crowded sandy beach. Looking down on the town you can pick out the red-roofed Byzantine church of *Panagia Lindou*, and try to work out a way of reaching it through the maze of narrow crowded streets.

The acropolis was of course used in classical times both for ceremony and a refuge for the people in time of war. The Knights of St John saw both advantages, though its real importance was as a military stronghold of the Order second only to Rhodes itself. The splendour of its fortifications is obvious on all sides, and most especially in that view from the road as you approach or leave Lindos.

If you are still feeling adventurous and have time in hand, it can be worth while to continue south for a bit longer. The still fast and well metalled highway can rush you on through the resort of Gen-

---

* St Paul is said to have found miraculous shelter here when in danger (not for the first or last time) at sea.

nadi and right on down to Kattavia, which is about as far south as you can go in Rhodes. However, given that you cannot as yet continue the circuit (except on rough roads) and return up the west coast, you could well finish the day by taking a right-hand turn before Gennadi to the hill village of **Asklepieio**.

It is built on an airy moorland hillside which is known to have attracted a school for the followers of Asklepios. There are no signs of a classical shrine, but the central site is occupied by a most unusual church – the *Panagia* of the Dormition (*Koimisis tou Theotokou*). It is now a three-aisled church, of which the two outer ones were added in the eighteenth century to fill in the western arm of an extended Greek Cross plan. The original short-armed cross is dated as early as 1060, with a cupola enclosed in a hexagonal tower, and the whole of the inside is covered in remarkable seventeenth-century frescos in good condition. The chief eye-catchers are a splendid St Michael trampling evil under foot; a biblical sequence on the upper wall of the central nave, beginning with Adam and Eve in a delightful garden, she proffering an apple from a delicious-looking treeful; and on a lower level a Last Supper, the apostles sitting for a change at a round table, suitably laid with dishes of food, and Judas stretching out to dip his bread in the sop. In the south transept are some extraordinary surreal scenes of the Second Coming – a griffin, a dragon-like monster, bodies rising from tombs, the sea giving up its dead, and all manner of strange beasts to decorate the margins.

These two coastal excursions will still not have covered some of the most beautiful and interesting places in Rhodes. Fortunately the northern half of the island is crossed by some excellent roads which connect villages high among the foothills of the great mountains of the centre. Perhaps the best route to take is from Kremasti, just beyond Trianda on the north-west coast. The road is signposted to Maritsa; thereafter it climbs through pines and cistus bushes over the watershed of Mount Psinthos to the village of the same name, and on down to Archipolis. On the way you pass two small Byzantine gems, the churches of *Agios Trias* and the *Panagia Parmeniotissa*. The first is up a track to your left a mile south of Psinthos – a bright little whitewashed rectangle with a red roof. There are some interesting frescos, a little the worse for wear, but the clearest is an unusual row of military-looking saints with short tunics and bare or stockinged knees. Down a rough path below is a minute *cella* – just an entrance and a vaulted hut, now disintegrating, but clearly in the right place for a hermit, with a copious spring running past.

The second church is about the same distance further on, and not obvious from the road. With luck you will find a short track going left off a sharp right-hand bend, and just over the rise a small stone box (recently repointed) with a rough apse and no belfry. The frescos here are some of the most vivid in Rhodes, and they rival many in Crete. The sequence on the southern range of vaulting is particularly fine. An Arrest in the Garden has ranks of helmeted crusader soldiery with spears being directed by Judas – the faces clear and well drawn – while the disciples lie asleep. There is the Trial before Pilate, a Crucifixion with Mary and St John standing below the Cross, and an Entombment, all finely executed in a style which looks not later than the sixteenth century.

From Archipolis to Eleusa you are still in lovely country at never much less than 2000 feet. At **Eleusa** it may be a shock to find the monastery has been taken over by the army, but it looks to have been modern and ugly in any case. The village is at a crossroads, and the minor road (unmetalled but easy to drive) leading west is the one to follow – it may be signposted to Prophitis Ilias, a place which takes its name from the striking mountain range above it. About half way there is another Byzantine gem, an architecturally perfect Greek Cross on a tiny scale. The round tower has blind Roman-esque arches and a red-tiled topknot, and there is a charming bell frame with just one bell. This is the church of *Agios Nikolaos Phountoukli*, and it is fully frescoed in the Cretan manner, with many familiar scenes portrayed. The style of painting is cruder than the Cretan, but it makes a lively scene inside; outside, in spring, there were flowers, nightingales, and great peace.

You can carry on still further south to Embonas, on the slopes of Mount Ataviros, and thence to the coast at Kameiros Skala, but perhaps it would be wiser to turn north to Salakos and make a much shorter descent to join the main road beyond Kalavarda. In either case it should have been a revelation of what there is to be seen in Rhodes which is unseen by the hundreds of thousands of visitors who hardly leave the city except for a coach tour to Lindos or the Petaloudes valley.

Modern scholars will not accept that the name of the island is derived from the Greek word for rose, as in *rhododendron*. Pindar says it was born from the union of Apollo Helios and the lovely nymph Rhoda, and perhaps that is the best answer, if not the right one. The Knights of St John, after eight years in exile, were finally given the islands of Malta and Gozo by the emperor Charles V as a new home for the Order. It is said that, when they sailed across from Sicily in the autumn of 1530 and saw the barren limestone islands of the Maltese archipelago, they wept remembering Rhodes. It is not difficult to understand their feelings, though we may well wince to contemplate what twentieth-century man has done to parts of their island.

Access

There are daily ferries from Piraeus, though the voyage takes at least eighteen hours in all. There are daily air flights from Athens, and of course frequent charter flights from the UK.

Communications

The road system is extensive, though a good deal of it is mountainous. Buses, taxis, hire cars and mopeds make full use of it.

Accommodation

Nearly two hundred hotels are listed in the brochures in different parts of the island. It would be vain to select even a sample few, but it may be useful to know of ALEXIA (B) in Rodos town, which is under the management of the president of the Dodecanese hoteliers association and extremely well run. It has no restaurant, but an efficient breakfast saloon.

Restaurants

It is difficult to get away from the more blatant tourist bait, but a genuine family-run place is SEVEN SEAS, to be found on the corner of 28 Octobriou and G. Leontinou streets, and not far from the Alexia hotel.

Facilities

Banks: There is no lack in Rodos town, or in other sizeable towns.

443

The Greek Islands

Yachts: Mandraki harbour is extremely crowded, mostly with resident yachts. There is a good anchorage at Lindos, and a small exposed harbour at Skala Kameirou on the west coast.

TWENTY-SIX

Karpathos, Kasos and Kastellorizo

Though far away to the south and west of Rhodes, **Karpathos** belongs to the Dodecanese. Its Italian name, Scarpanto, has survived longer than those of other islands, and it was never controlled or claimed by the Dukes of Naxos. Instead it was directly ruled first by the Genoese and then by the Cornari of Venice; at the end of the Turkish occupation it had fallen, like Rhodes, to the Italians once more in 1912

The main harbour is at **Pigadia**, on the east side of the more fertile southern half of the island. The town itself was built in 1894 and has little interest, but the encircling bay of Vrontis is a fine sight, with an impressive sweep of sandy beaches to the north. Close to the sea are the ruins of a fifth-century Byzantine church – probably, as so often, on the site of a classical temple.

As you come in, the sight of green trees behind the harbour promises well. In fact as you go inland you will find dense plantations of orange and quince trees – the local quince jelly is excellent – and the whole of this area looks prosperous. Communications are good, too, and you can do an interesting circuit by road to take in several villages. The most attractive and natural is Piles; Arkassa and Phiniki have access to the coast; Othos, Volada and Aperi are really mountain villages on the lower slopes of Mount Kalolimni.

The most interesting is **Arkassa**. On a headland there you can find remains of the ancient capital Arkaseia, and traces of mosaic pavements which indicate the site of more than one Byzantine church. The best of these belonged to the fifth-century *Agia Anastasia*; this is the one we looked down on in the Archaeological Museum in Rhodes, where it was taken for restoration and safe keeping.

When Karpathos was a fief of the Cornari family, Arkassa was

445

still the principal town, and it retains some Venetian architecture and fortifications. The Cornari were here from 1306 to 1538, and linguistic experts say that more Venetian dialect words survive in Karpathos than anywhere else in the Aegean. The silver and iron mines here were famous in classical times, and were still being worked when the Knights of St John were occupying Rhodes. In Arkassa you may see women wearing fine coral and silver jewellery; it may be of Rhodian origin, but the silver itself could well be Karpathian.

One brooch the writer saw, made in filigree silver, had the eight-pointed cross as its motif – the cross which has since become known as the 'Maltese Cross', but which the Knights had borne as their emblem for centuries before they were driven from the eastern Aegean. When they finally reached Malta they had with them a number of Rhodians and other Greeks who had elected to share their exile. A similar type of filigree work in gold and silver is practised in Malta today, as it is in Rhodes, and the art could have been brought there by silversmiths from Rhodes or Karpathos.

This southern bulge is the most fertile and prosperous part of the island, but not the most interesting. From the peak of Mount Kalolimni a rocky finger of land runs northward to join another high mountain with the familiar name of Prophitis Ilias, leaving only two points where you can cross the peninsula. Only now, after centuries of isolation, is it possible to reach the few villages in the north by road – and it is as well to enquire about the state of any advertised road before driving on it. At the time of writing only the road up the west coast as far as **Mesochori** was really viable, but it makes a lovely journey and Mesochori is a delightful village, built high above the western coastline.

The aim of the northern extension will be to reach **Olimbos**, until recently a mediaeval mountain village preserved as it were in amber by its isolation. The inhabitants have hardly yet resigned themselves to modern European dress and customs – or indeed to the standard Greek tongue, for experts have detected Doric and Phrygian elements in the dialect they use. Unlike many remote Greek villages (particularly in the Dodecanese) it is beautifully kept, and this applies not only to the churches. Inevitably the idea of seeing 'national' costume worn regularly is attracting tourists from the

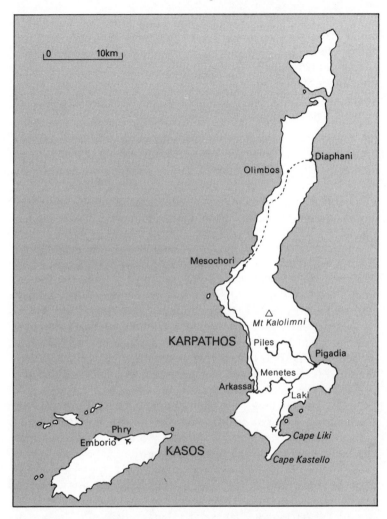

south, and so is the weekly event when the women gather on Saturday to bake bread in a communal wood-fired oven.

So far the only reliable approach to Olimbos is from the little port of **Diaphani** on the east coast opposite, which provides a lifeline for it and the few other northern villages. Neither it nor Pigadia are big

447

harbours, and both are exposed to the *meltemi* winds which in summer blow fiercely down on Karpathos from the north-west, with the whole fetch of the Aegean behind them. The weather around here was proverbial in Roman times, and Horace twice describes the danger of high winds in these waters. Yet it was the treacherous south wind, Notus, which he said could delay a young man's safe return home to his anxious mother:

> '*ut mater iuvenem, quem Notus invido*
> *flatu Carpathii trans maris aequora*
> *cunctantem spatio longius annuo*
> *dulci distinet a domo ...*'*

One suspects that Horace chose Notus rather than the north wind Boreas to suit the metre, but we are not told where the young man lived.

The ferry from Rhodes calls at Diaphani before Pigadia, and there is a road of sorts which carves its way up through the hills to Olimbos (the name, you will have guessed, is only the modern Greek orthography for Olympus). A better way, if you have the time and energy, is to walk up through a pine-clad valley beside a tumbling stream, and over the top to Olimbos – it takes about two hours without hurrying. A word of warning here: the boat from Rhodes may call only once a week, and that in fine weather, so there is a danger of having to spend longer in Diaphani than you planned.

The far south of Karpathos has been almost as difficult to reach by road. The opening of a small airport between Cape Liki and Cape Kastello has not made a great deal of difference, for there is still no road to join Pigadia to Kastello Bay, which is a more sheltered anchorage if the wind is northerly.

From here you look across to **Kasos**, a much smaller, less visited and less fertile island. It too was governed by the Cornari for over two hundred years, but they have left no signs of their rule. The population began to decline in the nineteenth century, when first of all a savage attack by Egypt (then in alliance with Turkey) killed most of the men and carried off women and children as slaves. Ironically this was followed by voluntary emigration to Egypt, and by 1860 we find

---

* *Odes* IV, v, 9–10.

Islanders, *Above left,* a monk of the *Zoodochos Pigi*
monastery on Poros; *right,* a street in Mykonos.
below left, a Samian shepherd; *right,* an
itinerant two-man band in Crete.

A gateway in the walls of Rhodes, built by the Knights of St John

thousands of Kassiots among the labour force building the Suez Canal. The deficit has not yet been made good by holiday traffic, so for its size Kasos is very much underpopulated.

What life there is confines itself to a few villages close to the north coast, in particular **Emborio**, which is the main harbour for ferries, and its near neighbour **Phry** where there is a smaller fishing and yacht harbour. (This curious name, pronounced '*free*', is an abbreviation of the classical *Othrys*.) The Dodecanese administrators have done their best to keep Kasos in the fold by building an airstrip which enables flights from Rhodes to land there after Karpathos. The airstrip is a charming little place served by a simple shed, and only a short walk or a few minutes drive out of Phry. The long distance ferries call at Emborio before reaching Karpathos on their way up from Crete, but sadly there is little to attract the summer visitor except the friendliness of the people who live here all the year round.

Kastellorizo has had the impudence to remain a Greek, or at least a European, island for a large part of its history, even though only a mile and a half from the mainland of Asia Minor and a long six hours' voyage from Rhodes, its nearest Greek neighbour. Those who know it well swear it has no rival as a holiday island, and the visitor who lands at the tight little harbour of Mandraki will quickly recognize its charm.

There is indeed no other place to land from in a ship, but from June onwards in the summer there is a daily air service from Rhodes which must be preferable to the long passage across an open and often stormy sea. Naturally there is much demand for seats in the small aircraft used, which makes it important to book well ahead. A small ferry comes twice a week from Rhodes, staying less than an hour before returning.

That such a tiny island – only three and a half square miles in area – should also be called Megisti ('the biggest') is not an example of Greek euphemism; it is easily the biggest of a group of twelve islets off the Turkish coast, and having such a fine deep-water harbour just there has given it an importance out of proportion with its size. The Rhodian Knights of St John valued it highly enough to build a castle there, even if they used it chiefly as a convenient place of exile

449

for difficult or rebellious members of the Order. Today we call them expatriates rather than exiles, but by all accounts there has been a considerable exchange of population between here and Australia, while many visitors from western Europe have found happy homes here.

The later history of Kastellorizo is not without interest. The Sultan of Egypt captured it in 1440, and used it as a springboard for his unsuccessful siege of Rhodes four years later. It was recaptured for the west in 1450 by Alfonso I, King of Naples, and remained a Neapolitan possession (the only one in the Aegean) until the inevitable Turkish conquest in 1512. What interest the King of Naples could have in this distant part of the Aegean needs explaining. His original title was Alfonso V of Aragon, and in the fourteenth century mercenaries of a merchant company from Cataluña near Barcelona had moved eastward from Sicily to disturb the balance of power in the mainland and islands of Greece. The Catalans made their violent presence felt from Corfu to Gallipoli, and after defeating the French Duke of Athens in 1310 they were able to appoint their nominee to the Duchy. In 1355 the title passed to Frederick III of Sicily, who was succeeded in 1377 by Pedro IV of Aragon. The Catalan rule was ended *de facto* by the Acciajuoli family from Florence eleven years later, but the Kings of Aragon never abandoned their claim *de iure* to be Dukes of Athens.

When the Italian Dukes were threatened by the Turkish invasions of the fifteenth century, Alfonso put in a formal claim to the title, and in 1442 he strengthened his position by capturing Naples and adding the crown of Sicily to his titles. He clearly hoped to win more lands in the Aegean, but in the face of continuing Turkish conquests all he achieved was to unite little Kastellorizo with the distant kingdoms of Aragon, Naples and Sicily. While Athens fell to Mehmet II in 1456, Kastellorizo – perhaps with the help of the Knights from Rhodes – survived for another fifty years. Even then Venice won it back briefly from the Turks in the sixteenth and seventeenth centuries.

No wonder that the original Knights' castle was destroyed and rebuilt several times, but you can still follow the line of the curtain wall, and three towers of the Venetian period survive. The Order of St John is remembered in the 'Street of the Knights' which leads

from harbour to castle, but it can hardly rival its prototype in the Collachium of Rhodes.

The chief monument today in the town (which is little more than a village) is the 'cathedral' church of *Agios Konstantinos and Agia Eleni*, that famous pair of royal Byzantine saints. It is impressive rather than beautiful, with a line of granite pillars dividing the nave from each of its two side aisles. The pillars are said to have come from a temple of Apollo on the mainland, though it is not clear when or how they made the journey. The only other inland visit possible is to **Palaiokastro**, nine hundred feet up on a rocky height away to the north-east. This was a classical Greek stronghold, with few traceable remains but a marvellous view of Mandraki below and across to the mountainous Turkish coast.

The most popular day trip is by boat to the 'Blue Grotto' at **Parasta** on the south-east coast. It was known locally as Phokiali, or 'sealhaven', but boatloads of tourists must have driven the seals away. Grottos may not be everyone's pleasure, and the writer has never seen this one, but they say it is finer than the one on Capri or at Bonifacio in Corsica. The drawback to this trip is that it takes

451

three hours, and if you have spent six hours in reaching Kastellorizo that might seem too long.

But the joy of Kastellorizo is its harbour and the semicircle of old balconied houses which surrounds it. A bright and friendly place, which stands out against the more sombre background of a different continent.

Access

None of these islands is easy to reach by sea. One long ferry route from Piraeus through the Dodecanese eventually reaches KARPATHOS and KASOS on the way to Crete, but seldom more than once a week. There is however a local ferry service twice a week from Rhodes which calls at both Diaphani and Pigadia on Karpathos and Emborio on Kasos. There are also daily air flights from Rhodes and Crete (Heraklion) which suggest easier access, but seats have to be booked at least a week ahead.

KASTELLORIZO has a ferry service twice a week from Rhodes; the passage takes six hours. From June to September only there are flights from Rhodes, subject to the same problem as above.

Communications

The roads in the south of KARPATHOS take a few buses, and there are taxis which serve the airport. Transport in KASOS is minimal. KASTELLORIZO has no roads outside the capital, but there are day excursions by small boat.

Accommodation

KARPATHOS   In Pigadia, ROMANTIKA (B) and PORPHYRIS (C) offer reasonable comfort.

KASOS   In Phry, ANAGENNISIS (C) promises rather more than it performs; ANESSIS (C) is friendly but has little modern comfort.

KASTELLORIZO   The visitor relies on a few 'pensions' and private rooms to let. There is promise of one or two hotels being built.

Restaurants

KARPATHOS   Near the ferry terminal at Pigadia TO KYMA is the most popular.

KASOS   There are tavernas at both Emborio and Phry, but none out of the ordinary.

KATELLORIZO   There are several good bar-restaurants in Mandraki, and fish meals are particularly good.

Facilities

Banks: The only bank proper is in Pigadia on Karpathos. There are agencies which handle exchange at Phry on Kasos and Mandraki harbour on Kastellorizo.

Yachts: Karpathos has two well equipped harbours at Pigadia and Diaphani. Kasos also has two, a modern one with a slipway at Emborio and a nice small boat harbour at Phry. Mandraki on Kastellorizo is a delightful place with excellent shore facilities.

Crete

CRETE

In trying to present a portrait of Crete as just one of the Greek Islands the writer's limitations are obvious – even a whole book will seem inadequate to cover all its aspects. Cretan history can be traced on the island for something like eight thousand years. There are remains of the Neolithic, Bronze and Iron ages; of Classical, Hellenistic and Roman times; of the early Christian and Byzantine eras; of the Venetian and Turkish occupations; of the struggles, revolutions and wars of the nineteenth and twentieth centuries. Meeting the people of Crete you can imagine them involved in scenes from almost any of these times.

Crete is as geographically intractable as its people have proved themselves in centuries of resistance to foreign invaders. The three mountain ranges of Dikti, Ida and the White Mountains form a backbone which effectively divides the island into two parts, though – perhaps fortunately – only on the northern coast is there room between mountains and sea to allow large towns or a continuous road system to develop. So uncompromising are the mountains that only a few roads manage to connect the north and the south coast, but it is along these that some of the most glorious scenery is found, and where the range of wild flowers from early spring to autumn is unparalleled in the Aegean.

The first of two chapters is designed to cover the principal city of Heraklion, its remarkable Archaeological Museum, and the chief sites connected with the Minoan civilization. The second chapter has a wider purpose, to introduce the traveller to some of the peculiar glories of the island – its scenery, its wealth of Byzantine and mediaeval churches, its countryside and not least its very individual people. Inevitably there are omissions in both chapters, but we hope there is enough in them to encourage readers to explore further; sometimes to leave the increasingly developed coastal resorts and discover the real Crete which has changed so little and has so much to delight the traveller who keeps his eyes open.

TWENTY-SEVEN

Crete I

The traveller coming in to Crete from the north has in all ages been most likely to arrive first at Heraklion. Today there is a choice – by sea or by air? – but the destination will usually be the same. Other possible landing places are at Chania, which also has an airfield, and at Agios Nikolaos or Sitia away to the east, where regular ferry ships put in after the long passage south through the Kyklades. Sometimes contact with Heraklion is fleeting, for tour operators run coaches direct from the airport to holiday bases. Nevertheless Heraklion is the logical place from which to begin to explore the island, if only because the principal sites of the great Minoan civilization are within easy reach – and they are the logical starting point for any study of Crete. The chapter which follows this will open up many other possibilities, but for the moment we are with the traveller as he comes out of the airport building to find the car he has hired, or to board taxi or bus to take him into the city.

Heraklion is still a walled city. The massive walls, now in places ruinous, are a legacy from four hundred years of Venetian rule, and date mainly from the sixteenth century. The road from the airport enters through a gap in the Venetian ramparts, and lands you immediately in the *Plateia Elevtherias* ('Liberty Square') in the most spacious and attractively laid out quarter of Heraklion. To the south, just below the section of wall which ends in the Vituri bastion, are the public gardens; to the north, standing in its own grounds, is the Archaeological Museum, where every visitor should spend the best part of a day at least.

Other open spaces you will come across inside the walls are the *Plateia Kornarou*, on the inner ring road which takes you past the Cathedral, and the El Greco Park, which is just off the main north-to-south street of *25 Avgoustou*. The Cathedral of *Agias Minas* is one of the largest churches in Greece, but from the date of its building, 1862 to 1895, we cannot expect much character or charm. On the other hand just to the north of it, across the *Plateia Agia Ekaterini*, is the sixteenth-century church dedicated to St Catherine. It was much altered in the seventeenth century, and the basilica itself is now a museum with an interesting collection of ikons and other relics. The ikons include six by Michailis Damaskinos, a great sixteenth-century artist.

The name of the Park – not unlike a green London square – commemorates an even greater artist of that century. His real name was Domenico Theotokopoulos, and he was born in Kandia (as Heraklion was then called) about 1547. As a young man he went to Venice to study under Titian, and worked for a time in Rome. In his thirties he settled at Toledo in Spain, where he won both his reputation as a painter and the by-name of 'El Greco' by which he is universally known. To the north of the Park is a group of quiet and unpretentious hotels, which are easily reached by side streets leading south from the sea front boulevard of *Sophocles Venizelou*; this means they are quickly accessible from the commercial harbour where the ferries berth. The street leading to the Park is appropriately the *Odos Theotokopoulou*.

Should you arrive by sea you will see at first only the functional quayside buildings. The commercial harbour was constructed in its present form to take the shipping which reached Crete during the reconstruction after the last war. To your right, though, as you come in, there is a more interesting area. The old Venetian harbour is almost landlocked, with a massive fortress, the *Rocca al Mare*, commanding the entrance. Now it accommodates only private yachts and fishing boats, but set back across the coastal carriageway are the huge structures which comprised the Venetian Arsenal. Not on the scale of the Arsenale at Venice itself, they would have allowed for the repair or winter stowage of the galleys which ruled the Aegean sea routes for four hundred years.

You will be reminded again of the Venetian past whenever you take one of the main roads out of the city, for they all pass through one or other of the original gates in the walls. If you are bound for Knossos you will be following the long south-bound street named

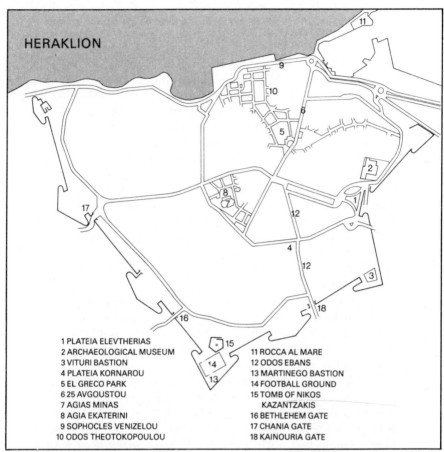

HERAKLION

1 PLATEIA ELEVTHERIAS
2 ARCHAEOLOGICAL MUSEUM
3 VITURI BASTION
4 PLATEIA KORNAROU
5 EL GRECO PARK
6 25 AVGOUSTOU
7 AGIAS MINAS
8 AGIA EKATERINI
9 SOPHOCLES VENIZELOU
10 ODOS THEOTOKOPOULOU
11 ROCCA AL MARE
12 ODOS EBANS
13 MARTINEGO BASTION
14 FOOTBALL GROUND
15 TOMB OF NIKOS
   KAZANTZAKIS
16 BETHLEHEM GATE
17 CHANIA GATE
18 KAINOURIA GATE

after its first excavator, Sir Arthur Evans – though you may not immediately recognize the Greek form of his name on the street signs. The *Odos Ebans* leaves the city by the Kainouria Gate, and there you can see the quite extraordinary width of the walls.

A little further west is the southernmost point of the fortifications, the Martinengo Bastion, which contains within its triangular compass not only a full-size football ground but also an enclosure for the tomb of the Cretan author of *Zorba the Greek*, Nikos Kazantzakis, who died in 1957. The next gap in the walls is the Bethlehem Gate, but the main western outlet is through the Chania

Gate, by which you must pass if bound for Rethymnon, Chania, Phaistos, Matala or Agia Galini.

Driving in Heraklion is not easy. The main thoroughfares are busy and crowded, and in between is a maze of narrow one-way streets. Yet in the past few years the city has lost much of the dusty inhospitable character it had. Gardens and trees have been planted, and here and there you can recapture the insouciant atmosphere it must have enjoyed during its long occupation by the Turks. Their legacy, though it was marked by stagnation in the island's economy, included a love of gardens, fountains and good food. In Heraklion now you can find all three.

The principal Minoan harbour was a little to the east of the Venetian and modern ones, at Katsamba in the suburb of Poros. Strabo tells us that *Heracleium* was the name of the city and its harbour in Roman times. The Saracens, who overran Crete in the early ninth century, called it *Kandak*, from the defensive ditch dug round it; under Byzantine influence this was corrupted to *Kandax*, a more recognizably Greek form. The English form 'Candy', with its derived meaning of crystallized sugar, was a later mediaeval shift – possibly when Henry the Navigator started the wine and sugar industry in Madeira in 1425, with sugar canes and vines brought from Crete. It was the Venetians who made it their capital in 1210, calling it and the whole island *Kandia*.

Venice in fact bought the island from Boniface of Montferrat, the military leader of the Fourth Crusade, and it remained in Venetian hands for over four centuries. Whatever the Cretans may have felt about their Latin masters, this was probably the most prosperous time in the island's modern history. In 1645, however, the Turks landed an army of 50,000 men and reduced Chania and Rethymnon. Three years later they invested Kandia, and thus began a siege which lasted twenty-one years – surely the longest in recorded history. Towards the end relief forces were sent by Louis XIV, but they were ineffective and soon withdrew. The Knights of Malta, an Order dedicated to fight the Muslim wherever he might be found, stayed with the Venetians to try to hold the crumbling ramparts. It was only at the last moment, when the fate of Kandia was sealed, that the Knights embarked in their ships to carry on the struggle for Christianity elsewhere. Francesco Morosini, the Venetian commander, said in a letter to the Republic, 'I lose more by the departure of these few but most brave warriors than by that of all the other forces'.

When Kandia finally fell in September 1669 the whole of Crete, with the exception of Suda, Grabusa and Spinalonga, passed into Turkish hands. The last three garrisons fell within the next few years, and Crete remained a Turkish possession in spite of many revolutions until 1898. Then, with the collapse of the Sublime Porte, the great powers of Britain, France and Russia set up an independent state under a High Commissioner from the Greek royal family, Prince George. It was finally ceded to Greece by the Treaty of London in 1913.

It is in the **Archaeological Museum** that the visitor will be able to trace the early history of Crete, thanks to a collection of some of the most remarkable artefacts to be found anywhere in the world. Scholars, artists and tourists of all nations come here to learn and to marvel. There is evidence here (in Gallery I) of the earliest human occupation of Crete in the Neolithic Age – probably about 6000 BC, according to a recent radiocarbon dating from Knossos. From the Bronze Age of 3000 BC onwards are finds associated with the various periods we have come to identify as Minoan, expertly displayed and catalogued.

Students of ceramics will find the finest display of early European work, from simple stone or terra cotta vessels to the delicate 'eggshell' vases found at Knossos and Phaistos. In Gallery VII you can see three wonderful vases decorated in serpentine relief, the 'Chieftain' cup and the 'Boxer' and 'Harvester' vases, which were found at the villa site of Agia Triada. There are magnificent examples of Minoan goldsmiths' work, with a delicacy and a sophistication which has never been surpassed. Perhaps the loveliest is an ornament found near the palace of Mallia, now also in Gallery VII. Two golden bees are joined round a golden ball, which encloses another smaller gold ball. Could it be another clue to the Golden Honeycomb of Daedalus?

There are also the restored frescos from Knossos. These more than anything seem to have the essence of the Minoan world. They have an elegance which never perhaps existed, any more than did the 'world' of Watteau or Fragonard, but their creators were artists in the tradition of Daedalus.

Less artistic, but fascinating in their implications, are a series of clay tablets incised with the partly pictographic scripts known as Linear A and Linear B. Examples of the latter have also been found on the Greek mainland at Mycenae and Pylos, so that these finds at Knossos have helped to date their levels of provenance to the period when Aegean power seems to have shifted to the mainland dynasties we meet in Homer, such as the houses of Agamemnon and Nestor. Linear B, for long considered impenetrable, was triumphantly deciphered soon after the last war by the brilliant deductions of Michael Ventris and John Chadwick – a story as intriguing in its way as the cracking of enemy codes during the war.

All the tablets so inscribed proved to be part of a very elaborate system of store-keeping and records of production. This had been anticipated, but what was unexpected, and in some ways more exciting, was that the language used was recognizable as an early form of Greek. Linear A tablets, found here and elsewhere at levels of an earlier period, have so far been only partially deciphered, but are assumed to have had the same function. Examples of both can be seen in Gallery V.

Gallery III contains an earlier and more puzzling object, the Phaistos Disc, which was found in a room of the palace of Phaistos dated to the seventeenth century BC. It has characters stamped on terra cotta by no fewer than forty-five different metal signs – perhaps the first known example of printing by moveable type. The characters, which spiral inwards towards the centre in rows divided by incised lines, are in an unknown hieroglyphic script. Can one hope that this is a work of art or literature, and not another example of Minoan book-keeping?

The early history of Christian and mediaeval Crete is well illustrated in the **Historical Museum**, just across the road from the Xenia hotel, which occupies a fine site looking out to sea to the west of the harbour area. The Museum was established in what was once the family home of Andreas Kalokairinos, the archaeologist and benefactor who presented it to the city for this purpose. His name was also given to the principal street leading out to the west from the centre of Heraklion. Modern times are represented too, for one of the rooms is fitted out as the study and library of Nikos Kazantzakis the novelist, and there is a collection of photographs taken during the battle for Crete in 1941.

Certainly Heraklion provides the best opportunity to explore the Minoan heart of Crete, whether you prefer to do this before or after your visit to the museums. Buses leave regularly for **Knossos** from the terminal off the *Plateia Elevtherias*, but most visitors will probably go either by their own transport or on one of the many guided coach tours which operate from Heraklion. The approach is prosaic, and it is not until one reaches the side road to the right which leads to the **Villa Ariadne**, which Sir Arthur Evans built for his home, that one is within striking distance of the goal. The Villa itself is a cool if sombre building well hidden in trees a hundred yards up the narrow lane. For many years it has been the headquarters of the British School of Archaeology in Crete, as Sir Arthur himself wished it to be.

Schliemann, whose flashes of insight seem to have derived more from psychic apprehension than from logic, was the first to divine that the mound at Knossos might hold a secret even greater than did Hissarlik in the Troad. Had it not been for Turkish opposition his might have been the name associated with the discovery and elucidation of Knossos. But it was Evans who acquired the site after some complicated negotiations, and in 1900 he began the excavations which produced in each successive week more and more evidence of a civilization that few except Schliemann and Kalokairinos had imagined.

Anyone visiting the remains of the great Minoan palaces of Crete should remember they are looking at an amalgam of structures built over a period of four or five hundred years, and in two distinct periods. We owe to Evans the division of the Cretan Bronze Age into three main periods, which he called Early, Middle and Late Minoan, after the legendary King Minos who ruled at Knossos.

The royal palaces at Knossos, Phaistos and elsewhere were not founded until about 1950–1900 BC, the early part of the Middle Minoan period. They stood intact for only 200–250 years, for in about 1700 BC came the first of the two catastrophes which destroyed the populated centres of the island. This one, the lesser of the two, has been attributed to a series of earthquakes. That it was not total is proved by the quick rebuilding which took place at the end of the Middle Minoan period. This was the greatest age of ancient Crete, and from that time we can date the grand and elaborate buildings whose ground plans we are looking at today – in some cases a good deal more than a ground plan.

Then around 1500–1450 BC came the biggest disaster of all; this was the one, whatever its cause, which ended for good the Minoan power in the Aegean, though it did not immediately wipe out the civilization which went with it. One school of thought today links this event with the enormous volcanic explosion of Santorin, sixty miles away to the north. Only at Knossos was there any substantial recovery, and the Late Minoan palace is thought to have been rebuilt for Mycenaean rulers from the mainland of Greece. For we are now approaching the almost historical age of Agamemnon, Achilles and Odysseus, when Idomeneus King of Crete was called upon to contribute to the Greek expedition against Troy – that same Idomeneus whose rash vow to ensure a safe return precipitated the near tragedy of Mozart's opera.

The key to this conclusion lay in the discovery of clay tablets in the Linear B script of the same period as those found at Mycenae and Pylos, examples of which we may have seen in the Archaeological Museum of Heraklion. However the recovery at Knossos was comparatively short-lived, for soon after 1400 BC the whole complex was finally destroyed by a great conflagration, the cause of which is still unexplained.

At the height of Minoan power the palace was the centre of administration and religion. But it was no more than the largest building in a city which some scholars have estimated may at one time have contained as many as 100,000 people – an immense number for so early a period, and one which indicates the prosperity which Cretan sea power had won from the eastern Mediterranean. Fertile though large parts of the island still are, they could never have given rise to the splendour of such a civilization. No, it was the ships of Crete, the merchantmen, the traders with east and west, who created the wealth which made Minoan culture a possibility, and helped to disseminate it.

Knossos has rightly been described as the archetype of Minoan palaces. Its heart is the main court, measuring no less than fifty-eight yards by twenty-nine, where business was transacted and where people strolled, idled and discussed life. It was the model for most subsequent Mediterranean architecture. The living apart-

ments usually surround a rectangular space where there may have
been a pool, fountains and flowers – all of which one could enjoy
while walking in the shadows of a colonnade, secure from the sun's
harsh eye. In autumn or winter one could still enjoy a promenade,
happily aware that log fires, spiced wine, hot lamb and other comforts were within reach of a convenient doorway.

The restorations which Evans carried out, setting whatever
authentic pieces that remained into their appropriate places, have
been much criticized. But without these additions there would be
little that the layman could read. At Pompeii and Herculaneum, and
even at Akrotiri on nearby Santorin, the seething ash and scorching
lava settled almost gently over the city and preserved it. Knossos
was twice thrown down by the roar of that very bull god to whom
they had always paid tribute and respect. The Cretans, like many
modern Greeks, lived in an area that was part of the earthquake belt
which stretches from Vesuvius, far to the north-west, past the Lipari
islands and fiery Stromboli, past Mount Etna in Sicily, then eastward through the Ionian islands and mainland Greece, and on
across the Aegean into what is now Anatolian Turkey.

A visit to Knossos can quite conveniently be combined with one
to Phaistos. Indeed many coach tours do this, and include also the
smaller royal summer residence at Agia Triada. A good road leads
down from Heraklion to both these places, and a combined visit can
be made well within the compass of a day, though ideally it is more
comfortable to explore at greater leisure.

Phaistos seems more moving than Knossos, mainly because of the
site. The palace, built in tiers, overlooks the gracious bay of Messara
– a good anchorage in summer, and one of the few places on the
south coast where a small boat can lie in any security. The last stage
of the road to Phaistos winds up a steep hill, and there – a fabulous
site even if there were no building to grace it – one stands and
surveys a huge area of Crete. Eastward lies the rich Messara plain,
which is brought to a close in the peak of Mount Dikti, the reputed
birthplace of Zeus. Between Phaistos and those mountains lay
much of the internal wealth of Crete. There can be little doubt that
the Messara plain alone yielded a wealth of grain which was in
excess of the needs of the islanders. North of the site rises the Ida
range of mountains, in one of whose many caves were found sam-

ples of the exquisite black-based pottery which can be seen in the Heraklion museum.

Despite its height above the sea, and its difficulty of approach, Phaistos has been a site attractive to man since Neolithic times. To the Italian Professor Federigo Halbherr should go much of the credit for discovering its secrets. As early as 1884, ten years before Evans made the first of his finds at Knossos, the Italian team discovered Minoan remains in the caves of Ida above the village of Kamares. By 1900 they were excavating on a large scale at Phaistos, where they discovered a second palace that rivalled, if it did not equal, Knossos. There is less reconstruction than at Knossos, and since most of the recently excavated areas have been left much as they were found the imagination can exercise itself more freely.

The basic similarity is immediately apparent, with the great central courtyard, but the feature which evokes the most vivid picture of its times is the sequence of broad processional stairways leading down to the lustral basins at their foot. You can see those stairs filling with solemn, slow-moving figures in the lovely fresh light of the hill top. The air seems fresher, too, than at Knossos.

At least three, and possibly all four sides of the courtyard gave access to living quarters of two or three storeys. The King's apartments were separate, as was an area set aside for the women. There was also a 'library' (these Cretans were methodical people) for the archives – records kept on clay tablets of tithes, harvests, taxes and production. The Minoans may have learnt from Egypt (with which much of their trade was conducted) the need for accurate records and the means of keeping them.

On the slopes of the hills around and below the palace the remnants of a number of Minoan houses and graves have been found. These areas are still being excavated, and there is a great deal of work yet to be done to provide further evidence of the life which surrounded so important a centre.

Westward along the ridge, quite close to Phaistos, lie the ruins of **Agia Triada**, so called on account of the delightful little Byzantine church close by, dedicated to the Holy Trinity. The Minoan name for it is not known. It was not the centre of any town, but almost certainly a summer palace for some member of the royal family. The view from here, as at Phaistos, is superb, with the added attraction that right at one's feet lies the rich plain through which the river Giophoros indolently wanders. It is an ideal summer view, and this area which bristles with fruit trees is locally known as 'Paradise' (which was the Greek word used originally to describe a Persian garden or park). It was near Agia Triada that some of the finest exhibits we have seen at Heraklion were uncovered. These included some vivid wall paintings and a painted sarcophagus, as well as those three famous steatite vases we have already noted in the museum – the 'Boxer', the 'Harvester' and the 'Chieftain Cup'.

There are two other important pieces of the Minoan pattern to be found within easy range of Heraklion, but these will involve separate expeditions. The nearest is at **Tylissos**, a village about ten miles to the south-west. The site, signposted half way up the main street, lies a hundred yards or so above it, past some houses with pretty gardens. Unlike the great palace complexes it is a neat and compact place, and shows just three examples of the country houses which were built in the gentler parts of Crete during an age of prosperity.

The three buildings are distinct, but with connecting features. It is not clear whether they had separate owners, or were successive adaptations by the same family. But the main elements can all be dated between 1600 and 1500 BC. All three were destroyed in the general cataclysm – possibly connected with the explosion of Santorin – which hit Crete around 1450. The most northerly of the three, possibly the last to be built, was reoccupied during the Late Minoan period and lived in as late as classical Greek times.

Much of what you see is below the original floor levels, but the elaborate arrangements for drainage and water supply indicate an enviable life-style in a comfortable climate. Artefacts found there show yet again what artists and technicians these people were. It is as though one of our smaller country houses of the eighteenth century were to be excavated and opened again to visitors in the year AD 5300.

Then there is the third of the great palaces, at **Mallia**, about twenty miles along the main coast road to the east. Its history and its layout are much the same as at Knossos, though there have been no reconstructions and only the ground plan survives. It was first discovered by the Greek archaeologist Ioannis Chatzidakis, and carefully excavated by the French School in the 1920s.

The central court is only just smaller than the one at Knossos, and contains in the exact centre a shallow pit, or *bothros*, whose purpose is not clear, but was probably sacrificial. The living quarters around it are just as elaborate. More clearly even than at Knossos, at Mallia you can see how confident its builders were that they could never be attacked. The palace lies in the coastal plain only a few hundred yards from the sea, and was obviously indefensible. During this middle period of Minoan power there was never a thought that enemies existed powerful enough by sea or land to attack and destroy its headquarters. They may have been right, if the most commonly held theory of a final destruction by volcanic explosion and tidal wave is correct.

An interesting feature at Mallia is that it has been possible to excavate a number of small connected sites close by. Some are of houses standing in their own grounds, or part of suburban quarters, and one is a big rectangular burial enclosure – a sort of Frogmore, the royal mausoleum at Windsor. Here was found the beautiful golden bee ornament which graces Gallery VII in the Heraklion museum.

There is one feature in all these Minoan palaces and country villas which illustrates the continuity of Mediterranean life. Everywhere there have come to light the large pottery jars, which like the later and more familiar *amphorae* served as the general receptacles of the time. In relief on their necks are the patterns of rope handles such as would actually have been used to move them. Lying at anchor at Matala, south of Phaistos, the author saw almost identical jars being loaded aboard a *kaïki*. Not only had their shape remained unchanged over 3000 years, but there on the rough clay sides were the same patterns of looped rope.

The modern *kaïki* itself, with its traditional prow strengthened to take the forestay, must be another example of continuity of design. The mainsail, if it is still there, is clumsily practical and used only as an auxiliary to engine power – just as the merchantmen and galleys of early Crete would have set out from harbour at Katsamba, Heracleium or Kandia under oars, making sail only later and if the wind was fair.

The problems facing the yachtsman today will not be greatly different from what they were in the days of King Minos. Always along the south coast of Crete one must keep an eye out for clouds gathering on the mountain peaks. Squalls, white or black, bursting down from the hills, are a regular feature of the Aegean, but the Cretan squalls are something that no one who has experienced them is likely to forget. It was off this coast that, as St Luke tells us, the vessel carrying him and St Paul to Rome ran into trouble:

> 'And when the south wind blew softly, supposing that they had obtained their purpose, loosing thence they sailed close by Crete. But not long after there arose against it a tempestuous wind, called Euroclydon. And when the ship was caught, and we could not bear up into the wind, we let her drive. And running under a certain island which is called Clauda, we had much work to come by the boat: which when they had taken up they used helps, undergirding the ship; and fearing lest they should fall into the quicksands, struck sail, and so were driven.'*

Clauda is the modern **Gavdo**, a small island about thirty miles south-west from Matala, where St Paul's ship hoped to winter.

It is clear from the narrative that 'Euroclydon' is the north-easter, known nowadays as the *Gregale* or *Grego* – the Greek Wind. It was this Greek wind astern of his ship which drove the Apostle across the sea to the westward, finally to run aground on the island of Malta. Not only yachtsmen feel the force of the *Gregale*. Its roughness and its violence is always liable to take one unawares when climbing or descending a mountain valley in Crete. That is the Cretan paradox – how often since Minoan times has sudden violence erupted to disturb a rich and gracious land.

In this chapter we have covered a time span of several thousand years, yet we have so far discovered only a small part of what Crete has to delight and astonish the traveller. In the next chapter you are invited to follow the author through the length and breadth of an island where every turn of a road can bring surprise and wonder.

---

* *Acts of the Apostles, xxvii.*

TWENTY-EIGHT

Crete II

Crete is 160 miles long, and we know something of its history for over 8000 years. To explore only the relics of fifteen hundred years of Minoan life would be a mistake, and so it would be to consider only those sites which are within easy reach of Heraklion. To look further in space and time calls either for a leisurely – and patient – use of the Cretan bus services or for the hire of a car for a week or more. Here we propose the outline of a sensible though by no means comprehensive tour, which can be varied at any point, or put into reverse order when that proves more convenient. Alternatively, from a succession of bases in Heraklion, Rethymnon, Chania or Agios Nikolaos, it can be joined at different stages. In any case a good motoring map is essential.

South from Heraklion

If you drive south by the road signposted early on to Mires and Phaistos, you will soon find yourself in lovely country. In spring there are fruit trees in flower, and the usual glorious mixture of roadside flowers is joined by more exotic varieties – banks of the white Turban Buttercup (*Ranunculus asiaticus*) and splashes of the light purple *Gladiolus segetum*. At Agia Varvara a road leads off to the right for Gergeri and Zaros. Outside **Zaros**, about half a mile up a bumpy lane (ask in the village) is the small hotel *Idi*, converted from an old mill house, where they will serve you with grilled trout from their own reservoir. This is not a bad base for exploration to the south and west.

Whether you go straight on through Agia Varvara or make the

detour to Zaros, you should spend time at **Gortyna** before going on to Phaistos and Agia Triada. There is no mistaking the principal site here, the ruined **Basilica of Agios Tito**, because you will see tourist coaches lined up by the road just west of the uninspiring town of Agii Deka. (With a few exceptions the modern towns and villages of Crete are untidy, cluttered and badly maintained.)

Gortyna, or Gortys, became the capital of the Roman province of Crete and Cyrenaica, but it was already a flourishing Greek city in the sixth century BC. The Basilica was dedicated to Titus, the first bishop of Gortyna, and dates from the seventh century AD. Apart from its size its ground plan is like other Byzantine churches of the period. The central apse and its dome are intact, leaving good nesting opportunities for the swallows which are constantly flying in and out of the ruins. Otherwise some broken pillars and a few Ionic capitals suggest the style in which the church was built.

Further back from the road is the little Roman **Odeum** rebuilt from earlier structures by Trajan in AD 100. A charming place itself, it incorporates behind it a brick building into the back wall of which are let the famous stone tablets of the Law Code of the Greek city. These date from 500 BC and are beautifully inscribed in a Dorian dialect of Greek, with the lines running *boustrophedon* – that is to say like the furrows of an ox-drawn plough, alternately from left to right and right to left. The lettering is still astonishingly clear against the buff-coloured stone.

To the west of the site a stream runs, partly channelled into a modern aqueduct. Beyond the stream rises the hill where once stood an older acropolis. It would be hard now to trace the outline of an eighth-century temple, though the circle of seating for a later theatre is just discernible from below. However, it is worth just crossing the stream to look at a handsome plane tree with a board fixed to its trunk recording that (to translate) 'Zeus took on the shape of a bull, carried off Europa, married her here, and she gave birth to Minos'. Disappointingly the tree itself is a *Platanus orientalis* of Spanish origin and no great age, but this is a place where anything might happen.

So far the ground is covered by thousands of tourists every week of the summer. But if you cross the main road from the car park and walk back 500 yards towards Agii Deka you will find a narrow path

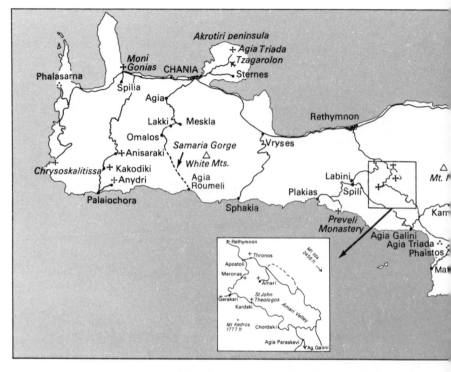

on your right signposted to the temples of Pythian Apollo and the Egyptian deities Isis and Serapis. It leads through an olive plantation, paved in places and easy to follow for a time. First on the right you see the little temple of **Isis and Serapis**, the old ground level well below you, with bases of pillars and the torso of a female statue preserved. An architrave lying on the ground records that the temple was built by one Flavia Philyra and her two sons. For we have now entered the main part of the Roman capital city, and if you now turn left after about fifty yards you come upon the vast excavations of the **Praetorium**, laid out with all the precision of Roman site planning. A more attractive sight opposite is a little **Nymphaeum** of the second century AD, which in the Byzantine period was converted to a public fountain.

If you go back along the same path you reach the temple of **Pythian Apollo**, which was a very big structure indeed, and further

474

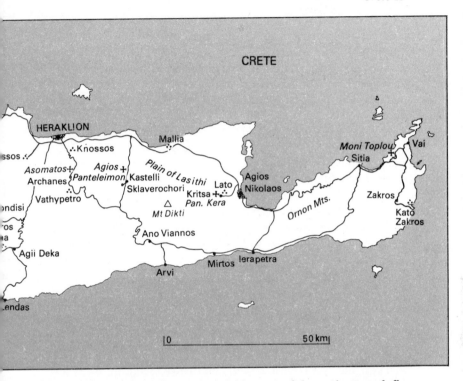

on still a few chunks of masonry sticking out of the undergrowth fix the site of a huge brick-built Roman theatre. The extraordinary thing is that most conducted tours leave out this part of Gortyna completely, so that you can wander undisturbed among the olives and grassy banks which conceal a Roman city of the scale of Verulamium.

From Gortyna you can carry on along the road through Mires (another ugly small town) to Phaestos and Agia Triada. Or you can take the minor road leading due south opposite the car park which winds its way through the dusty little villages of the Messara plain, and across a bare but imposing range of hills, to descend to the seaside village of **Lendas**. The beach here is of grey sand and not much joy, but you could swim off the rocks and there is a bar-restaurant which serves good food. Lendas (ancient Lebena) was the harbour for Gortyna in Roman times, and was once a healing

475

sanctuary with a fourth-century BC temple of Asklepios. The site of this is above the harbour and surrounded by a wire fence, but is now much overgrown. There is no trace today of the classical Treasury or its Hellenistic mosaics, or the porticos with their marble stairway, all recorded in earlier guides.

Returning to Zaros, you can take the road leading westward to **Kamares**. This takes you past the foothills of the great Mount Ida massif, the centrepiece of all Crete, which will never be out of sight now as you travel to the west. Kamares is in fact the village where you can find a guide for parties wanting to climb into the fastnesses of Psiloritis, the main peak of the range, though the easier route to the Mount Ida cave (*Ideon Antron*) is south from the village of Anogia on the north-eastern slopes. At the end of the track from there you will even find a tourist pavilion.

However, if you prefer to stay at a lower level, turn sharp right a mile or so out of Zaros to the monastery of **Vrondisi**, and you will not be disappointed. Before the monastery gate you can park in a little *plateia* with two huge plane trees, at the end of which there is a delightful sixteenth-century Venetian fountain with battered reliefs of Adam and Eve (their heads chopped off by the Turks). The inner courtyard is entered through a gateway watched over by a most hospitable *gardien*, and there you will find a simple little church with a square bell tower. Inside there are two vaulted aisles with corresponding apses – one dedicated to St Thomas and the other to St Anthony. The apses contain some rich dark-toned frescos of the fourteenth century. If this is your first sight of Cretan Byzantine frescos it will whet your appetite for more.

A little further along the road to Kamares is the village of Voriza. Here you should do your best to find the monastic ruins of **Valsamonero**, which lie about half a mile down a track to the left below the village. The key to the church is held by the Pappas of Voriza, and from his house you can get directions or perhaps a guide. Of the monastery itself there is practically nothing to see, but the church next door of *Agios Phanourios* is a treasure. There are charming exterior details, a belfry with one huge bell and Ionic volutes below it. The inside is covered (almost literally) with fine fifteenth-century frescos of the Cretan school, attributed to Konstantinos Rikos – scenes from the life of the Virgin and of St John the Baptist in the desert. All around is lovely mountain scenery, upland pasture for the big flocks of sheep and goats kept by walnut-faced, head-banded, moustachioed, aristocratic Cretan farmers, always ready for a bout of repartee with the visitor, especially if English.

After Kamares the road continues along the southern slopes of Psiloritis until it reaches the foot of the **Amari Valley**. This opens up one of the most beautiful drives in all Crete, and you have a choice of a clockwise or anti-clockwise circuit – up the west side and down the east, or *vice versa*. The western road is the more interesting, and begins only a mile or so further on, so if time is short you can concentrate on that. It is simply glorious country. The flower-banked road climbs steadily above a fertile valley, and at every turn you have a fresh view of the snow-capped dome of Ida – snow lies up there for most of the year.

Apart from its natural beauties the Amari valley has the biggest concentration of frescoed Byzantine churches in the island. There were two periods when Cretan churches were built and decorated in the Byzantine tradition. From the earlier Christian period (the fifth to the ninth centuries) you can find quite a few built in basilica form with mosaic decorations and columns with classical capitals – though many of these are now romantic ruins. After the liberation of the island from the Saracens, and the fall of Byzantium itself in 1204 to the Latin armies of the fourth crusade, Crete (now under the control of Venice) became a centre for Byzantine artists who over the next four hundred years enriched even the tiniest churches with a variety of wall paintings unrivalled anywhere in the world save in certain parts of Italy. The process was intensified after the final fall of Constantinople to the Turks in 1453, when more refugee artists arrived and Venetian influence became stronger.

Your first sight of this captivating form of art may have been at Vrondisi and Valsamonero, but you will be hardly prepared for what you will find at **Kardaki**, about half way up the west side of the Amari valley. In the village itself (not to be confused with Chordaki, which you will have passed through earlier) you will find a dear little church standing on its own in a pretty courtyard, but this should not detain you. About half a mile further on you will see standing just above the road on your right the monastery church of **St John Theologos** (the Evangelist), dating from the eleventh and twelfth

477

centuries. It is only twenty-five yards long, so it must have served a very small establishment of monks. It is quite enchanting outside, with a round red-tiled tower rising only about six feet above the roof at the west end, and set in what looks like its own private garden of wild flowers.

The frescos inside are magnificent, covering every foot of vaulting and walls. Considering that the church has no doors but stands wide open in all weathers, they are astonishingly well preserved. Notes written at the time give some idea of their vividness: 'Here is Mary Magdalene washing Christ's feet; a clear picture of a towered city with people popping out of chimneys holding out hands in supplication; a fierce-looking angel in white; all faces have long Cretan nose.' But there is far more than that to take in.

Beyond Gerakari, where you could take a pleasant break for lunch, is another frescoed church at **Meronas**. The outside is striking, with three apses marking its three separate aisles, each lit by arched openings supported by little columns. These openings half way up the apse are designed to give a back light to the crucifix standing above the altar in the sanctuary (which in the Orthodox plan is always concealed by the sanctuary screen, or *templo*). They are decorated either by this pattern of arches, rather reminiscent of Saxon work in England, or by stone grilles which may be based on a simple cross or formed by elaborate patterns in basket-work or geometric designs. At Meronas examples of three different kinds of grille can be seen in the wall of the north aisle.

The road goes on north-westward through Apostoli to connect with the outskirts of Rethymnon on the north coast, but it would be a pity not to carry on across the valley at least as far as **Thronos**, a little way up a side road to the left. The church there is a *Panagia* – that is to say it is dedicated to some aspect of the life of the Virgin Mary, in this case what is known as the Dormition, or 'falling asleep', which was the first stage in her Assumption, as it is called in the West. Fragments of a mosaic pavement are preserved outside, confirming that the present church was built over the site of an early Byzantine basilica. The west door shows western influence, with pointed arches in the Early English style, and multiple mouldings of rope and nail patterns. Inside, walls and vaulting are again richly covered with frescos, of which the most prominent is a fine

St George on a white horse wielding a spear to good effect. The actual Dormition is represented by the figure of the Virgin semi-recumbent in a shell-like cradle.

You now have the choice of continuing back to the south by the east side of the valley, or retracing your steps as far as Gerakari. If you decide to compromise by turning aside at the Asomaton monastery for the so-called 'capital' of the eparchy, the village of **Amari**, a word of warning. The monastery now houses a large agricultural school, and Amari itself, with under two hundred inhabitants, has nowhere to stay. On the other hand the *Asomatos* church in the village has the earliest dated frescos in Crete – the date is 1225.

The Amari valley is easily reached from the south coast resort of **Agia Galini**. This has become a very popular place with holidaymakers, and there are more hotels, bars and restaurants than any other kind of building. There is a good harbour down below and reasonable swimming near by – though there are many factors which limit the attraction of swimming in Crete. For the visitor who has chosen Agia Galini for a holiday, a tour of the Amari valley would be a pleasant diversion. The same applies to **Plakias**, another fast developing resort further up the coast to the west. Between the two, along a rather confusing minor road from Plakias, is a place not to be missed if you are based anywhere in the neighbourhood – the **Preveli Monastery**.

This is the nineteenth-century, or *Piso Moni*, of Preveli, which occupies a superb site above the Libyan sea. A large establishment, it is still in limited occupation, and the monastery church of St John *Theologos* is beautiful and well maintained. The west end is particularly handsome, with two doors each crowned by a marble architrave. Inside is a fine wooden *templo*, intricately carved and gilded, but no frescos.

On the wall of the courtyard facing the church is a tablet recording (in Greek and English) how the monastery became the rallying point for hundreds of British, Australian and New Zealand servicemen after the fall of Crete to the Germans in 1941, and how the monks 'fed, protected and helped them to avoid capture, and guided them to the beaches where they escaped to the free world by British submarines'. For this 'ferocious reprisals' were inflicted on the monks and the local population.

479

On the way there you will have passed the ruins of the earlier monastery of **Kato Preveli**, abandoned in 1821 after its destruction by the Turks and the martyrdom of its Abbot, Isaiah Ieromachos, with 'a worthy disciple of his' – so says a plaque on the west wall of the tiny church inside. It is an attractive huddle of ruins, with distinctive chimneys rising above the secular buildings, and a trellised vine outside the church, but the history of both monasteries illustrates how violence has been a part of Cretan life for century after century.

At Plakias you have come almost as far as you can drive to the westward along the south coast. A very doubtful road does lead on to **Sphakia**, or Chora Sphakion, but this popular swimmng resort is best reached by the main road which descends through a narrow gorge from the north coast between Chania and Rethymnon. It was through here that in May 1941 more than 10,000 allied troops came down to be taken off by the British navy to rejoin the forces in Egypt.

The time has come to switch to the north coast if you want to go any further west. You can do this from either Plakias or Agia Galini, but in either case it is worth stopping at **Spili**, one of the few really attractive villages in Crete. There is one comfortable-looking hotel, and a good simple restaurant close to the show piece of Spili, a fountain spouting water from a row of nineteen cast iron heads. Mountainous Crete is never short of water.

Two or three miles west of Spili, just before you come to the nicely named Mixorrouma, is a turning to the right which leads to **Labini**. Here is the fourteenth-century church of the *Panagia*, built in the squared-off cruciform style with an octagonal central tower over an interior dome. On the lintel of a window on the south side is a lovely carving of a dove with outspread wings, with roundels to left and right. The apsidal grille is a geometric design of intersecting circles. It may be difficult to find the key, but there are fine contemporary frescos inside.

The natural route is now northward to **Rethymnon**, which at its heart is the most attractive of the northern cities, but a better base for exploring western Crete is **Chania**, which can be reached very rapidly along the new coastal highway. The old town still has lots of charm and character, and the Venetian harbour is a place to loiter or

Rhodes. Hellenistic *stoa*, Lindos

Above, Church of the *Panagia* at Labini, Crete;
below, Minoan *pithoi,* showing rope patterns

find an evening meal. The *Doma* hotel, a traditional family-run place outside the old walls to the east, is a haven of civilization. In 1912 it housed the British Embassy to independent Crete, and in 1942 the German Commandant of the area. The family who still run it display in the dining room the original deeds of the property in Turkish.

West from Chania

From Chania you can quickly reach the **Akrotiri** peninsula which is not very interesting in itself, but contains two monasteries, the more important being *Agia Triada Tzagarolon*, away towards the northern edge of the peninsula. The airport is at Sternes to the east, and on the hill of Prophitis Ilias stands the simple tomb of the father figure of Cretan politics, Elevtherios Venizelos, who died in 1936.

A good coastal road runs westward through typical examples of north coast development at Platanias and Maleme (the wartime airfield) to a quieter area around **Kolymvari**. A right turn there brings you to the monastery of **Gonia**, a seventeenth-century foundation with many good ikons in its church. Only two of the handsomely carved contemporary wooden stalls survived the attentions of the Turks, who burned the rest. The Turks left their mark too on a little terrace behind the main courtyard, overlooking the sea. There is mounted a plaque which reads '*Blima Tourkiko 14 June 1867*', and four cannon balls have been set at intervals in the parapet.

To my mind there is greater pleasure to be found if you cross the road opposite the monastery gate and follow a narrow path uphill between banks of wild flowers (anchusa, scabious, yellow sage among them) to the thirteenth-century church of the *Panagia tis Koimisis* (Dormition of the Virgin). This is all that remains of the original monastery, destroyed in the sixteenth century. The frescos have deteriorated, but there is plenty of life in those you can make out – a coastline or harbour with a ship dashed on the rocks (St Paul?) and some elaborate pictures of city life. The colours are lovely – lighter than in Vrondisi or the Amari churches.

The road back from Gonia crosses the main road at Kolymvari and takes you first to **Spilia**. At the back of the village you will find a small *plateia* with six ancient plane trees, and from there a path brings you after nearly a mile to the tiniest church imaginable – it measures just eight yards by four – with some of the liveliest frescos. This is another *Panagia* of the Dormition, so it has that as one subject, a very complete Crucifixion, a Raising of Lazarus (a favourite subject of Cretan frescos) and a Presentation in the Temple. The Pappas says the church was built in the sixth century, but obviously the frescos belong to the later Byzantine period.

Returning to the main road and continuing westward, a right turn at Platanos takes you down to a coastal plain with a long curving sandy beach. All along behind it, rectangles of plastic sheeting gleam in the sun as you look down from the hills above – one of the new Cretan industries is market gardening on a huge scale. At the far end of the beach is the site of the ancient city of **Phalasarna**, now overgrown and not easily intelligible. The adventurous driver or the hardy walker may continue south beyond Platanos, and if he has a really tough vehicle or strong legs he may even reach the astonishing isolated monastery of **Chrysoskalitissa**, poised above the lovely Stomio bay. He could then return via Elos to Kastelli Kissamou, which makes an exciting run.

If you should be staying at the now developed resort of **Palaiochora** (which has a fine sandy beach, but can only be reached by the spectacular road due south from Chania) you will be close to another concentration of Byzantine churches, equalled in interest only by those in the Amari Valley. The most notable frescos are at **Anydri**, a few miles to the north-east, at **Kakodiki**, just off the main road north, and at **Anisaraki**, a little to the east of Kandanos.

There is one more expedition from Chania which should not be missed. If you leave the city by the main Kissamou highway to the west you will very soon see a left hand turn signposted to Omalos. This village is at the head of the famous **Samaria Gorge**, through which an eleven-mile trek on foot takes you down to Agia Roumeli on the south coast. (You must either face the return journey on foot or wait for a boat to take you round to Chora Sphakion; to save your car from being stranded at the top, there is a regular bus service from Chania.)

However there is much to see on the way to Omalos. First, stop in the village of **Agia**, about twelve miles down the road. Notice the spelling, for you will have passed earlier a village called Agias, where there is nothing to detain you. At Agia there was said to be a fourteenth-century church, but the only one you will see in the village is modern and garish. In it we were lucky to find the young Pappas getting the inside ready for the Easter celebrations. Asked about a *'palaia ekklesia'* he said there was indeed one *'poli palaia'* but difficult to find. Most obligingly he despatched two of his young helpers on a motor cycle to guide us along a winding lane to the right of the main road till we could see masonry standing in an overgrown flowery patch in the middle of an orange plantation.

What we saw was certainly *palaia*, and far older than the four-teenth century. It was a ruined basilica church of the early Byzan-tine period. It has a wide nave with two rows of columns, five still standing, and two side aisles. The north wall is well preserved, with four window openings carrying semicircular brick arches. All the remaining wall structure is of stone bonded with narrow brick tiles in the Roman manner – including the main apse, which is intact up to twelve feet or more. In any other country it would be a historic monument; here its existence is known only in the nearby village. There is a drenching scent of orange blossom and the 'murmur of innumerable bees'.

Beyond Agia the road ambles through a huge area of orange plantations. Empty wooden crates are stacked on the verges waiting to be filled and carried away by fleets of trucks. This is one of the major industries of Crete, and here is its centre. The internal economy of Crete is worth a thought. Only in the over-developed strip along the north coast, and at a few isolated points in the south, has the tourist industry taken a dominant hold. Over most of this land of tough mountains and green valleys the people earn their living as they always have, from their flocks of sheep and goats. You never drive far without passing or meeting one, or having to wait while a woolly river pours across the road from one pasture to another, or waving as you pass an old woman urging her three goats back to the village for the evening milking.

There are other traditional industries too. You notice especially in western Crete that hundreds of acres of young olive trees have been planted to join the gnarled veterans, which will continue to supply the oil which has been pressed out here since the time of King

Minos. Elsewhere in sunny well watered places you will come across huge concentrations of big plastic sheds – seen from the hills above they look like flooded rice fields or reservoirs. Inside them are grown thousands of tons of ingredients for the great Greek Salad, and for a thriving export trade in tomatoes, cucumbers, onions, lettuces, aubergines, courgettes, beans – even bananas. Cretan wines are not much exported, but are rightly enjoyed by the inhabitants and by more and more visitors. It can be powerful stuff, not resinated, with an earthy tang and never too sweet. The centre of viniculture is a wide area of central Crete around Archanes, south of Heraklion. It is not usually bottled, but served in tall open flagons or carafes.

The main road to Omalos forks at Phournes. The left hand road leads to **Meskla**, where no fewer than three churches are listed. In fact only one is of much interest. Round the first corner after the village sign is a track leading off left. Fifty yards up this stands the whitewashed rectangular church of *Christos Sotiros* (Christ the Saviour). Inside there are some arresting frescos. Facing you on entry is a fine Christ in Glory, and on the vaulting to your right are well preserved scenes from the Gospels – especially a lifelike study of the disciples hauling in their nets on the sea of Galilee.

To reach **Omalos** you have to go back to Phournes and take the other fork past Lakki. Like all drives in central Crete it has dramatic moments before reaching the strange upland plateau which leads to the Samaria Gorge. One imagines that an enormous quantity of water was trapped up here to form a prehistoric lake, which then forced its way out through this cleft, a thousand feet deep and in places only a few yards wide, till it reached the southern sea. Now the plain provides pasture for sheep in large numbers.

By the side of the road up from Lakki you can see a plaque put up in memory of Dudley Perkins, a New Zealander who got away after the fall of Crete, but came back to help in the resistance. He was eventually caught by the Germans and shot. At the head of the gorge itself there is a little pavilion, but the shepherds gather in a *kapheneion* by the road in the village of Omalos, and a cheerful boisterous lot they are after an hour or two on Cretan wine. Good resistance material.

East from Heraklion

The time has come now to turn eastwards. Thanks to the new coastal road it takes under two hours to cover the 85 miles from Chania to Heraklion, and a pleasant drive it is, with the sea at your left elbow nearly all the way. After Heraklion, though, you are exposed to one of the messiest ever developments of a coastline. Ugly blocks of modern hotels and half-finished concrete structures rise out of what looks like a twenty-mile long building site.

The road does however take you close to the third big Minoan palace of **Mallia**, already described in the previous chapter. Before you get there, a welcome escape from the concrete jungle is to take the road to the right just before Chersonisos, which leads to **Kastelli** in the Pediada district. It is also the way to the much written-up **Plain of Lasithi**, an extraordinarily lush upland plateau. The hundred of wind-driven pumps which irrigate it feature in all tourist literature and postcards of the area, but it is spectacular enough without them, surrounded as it is by the ring of mountain peaks – all over 5000 feet high – which make up the massif of the Dikti mountains.

The road to Lasithi forks left after about four miles, but if you carry straight on for Kastelli there are two notable and surprising things to see. First of all, just before you reach the little town, a rough signpost will guide you down a left-hand lane to the Byzantine basilica of **Agios Panteleimon**. This is watched over by a remarkable family who live in the little taverna just below it. The church is kept locked, but the hostess of the taverna will ring an enormous cowbell to summon the keeper of the key from a nearby farm – her 'telephone', she calls it.

While we waited for him we drank coffee with the three generations of the family present. Youngest was a pretty dark girl of sixteen, daughter of the hostess and her cheerful well educated husband. Oldest were the grandparents, sitting huddled – it was a chilly afternoon – over a brazier in the sitting room. Grandfather, now 81, had served as a messenger between the Cretan and British resistance forces after the fall of Crete. Not for the first time we registered how long are Cretan memories of British friendship in arms.

The *gardien* himself proved an informative guide. He showed us proudly over what had been a large and splendid church, in which some remarkable frescos have lately been uncovered. There are two colums each side of the nave, one of which is built up from four superimposed Corinthian capitals, taken it is said from the nearby first-century Roman site at Lyttos. The centrepiece of the apse is a kingly *Christos Pantokrator* surrounded by angels, and above you can make out a brilliantly drawn house – Abraham's *spiti*, we were told. There are good military portraits of St George and St Michael, a St Nicholas and two splendid hermits. On either side of the *templo* stand St Stephen and St Panteleimon, both showing bullet holes from Turkish rifles.

In the Orthodox church much more is made of the Virgin's mother, St Anne, than we are used to in the west. Often a whole aisle is made over to illustrate her story, and here in the south aisle is a lovely painting of St Anne, a sweet face and slim figure holding the infant Mary. Another popular scene in the Gospel story, the Raising of Lazarus, is well represented – the burial bindings just coming away from the body.

As we came down past the taverna the old 'postman' was standing to attention outside – a straight six feet. An emotional handshake was all I could manage, though I felt like saluting.

About half a mile outside Kastelli to the west – the road signposted **Sklaverochori** – is the little fifteenth-century church of the Presentation of the Virgin (*Panagia tis Eisodias tou Theotokou*). An obliging lady with a well informed young family has the key in a house beyond. The beautiful frescos include a handsome St George transfixing his dragon before an admiring audience of princesses looking on from a tower, while trumpets sound from the battlements. There is a Baptism in a river full of fish, another Raising of Lazarus, and an Entry into Jerusalem.

The next stage of the journey, perhaps after making the detour to Lasithi, will inevitably take you to **Agios Nikolaos**, perhaps the most popular of all Cretan resorts. It is deservedly popular, with its romantic double harbour surmounted by red-tiled houses, but its popularity has brought disadvantages, including a chaotic traffic system. It could however be another centre for exploring the little-known eastern section of Crete.

In that case the first priority is to travel the few miles out to **Kritsa**, where there will be heavy competition from other tourists to get inside the church of *Panagia Kera*. A visit early in the day is best, before the coaches start lining up outside – the church stands only about twenty yards back on the right hand side as you enter the village. The reason for the crowds is that it contains the most splendid sequence of Byzantine wall paintings in the whole of Crete, which is saying a lot.

There are three aisles, low and broadly spaced, supported by three very strong buttresses on each side. The centre and south aisles date from the thirteenth century, the north aisle being added later. The arrangement of frescos inside is a classic example of the Byzantine tradition: in the central aisle and apse is *Christos Pantokrator* and scenes from the New Testament; the south aisle is devoted to the story of St Anne, mother of Mary; the north one to projected scenes of the Second Coming. For a detailed and beautifully illustrated account, you can buy on the spot the booklet by Manolis Borboudakis, which has been conveniently translated into English, French and German. Among the finest of this glorious collection is the huge head of St Anne which dominates the south apse with its long nose and piercing eyes, both hands outstretched in blessing. In the aisle her husband Joachim is being congratulated by local farmers, one of whom carries the curly Cretan staff. In the central aisle there is a delightful Journey to Bethlehem, with an obviously pregnant Mary unexpectedly riding a horse, and her stepson James walking ahead with a bag slung over one shoulder while a young servant walks ahead. The Last Supper takes place on a table elegantly appointed with implements for a meal in the Italian style. The traditional figures of saints on the walls are no stereotypes, but obviously portraits of contemporary men.

The north aisle has some of the most interesting painting, perhaps because it now shows a strong Venetian tendency towards naturalism. There is a charming view of Paradise at the time of the Second Coming, with Mary seated among the saints in a flowery garden with birds flying around the trees, and there are lifelike full-length portraits of the amiable couple who paid for the decorations of this aisle.

Having seen all this early enough in the day, you should have time to take the track which leads off to the right not long before you come to the Panagia Kera. It is signposted to **Lato**, the lovely and evocative site of a small archaic Greek town founded in the seventh century BC. A 'motorable track' is a fair description of a bumpy ride of about two miles, but the journey is worth it. You arrive at the top of the track to step over a ruined wall into what must have been one of the most delectable places to inhabit in the ancient world. The ground plan is not difficult to follow, and it shows a sensible arrangment of public and private buildings, but the joy of the place is that it is poised on the lip of a deep rock-lined basin, with a clear view down to the roofs of Agios Nikolaos and the sea beyond. Whatever it may have been like to live in, it makes a perfect place for a picnic. The terraces sloping away towards the basin are covered in spring with the full range of Cretan wild flowers, and up from below comes the song of blackbird and chaffinch.

The traveller now has the choice of continuing to the eastern limits of the island or taking the short cut to the south coast at Ierapetra. In either case he will pass on his right hand, just before the seaside village of Pachia Ammos, another major Minoan site. **Gournia**, like Mallia, was built in an open position sloping gently down towards the sea. Unlike Mallia and Phaistos it was not a palace, but a populous town, and therein lies much of its interest. The ground plan can be easily followed in any of the archaeological guide books, and finds from the site are displayed in Galleries IX and X of the Heraklion museum.

East from Agios Nikolaos

Beyond Gournia the road forks. Straight ahead it winds among the foothills of the forbidding Ornon mountains to another fast-developing resort at **Sitia**, which still keeps a good deal of character. Beyond Sitia a left-hand turn after ten miles brings you first to the famous monastery of **Toplou** and later to the overrated seaside resort of **Vai** – chiefly remarkable for the grove of wild date palms, indigenous to Crete, which fringe the admittedly long sandy beach. The monastery was founded in 1365 and originally called the *Panagia Akrotiriani* after the cape on which it stands, but from incidents during the Turkish occupation it became known as *Toplou* (or 'cannon-ball'). It is a notable building in a fine isolated position, and it contains a fine eighteenth-century ikon by the Cretan artist Ioannis Kornaros, which celebrates the greatness of Christ.

The end of the long road to the east comes at **Zakros**, where the small hotel could be a welcome resting place. From there a steep valley leads down to the sea, well known to botanists for some rare varieties of wild flowers, and at **Kato Zakros** we reach the most distant of the Minoan sites, partly town and partly palace – the latter so near the sea that it is often partly covered by it. It was destroyed by the same tremendous catastrophe which has been linked with the eruption of Santorin around 1450 BC, and never rebuilt.

West from Ierapetra

From Zakros there is nowhere to go but back to Sitia, from where you can take the long diagonal across to the south coast at Makryalos, still a pleasant little spot, and on to **Ierapetra** where it joins the much shorter route from Gournia. Here is the largest development on the south coast. The smaller villages of this coast are far between and hard to reach, but two of the most agreeable are **Mirtos** and **Arvi**, both with small hotels. Arvi is reached from the main road by a turning south just before the attractive hill town of Ano Viannos. The monastery shown nearby on the map is a modern restoration and does not admit visitors.

The last lap of our journey through the length and breadth of Crete follows a lovely cross-country road round the western foothills of the Dikti mountains, by way of Panagia and Arkalochori to Archanes. Actually, if you take the southern approach to Archanes you will come to the pleasantest of all the Minoan sites, **Vathypetro**. On nothing like the scale even of Tylissos, it is just a hill-top country house, with lovely views all round. Inside you can see how they pressed their oil and grapes, wove their materials and fashioned their pottery. Implements and machinery for these 'cottage' industries are shown inside roofed sheds by the resident *gardien* – provided you avoid arriving on a public holiday or out of season.

Archanes is the centre of the main vine-growing area – a business-like industry which produces some excellent wines. It also has three Byzantine churches, the biggest of which is the *Panagia*, on the main road through the town, with three aisles. The northern apse has a fine tracery grille formed by the figures of Adam and Eve holding a Tree of Life between them, and there are some good Byzantine ikons inside. The tall bell tower in classical style dates from 1870, but it has clean harmonious lines.

Up a steep side street to the west is the much smaller church of *Agia Triada*, the key to which is held by a nice young housewife close by. The little nave has early fourteenth-century frescos, much faded and damaged by water leaking through the roof, an unusual circumstance in Crete. You should be able to make out the now familiar Dormition, a Nativity, and the less familiar St Phanourios at the well.

The most difficult church to find is the *Asomatos*, about a mile to the south of the road to Vathypetro. The key is kept by the proprietor of a very good restaurant (the café-bar Myriophyton, kept by Georgios Elevtheraki) in a shady *plateia* at the bottom end of the town. It would be as well to ask him for directions, too, as it is so small as to be almost invisible in the trees at the end of a rough track. The church measures only six yards by four, the smallest yet, and contains some of the most arresting frescos, said to be the work of Michailis Patsidiotis in the early fourteenth century. On the south side of the vaulting is a moving Crucifixion, with Christ's body limply bent, as in the great Cimabue crucifix, and a mourning Mary beside. Lower down on the south wall is a splendid figure in Frankish armour with a drawn sword, who represents Joshua besieging Jericho! On the west wall is a feature we have not seen a lot of in Crete, a Day of Judgment, only partly preserved and somewhat obscure in its symbolism. To the left of the door is a figure riding a lion, of which only the hindquarters are visible, with a dog at heel. To the right a naked man is riding a horse, with an oar over his shoulder, and the symbolism becomes clearer when we see that the horse is disgorging the naked torso of a woman hanging upside down from its mouth – a dramatic version of The Sea Bringing Forth its Dead. Above this group is a beautifully drawn ship under sail, a steersman with two paddles and the master tending the mainsail sheets.

You are now only twelve miles from Heraklion, where our tour began. If you had imagined that Crete, apart from its magnificent mountain scenery, contained only a few Minoan sites excavated long ago, you will have learnt better. The continuous scenic excitement is equalled perhaps in Corsica, but the vigour and charm of its mediaeval art and architecture will be something quite new to most travellers. With it goes the inextinguishable spirit of a strong, proud people. From north to south, west to east, Crete is the most thrilling of all islands.

Access

Sea passages from Piraeus take about twelve hours, and follow several different routes. Ports of arrival are Heraklion, Chania, Agios Nikolaos and Sitia. There are airports at Heraklion and Chania, where both scheduled and charter flights arrive regularly from many countries. There are sea and air connections with Santorin on most days of the week.

Communications

The road system is limited by the mountainous terrain, but there is a continuous modern highway, dual in places, along the north coast between Agios Nikolaos in the east and Kastelli in the far west. There is no continuous road along the south coast, and only a few which penetrate the mountain ranges from north to south. Minor roads can be very rough. Regular buses are outnumbered by tourist and excursion coaches, but are cheap and efficient. Cars and mopeds can be hired in all towns.

Accommodation

It is impossible to assess the many hundreds of hotels, pensions and rooms all over Crete. Here are just a few suggestions based on limited personal experience in different parts of the island; nearby restaurants are included if the hotel is without one.

HERAKLION   KASTRO (B) in a side street just north of El Greco Park is modern, quiet and obligingly run. It has no restaurant, but close by is ALEXANDRE, with good food, local wine and some style.

CHANIA   DOMA (B) just outside the walls to the east of the harbour is outstanding for its long-established comforts and atmosphere, and for the excellent traditional Greek cooking of its dining room. For a change, or a cheaper meal, LERIERE, half way along the Venetian harbour front, is more lively and good value, with local wines.

491

ZAROS   IDI (C) is an attractively converted mill house with a good restaurant and a well stocked trout pool.

CHERSONISOS   VASSO (C) at the entrance to the town is modern, quiet and unpretentious. It has no restaurant, but there are several along the harbour front (where parking is not allowed in the evening).

ARVI   ARIADNI (C) is a small friendly hotel right on the sea front. It has no restaurant, but one can eat well at the far end of the front.

ZAKROS   ZAKROS (C) is a simple and welcoming hotel in this seldom visited part of Crete.

Facilities

Banks: There are plenty of branches in all the main towns and resorts.

Yachts: For the general picture see Crete I (p. 470). Agios Nikolaos is the most popular harbour for yachtsmen, Suda Bay the most sheltered anchorage.

FOOD AND DRINK

The first objective of this chapter is to refute the criticism so often heard of Greek island food – that it is monotonous, dull and of poor quality. Obviously no cramped little kitchen in an island village can produce the range of food offered in a French provincial town; equally the refinements we may be used to in the presentation of food at table would seem pretentious and even ridiculous in the happy-go-lucky atmosphere of a quayside restaurant. Quality can certainly vary, but what the Greek kitchen has to offer is food derived mostly from the resources of the island; it is only when the owners try to meet the tastes of less discriminating visitors by using a variety of imported products – which may have been frozen on the way – that their standards fall. From their mountain slopes, from the green valleys between, and above all from the rocks and the seas which surround them, the islanders can produce one of the healthiest and most appetising diets one could wish for.

The almost universal custom of inviting the customer to see 'what's cooking' before they choose is an excellent start. In all but the smallest places an *à la carte* menu is provided, but the best use for this is to check the price of a dish; the important thing is to know what you are getting. Once behind the scenes you need never be afraid to ask whether something not on display can in fact be provided. Local customers in the know will probably have already detected it, and there is no need for you to be left out.

Of course there are bad restaurants as well as good ones. The most important test is whether the Greeks themselves go there with their families, and are not hopelessly outnumbered by tourists whose tastes are often responsible for lower standards of food and service. Look too for signs that the management – and the best are

493

always a family team – is taking its customers seriously: look for proper straight-backed wooden chairs with rush seats; ignore places where deafening 'music' interferes with the quieter pleasures of the table, or the television set seems to be a bigger draw than the cooking. (Exceptions to this rule may have to be made when World Cup football is on!)

In the individual chapters which precede this, some limited guidance has been given about particular restaurants, based on personal experience, but it may be helpful here to suggest what is most likely to please in the different categories of food and drink.

Fish and Crustaceans

This is and always has been the mainstay of Greek island food. King of the rocks is the Mediterranean lobster – the French *langouste* or the Greek *astakos*. He is sold by the kilo, as are all fish except the smaller varieties, and it is still possible to find (if previously ordered) a creature big enough for two for around £10. Next in esteem are the large prawns (*garides*), which as a separate dish tend to be expensive for their bulk but make delicious kebabs grilled on spits with pieces of onion, bacon and green pepper. *Salingaria*, or edible snails, are also delicious if you can find them, and the juices of the sea-urchin *echinos* are a marvellous aperitif when combined with *ouzo* – though neither of these delicacies is normally to be found in restaurants.

As for fish proper, there is an enormous variety, always good eating when fresh; it is not sensible to ask for fish after a day or two of stormy weather. On the whole the larger the fish the more expensive they are by the kilo, because it takes more fuel to reach the deeper fishing grounds, and it is always wise to have your choice weighed and priced before ordering. The same is true of the red mullet (*barbounia*) even when small, for they too live in deep waters. Of medium to large size are the bream family (among them *sinagrida*), excellent eating; but the best value of all are the small inshore fish whose names are legion. These you can order by the plate or helping, and they cost absurdly little. For a first course (or even a main course if economizing) the infant *mikra psaria* which resemble whitebait, crisply fried with lemon, are uplifting, though they should be eaten the same day as caught.

The many-tentacled family is mainly represented by the conventional *kalamares*, a medium-sized squid fried with the body cut into strips and the tentacles separate. Properly treated both before and during cooking it can be a very appetizing dish, but for real lightness and flavour the smaller tentacles (*kalamarakia*) fried in very hot oil are exceptional. The larger creature properly known as *oktapous* is best eaten cold after marination, and can be a delicious midday dish.

Meat

The natural meat of the islands is lamb, especially in the spring, and if properly cooked it is far superior to any you find in France. Stewed lamb (*arni*) is always good, and so are grilled lamb cutlets (*paithakia*) provided they are cut fairly small. Beef is not natural to the islands; even if disguised as veal (*moskari*) it is usually tough or stringy – though stewed in red wine sauce, which is a traditional recipe (*moskari kokkinisto*), by expert hands it can be delicious. Pork is a safer choice, though better served as slices from a spit than as *britsoles*, or chops. Stews are the standby of the humbler restaurant, and few dishes are better than young kid (*katsikaki*) or rabbit (*kouneli*) slowly cooked in this way. *Souvlakia* (kebabs) whether of lamb or pork tend to be made from the tougher off-cuts and can be disappointing. If you like grilled calves' liver (*sikoti*) you will find no better anywhere, but ask for it *ligo psito* (rare) or it will be hard at the edges. *Kokkoretsi* are indefinable strips of pork or lamb well seasoned and wound round a roasting spit, and quite delicious. Once a popular weekly Greek dish (when the butcher cleans up his scraps), it takes trouble to prepare, and sadly is less and less to be found.

Of the made-up dishes, the universal 'meat-balls' (*kephtedes*) can vary from delicious mouthfuls to stodgy affronts, while *tsoutsoukakia* (sometimes confusingly called *bifsteki*) are a flatter form with the same ingredients. The best known Greek dish is probably *moussaka*, which too often turns out to be a soggy cube. To eat one properly made and cooked by a light-handed expert is a revelation rarely vouchsafed. *Dolmades* properly contain only rice and herbs within the vine leaves (not meat) and are served with a lemon sauce. Most of these dishes are Turkish in origin.

Local chickens seem rarely to be killed for eating, and most of those on offer in restaurants have been imported frozen.

Vegetables

This is where most islands score heavily. Runner or French beans (*phasolakia*), carob beans (*banies*), broad beans (*koupia*), spinach (*chorta*), carrots (*karota*), aubergines (*melitsanes*) and courgettes (*kolokithi*) are nearly always to be had, though not necessarily in the same place at the same time. Except for the spinach they are usually served with light oil and tomato additives, which is by no means disagreeable. If you want either meat or vegetables kept hot and served in succession, say so.

Salads

The Greek Salad (*choriatika*) is a great invention, and can be exactly what you want for lunch on a hot day. But Greek salads do not stop there. In many islands, and in season, a plain lettuce (*marouli*) or cucumber (*angouri*) salad with or without onions and green peppers is readily prepared. Then there are the flour-based dishes such as *taramasalata*, *melitsanisalata* and the garlicy *skordalia*, as well as the familiar *tsatsiki* with its creamy yoghurt, cucumber and garlic.

Cheese and Fruit

The goat cheese is paramount, of course, and though the quality of *tiri pheta* varies, you can hardly improve on fresh goat's cheese pressed that morning and eaten in a hill farm. Of matured cheeses the goat is very hard, but *tiri kasseri* is not unlike the French *cantal* and makes a change from *pheta*. Fruit is not often displayed or offered in a restaurant, but some Ionian islands specialize in wild strawberries (*phraoules*), and the melon (*peponi*) can be found for

496

most of the year both on fruit stalls and in restaurants; it makes a lovely fresh finish to a Greek meal.

Wine

One of the sadder changes in the islands has been the disappearance of many of the local wines which used to be stored in or drawn from the wood (*bareli*). However, the quieter and more remote the venue the more likely they are to appear, whether served in carafes or in those gleaming copper cans which remind old sailors of rum issues in the Royal Navy. The truth is that these wines are still widely made, but in small uncommercial quantities, so that not unreasonably the inhabitants tend to keep them for themselves, rather than casting them before tourists. By no means all local wines are resinated, and you can find excellent natural red wines in islands as far apart as Crete, Andros and Kea. The true red Samian, though, and the deep red *mavro* of Paros have vanished from the restaurants. There is a wide variety of bottled wines, resinated and unresinated, too wide to cover here, but the best of the whites come from Santorin, where viniculture is a big industry.

They say that *retsina* is an acquired taste, but there are few better dust-layers in a hot dry climate. The little metal-capped bottles of Kourtaki or Marko are just as good for the purpose as the more pretentious Boutari, and half the price. *Ouzo*, perhaps the most drinkable of all the anise-based liquors, is another sovereign dust-layer, and incidentally goes marvellously well with strawberries! If you should come across *tsikoudia*, treat it with respect: it is a colourless grape distillation with all the qualities of a French *marc* or *eau-de-vie* only more so. The Greek brandies are limited to the Metaxa range, of which 'three-star' is as rough as they come, 'seven-star' is distinguished only by its price, which leaves 'five-star' as an invigorating companion for the last hours of the day.

This leaves Water, the most treasured drink in the islands, whose inhabitants will argue fiercely to assert the supremacy of their own product. The first act of hospitality is still to offer the visitor a glass of water, a sweet and a cup of coffee, to be attended to in that order. The water should be given the same attention as a glass of wine in the Medoc, and your approval will be well received. Although many islands have to depend on stored rainwater for practical uses, the organized water supply in hotels, towns and villages is perfectly drinkable (unless there is a notice to say it is not) while a monastery or a farm in the country will nearly always have its own well or spring for you to savour and praise.

INDEX

499

Index

Index

Index